THE OXFORD REGION

Copyright Oxford University Department for
External Studies 1980

Book Number: ISBN 0 903736 10 1

Oxford University Department for External Studies

THE OXFORD REGION

Edited by

TREVOR ROWLEY

(Staff Tutor in Archaeology and Local Studies,
Oxford University Department for External Studies)

Papers presented to a conference to mark
100 years of Adult Education in Oxford.

CONTENTS

Page

LIST OF CONTRIBUTORS

J.M. Bailey, BSocSc, BPhil,
Transport Studies Unit, University of Oxford

J.F. Barrow, BA, MRTPI,
County Planning Officer, Oxfordshire County Council

C.J. Bond, BA, FSA,
Oxfordshire County Council Department of Museum Services, Woodstock

M.J. Breakell, BA, DipTP, MPC, MRTPI,
Oxford Polytechnic Department of Town Planning

Sir Norman Chester, CBE, HonLittD, MA,
Fellow of Nuffield College, Oxford

E.J.S. Clarke, TD, MA,
United Kingdom Atomic Energy Authority, Harwell

M.J. Day, MA, DPhil,
Associate Professor of Geography, University of Wisconsin - Milwaukee

J.P.D. Dunbabin, MA,
Fellow of St. Edmund Hall, Oxford

A.S. Goudie, MA, Phd,
School of Geography, University of Oxford

M.G. Hart, MA,
School of Geography, University of Oxford

T.G. Hassall, MA, FSA,
Fellow of St. Cross College, Oxford

A. Kadish, BA, DPhil,
Wolfson College, Oxford

J. Minett, DipArch, DipTP, MRTPI,
Oxford Polytechnic Department of Town Planning

F.V. Pickstock, MA,
Fellow of Linacre College, Oxford

R.T. Rowley, BA, MLitt, FSA,
Oxford University Department for External Studies

D.I. Scargill, MA, DPhil,
School of Geography, University of Oxford

C.G. Smith, MBE, MA,
School of Geography, University of Oxford

R.C. Whiting, MA, DPhil,
School of History, University of Leeds

LIST OF ILLUSTRATIONS

FOREWORD

In 1954 <u>The Oxford Region: a Scientific and Historical Survey</u>, edited by
A.F. Martin and myself, was published for the British Association for the
Advancement of Science by the Oxford University Press. The occasion was the
meeting of the British Association in Oxford in September 1954 and, as the then
Vice-Chancellor of the University of Oxford, Sir Maurice Bowra, said in his
Foreword to the volume, it was "a happy opportunity for producing a book in
which distinguished men of science and learning give us the history of our
region on broad and impressive lines". He also pointed out how "most of us
take for granted the places in which we live and do not trouble to ask how or
why they have become what they are".

The sub-title of the British Association - a scientific and historical survey -
underlined the nature and purpose of the book. It indicated the kinds of scholars who would be invited to contribute to the survey, as well as the nature
of the audience for which the book was primarily and initially intended, those
attending the Annual Meeting of the British Association. Both editors were
geographers, as were ten of the twenty-nine authors. But there were also
geologists, botanists, foresters, historians and archaeologists as well as
those who wrote about the growth of the university, the university as it was in
the 1950s, and the museums and libraries of Oxford and its Science Area.

Editors are too close, and too committed, to their work to be able to assess
the true worth of the collection of essays for which they are responsible, but
I understand that what we produced, with a certain amount of hurry because of
the timing of the meeting, has proved to be a useful background survey of the
Oxford Region. These regional surveys done year by year over a long period
for successive meetings of the British Association have undoubtedly contributed greatly towards our understanding and appreciation of the country in which
we live. I like to think that <u>The Oxford Region</u> has done at least as much as
any of the others in this series, even though it is considerably smaller and
less lavish than some that have been produced!

More than twenty-five years have elapsed since the publication of the 1954
survey and there have been many significant changes in the Oxford Region in
that period. Developments in transport and shopping, for example, have greatly
extended the influence of the city of Oxford in the surrounding area. Motorways and high speed trains have also increased the effects of the proximity
of Greater London which, in many respects, is now much closer to Oxford than
it used to be. There have been many developments in industry, by no means
restricted to the motor industry, and a tremendous spread of housing, particularly in the areas immediately adjacent to Oxford itself. There have been important modifications in the nature of the administrative relationships between the
County and City of Oxford, and between the City and the University of Oxford.
Even that most modified of institutions has not been immune from changes, some
of them - though not all - arising from Lord Franks' Commission of Inquiry into
the University.

The Franks Report stressed the University's national and international obligations. To these its extra-mural department adds a regional responsibility.
As one who was until a few months ago Chairman of the Universities' Council
for Adult Education, I am particularly pleased that the Department for External Studies of the University of Oxford chose as part of the celebrations of
its centenary to pick up the theme of the Oxford Region survey of a quarter
of a century before.

In mounting the centenary conference which gave rise to this collection of essays, the Department had two aims: first, to stress its commitment to the region of Berkshire, Buckinghamshire and Oxfordshire, in which it has the responsibility for running courses; secondly, to demonstrate by the subjects covered and the analysis adopted, that application of scholarship to matters of public concern which has been a vital part of the extra-mural tradition from Sadler and Mackinder, through Tawney, to the present day.

These two concerns, for the region, and for the application of rational analysis to public problems, interweave in a variety of patterns. Within the University itself we examine college finances and property; within the City, we trace the impact of the University councillors, abolished on local government reform in 1974; within the County we look at the development of adult and community education - which takes us back to the aspirations of the group of young economists who were so active at the start of the Extension Movement. They, who travelled north to teach industrial economics to working men, would have been fascinated to see the impact of industry on Oxford itself. One essay here analyses industrial relations in the early car factories; whilst a second considers the impact of the Atomic Energy Authority's research site at Harwell.

This interplay of town and gown, of the University, the city, and the surrounding region, produces acute problems, fascinating to the geographer and planner, but deeply frustrating to the citizen or tourist. I am delighted that my fellow geographers are thus again well represented - including C.G. Smith, who has the unique distinction of contributing to both this and the earlier, 1954, volume - writing on subjects that range from the physical environment to the problem of conservation in the Oxford Green Belt. Oxford is a beautiful city, set in a lovely region of small towns, whose nineteenth-century development is traced here. How can this beauty be preserved in a way which is compatible both with prosperity for the region and with reasonable access for tourists to its sites? What are the effects of new archaeological finds, of transport policy, of the Green Belt, of Structure Plans and their predecessors? Here, surely, is a problem of public policy requiring cool analysis and informed public opinion: the ideal setting for a good extra-mural class!

There will, I am sure, be a very warm welcome for this volume, and I trust that it will prove to be as useful and as lasting as The Oxford Region appears to have been over more than a quarter of a century. As many people have more leisure, as more of us are prepared to study and to analyse conditions in the physical and social environment in which we live in some depth, and as there is a wider appreciation of the problems and the challenges that society faces - in the Oxford region no less than anywhere else - these papers will summarize the position in 1980 and in some instances may point the way towards the solutions that must be found in the coming years.

ROBERT W. STEEL

Vice-Chancellor, University of Wales;
Principal, University College of Swansea

November 1980

ACKNOWLEDGEMENTS

Thanks are due to Linda Rowley for producing the typescript,
Miller, Craig and Cocking Design Partnership for the cover design
and to Aero and Industrial Photographic Services, B.L.S.L. Photographic Services, Cowley, Oxford, Cambridge University Committee
for Aerial Photography, Oxfordshire County Libraries, Westgate,
Oxford and Mr. J.D. Peacock, Oxford, for permission to reproduce
photographs.

The Oxford University Department for External Studies wishes to
express its gratitude to the contributors and to everyone who has
made the production of this volume possible.

R.T. ROWLEY

November 1980

DEVELOPMENTS IN THE GEOMORPHOLOGY OF THE OXFORD REGION

A.S. Goudie, M.J. Day and M.G. Hart

The geomorphology of the Oxford Region (Fig. 1) has been the subject of various earlier reviews, notably by Sandford and Beckinsale (1954) and Beckit (1926). Likewise the Quaternary deposits, especially the river terraces, the old river channels, including that at Sugworth, and the solifluxion deposits have recently been discussed elsewhere (Goudie and Hart, 1975; Quaternary Research Association, 1976). This paper, therefore, does not aim to provide a comprehensive description or analysis of the geomorphology of the area, but rather to discuss selected features which have been the subject of recent attention: Karstic phenomena, the morphometry of the valley net, the origin of dry valleys, the fluted chalk scarps, and the sarsen blockfields.

KARSTIC FORMS AND PROCESSES

Introduction

The limestone and chalk terrains of the Oxford region are not well known for the development of classic karstic terrain. Closed depressions and caverns are rare, though fluvio-karst, in the form of dry valleys, is widespread. Arkell (1947) refers to some "swilly holes" developed in the Coral Rag which receive runoff from Shotover, Boars Hill and Cumnor Hurst, and to some small depressions in the Forest of Wychwood. Other depressions occur in association with patches of Tertiary deposits on the chalk near Great Bedwyn and in the Chilterns, while some small caves occur in Inferior Oolite of the Cotswolds, notably at Isaac's Cave, Cleeve Hill. Certain dip slope streams on the Cotswold Cuesta have underground courses, such as the Leach upstream from Eastleach.

One reason which is often cited to account for the paucity of karstic forms in the English scarplands is that the rocks themselves lack the mechanical strength to support large-scale solutional features. This may be one important factor in the lack of underground or collapse forms, but seems of limited importance in explaining the lack of surface solution dolines and other such phenomena, for these are known from elsewhere in lowland England both on the Chalk (Sperling, et al, 1977) and on the Jurassic limestone (Hindley, 1965). Likewise, as studies of water chemistry show, the lack of karstic phenomena cannot be explained in terms of low rates of solution, for rates in the Oxford region are of the same order as those in more 'classic' karst terrains (see p. 3). A more likely reason for the paucity of Karstic forms, especially dolines, is that there is a relative absence of impermeable or acidic non-calcareous rocks in the area such as would localise runoff and promote solution. The Oxford region has neither the widespread superficial Tertiary and Pleistocene sands and gravels of Dorset or East Anglia (where Chalk Karst is well developed) nor the overlying shale or sandstone bedrock such as characterises the Mendips, Ingleborough, and the Burren.

The Fluvio-karst of the River Leach

The influence of the limestone rocks of the region on river discharge and morphology is illustrated most clearly by a consideration of one of the intermittent streams of the Cotswold dip-slope, the Leach.

The hydrology of the River Leach was studied in some detail during the period August to December 1972 and two important and contrasting events occurred at this time. In early November the river reached an unusually low stage, and one month later it flooded. Details of the gauging stations used on the Leach appear in Table 1.

1

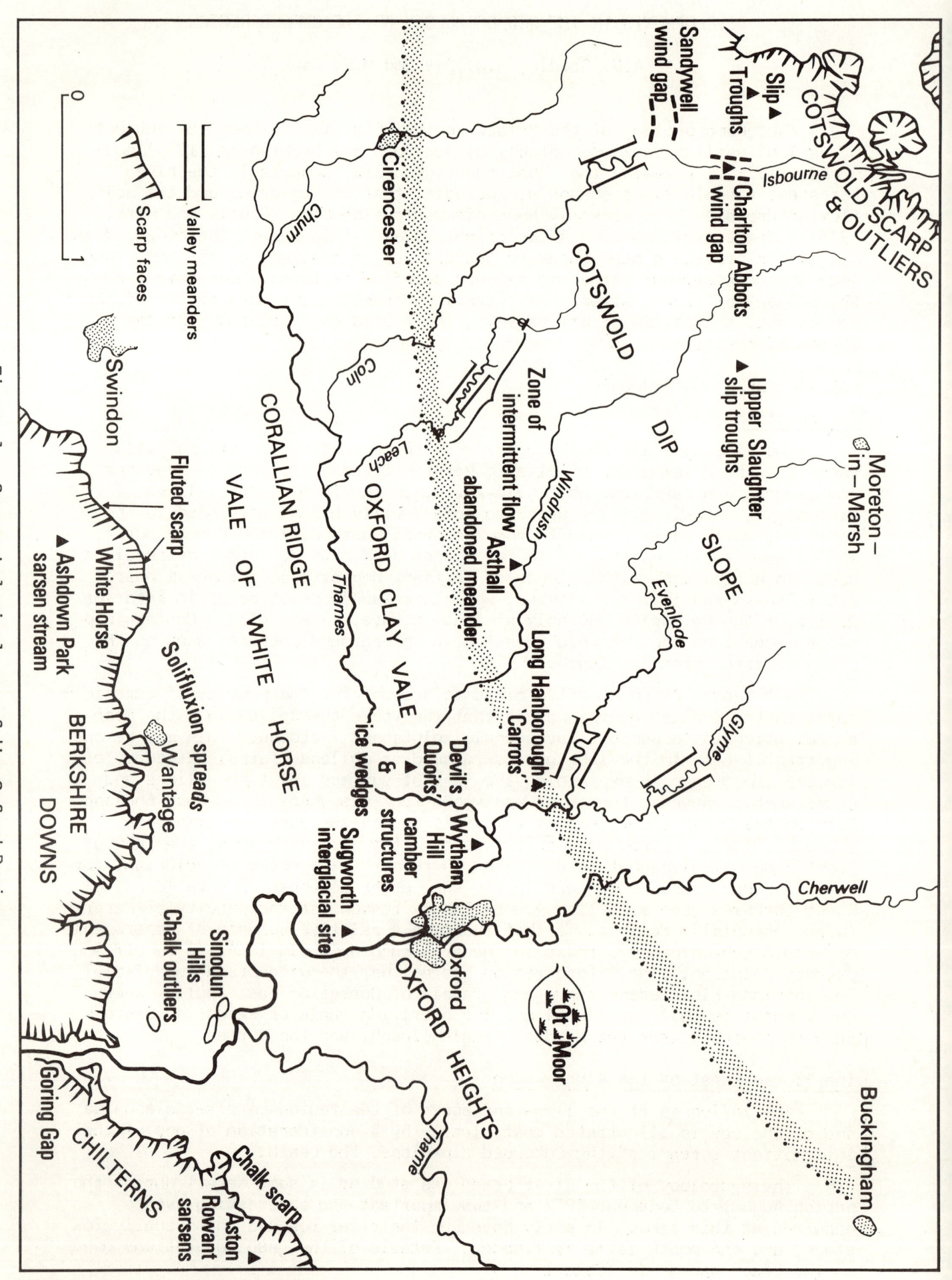

Figure 1. Geomorphological map of the Oxford Region

In the Leach valley the effect of the surface outcrop of Inferior and Great Oolites on the stream is seen in its most extreme form, for at times of low flow the stream becomes intermittent. At the beginning of November, 1972, for example, the channel was dry for about 14 km from just below Larkethill Wood to just above Eastleach village. The dry reach so formed coincided approximately with the surface outcrop of the Great Oolite. At its lower end the dry reach was terminated by some muddy ground with occasional stagnant pools of deep water, and the stream was flowing at the surface again in Eastleach village.

Heavy rain during the first week of December produced an overbank flood along most of the river, including the reach developed in the Great Oolite that had been dry one month earlier. This flood was closely monitored until the end of the month. The measurements obtained are presented in Table 2 as discharges and in Table 3 as discharges per unit drainage area. From 8th December, when monitoring began, until 16th December, the flood wave passed gradually downstream. Measurements of discharge and observation in the field showed that it reached Sheepbridge Barn on the 10th, Eastleach on the 12th and the mouth of the Leach at Lechlade on the 16th. This indicates that the flood wave reached Lechlade two weeks after the very heavy rainfall of the 1st December that initiated the flood, and took six days to clear the lower 15 km or so of the stream alone. It is usual, however, for flood waves to pass only slowly downstream on permeable lithologies, and it should also be noted that there were further falls of rain in the area until mid-month.

The measurements of discharge show that during the flood there was a gradual increase in discharge downstream, even along the reach that was dry at low flow. The data in Table 3 show, however, that the surface discharge at Sheepbridge Barn was lower than that to be expected in view of the additional increment of drainage area acquired below Swyre Farm. In other words, a greater proportion of the discharge was flowing as surface runoff at Swyre Farm than at Sheepbridge Barn. The Great Oolite reach begins, however, near Larkethill. For some reason, therefore, when the Leach is in flood the progressive loss of water underground is delayed until the section downstream of Swyre Farm is reached.

The behaviour of the river as the flood was going down was particularly interesting. From measurement and observation it was clear that from about the 17th onwards the discharge was decreasing at a much faster rate at Swyre Farm and especially Sheepbridge Barn than elsewhere on the stream. On the 27th the Leach became an intermittent stream once again. A very short dry reach, about 80 metres long, had developed at Sheepbridge Barn. Over the next few days, as the river-stage elsewhere continued to fall, the dry reach gradually lengthened. It lengthened quickly in an upstream direction but only slowly downstream, such that on January 10th 1973 it extended from just below Swyre Farm to about 200 metres below Sheepbridge Barn. This clearly represented a transitional stage between the continuous stream of the earlier part of the month and the state of the stream at low flow, when the dry reach extended from Larkethill to Eastleach.

There is reason to believe, however, that the interesting behaviour of the Leach owes something to human interference. Phillips (1871) in an otherwise comprehensive description of the general characteristics of the dip-slope streams of the Cotswolds, does not refer to the Leach as an intermittent stream, and the 6" sheets of the Ordnance Survey, last fully revised between 1919 and 1924, show the Leach as a continuous stream.

Spring Water Chemistry

Springs, on account of the alternation of permeable limestones and impermeable clays are widespread in the Oxford Region and the study of their

3

water chemistry enables an assessment of the importance of solutional activity. A summary of the results of water hardness determinations is presented in Table 4.

The waters of all the limestone formations show high hardness values. Paterson's (1970) values are highest from the Corallian and lowest from the Chalk. Goudie (1967), however, finds lower mean values for the Jurassic of the north Cotswolds than are quoted by Paterson for the Chalk. Smith's (1965) values for the south Cotswolds seems comparable to those of Paterson for the North Oxfordshire Heights. The values of Paterson and the authors for the Chalk are very similar.

TABLE 1

Details of Gauging Stations on the River Leach

	Map Reference	Drainage area (km^2)	Bedrock			
Larkethill	139114	14.73	Alluvium overlying Great Oolite			
Swyre Farm	151088	26.88	"	"	"	"
Sheepbridge Barn	191069	58.95	"	"	"	"
Lechlade	226992	82.77	"	"	Oxford Clay	

TABLE 2

The discharge of the River Leach (Cumecs)

	Larkethill	Swyre Farm	Sheepbridge Barn	Lechlade
8.12.72			0.676	0.431
10.12.72	0.329	1.004	1.069	2.187
11.12.72	0.263	0.821	1.043	2.670
12.12.72	0.226	0.672	1.016	2.537
14.12.72	0.181	0.801	0.925	2.500
17.12.72	0.212	0.651	0.988	2.634
20.12.72	0.129	0.285	0.425	2.086
22.12.72	0.101		0.213	1.728
24.12.72			0.096	1.507
27.12.72	0.065		Nil	1.396
29.12.72	0.065		Nil	1.277
1. 1.73			Nil	1.106
3. 1.73			Nil	0.991
5. 1.73			Nil	0.956
10. 1.73			Nil	0.837

TABLE 3

The discharge of the River Leach
(Cumecs per square kilometre of catchment area)

	Larkethill	Swyre Farm	Sheepbridge Barn	Lechlade
8.12.72		0.011	0.011467	0.005207
10.12.72	0.022335	0.037351	0.018134	0.026422
11.12.72	0.017854	0.030543	0.017692	0.032258
12.12.72	0.015342	0.025000	0.017234	0.030651
14.12.72	0.012287	0.029799	0.015691	0.030204
17.12.72	0.014392	0.024218	0.016759	0.031823
20.12.72	0.008757	0.010602	0.007209	0.025202
22.12.72	0.006856		0.003613	0.020877
24.12.72			0.001628	0.018207
27.12.72	0.004412		Nil	0.016866
29.12.72	0.004412		Nil	0.015428
1. 1.73			Nil	0.013362
3. 1.73			Nil	0.011972
5. 1.73			Nil	0.011550
10. 1.73			Nil	0.010112

TABLE 4

Water chemistry data for different lithologies in the Oxford Region

Area	Hardness (ppm) Total	Calcium	Magnesium	No. of samples	Ca/Mg ratio	Source
Oxford Heights (Corallian)	431	424	7	120	60.57	Paterson (1970)
North Oxfordshire Heights (Jurassic)	344	334	10	392	33.40	Paterson (1970)
North Cotswolds (Jurassic)		257	–	109	–	Goudie (1967)
South Cotswolds (Jurassic)		260–370				Smith (1965)
Berkshire Downs (Chalk)	269	264	5	138	52.80	Paterson (1970)
Chiltern Hills (Chalk)	267	260	7	24	37.14	Authors

Paterson accounts for the variations in hardness between the rock types in terms of variation in residence time of the water, lithological variation and variation in CO_2 concentration with differing soil type. The mechanism of flow in the rock masses is, however, obscure. Paterson's data for tritium dating of water from the Berkshire Downs at the Woolston Wells indicates residence times in excess of fifteen years. At the same time, however, a flushing out of the higher-hardness water is indicated after times of heavy rainfall. It may be that two distinct types of flow exist in the chalk, a diffuse flow involving very slow seepage through pore spaces and a rapid flow along well-defined lines which may be in the form of conduits.

Observations of pH of the waters issuing from the limestones indicates that there are not significant differences between the values of the different lithologies. Paterson (1970) gives the following values:

Formation	Mean pH	Number of Samples
Jurassic (N. Oxon. Hts.)	7.3	365
Corallian (Oxford Hts.)	7.0	119
Chalk (Berks. Downs)	7.3	136

Smith (1965) indicates a range from 6.85 to 7.95 for the Jurassic of the south Cotswolds. Preliminary results from the Chalk of the Chilterns show a mean pH value of 7.2.

Within any of the major rock types of the area there may be a considerable range in hardness values. Monitoring of spring hardness values in the Cotswolds, for example, indicated that some springs were consistently low (see, for instance, Postlip and Guiting Power) while others (see for instance Chedworth Manor and Spring Bottom) were higher. This spatial variability of spring water chemistry (Table 5) illustrates the need for detailed spatial sampling to determine regional denudation rates.

Hardness as a proportion of total dissolved solids

The calcium and magnesium hardness determinations of the spring waters only give a partial indication of net rates of solute removal. Data obtained from the North West Gloucestershire Water Board and the Cotswold Water Board (Goudie 1967) indicate that other constituents are important (Table 6). Thus, for example, calcium carbonate only makes up 66% of the total dissolved solids at Seven Springs (967169), 67% for Upper Swell (177269), 65% for Lower Swell (174256), 61% for Northfield (984221) and 64% for Dowdeswell (988197). The Magnesium carbonate content is also much lower than that of calcium carbonate: the Ca/Mg ratio varies between 33.40 and 60.57 (Table 4).

One feature of the spring water chemistry of the region is the relative constancy of its dissolved load content through time. This relative constancy in values reflects the relative importance of the percolation contribution to groundwater flow, for although a conduit-type flow has been recognised for example, in Chalk areas (Smith, 1976), the springs of the Oxford region are not true resurgence types. Likewise spring temperature values appear to remain moderately constant. Values for December 1966 (in Table 7) are, for instance, almost identical to those in July. More work on the correlations between environmental variables and spring water chemistry of the type developed by Paterson (1972) needs to be undertaken.

Rates of Limestone denudation

Utilising the water chemistry data, rock density determinations, and annual rates of runoff, overall rates of net surface denudation have been obtained for the Oxford Region following the method of Williams (1963). These are summarised in Table 8.

Some comparable data for elsewhere in Britain are summarised in Table 9. From these it is clear that while there is some variation in denudation rates within the Cotswold region, the values are broadly similar to those found in highly developed karstic areas such as the Peak District, Craven, the Mendips and South Wales.

TABLE 5

Calcium carbonate values for Cotswold springs (1965 and 1966)

Location	G.R.	1965					1966					
		Aug	Sept	Oct	Nov	Dec	Jan	Feb	Mar	Apr	July	Dec
Chedworth Manor	052121	305	257	264	220	320	321	–	–	–	–	–
Chedworth Villa	053135	220	–	–	–	–	–	–	–	–	–	–
Cleeve Nutterswood	982255	–	–	–	–	–	–	–	–	–	148	148
Cleeve Postlip	996262	128	129	123	123	123	–	–	–	–	–	–
Cleeve Rising Sun	984269	–	–	–	–	–	–	–	–	–	190	195
Cleeve Table	983249	–	–	–	–	–	–	–	–	–	337	353
Coberley	962160	–	–	–	–	–	–	–	–	–	217	220
Combend	984118	–	274	–	–	–	–	–	–	–	–	–
Compton Abdale I	061165	249	142	238	236	264	265	–	258	264	251	263
" " II	060165	–	–	–	–	–	–	–	305	–	287	303
" " III	063164	–	–	–	–	–	–	–	–	–	250	263
Upper Cowley	961142	–	–	–	–	–	–	–	–	–	276	339
Lower Cowley	957138	288	–	–	–	–	–	277	322	–	274	–
Crippets	938182	–	–	–	–	–	–	–	–	–	287	320
Guiting Power	095250	198	197	190	150	197	219	–	–	–	190	192
Hampnett	099159	–	–	–	–	–	–	–	–	–	287	313
Hilcot	997168	–	–	–	–	–	–	–	–	–	175	169
Kineton Ford	007260	230	258	285	229	275	–	–	–	–	–	–
Lower Swell	174256	210	209	209	170	229	203	–	–	–	209	223
Salperton	075209	–	–	–	–	–	–	–	–	–	240	285
Sandy Well	009203	–	–	–	–	–	–	–	–	–	293	285
Seven Springs	967169	211	215	209	210	210	208	208	210	208	215	210
Shipton Oliffe	041188	–	–	–	–	–	–	–	–	–	284	285
Spring Bottom	966208	413	388	370	370	402	–	355	401	401	393	400
Ullenwood I	933175	–	–	–	–	–	–	–	–	–	288	303
" II	933173	–	–	–	–	–	–	–	–	–	293	231
" III	932171	–	–	–	–	–	–	–	–	–	231	245
Whittington	010211	–	–	–	–	–	–	–	–	–	398	338

NOTE: Values obtained by E.D.T.A. titration

TABLE 6

Chemical content of Cotswold Springs (ppm)

	Spring (1)	(2)	(3)	(4)	(5)	(6)	(7)	(8)
$CaCO_3$	190	220	205	180	180	225	190	180
Calcium Sulphate	37	27	47	31	34	47	61	31
Calcium Chloride	8	-	-	14	6	17	11	2
Magnes. Chloride	8	2	12	-	9	-	5	10
Magnes. Nitrate	7	-	10	15	7	14	15	5
Magnes. Sulphate	-	21	-	-	-	-	-	-
Sodium Chloride	-	12	-	-	-	-	-	-
Sodium Nitrate	21	4	18	21	18	21	21	27
Potassium Chloride	4	4	2	4	1	2	4	2
Silica	8	7	8	9	8	5	7	8
Various	-	-	8	-	-	19	-	-
Total	283	297	310	274	263	350	314	265

		Date	O.S. Grid Reference
(1)	= Upper Swell	24.5.65	177269
(2)	= Bibury	4.10.66	
(3)	= Seven Springs	1.5.62	967169
(4)	= Lower Swell	24.5.66	174256
(5)	= Swyreford	30.4.64	029203
(6)	= Coates	1.5.62	
(7)	= Seven Springs	24.5.66	967169
(8)	= Lower Swell	30.4.64	174256

TABLE 7

Spring Water Temperature Variations

Location	O.S. Grid Reference	Sept	Oct	Dec	Jan	Feb	Mar	July
Postlip	996262	8.75	8.00	8.75	–	–	–	–
Chedworth Manor	052121	–	10.00	10.00	9.00	–	–	–
Compton Abdale I	061165	9.00	12.00	9.50	9.00	–	8.75	9.00
" " II	060165	–	–	–	–	–	9.00	9.50
" " III	063164	–	–	–	–	–	–	9.50
Lower Cowley	957138	–	–	–	–	6.00	7.00	–
Guiting Power	095250	–	10.00	9.50	8.75	–	–	9.25
Coberley	962160	–	–	–	–	–	9.00	–
Kineton	087260	10.50	7.50	–	–	–	–	–
Lower Swell	174256	9.50	10.50	9.00	–	–	–	9.25
Sandywell	009203	–	–	–	–	–	–	10.50
Seven Springs	967169	8.75	11.00	9.75	10.00	7.50	7.50	9.75
Shipton Oliffe	041188	–	12.00	–	–	–	–	9.00
Spring Bottom	966208	–	–	11.00	–	8.00	9.00	10.00

TABLE 8

Rates of Solutional Denudation in the Oxford Region

Area	Rate $(m^3/km^2 yr)$	Source
Jurassic limestone of the North Cotswolds	35	Goudie (1967)
Berkshire Downs (Chalk)	67	Paterson (1970)
North Oxford Heights (Jurassic)	60-66	"
Corallian Scarp	74	"
Thames Basin at Eynsham	60	Douglas (1964)

TABLE 9

Rates of Solutional Denudation in Britain Exclusive of the Oxford Region

Area	Year $(m^3/km^2/yr)$	Source
Peak District	75-83	Pitty (1968)
Craven	40	Sweeting (1965)
Fergus and Shannon	51-53	Williams (1963)
East Anglia	25	Perrin (1955)
Mellte, S. Wales	16	Groom and Williams (1965)
Lismore, Scotland	150	Corbel (1959)
Lismore, Scotland	100	Smith (1965)
Mendips	40	Corbel (1959)

TABLE 10

Miscellaneous Basin Morphometric Characteristics

For The Oxford Region

	Chalk	Corallian	Oolite	Clay
Bifurcation Ratio	3.34	3.32	3.77	3.32
Mean Stream Lengths (km) Order 1	5.10	4.69	4.35	3.62
2	3.16	2.83	1.79	2.03
3	1.79	2.48	1.27	1.90
Channel Frequency	1.80	1.25	1.92	1.65
Melton's Basin Infilling Index	0.16	0.18	0.20	0.19
Valley Density (km/km^2)	0.96	1.00	0.88	0.85

From de Courcy Wheeler (1974)

TABLE 11

Morphometric Data for Small English Catchments

Source	Location	Mean Bifurcation Ratio	Mean Valley Density (km/km^2)
Morgan, 1971	English Chalk	4.0	-
Brown, 1969	Chilterns	-	2.66-3.84
Morgan, 1971	Weald Clay	-	2.3
"	Ashdown Sand	-	2.0
"	Tunbridge Wells Sand	-	1.7
Gregory, 1966	Otter Basin	-	2.14
"	South Devon (5 basins)	-	3.03
Brunsden, 1968	Dartmoor Granite	3.5-3.9	1.61-2.24
"	Middle Devonian	3.8-4.2	2.92-2.98
"	Lower Devonian	3.9	2.86
"	Culm Measures	3.4-3.7	3.23-4.78
Chorley & Morgan, 1962	Dartmoor		2.14

FLUVIO-KARSTIC LANDFORMS OF THE OXFORD REGION

The nature of the Valley Net

Morphometric analysis of 1:25,000 O.S. maps of the Oxford region has been undertaken to ascertain the nature of the valley networks on different rock types. Data from this work are summarised in Table 10. Analysis was restricted to third order basins in which there was no obvious evidence of artificial surface streams. Stream ordering followed Strahler's method, and for the construction of valley networks, courses were drawn through the crenulations of the contours. This is the method utilised by Morgan (1971) and Paterson (1970).

The main feature of the work is that there appears to be no statistically significant differences between the bifurcation ratios, drainage densities, channel frequencies and Melton infilling indices between the four main rock types of the region (de Courcy Wheeler, 1974). In essence, therefore, the valley nets, whether they be on Chalk, Corallian beds, Oxford and Kimmeridge Clays, or Cotswold oolitic limestone, appear to be similar. Thus, for example, drainage density (in km/km^2) only ranges from 0.85 on the clays to 1.00 on the Corallian. In that the great bulk of the valley network is a relict Pleistocene feature it may be that this remarkable similarity was imposed by formerly less marked permeability differences produced by a permafrost cover.

Overall, the valley densities of the Oxford region are low in comparison with those of many sedimentary rock types elsewhere in England (Table 11), though densities in lowland England generally tend to cluster around 2 to 3.

Dry Valleys and Misfit Streams

Introduction: One of the most striking features of the fluvial geomorphology of the Oxford Region is the presence of dry valleys and misfit streams. Misfit streams are streams which are much smaller (by a ratio of about 10:1) than the valleys (often referred to in the local geomorphological literature in a somewhat exaggerated way as 'gorges') in which they flow in respect of width and meander wavelength, and the Cotswold Hills are particularly notable for misfits. The relationship between stream- and valley-size is most impressive where the valley itself describes regular and symmetrical meanders. Such valley-meanders are particularly well displayed in the lower part of the so-called Evenlode Gorge, between Stonesfield and Long Hanborough, and by the Leach Valley between Swyre Farm and Eastleach (Fig 1). Most valley meanders are currently occupied by the small modern streams but in the case of the Windrush at Asthall the stream has abandoned one of its meanders and has shortened its course by cutting across a neck of land between Asthall and Swinbrook. The Chalk cuestas of the Berkshire Downs and Chiltern Hills are, on the other hand, especially well known for their systems of dry valleys. It must be pointed out, however, that both misfit streams and dry valleys occur on both the Cotswolds and on the Chalk. The misfit streams of the Cotswolds usually have tributary systems of dry valleys, and some of the valleys of the Chalk carry perennial misfit streams. The characterisation of the chalk by dry valleys and the Cotswolds by misfit streams is a matter of emphasis only.

There is no common consensus as to the causes of valley meander, misfit stream and dry valley development. Table 12 shows some of the main theories which have been postulated. They can be categorised into the uniformitarian hypotheses (those requiring no major changes of climate or base level but merely the operation of normal geomorphic processes through time), the marine (related to base level changes) and the palaeoclimatic (associated primarily with the climatic changes of the Pleistocene). Some of the hypotheses have broad applicability throughout the region (eg. 2,7,8, 13,14,15) while others may account for individual cases (eg. 5,6,10,11). It is not possible to state with certainty which of the general hypotheses is likely to have been most important but dated solifluction deposits and terrace spreads suggest that the cold phases of the Pleistocene did see intense fluvial erosion, frost weathering and mass movement of the Chalk and the limestones.

TABLE 12

Hypotheses of Dry Valley Formation

Uniformitarian

1. Superimposition from an impermeable cover of Tertiary Beds, Plateau Drift or Fullers Earth

2. Joint enlargement by solution through time

3. Cutting down of major through-flowing stream

4. The Chandler-Fagg hypothesis of scarp retreat

5. Cavern Collapse

6. River Capture (eg. of Thames tributaries by Severn/Avon tributaries)

7. Rare events of extreme magnitude (eg. extreme floods)

Marine

8. Non-adjustment of stream to a falling Pleistocene sea-level and associated fall of ground-water levels

9. Tidal Palaeomorphs

Palaeoclimatic

10. Overflow from proglacial lakes (such as Lake Harrison)

11. Glacial scour, possibly during the Anglian

12. Glacial meltwater

13. Higher rainfall and/or reduced evaporation

14. Spring snow melt under periglacial conditions

15. Runoff from impermeable permafrost

Within the Oxford Region, some of the escarpment dry valleys of the Berkshire Downs are attributed to niveo-fluvial processes during Zone III by Paterson (1970, 1971, 1977). At the foot of these dry valleys lie fans of chalky solifluxion deposits assigned to this period. The sites reveal a stratigraphy comparable with that found elsewhere in southern England (Kerney, 1963; Kerney, Brown and Chandler, 1964; Evans, 1966).

Support for the periglacial origin of some escarpment dry valleys of the Chilterns comes from Brown (1969), who studied the relationship between joint- and dry valley-orientations near Ivinghoe. He found little or no correlation between the orientations of joints and dry valleys, and went on to show that the valleys tended to be orientated normally down the scarp. He concluded that these two pieces of evidence supported a periglacial rather than a spring-sapping origin for those valleys, since while spring-sapping might be expected to pick out the joint pattern, periglacial torrents could have their direction determined mainly by the line of greatest slope.

DEVELOPMENTS IN THE GEOMORPHOLOGY OF THE OXFORD REGION

A.S. Goudie, M.J. Day and M.G. Hart

The geomorphology of the Oxford Region (Fig. 1) has been the subject of various earlier reviews, notably by Sandford and Beckinsale (1954) and Beckit (1926). Likewise the Quaternary deposits, especially the river terraces, the old river channels, including that at Sugworth, and the solifluxion deposits have recently been discussed elsewhere (Goudie and Hart, 1975; Quaternary Research Association, 1976). This paper, therefore, does not aim to provide a comprehensive description or analysis of the geomorphology of the area, but rather to discuss selected features which have been the subject of recent attention: Karstic phenomena, the morphometry of the valley net, the origin of dry valleys, the fluted chalk scarps, and the sarsen blockfields.

KARSTIC FORMS AND PROCESSES

Introduction

The limestone and chalk terrains of the Oxford region are not well known for the development of classic karstic terrain. Closed depressions and caverns are rare, though fluvio-karst, in the form of dry valleys, is widespread. Arkell (1947) refers to some "swilly holes" developed in the Coral Rag which receive runoff from Shotover, Boars Hill and Cumnor Hurst, and to some small depressions in the Forest of Wychwood. Other depressions occur in association with patches of Tertiary deposits on the chalk near Great Bedwyn and in the Chilterns, while some small caves occur in Inferior Oolite of the Cotswolds, notably at Isaac's Cave, Cleeve Hill. Certain dip slope streams on the Cotswold Cuesta have underground courses, such as the Leach upstream from Eastleach.

One reason which is often cited to account for the paucity of karstic forms in the English scarplands is that the rocks themselves lack the mechanical strength to support large-scale solutional features. This may be one important factor in the lack of underground or collapse forms, but seems of limited importance in explaining the lack of surface solution dolines and other such phenomena, for these are known from elsewhere in lowland England both on the Chalk (Sperling, et al, 1977) and on the Jurassic limestone (Hindley, 1965). Likewise, as studies of water chemistry show, the lack of karstic phenomena cannot be explained in terms of low rates of solution, for rates in the Oxford region are of the same order as those in more 'classic' karst terrains (see p. 3). A more likely reason for the paucity of Karstic forms, especially dolines, is that there is a relative absence of impermeable or acidic non-calcareous rocks in the area such as would localise runoff and promote solution. The Oxford region has neither the widespread superficial Tertiary and Pleistocene sands and gravels of Dorset or East Anglia (where Chalk Karst is well developed) nor the overlying shale or sandstone bedrock such as characterises the Mendips, Ingleborough, and the Burren.

The Fluvio-karst of the River Leach

The influence of the limestone rocks of the region on river discharge and morphology is illustrated most clearly by a consideration of one of the intermittent streams of the Cotswold dip-slope, the Leach.

The hydrology of the River Leach was studied in some detail during the period August to December 1972 and two important and contrasting events occurred at this time. In early November the river reached an unusually low stage, and one month later it flooded. Details of the gauging stations used on the Leach appear in Table 1.

1

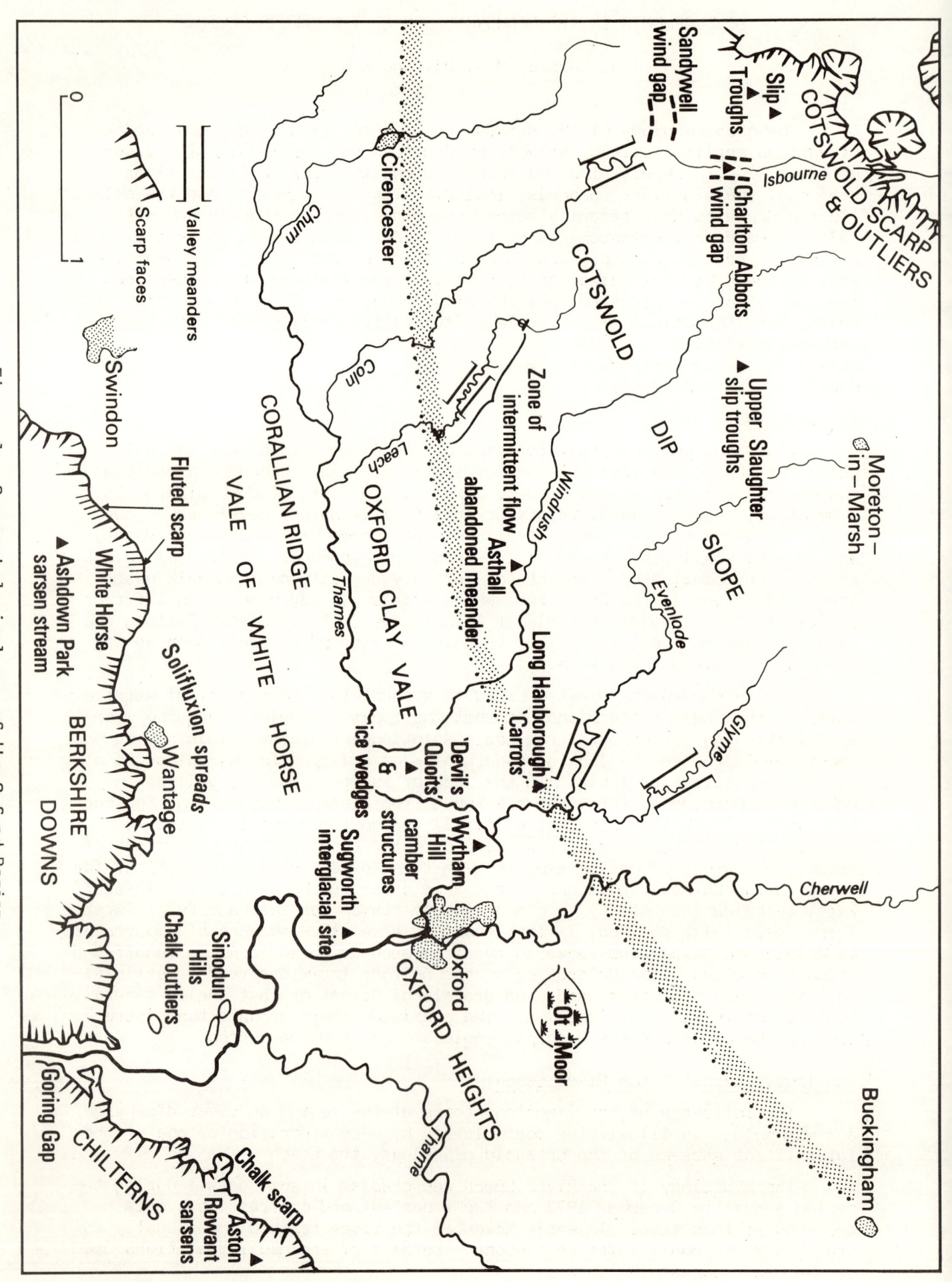

Figure 1. Geomorphological map of the Oxford Region

In the Leach valley the effect of the surface outcrop of Inferior and Great Oolites on the stream is seen in its most extreme form, for at times of low flow the stream becomes intermittent. At the beginning of November, 1972, for example, the channel was dry for about 14 km from just below Larkethill Wood to just above Eastleach village. The dry reach so formed coincided approximately with the surface outcrop of the Great Oolite. At its lower end the dry reach was terminated by some muddy ground with occasional stagnant pools of deep water, and the stream was flowing at the surface again in Eastleach village.

Heavy rain during the first week of December produced an overbank flood along most of the river, including the reach developed in the Great Oolite that had been dry one month earlier. This flood was closely monitored until the end of the month. The measurements obtained are presented in Table 2 as discharges and in Table 3 as discharges per unit drainage area. From 8th December, when monitoring began, until 16th December, the flood wave passed gradually downstream. Measurements of discharge and observation in the field showed that it reached Sheepbridge Barn on the 10th, Eastleach on the 12th and the mouth of the Leach at Lechlade on the 16th. This indicates that the flood wave reached Lechlade two weeks after the very heavy rainfall of the 1st December that initiated the flood, and took six days to clear the lower 15 km or so of the stream alone. It is usual, however, for flood waves to pass only slowly downstream on permeable lithologies, and it should also be noted that there were further falls of rain in the area until mid-month.

The measurements of discharge show that during the flood there was a gradual increase in discharge downstream, even along the reach that was dry at low flow. The data in Table 3 show, however, that the surface discharge at Sheepbridge Barn was lower than that to be expected in view of the additional increment of drainage area acquired below Swyre Farm. In other words, a greater proportion of the discharge was flowing as surface runoff at Swyre Farm than at Sheepbridge Barn. The Great Oolite reach begins, however, near Larkethill. For some reason, therefore, when the Leach is in flood the progressive loss of water underground is delayed until the section downstream of Swyre Farm is reached.

The behaviour of the river as the flood was going down was particularly interesting. From measurement and observation it was clear that from about the 17th onwards the discharge was decreasing at a much faster rate at Swyre Farm and especially Sheepbridge Barn than elsewhere on the stream. On the 27th the Leach became an intermittent stream once again. A very short dry reach, about 80 metres long, had developed at Sheepbridge Barn. Over the next few days, as the river-stage elsewhere continued to fall, the dry reach gradually lengthened. It lengthened quickly in an upstream direction but only slowly downstream, such that on January 10th 1973 it extended from just below Swyre Farm to about 200 metres below Sheepbridge Barn. This clearly represented a transitional stage between the continuous stream of the earlier part of the month and the state of the stream at low flow, when the dry reach extended from Larkethill to Eastleach.

There is reason to believe, however, that the interesting behaviour of the Leach owes something to human interference. Phillips (1871) in an otherwise comprehensive description of the general characteristics of the dip-slope streams of the Cotswolds, does not refer to the Leach as an intermittent stream, and the 6" sheets of the Ordnance Survey, last fully revised between 1919 and 1924, show the Leach as a continuous stream.

Spring Water Chemistry

Springs, on account of the alternation of permeable limestones and impermeable clays are widespread in the Oxford Region and the study of their water chemistry enables an assessment of the importance of solutional activity. A summary of the results of water hardness determinations is presented in Table 4.

The waters of all the limestone formations show high hardness values. Paterson's (1970) values are highest from the Corallian and lowest from the Chalk. Goudie (1967), however, finds lower mean values for the Jurassic of the north Cotswolds than are quoted by Paterson for the Chalk. Smith's (1965) values for the south Cotswolds seems comparable to those of Paterson for the North Oxfordshire Heights. The values of Paterson and the authors for the Chalk are very similar.

TABLE 1

Details of Gauging Stations on the River Leach

	Map Reference	Drainage area (km^2)	Bedrock
Larkethill	139114	14.73	Alluvium overlying Great Oolite
Swyre Farm	151088	26.88	" " " "
Sheepbridge Barn	191069	58.95	" " " "
Lechlade	226992	82.77	" " Oxford Clay

TABLE 2

The discharge of the River Leach (Cumecs)

	Larkethill	Swyre Farm	Sheepbridge Barn	Lechlade
8.12.72			0.676	0.431
10.12.72	0.329	1.004	1.069	2.187
11.12.72	0.263	0.821	1.043	2.670
12.12.72	0.226	0.672	1.016	2.537
14.12.72	0.181	0.801	0.925	2.500
17.12.72	0.212	0.651	0.988	2.634
20.12.72	0.129	0.285	0.425	2.086
22.12.72	0.101		0.213	1.728
24.12.72			0.096	1.507
27.12.72	0.065		Nil	1.396
29.12.72	0.065		Nil	1.277
1. 1.73			Nil	1.106
3. 1.73			Nil	0.991
5. 1.73			Nil	0.956
10. 1.73			Nil	0.837

4

TABLE 3

The discharge of the River Leach
(Cumecs per square kilometre of catchment area)

	Larkethill	Swyre Farm	Sheepbridge Barn	Lechlade
8.12.72		0.011	0.011467	0.005207
10.12.72	0.022335	0.037351	0.018134	0.026422
11.12.72	0.017854	0.030543	0.017692	0.032258
12.12.72	0.015342	0.025000	0.017234	0.030651
14.12.72	0.012287	0.029799	0.015691	0.030204
17.12.72	0.014392	0.024218	0.016759	0.031823
20.12.72	0.008757	0.010602	0.007209	0.025202
22.12.72	0.006856		0.003613	0.020877
24.12.72			0.001628	0.018207
27.12.72	0.004412		Nil	0.016866
29.12.72	0.004412		Nil	0.015428
1. 1.73			Nil	0.013362
3. 1.73			Nil	0.011972
5. 1.73			Nil	0.011550
10. 1.73			Nil	0.010112

TABLE 4

Water chemistry data for different lithologies in the Oxford Region

Area	Hardness (ppm) Total	Calcium	Magnesium	No. of samples	Ca/Mg ratio	Source
Oxford Heights (Corallian)	431	424	7	120	60.57	Paterson (1970)
North Oxfordshire Heights (Jurassic)	344	334	10	392	33.40	Paterson (1970)
North Cotswolds (Jurassic)		257	–	109	–	Goudie (1967)
South Cotswolds (Jurassic)		260–370				Smith (1965)
Berkshire Downs (Chalk)	269	264	5	138	52.80	Paterson (1970)
Chiltern Hills (Chalk)	267	260	7	24	37.14	Authors

Paterson accounts for the variations in hardness between the rock types in terms of variation in residence time of the water, lithological variation and variation in CO_2 concentration with differing soil type. The mechanism of flow in the rock masses is, however, obscure. Paterson's data for tritium dating of water from the Berkshire Downs at the Woolston Wells indicates residence times in excess of fifteen years. At the same time, however, a flushing out of the higher-hardness water is indicated after times of heavy rainfall. It may be that two distinct types of flow exist in the chalk, a diffuse flow involving very slow seepage through pore spaces and a rapid flow along well-defined lines which may be in the form of conduits.

Observations of pH of the waters issuing from the limestones indicates that there are not significant differences between the values of the different lithologies. Paterson (1970) gives the following values:

Formation	Mean pH	Number of Samples
Jurassic (N. Oxon. Hts.)	7.3	365
Corallian (Oxford Hts.)	7.0	119
Chalk (Berks. Downs)	7.3	136

Smith (1965) indicates a range from 6.85 to 7.95 for the Jurassic of the south Cotswolds. Preliminary results from the Chalk of the Chilterns show a mean pH value of 7.2.

Within any of the major rock types of the area there may be a considerable range in hardness values. Monitoring of spring hardness values in the Cotswolds, for example, indicated that some springs were consistently low (see, for instance, Postlip and Guiting Power) while others (see for instance Chedworth Manor and Spring Bottom) were higher. This spatial variability of spring water chemistry (Table 5) illustrates the need for detailed spatial sampling to determine regional denudation rates.

Hardness as a proportion of total dissolved solids

The calcium and magnesium hardness determinations of the spring waters only give a partial indication of net rates of solute removal. Data obtained from the North West Gloucestershire Water Board and the Cotswold Water Board (Goudie 1967) indicate that other constituents are important (Table 6). Thus, for example, calcium carbonate only makes up 66% of the total dissolved solids at Seven Springs (967169), 67% for Upper Swell (177269), 65% for Lower Swell (174256), 61% for Northfield (984221) and 64% for Dowdeswell (988197). The Magnesium carbonate content is also much lower than that of calcium carbonate: the Ca/Mg ratio varies between 33.40 and 60.57 (Table 4).

One feature of the spring water chemistry of the region is the relative constancy of its dissolved load content through time. This relative constancy in values reflects the relative importance of the percolation contribution to groundwater flow, for although a conduit-type flow has been recognised for example, in Chalk areas (Smith, 1976), the springs of the Oxford region are not true resurgence types. Likewise spring temperature values appear to remain moderately constant. Values for December 1966 (in Table 7) are, for instance, almost identical to those in July. More work on the correlations between environmental variables and spring water chemistry of the type developed by Paterson (1972) needs to be undertaken.

Rates of Limestone denudation

Utilising the water chemistry data, rock density determinations, and annual rates of runoff, overall rates of net surface denudation have been obtained for the Oxford Region following the method of Williams (1963). These are summarised in Table 8.

The application of the periglacial hypotheses to back-slope chalk dry valleys has been on a limited scale only. However, dry valley asymmetry observed on the Chilterns (Ollier and Thomasson, 1957), and the Marlborough Downs (Small, Clark and Lewin, 1970) is attributed to periglacial conditions. Under periglacial conditions, the aspect of a slope may have a considerable influence on its form and development. In the Chilterns, where in general the valleys run from north-west to south-east, the valley slopes facing south-westwards are usually much steeper than those which face north-eastwards. Ollier and Thomasson suggest that the slopes facing south-west are more prone to frost-weathering and solifluxion than the slopes facing north-east because they receive greater amounts of insolation. They are therefore "active" and undergo both retreat and steepening of angle. It is interesting that in the Clatford Bottom region of the Marlborough Downs, the dry valley asymmetry is typically reversed: long, gentle (3-4°) south-south-west-facing slopes face steeper north-north-east-facing slopes. The asymmetry is still attributed to differential receipt of insolation, but in this area the "active" processes operating on the south-south-west-facing slopes are supposed to have degraded the slope rather than to have steepened it. There seems to be a fundamental doubt as to whether "active" periglacial processes do or do not steepen slopes. It has further been postulated for the Clatford Bottom area (Small et al, 1970) that the tongues of solifluxion debris moving down the gentler slope will actually push any stream that may have flowed along the valley bottom into the base of the opposing slope, which may thus be steepened by under-cutting and the valley asymmetry accentuated. French (1973) has suggested that cryo-pediments are one component of the asymmetry.

The hypotheses of erosion by niveo-fluvial processes has been successfully applied to the oversize valleys of the Cotswolds by Beckinsale (1953, 1970). He lays great stress on the regime of the streams that would have existed during periglacial conditions - a "nival" regime, with the annual discharge strongly concentrated into spring snowmelt runoff, when great valley-erosion would occur. This theory is in accord with the "cold-condition" origin of most of the terraces of the upper Thames (Goudie and Hart, 1975). It is possible that, under periglacial conditions, material was eroded from the Cotswolds and deposited in the Thames valley to form terraces.

More recently it has been suggested that the drainage system of the southern Cotswolds and South Oxfordshire may have been influenced by early glaciation (Kellaway, et al 1971; Beckinsale and Beckinsale, 1976) and various possible glacial erratics have been noted by Whittow in a wind-gap in the scarp crest of the Downs south of Chilton village (see Beckinsale and Beckinsale, 1976, p.53).

Fluted Valleys of the Chalk Scarp

Examination of the northward-facing scarp faces of the Chalk escarpments of Berkshire reveals the existence of highly localised, short, narrow, parallel or sub-parallel, seldom branching, steep gulleys. These occur either as crenulations on unbroken scarp faces or as serrated indentations on scarp-slope dry valleys.

At various locations along the chalk scarps of Berkshire, measurements were made by tape and clinometer of the morphology of flutings. At the Manger (White Horse Hill, G.R. 297863), the distance between the bases of the flutes averaged (mean of 9) 50.59 m, and the distance between the ridge crests between them averaged 52.77 m. At Kingstone Coombes (G.R. 273854) another 9 flutes were measured. The mean spacing between bases was 43.88 m and between ridges 41.11 m. Taking the two groups together the mean values were 47.21 and 46.94 m respectively. The range of values involved for individual flutes was 25-85 m for the bases and 25-85 m for the ridges.

The long profiles of some flutes were also measured. At the Manger the flutes were 105-145 m long and the mean slopes were between 17.97° and 24.07°. Locally, however, the angle of 5m segments exceeded 30° and sometimes attained over 36°. At Kingstone Coombe the flutes were 65-135 m long and the mean slopes were between 13.42° and 24.26°. Once again the angle of 5 m segments sometimes exceeded 30°. At Coombe Gibbet (G.R. 365623) flutes were 100-130 m long and had long profile segments of up to 34°.

The general forms revealed by these measurements are illustrated in Figures 2, 3, 4 and 5. Figures 2 and 3 are sequences of surveyed cross profiles taken half-way down the surveyed long profiles shown in Figures 4 and 5. They give an impression of their irregular wave-like form. Such a frequency of relatively regular crenulation appears to be rare on the chalk scarps.

The orientations of the troughs is somewhat variable. They are more or less parallel to the maximum slope of the terrain on which they are developed. At the Manger their aspect ranges from 315° round to 80° and at Kingstone Combes from 271° round to 321°. The aspect of two troughs at Coombe Gibbet was between 355° and 360°. This reflects the trends of the scarps in the parts of Berkshire studied, and further study would have to be made in other parts of Southern England with other scarp orientation to assess whether this range of aspect has any significance.

One further possible factor in accounting for their location is the general slope of the scarp faces where they are developed. The three localities which we discuss happen to possess the steepest angles of the scarp faces which we have examined. Parts of the escarpments with lower angle slopes are free of such closely spaced and relatively regular crenulations.

Just as it is difficult to put forward an agreed hypothesis to explain normal dry valleys, so it is difficult to explain the origin of these highly localised flutings. They are morphologically very similar to the Caulées of South Alberta, Canada (Beaty, 1975) which are thought to have formed after drainage incision had given sufficient initial relief by the action of wind-driven snow and rain carving furrows that were later enlarged by surface runoff and preferential snow accumulation. Likewise, similar roughly parallel chutes (rasskers) have been formed in Fennoscandia and elsewhere by avalanche activity (Markgren, 1964) while Lewis (1939, pp 156-7), in his examination of snow patch erosion in Iceland, drew attention to the fact that in his study area, most of the snow-patches were longitudinal. Alternatively they may merely be fluvial valleys caused by incision of small streams into Chalk rendered impermeable by the presence of permafrost.

Sarsen Blockstreams

Another striking feature of the valley systems of the Oxford Region, and one which once again is highly localised, is the presence of the sarsen block streams.

The sarsen themselves, sometimes called greywethers, are quartiztic sandstones, flint breccias and conglomerates (puddingstones). They are thought to have originated as a siliceous demicrust under warm, semi-arid conditions similar to those now found in the Kalahari (Kerr, 1955).

They occur as blocks up to 200 tons in weight, 600 cubic feet in volume, and 4-5 metres long. They have thicknesses up to 2 m. The blocks are generally tabular and rectangular in shape (although often with irregular surfaces) and give the impression of being slabs which are the remnants of a formerly jointed and more continuous stratum. Many of the blocks have

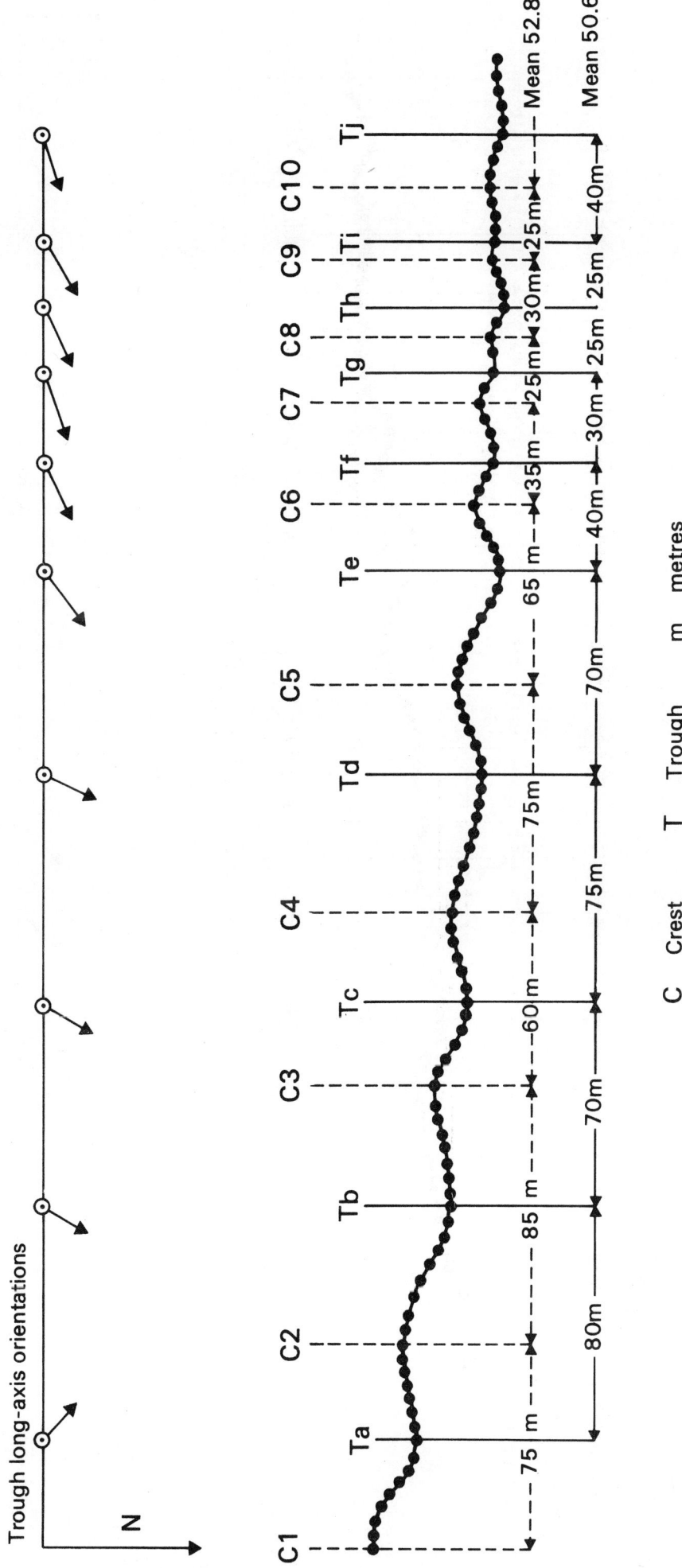

Figure 2. Surveyed cross profiles of selected flutes

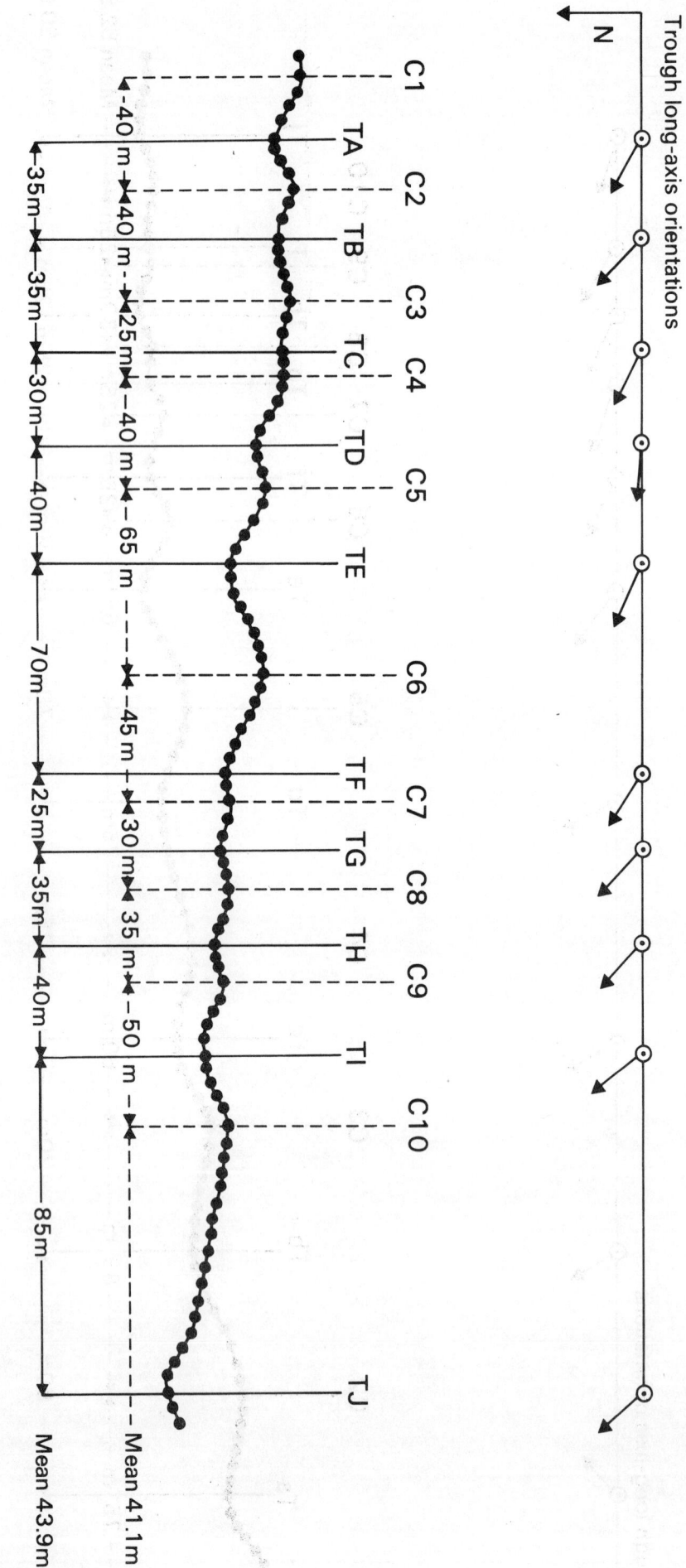

Figure 3. Surveyed cross profiles of selected flutes

C Crest   T Trough   m metres

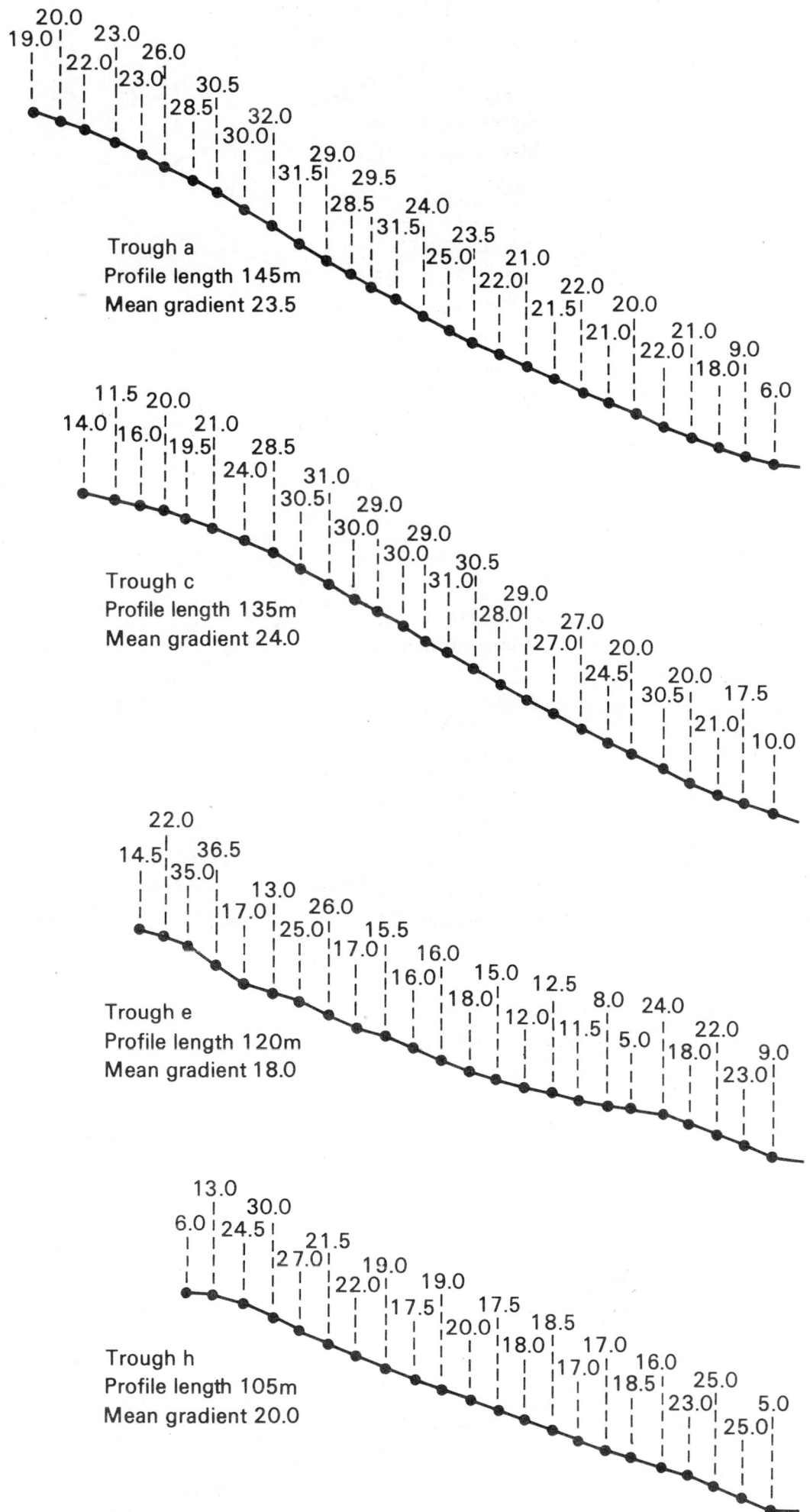

Figure 4. Long profiles of selected flutes

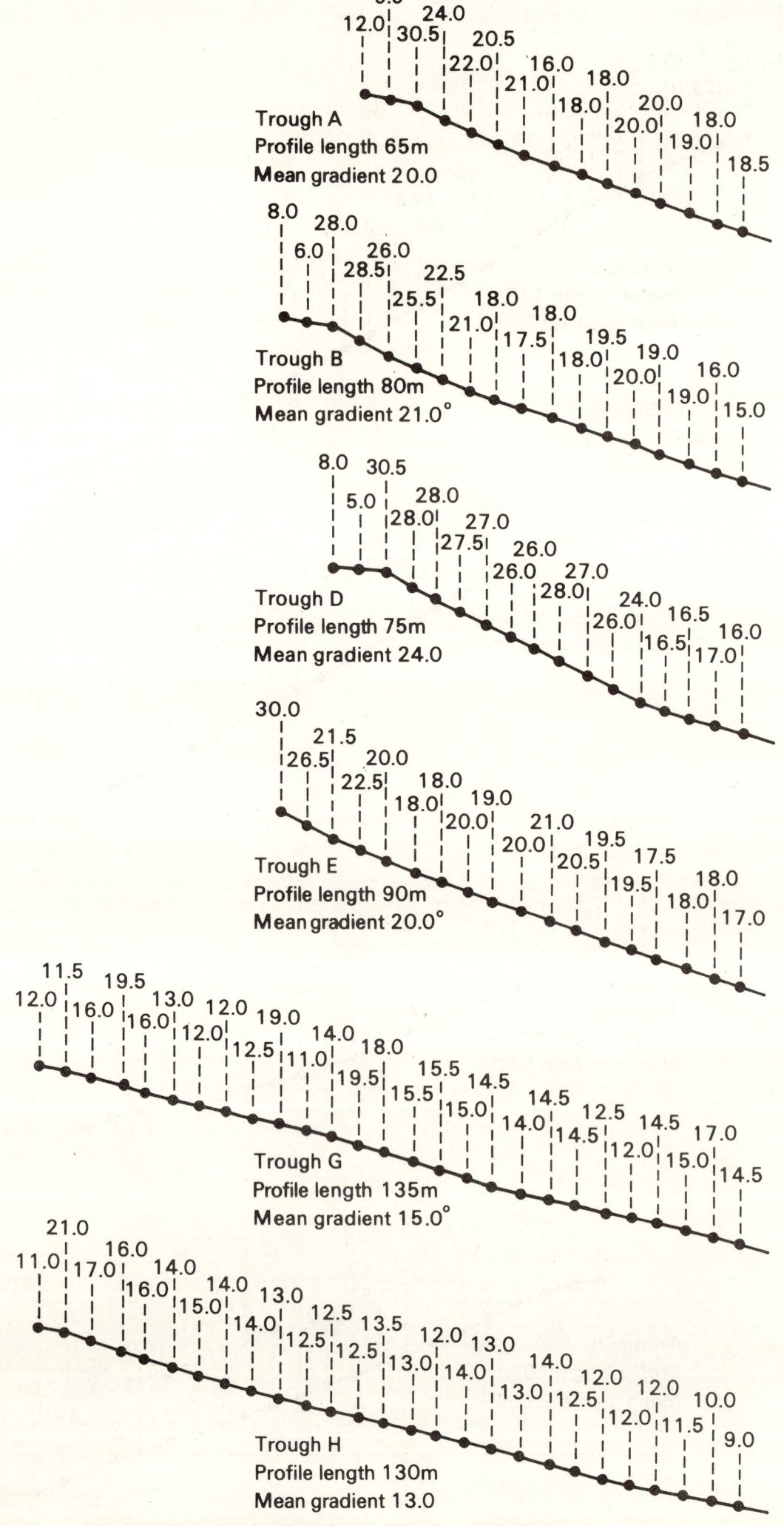

Figure 5. Long profiles of selected flutes

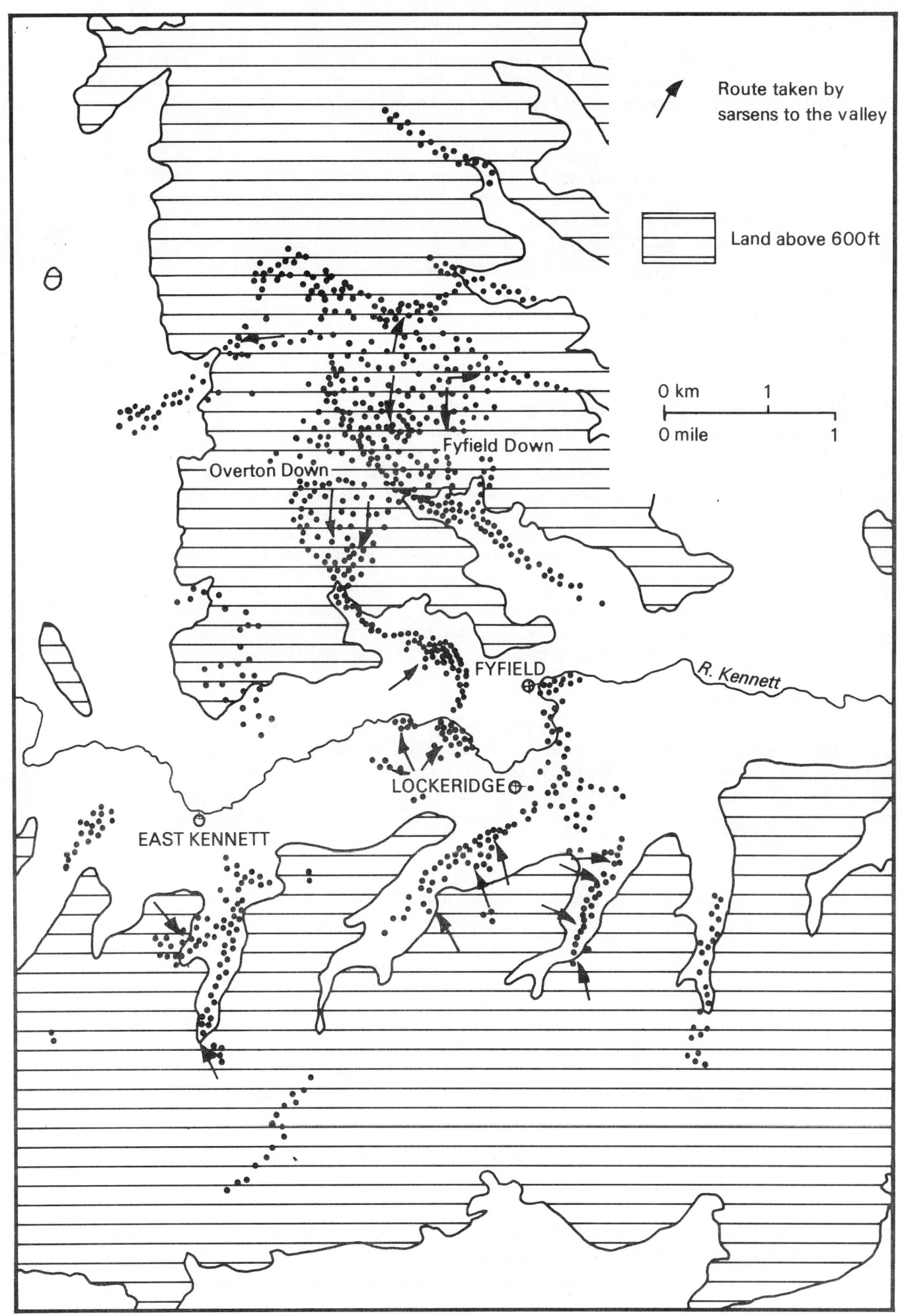

Figure 6. Distribution map of block streams on the Marlborough Downs and Ashdown Valley

been removed for building such edifices as Windsor Castle and for the setts in front of Hertford College, Oxford. In spite of this (Small et al 1970) calculate that at Clatford Bottom there are still 8000-10,000 sarsens in a 60 x 750 m strip.

Sarsens occur widely in southern England (Summerfield and Goudie, in press) from Staple Fitzpaine in Somerset, to Sudbury in Suffolk, but in the Oxford area are most frequent in the Marlborough-Lambourn district and in the Chilterns near Walter's Ash. Good examples occur at the ends of the M.40 cutting at Aston Rowant.

The distribution of the block streams which are thought to have been formed by periglacial action - frost weathering and solifluxion - is shown in Figure 6. They play a role in the development of the marked assymmetry of the dry valleys of the Marlborough Downs and the Ashdown Valley.

The age of the sarsens is still a matter of controversy for the number of reliable in situ occurrences that have been recorded is small, but they may be related in age to the Reading and Bagshot beds. Comparable deposits occur in situ in the Paris Basin and elsewhere in western Europe and occur during several phases of the Tertiary, notably the Eocene. Clark et al (1967) postulate, however, that the main episode of silification in the Marlborough area may have occurred in association with the development of an erosional surface - the Eogene peneplain of Oligocene and/or Miocene times - transecting various Eocene formations. In some localities the surface may well have passed onto the Chalk, on which Tertiary remanié deposits would have been cemented to give a sarsen-crust.

The exact mode of origin and the age of the sarsens is therefore still obscure but they probably hold an important clue as to the history of Tertiary deposition and erosion in the Oxford Region.

Acknowledgements

MGH and MJD gratefully acknowledge that some of this work was undertaken while they were in receipt of research studentships from the Natural Environmental Research Council.

BIBLIOGRAPHY

Arkell, W.J. (1947), The Geology of Oxford.

Beaty, C.B. (1975), 'Coulée alignment and the wind in southern Alberta, Canada', Bulletin, Geological Society of America, 86, pp.119-28.

Beckinsale, R.P. (1953), 'Some morphological features of the Valleys of the North Cotswolds: the Windrush and its tributaries', Proceedings, Cotteswold Naturalists' Field Club 31, pp.184-195.

Beckinsale, R.P. (1970), 'Physical problems of Cotswold rivers and valleys', Proceedings, Cotteswold Naturalists' Field Club 35, pp.194-205.

Beckinsale, R.P. & Beckinsale, R.D. (1976), 'Glaciation and periglaciation in the Cotswolds', Proceedings Cotteswold Naturalists' Field Club 27, pp.46-57.

Beckit, H.O. (1926), 'Physiography of the Oxford Region', in J.J. Walker (ed.), The Natural History of the Oxford District, pp.1-20.

Brown, E.H. (1969), 'Jointing, aspect, and the orientation of scarp face dry valleys, near Ivinghoe, Buckinghamshire', Transactions, Institute of British Geographers 48, pp.61-73.

Brunsden, D. (1968), Dartmoor, British Landscapes through Maps, No.13.

Chorley, R.J. & Morgan, M.A. (1962), 'Comparison of morphometric features, Unaka Mountains, Tennessee, and North Carolina, and Dartmoor, England', Bulletin Geological Society of America 73, pp.17-34.

Clark, M.J., Lewin, J. & Small, R.J., (1967), 'The sarsen stones of the Marlborough Downs and their geomorpholigical implications', Southampton Research Series in Geography 4, pp.3-40.

Corbel, J. (1959), 'L'érosion en terrain calcaire', Annales de Géographie 68, pp.97-120.

De Courcy Wheeler, L. (1974), 'Aspects of the morphometry of the Oxford region', Unpublished B.A. dissertation, University of Oxford.

Douglas, I. (1964), 'Intensity and periodicity in denudation processes with special reference to the removal of material in solution by rivers', Zeitschrift für Geomorphologie NF 8, pp.453-73.

Evans, J.G. (1966), 'Late-Glacial and Post-Glacial Sub-Aerial deposits at Pitstone, Buckinghamshire', Proceedings, Geologists' Association 77, pp.347-64.

Evans, J.G. (1975), The Environment of Early Man in the British Isles, pp.216.

French, H.M. (1973), 'Cryopediments on the Chalk of Southern England', Biulteyn Peryglacjalny 22, pp.149-156.

Goudie, A.S. (1967), 'Solutional rates, processes and forms in the country between Cheltenham and Stow, Glos.', Unpublished B.A. dissertation, University of Cambridge.

Goudie, A.S. & Hart, M. (1975), 'Pleistocene events and forms in the Oxford Region', in C.G. Smith & D.I. Scargill (eds.), Oxford and Its Region, pp.3-13.

Gregory, K.J. (1966), 'Dry valleys and the composition of the drainage net', Journal of Hydrology 4, pp.327-40.

Groom, G.E. & Williams, V.H. (1965), 'The solution of limestone in South Wales', Geographical Journal 131, pp.37-41.

Hindley, A. (1965), 'Sinkholes on the Lincolnshire limestone between Grantham and Stamford', East Midland Geographer 3, pp.454-60.

Kellaway, G.A., Horton, A. & Poole, E.G. (1971),'The development of some Pleistocene Structures in the Cotswolds and Upper Thames Basin', Bulletin, Geological Survey of Great Britain 37, pp.1-28.

Kerney, M.P. (1963), 'Late Glacial deposits on the chalk of south-east England', Philosophical Transactions Royal Society of London B, 246, pp. 203-54.

Kerney, M.P., Brown, E.H. & Chandler, T.J. (1964), 'The Late-Glacial and Post-Glacial history of the chalk escarpment near Brook, Kent'. Philosophical Transactions Royal Society of London B, 248, pp.135-204.

Kerr, M.H. (1955), 'On the origin of silcretes in Southern England', Proceedings Leeds Philosophical and Literary Society (Scientific Section) 6, pp.328-337.

Lewis, W.V. (1939), 'Snow-patch erosion in Iceland', Geographical Journal 94, pp.153-61.

Markgren, M. (1964), 'Geormorphological Studies in Fennoscandia. vol.II. Chute slopes in Northern Fennoscandia. B. Systematic Studies', Lund Studies in Geography, Series A, Physical Geography, No.28.

Morgan, R.P.C. (1971), 'A morphometric study of some valley systems on the English Chalklands', Transactions, Institute of British Geographers 54, pp.33-44.

Ollier, C.D. & Thomasson, A.J. (1957),'Asymmetrical valleys of the Chiltern Hills, Geographical Journal 123, pp.71-80.

Paterson, K. (1970), Unpublished D.Phil Thesis, University of Oxford.

Paterson, K. (1971), 'Weichselian deposits and fossil periglacial structures in North Berkshire', Proceedings Geologists' Association of London, 82, pp.455-67.

Paterson, K. (1972), 'Responses in the chemistry of spring waters in the Oxford region to some climatic variables', Transactions, Cave Research Group 14 (2), pp.132-40.

Paterson, K. (1977), 'Scarp-face dry valleys, near Wantage, Oxfordshire', Transactions, Institute of British Geographers NS 2(2), pp.192-204.

Perrin, R.M.S. (1955), 'Studies in Pedogenesis', Unpublished Ph.D. Thesis, University of Cambridge.

Phillips, J. (1871), Geology of Oxford and the Valley of the Thames.

Pitty, A.F. (1968), 'Some features of calcium hardness fluctuations in two karst streams and their possible value in geohydrological studies', Journal of Hydrology 6, pp.202-8.

Quaternary Research Association (1976), Field Guide to the Oxford Region.

Sandford, K.S. & Beckinsale, R.P. (1954), 'River development and superficial deposits and geomorphology', in A.F. Martin & R.W. Steel (eds.), The Oxford Region, pp.21-36.

Small, R.J., Clark, M.J. & Lewin, J. (1970), 'A periglacial rock-stream at Clatford Bottom, Marlborough Downs, Wiltshire', Proceedings Geologists' Association 81, pp.87-98.

Smith, D.I. (1965), Some aspects of limestone solution in the Bristol Region', Geographical Journal 131, pp.44-49.

Smith, D.I. (1976), 'The problems of limestone dry valleys - implications of recent work in limestone hydrology', in R. Peel, M. Chisholm and P. Haggett (eds.), Processes in Physical and Human Geography, pp.130-147.

Sperling, C.H.B., Goudie, A.S., Stoddart, D.R. & Poole, G.G. (1977), 'Dolines of the Dorset chalklands and other areas in southern Britain', Transactions, Institute of British Geographers, NS 2(2), pp.205-223.

Summerfield, M.A. & Goudie, A.S. (in press) 'The Sarsens of Southern England: their palaeoenvironmental interpretation with reference to silcretes', in D.K.C. Jones (ed.), The Shaping of Southern England, Academic Press.

Sweeting, M.M. (1965), 'Denudation in limestone regions: an introduction', Geographical Journal 131, pp.34-7.

Williams, P.W. (1963), 'An initial estimate of the speed of limestone solution in County Clare', Irish Geographer 4.

TWO HUNDRED YEARS OF OXFORD WEATHER

C.G. Smith

INTRODUCTION

Although it was at one time traditional for Oxford dons to complain about the city's climate; cold, raw and prone to fogs in winter and often humid and oppressive in summer, the object of this paper is not to suggest or prove that Oxford's local climate is particularly distinctive or extreme by British standards. In fact the climate of Oxford is similar to that of many other lowlying portions of the English midlands. By virtue of its central position in southern Britain, the Oxford region experiences a climate which reflects a balance between Atlantic and continental influences; two predominant factors responsible for local variations of climate within Britain. The highest ground within the region, in the Cotswolds and Chilterns, only approaches 300 metres above sea level and thus relief, a most important factor in local climatic differentiation in Britain, is hardly significant in modifying the climate of Oxford city or in producing large local variations within the district (Smith, 1954).

Distance from the sea gives Oxford a mildly continental climatic régime as compared with coastal regions of Britain, yet the absence of high ground in a northeasterly direction between Oxford and the North Sea renders the region more open to cold continental air masses in winter and spring than might at first be thought. The presence of the Welsh mountains and Cotswolds to the west provides significant shelter from maritime influences and consequently the annual rainfall of Oxford and its seasonal distribution is more characteristic of eastern Britain; it is on the low side with a slight summer and autumn maximum. Oxford's mean annual rainfall of 653 mm compares with 790 mm at Bristol, 803 mm at Southampton and 551 mm at Cambridge. In terms of temperature Oxford experiences conditions at all seasons which are more typical of continental influences; it is usually among the warmer places during summer heat waves; while during prolonged cold spells in winter, like much of the midlands and southeast, night minimum temperatures sink rather low. Similar continental effects are found when one examines the average number of days with radiation fog in winter and the number of days on which thunder is heard in summer. On the credit side, distance from the sea means that wind speeds recorded at Oxford are almost always much lower than in coastal regions and thus the frequency of damaging gales is not high. The relatively low rainfall in the district, combined with the extensive areas of permeable limestone in the basins of the upper Thames and its tributaries, result in these rivers having less turbulent and extreme régimes than rivers in western and northern Britain so that sudden and damaging floods are rather infrequent events. However, on occasions even the gentle Thames can flood large lowlying areas adjacent to the river. This is most likely to occur in winter or spring following a prolonged spell of wet weather or, as occurred in 1947, when a very wet spell and thaw followed a severe winter with a deep and extensive snow cover in the Cotswolds.

We are fortunate in possessing for Oxford one of the longest, reliable and best maintained meteorological records in Britain or in the world (Radcliffe Observatory). There is a continuous daily record of temperature and rainfall since 1814 and a discontinuous record of the same elements covering about half of the period 1767 to 1805. These readings were taken at the same site, the old Radcliffe Observatory, and are being continued today. For the earlier period these Oxford readings can be supplemented by a weather record maintained at Shirburn Castle by the Macclesfield family. This has a nearly complete daily record of temperature, pressure wind and weather from 1743 until 1786. There is also a rainfall record for Shirburn which enables monthly and annual totals to be calculated for the period 1780 to 1795 (Smith 1979a).

This essay examines the history and nature of the Oxford meterological record; makes use of this record to look at some extreme or unusual weather events at Oxford during the last 200 years; and considers whether such a long period record gives any positive evidence of changes or fluctuations of climate over this period.

THE HISTORY OF THE OXFORD METEOROLOGICAL RECORD

It is often stated that the oldest weather record or journal in Britain was maintained at Oxford between 1337 and 1344 by William Merle, a fellow of Merton College; but it is now generally held that for most of the time this record was maintained in Lincolnshire (Symons, 1891). The earliest attempts to compile a daily record of weather at Oxford seem to have been a consequence of a paper presented to the Royal Society by Robert Hooke in 1663 in which he proposed a scheme and a method for "making a history of the weather" (Sprat, 1667). Hooke was at this time much involved in the design and manufacture of early meteorological instruments, including the thermometer, barometer, hygrometer and rain gauge (Frisinger, 1977). A weather journal in the form of a diary was maintained at Oxford by John Locke from 1666 to 1667 (Locke MSS Bodleian) and a little later in 1684 Dr. Richard Plot maintained a similar record for a year.

These seventeenth century efforts to encourage the compilation of weather journals or records were sponsored by the Royal Society and some sixty years later, when this initial impulse had faded, renewed efforts were made by the Secretary of the Society, James Jurin, to encourage weather observers to make their observations in a standard form and submit their daily observations annually to the Society (Jurin, 1723). Quite apart from this specific encouragement to observe the weather for its own sake there was in the eighteenth century another, and sometimes related, reason for the commencement of systematic visual and instrumental meteorological observations; the close relationship that then existed between astronomy and meteorology. Astronomers found it necessary to measure air temperature at the time of their star observations in order to correct for atmospheric refraction, while they also found it useful to record the state of the sky in terms of cloud cover to explain why observations had not been taken at specific times.

This close link between the study of astronomy and meteorology is illustrated by the earliest systematic series of meteorological observations made in the Oxford district, those of Dr. Thomas Hornsby, Savilian Professor of Astronomy at Oxford from 1763 until his death in 1810, and those maintained by George Parker, second Earl of Macclesfield, at his private astronomical observatory at Shirburn Castle near Watlington from about 1740. The Shirburn observations were continued after the Earl's death in 1764 by those members of his domestic staff he had trained as competent astronomers. The Shirburn astronomical journals from 1743 to 1786 list, in addition to star observations, air temperature, atmospheric pressure, wind direction and state of the sky, (Savile MS Bodleian Library). A separate rainfall record for Shirburn from October 1779 until October 1794 apparently ceased with the death or infirmity of the last of these observers who must remain anonymous. The story of the Shirburn observatory is a particularly interesting one for several reasons. Its founder, George Parker, was not only an Oxfordshire notable but, as President of the Royal Society from 1752 until 1764 and a noted astronomer, he was much involved in the movement for the reform of the calendar which took place in 1752. He was also in regular and close scientific and social contact with two Savilian Professors of Astronomy at Oxford, James Bradley (1693-1762) and his successor, Thomas Hornsby (1733-1810). It would appear that in setting up and equipping his astronomical observatory at Shirburn the Earl leant heavily on Bradley's advice. Indeed until Hornsby was able to persuade the Radcliffe Trustees to provide sufficient money for the building and equipping of the Radcliffe Observatory at Oxford, facilities for astronomical observation at Shirburn were probably superior to those enjoyed by the Savilian Professor. The Radcliffe Observatory at Oxford was built between 1772 and 1794 but it was sufficiently advanced by 1776 for Hornsby to move into the adjoining observer's house and to begin the purchase of instruments. Apart from the central tower, which is a copy of the Tower of the Winds at Athens, the building was largely completed by 1779. The evidence of the Shirburn meteorological record and that of Hornsby's meteorological journal kept in his own hand is that Hornsby made regular visits to Shirburn and probably advised on the choice of instruments and methods of observation. Unfortunately Hornsby's early Oxford meteorological record is incomplete. It is not certain from those portions of his journal which survive whether the record for the missing years has been lost or whether his numerous duties prevented him from maintaining the record for long periods (Fig.1) His record is largely complete for the following years, except for short periods when he was away from Oxford usually in the summer vacation: 1760-1761, 1767-1776, 1794-1805. The existence of annual rainfall totals in Hornsby's own hand for the period 1784-1794 suggests that there may have been daily observations during this period too but that the original records have been lost, (Craddock and Craddock, 1977).

There is a gap in the Oxford meteorological record from 1805, when Hornsby's record ceased probably because of age and infirmity, and 1811 when his successors at the Observatory commenced a neat record of pressure, temperature, wind and weather in very similar form. From 1815 onwards these records, together with one of rainfall, are sufficiently well documented and continuous for reliable monthly means of temperature and rainfall to be calculated. When the Radcliffe Observatory moved from Oxford to Pretoria in 1935 the maintenance of these observations became the responsibility of the School of Geography which is justifiably proud of the fact that it has maintained a series of daily observations continuous from 1815. In 1935 the station was renamed "the Radcliffe Meteorological Station". Throughout the nineteenth century, as the science of meteorology developed, there were improvements in the type of instruments in use and observing methods became standardised so that observations from different stations might be comparable. Such improvements and changes were immediately adopted at the Radcliffe Observatory and the staff there were often responsible for the introduction of such new methods. There was frequent and regular contact with the staff at Greenwich and Kew Observatories and, after 1880, with the Meteorological Office. The Observatory pioneered the introduction of self-recording or autographic instruments which gave continuous records of temperature, humidity, and wind. For many years the principal instruments were read hourly, and throughout most of the period from 1815 until 1924 at least three times a day. Since 1 January 1925 the majority of daily observations have reverted to once daily eye readings, supplemented by the continuous record of the autographic instruments. With the growth of synoptic meteorological stations, largely staffed and administered by the Meteorological Office, which are part of the network required for weather forecasting purposes, the role of such stations as the Radcliffe has become climatological. As such it has a quite unique value because of the length of the record at one site.

The establishment of a number of R.A.F. airfields in the Oxford district, during and in the period immediately preceding the Second World War, has

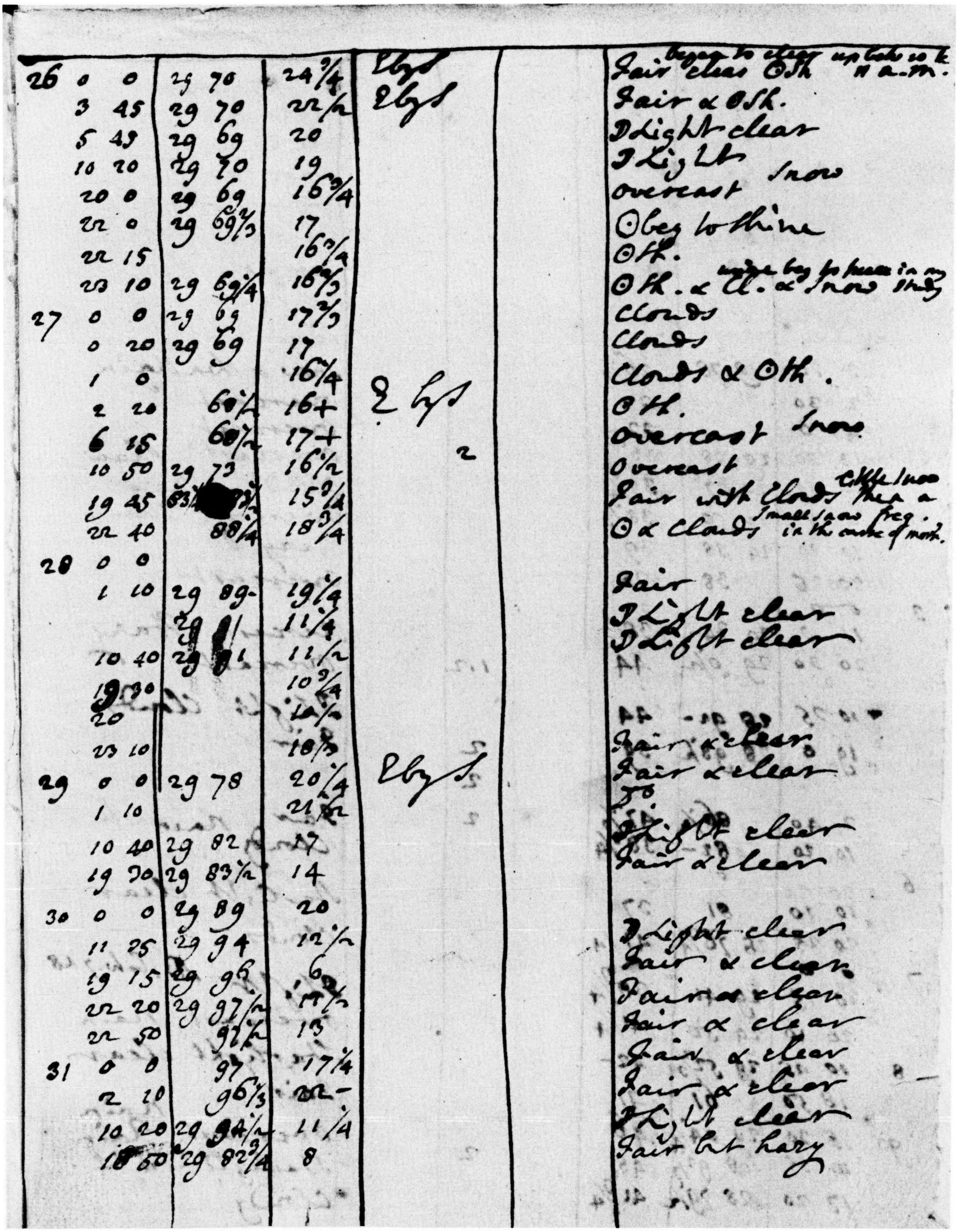

26	0 0	29 70	24 3/4	Ebys			Fair clear Oth (begun to clear up til ... 11 a.m.)
	3 45	29 70	22 1/2	Ebys			Fair & Oth.
	5 45	29 69	20				D Light clear
	10 20	29 70	19				D Light
	20 0	29 69	16 3/4				overcast Snow
	22 0	29 69 1/3	17				Obey to thine
	22 15		16 3/4				Oth.
	23 10	29 69 1/4	16 1/3				Oth. & Cl. & Snow
27	0 0	29 69	17 1/3				Clouds
	0 20	29 69	17				Clouds
	1 0		16 1/4	E bys			Clouds & Oth.
	2 20	68 1/2	16+				Oth.
	6 15	68 1/2	17+		2		overcast Snow
	10 50	29 73	16 1/2				Overcast
	19 45		15 3/4				Fair with Clouds (little snow)
	22 40	88 1/4	18 3/4				O & Clouds (small snow)
28	0 0						
	1 10	29 89	19 1/4				Fair
		29	11 1/4				D Light clear
		29	11 1/2				D Light clear
	10 40	29	11 1/2				
	19 30		10 3/4				
	20		10 1/2				
	23 10		10 1/3				Fair & clear
29	0 0	29 78	20 1/4	Ebys			Fair & clear
	1 10		21 1/2				Do.
	10 40	29 82	17				D Light clear
	19 30	29 83 1/2	14				Fair & clear
30	0 0	29 89	20				D Light clear
	11 25	29 94	12 1/2				Fair & clear
	19 15	29 96	6				Fair & clear
	22 20	29 97 1/2	14 1/2				Fair & clear
	22 50	97 1/2	13				Fair & clear
31	0 0	97	17 1/4				Fair & clear
	2 10	96 1/3	22-				Fair & clear
	10 20	29 94 1/2	11 1/4				D Light clear
	18 50	29 82 3/4	8				Fair but hazy

Figure 1. A page from the weather journal maintained at Oxford by Dr. Thomas Hornsby during the very cold January of 1776. The first column shows the date and time; the next columns from left to right, atmospheric pressure in inches, outside temperature in degrees Fahrenheit, wind direction, rainfall (blank for this period) and the state of the sky and weather.

increased the number of reliable meteorological records available. However in the last three years two of these meteorological stations have closed because of changing service requirements at Little Rissington and Abingdon, while for similar reasons the records at Brize Norton, Fairford and Upper Heyford are not continuous. The longest of these airfield records still being maintained is that at R.A.F. Benson which for most elements is uninterrupted since 1940. It is also of interest to note that a climatological station has been recording continuously at Shirburn since 1964; it is maintained by a local farmer who is a direct descendent of Thomas Parker, the second Earl of Macclesfield. In spite of several threats to the site of the Radcliffe Meteorological Station arising from plans to extend the Radcliffe Infirmary and the Medical School, the station has survived and the exposure of the instruments has changed little since Hornsby's day. It is impossible to say how long this situation will remain, or whether changes in the density of urban building in Oxford will eventually so modify the local and microclimate of the site as to render the readings not strictly comparable with those of the past. Suffice it to say that the site, now within the grounds of Green College, has been protected by a University Decree for as long as the meteorological observations are deemed to be of scientific value, and that a careful examination of recent rainfall and temperature values at this site indicates that they are consistent with the earlier observations so that they may be regarded as part of a homogeneous record, (Smith, 1975b, Craddock and Smith, 1978).

SOME NOTABLE WEATHER EVENTS AND SEQUENCES AT OXFORD

With a hundred and sixty five years of continuous daily weather observations at the Radcliffe site, and with a discontinuous record of rainfall, pressure and temperature extending back for over two hundred years, we have a formidable array of meteorological data. It might be compared with the mass of figures available to cricket statisticians in the volumes of Wisden, or to the British population data available in the volumes of decennial census reports. Much of it, and particularly that deemed to be most important in probing the climatic régimes of the past, is now on computer file, both in Oxford and at the Meteorological Office, while the original manuscript records are stored at the School of Geography. The remainder of this paper makes use of some of this data to illustrate that, while there have certainly been small fluctuations of climate at Oxford over this period, conditions have varied only slightly around a long term mean so that the more extreme or unusual weather sequences this century can be closely matched by events in the eighteenth and nineteenth centuries.

COLD SPELLS AND COLD MONTHS

A month with a mean temperature below freezing point is a very good indicator of a prolonged and severe cold spell in southern Britain. Such occasions are usually caused by a persistent high pressure belt to the north and northeast of Britain with low pressure to the south, thus permitting very cold continental air from eastern Europe to dominate the British Isles; this is a complete reversal of the more normal west to south-westerly airflow. These very cold conditions are unlikely to commence before late November, or to persist after the first week of March. During such spells Atlantic depressions are pushed either well north of Britain or take a more southerly track across northern France or up the English Channel. In the latter case they bring a brief period of heavy snow, or a temporary thaw with rain to the Oxford district. If the snow cover is thick and persistent it tends to produce a "positive feed back" situation by reflecting the weak winter solar radiation (the albedo effect) and thus intensifying the cold. On clear nights temperatures fall very low indeed, while a complete snow cover maintains very low daytime temperatures. The moderate to strong east to northeasterly winds which prevail during such synoptic conditions accentuate the physiological cold by introducing a wind chill effect. Such conditions, prevailing for a month or more, have been responsible for the longest and severest cold spells on record at Oxford.

Some of the best examples of this have been the long cold winters of mid-January to early March 1947 and late December 1962 to early March 1963. This most recent occasion was the coldest winter on record at Oxford both in terms of the duration of snow cover, 65 consecutive days, and the persistence of very low temperatures. January 1963 was the coldest month on record at Oxford with a mean temperature of -3.2°C, similar to the average January temperature at Warsaw! The coldest February on record at Oxford was in 1947 with a mean temperature of -2.6°C; this month also experienced the lowest night minimum temperature ever recorded at Oxford, -16.2°C. This very low temperature occurred at the end of a spell of fifteen consecutive days when the temperature remained below zero day and night and was a consequence of clearing skies and a calm night when the ground was covered with thick snow.

Figure 2 shows the mean winter temperatures at Oxford for every year since 1815 in terms of the departure of this value from the long period mean, together with the number of days on which snow fell. From this it can be seen that, although the winters of 1947 and 1963 were particularly severe they were not very different from some notable cold winters in the nineteenth century, such as 1830, 1879, 1891 and 1895. The graph also shows that, with the exception of the period from 1896 to 1938, during which there were relatively few severe winters, the recent frequency of cold winters has been similar to that prevailing for much of the nineteenth century. The less continuous, and probably less reliable, data for Oxford before 1815 also suggest that the frequency of cold winters in the late eighteenth century was similar to that in more recent years. January 1776 and January 1814 were probably the second and third coldest Januarys for which temperature records are available at Oxford, but the length of these cold spells did not match those of 1947 and 1963, (Smith 1979b). Unfortunately no records exist at Oxford for January 1795, which according to the table produced by Manley (1974) was probably the coldest month on record in Central England since 1659. It is likely that the conditions of the winter of 1962-63 were equalled or exceeded in much of central England during the winter of 1739-40, but this was before records were maintained at Oxford or Shirburn.

Figure 2 also reveals an interesting feature of the variation of winter conditions at Oxford, which applies to much climatological data: extreme events, whether cold or mild conditions, are not randomly distributed. There is a definite tendency for departures from the mean, either on the warm or cold sides, to be clustered. The sequence of mild winters from 1910 to 1916 and from 1971 to 1976, together with the number of cold winters between 1879 and 1895 are good examples of this. However, occasional severe winters such as those of 1917 and 1929 may occur during a long run of predominantly open or mild winters.

Short, but nevertheless equally severe, cold spells which occur in the middle of a month or overlap two months may occur during winters otherwise showing no great departure from average conditions of temperature or snowfall. The cold spell of late December and early January 1767-8, described by Gilbert White in his Natural History of Selborne, was particularly severe at Oxford where Dr. Hornsby's journal records midday maximum temperatures of -8°C on 29 and 30 December 1767. This is only a little above the midday maximum temperature of -9°C recorded by Hornsby on 27 January 1776 during one of the coldest Januarys on record at Oxford. On this day

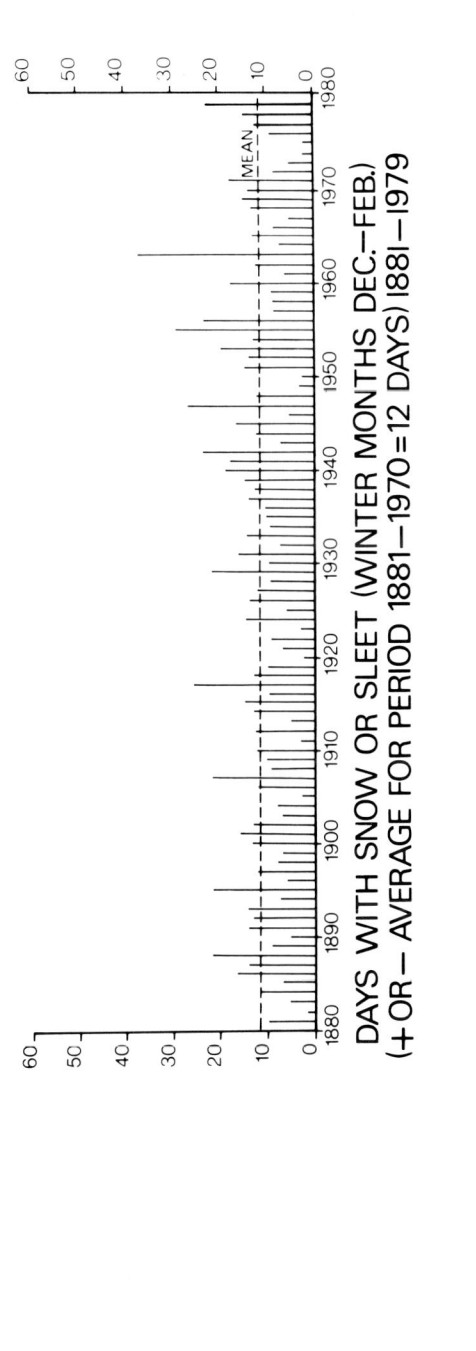

DAYS WITH SNOW OR SLEET (WINTER MONTHS DEC.–FEB.)
(+ OR – AVERAGE FOR PERIOD 1881–1970=12 DAYS) 1881–1979

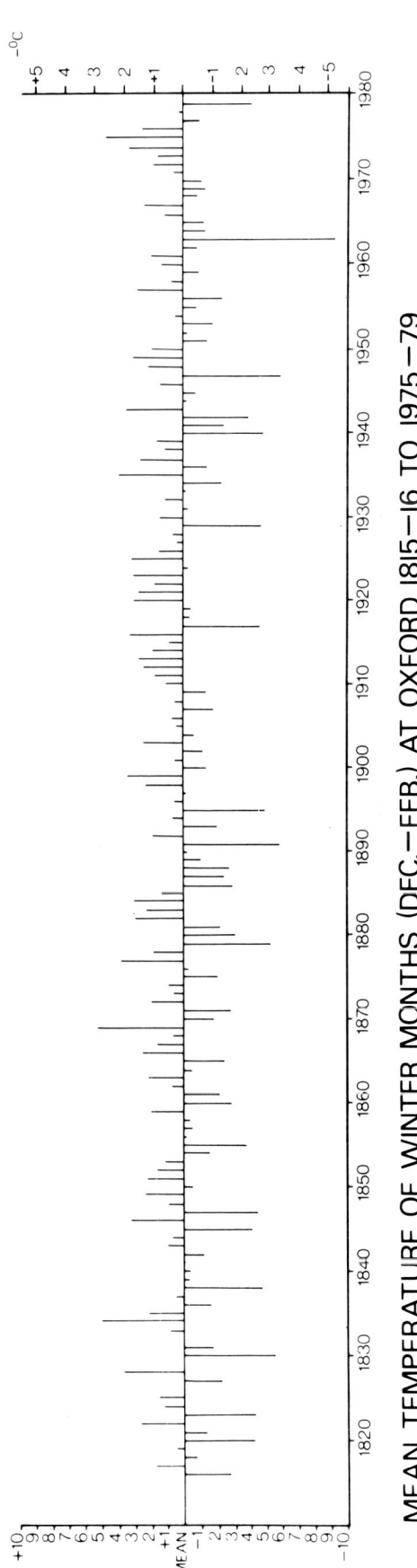

MEAN TEMPERATURE OF WINTER MONTHS (DEC.–FEB.) AT OXFORD 1815–16 TO 1975–79
+ OR – LONG PERIOD AVERAGE (1815–1964), 4°C (39·2°F)

Figure 2.   Winters at Oxford since 1815:   the lower diagram shows the departure of the mean winter temperature
from the long period average;   the upper diagram the number of days on which snow fell.

Hornsby was moved to add a personal note to his meteorological journal "wine keg froze in my study!" The lowest midday maximum temperature recorded in January 1963 was -7ºC.

However, these brief cold spells rarely produce such serious economic consequences or linger in the folk memory as when cold snowy conditions endure for a month or more. Therefore it is particularly useful to note the frequency of occurrence of months with a mean temperature below freezing point, or of two adjacent months with a temperature sufficiently below average as to be associated with prolonged snow and cold. There is a continuous record of daily temperatures at Oxford since November 1813 and from this it is possible to calculate monthly mean temperatures to the present day. During this period of 166 years there have been seventeen months with a mean temperature below zero. Divided arbitrarily into three approximately equal periods their distribution has been as follows:

TABLE 1

NUMBER OF MONTHS WITH MEAN TEMPERATURE BELOW 0ºC

	1814–1868	1869–1914	1915–1979	Total
December	–	1	–	1
January	4	2	3	9
February	1	1	5	7
Total months	5	4	8	17

As a footnote to this table it is worth adding that this gives a misleading impression of a more even distribution; no such months occurred between 1895 and 1929 but there were six in the 25 years from 1939 to 1963. A rather similar frequency of cold winters or prolonged cold spells is indicated by the test of two consecutive months each of which has a mean temperature below 1.8ºC. There have been seventeen such pairs of months since 1813 and they occurred as follows:

TABLE 2

CONSECUTIVE MONTHS WITH MEAN TEMPERATURE BELOW 1.8ºC

	1813–1868	1869–1914	1915–1979
Dec–Jan	1822–23	1870–71	1962–63
	1829–30	1878–79	
	1840–41	1879–80	
		1890–91	
Jan–Feb	1838	1895	1917
			1929
			1942
			1963
			1979
Dec–Jan–Feb	Nil	Nil	1962–63

Both Table 2 and Table 3 indicate a marked tendency for cold spells to continue into February this century. In the nineteenth century they began earlier in December.

30

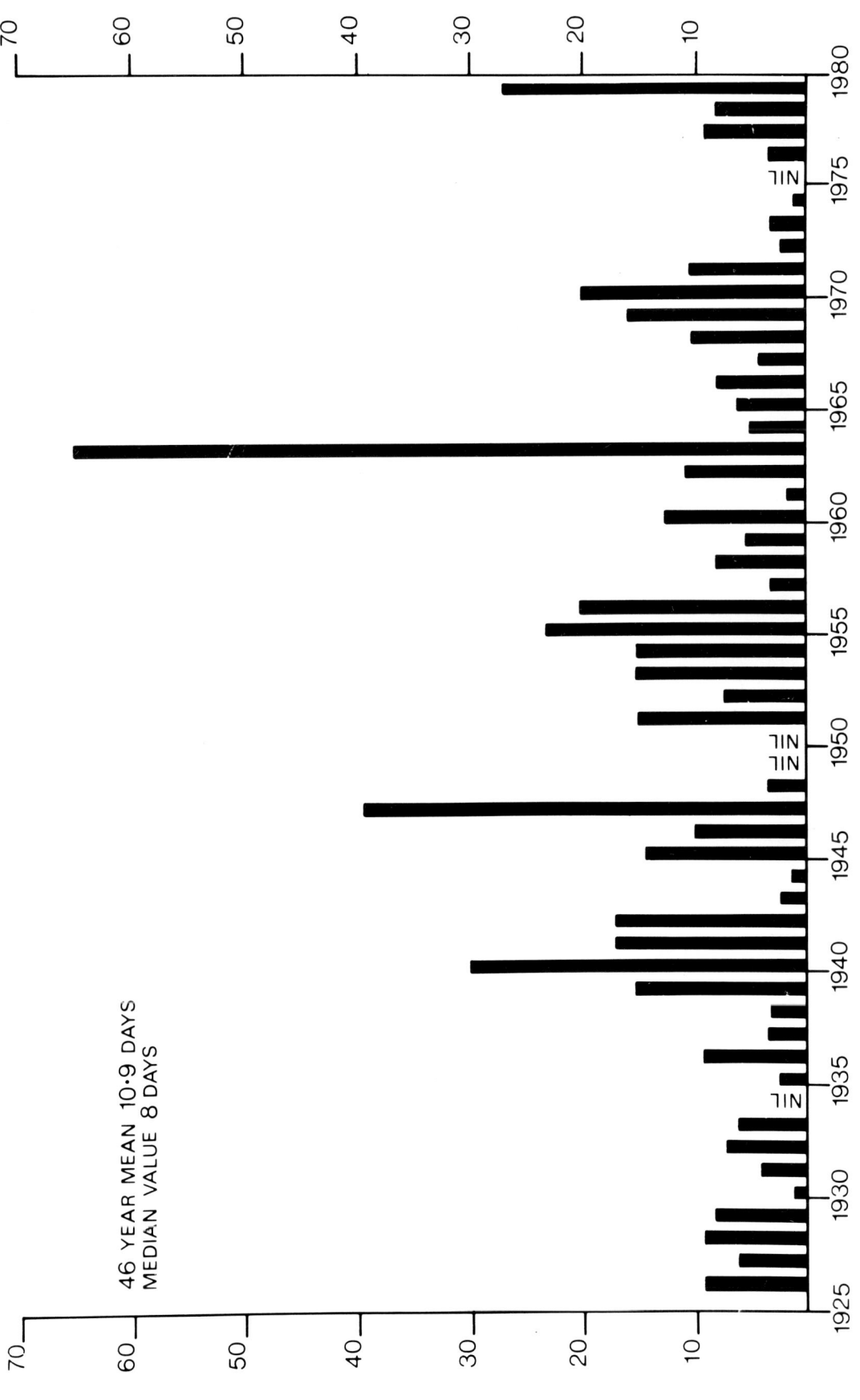

NUMBER OF MORNINGS WITH SNOW LYING AT 0900 HRS. G.M.T. AT OXFORD
WINTER MONTHS (DEC.–FEB.)

46 YEAR MEAN 10·9 DAYS
MEDIAN VALUE 8 DAYS

Figure 3. The number of days on which lying snow covered at least half the ground surface at
Oxford during the three winter months December to February.

A systematic observation of snow lying each morning at Oxford has only been maintained since 1926. For the 54 years of available record the frequency of such occasions during the winter months is displayed in Fig.3. This diagram shows the association of snowy winters with long cold spells and the marked change in the frequency of snowy winters after 1938 which is generally recognised as the end of the long spell of open winters which commenced after 1895. Bot Figs. 2 and 3 show that since 1963 there has been no recognisable trend either to a continuation of severe winters or to a return to the milder winters of the early part of this century. In any event the Oxford records since 1814 and before should provide sufficient warning of the dangers of climatic forecasting on the evidence of some apparent trend. Those who attempt to do so should be reminded of the fact that many trends have only been identified at the very moment they have been reversed. Likewise those who place confidence in the belief that a long period record only indicates a purely random pattern of events should bear in mind that an extreme event is often succeeded by one more or nearly as extreme. An example of this is the very hot dry summer of 1975 which was followed by that of 1976; even hotter and drier with an intervening mild dry winter!

SUMMERS AT OXFORD

While the meteorological definition of winter is generally satisfactory in that really severe cold spells rarely become established before the end of November or endure long into March, a similar arbitrary definition of summer as the three months June to August inclusive is rather less satisfactory to the layman. May and September often bring short hot sunny spells, the trees are in leaf and one expects to engage in such pursuits as cricket and tennis. A study of summers at Oxford since 1815 (Smith 1975a) examined the variation of summer conditions in terms of two different arbitrary periods: the months May to September inclusive and the conventional meteorological summer period June to August. Although this study showed that there were some notably hot dry summers which started rather late after a wet cool May, such as 1955, or terminated at the end of August and were followed by very wet Septembers, as occurred in both 1975 and 1976, there was a general tendency for notably fine summers to stand out whichever criterion was adopted: for example the very hot, sunny and dry summers of 1911, 1921, 1947 and 1959. While hot summers with a long duration of sunshine are usually dry, individual summer months may occasionally show a very high rainfall total at a particular place because exceptional local downpours associated with thunderstorms may give the average rainfall for the month in a few hours.

Figure 4 shows the mean temperature of the three summer months June to August at Oxford in terms of the departure from the long period mean. Above this diagram is another showing the total hours of bright sunshine recorded in each summer period since 1881 when this meteorological element was first recorded at Oxford. As is to be expected all the summers with mean temperatures significantly above average turn out to have been particularly sunny. As compared with the diagram showing the departure of winter temperatures from the long period average, the summer months show a smaller departure from the mean; in summer there is a smaller difference between the air temperature over the North Atlantic and that over the European continent than is generally the case in winter. Cool summers in Britain are usually associated with more cloudy, rainy and unsettled conditions with the frequent passage of Atlantic disturbances. Hot, sunny summers are associated with prolonged spells of anticyclonic conditions; what meteorologists describe as 'blocking situations' when cyclonic disturbances are either pushed southwards into the Mediterranean or deflected

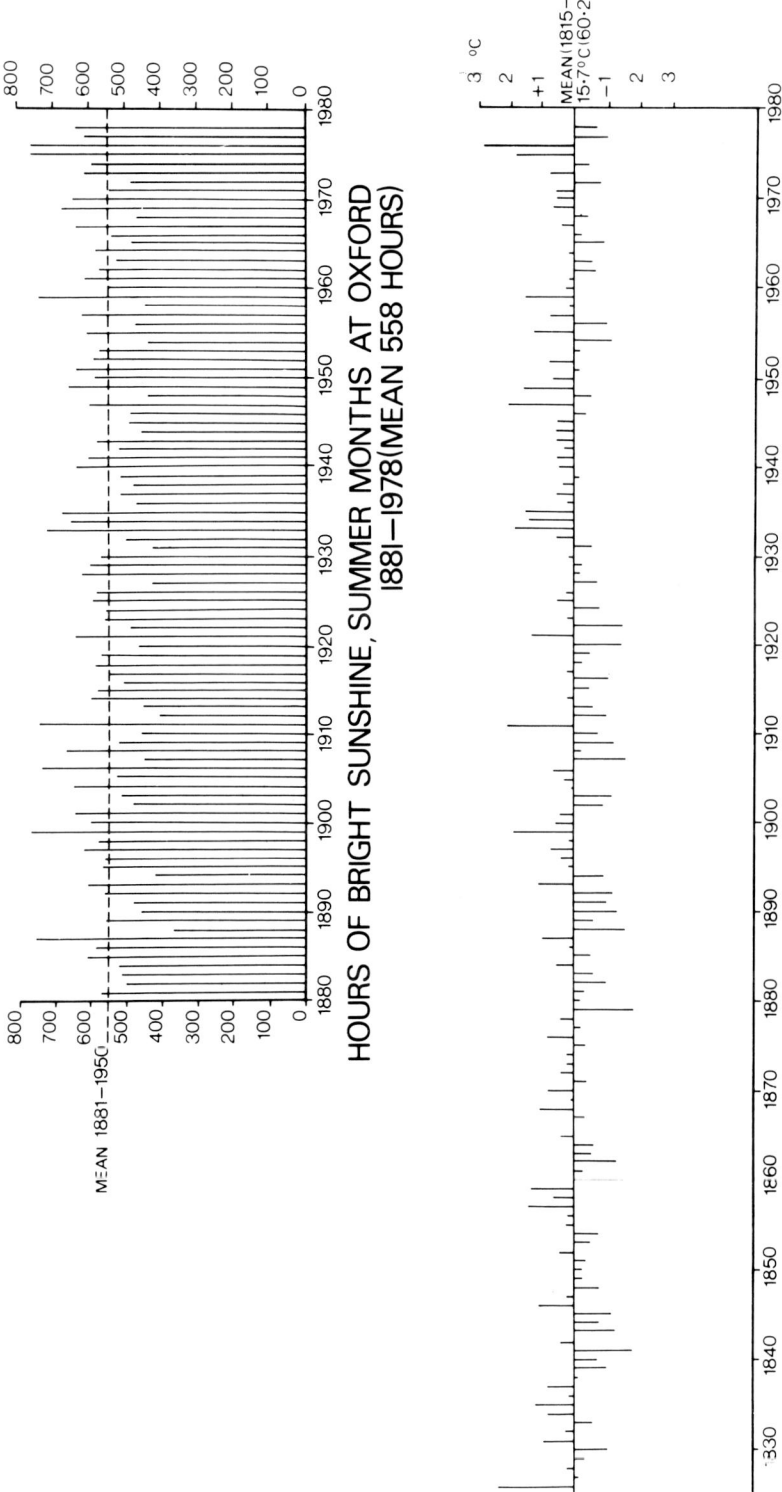

HOURS OF BRIGHT SUNSHINE, SUMMER MONTHS AT OXFORD
1881—1978 (MEAN 558 HOURS)

MEAN TEMPERATURE OF THE THREE SUMMER MONTHS AT OXFORD 1815—1978
EXPRESSED AS + OR — THE LONG PERIOD AVERAGE

Figure 4. Summer temperatures at Oxford shown as departures from the long period mean (lower diagram) and the number of hours of bright sunshine recorded at Oxford each summer since 1881.

far to the north around Iceland. Figure 4 shows that the incidence of warm and cool summers is not entirely random; there is some tendency to clustering as in and cool is not entirely random; there is some tendency to clustering as in the case of the run of cool summers in the 1840's and around 1880 and 1890. The run of summers with temperatures above average between 1930 and 1950 is an outstanding feature of this diagram. However, not all of these summers were relatively dry and sunny.

People's perception of a 'good summer' will vary to some extent. For example a very dry summer which is also hot may be welcomed by the cricketer and the tourist, but may be serious for some farmers and water authorities. However, wet cool summers are generally regarded as poor by most people. In an attempt to quantify such impressions and requirements, Poulter (1962) devised a "summer index" to take account of mean temperature, total rainfall and hours of sunshine in Britain. The higher the index the better the summer. By this test the six finest summers at Oxford since 1880 have been the follo- wing (ranked in order with the index score): 1976 (769), 1911 (751), 1975 (748), 1899 (744), 1949 (734), 1933 (733). The six worst summers similarly ranked have been: 1888 (587), 1912 (596), 1903 (604), 1927 (606), 1922 (607), 1954 (609). The driest three month summer period at Oxford since 1814 was 1818 with only 31 mm or rain; 1976 came second with 55 mm. 1976 was the warmest summer on record with a mean temperature of 18.4°C and 1911 came second with a mean temperature of 17.8°C. Since 1880 the sunniest summer was that of 1899 with 774 hours of sunshine; 1976, with 770 hours came second.

Figure 5 illustrates the trend of summer conditions at Oxford from 1815 in terms of ten year moving averages of summer rainfall and temperature (the two upper graphs). Below are similar moving averages for summer sun- shine and Poulter's Index. These graphs show a number of significant fea- tures: the very wet summers in the 1840's and around 1880 which were disas- terous for agriculture in some parts of England and the notable warmth and dryness of the summers from 1930 to 1950. Although this latter period does not stand out as being generally as sunny as the period around 1900, the low rainfall and higher temperatures significantly influence Poulter's Index for this period. Ten year moving averages can be misleading if they are particularly influenced by two or three very extreme years. Thus the recent trend of all four graphs is certainly affected by the two very fine summers of 1975 and 1976.

The drought of 1975 and 1976 was such an unusual event in much of Britain, and its consequences for the water supply industry and agriculture so serious, that it has been the subject of much subsequent investigation (Royal Society, 1978). Although some of its consequences in the Oxford dis- trict were fortunately mitigated by the timely construction of the Farmoor reservoir, which provided a significant storage reserve of Thames water, the flow of the river in the Oxford district dropped so low in August 1976 that water was actually being lost between Eynsham weir and Day's weir as it seeped into the flood plain gravels, normally a source of underground storage and seepage into the river. Although some other parts of south and south west England had a greater rainfall deficit than the Oxford area the follow- ing figures reveal the extent of this deficit at Oxford.

TABLE 3

Period	Total rainfall	Percentage of long period average
May 1975 - August 1976	448 mm	51%
August 1975 - July 1976	333 mm	51%
October 1975 - March 1976	126 mm	39%

These totals were the lowest for any equivalent 16, 12 and 6 month period at Oxford.

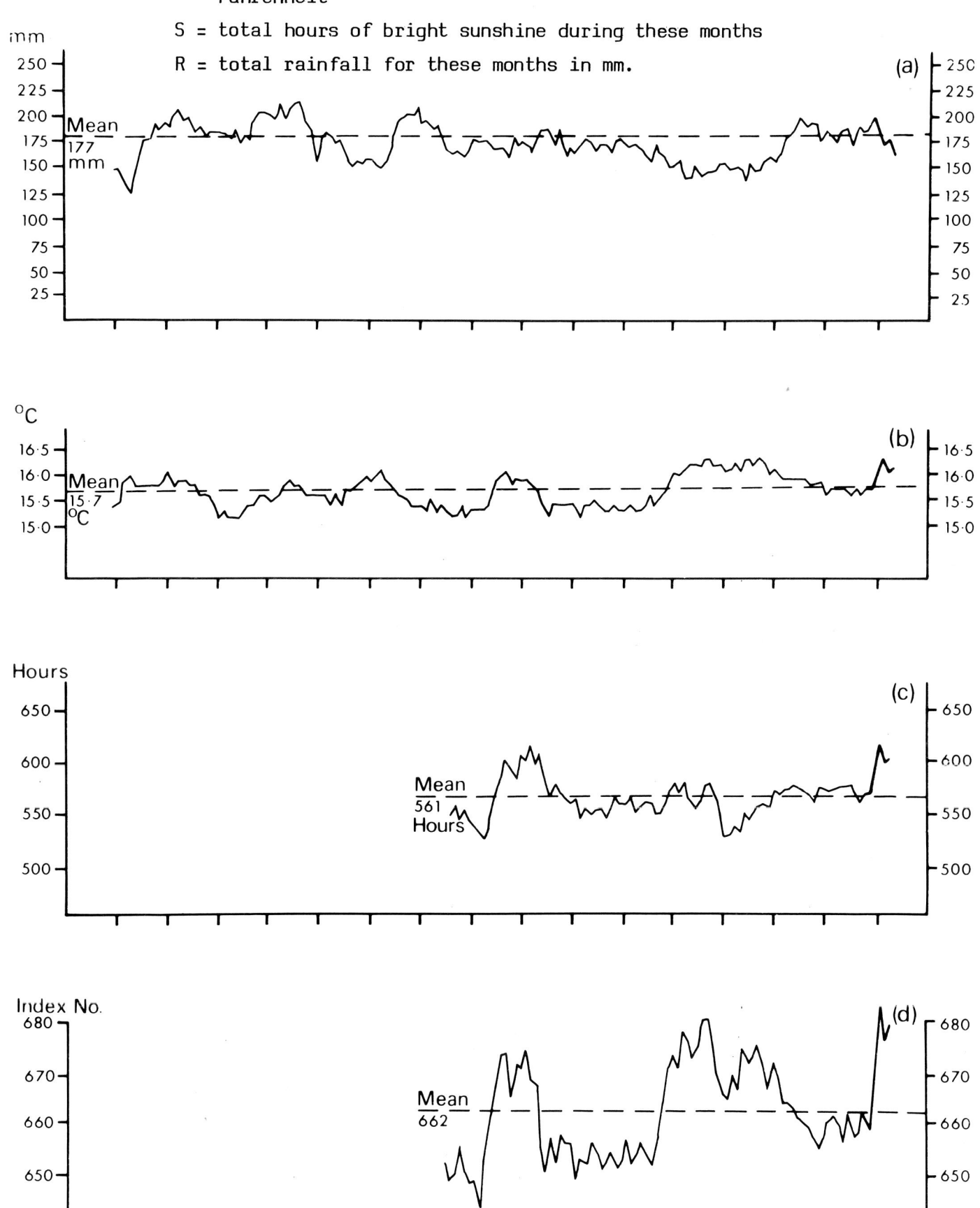

Figure 5. The fluctuation of summer conditions at Oxford shown by ten year moving means centred on the fifth year of each decade: (a) Rainfall; (b) Temperature; (c) Hours of bright sunshine; (d) Poulter's Index.

Poulter's Index = $10T + \dfrac{S}{6} - \dfrac{R}{5}$

where T = mean temperature of the 3 months, June to August, in degrees Fahrenheit

S = total hours of bright sunshine during these months

R = total rainfall for these months in mm.

SOME NOTABLE SHORT PERIOD WEATHER EVENTS AT OXFORD

The inland situation of the Oxford district and the absence of high
relief and steep slopes which frequently produce flash floods in mountain
catchment areas has spared it from weather disasters of the magnitude of
those which, from time to time, cause extensive damage and loss of life in
other parts of Britain. Examples of such extreme events are the Lynmouth
flood caused by torrential rain over Exmoor in August 1952; the North Sea
gale and storm surge of January 1953 which flooded large areas along the east
coast; and the gale which damaged 60% of the buildings in the Sheffield area
on 16th February 1962. The events described below as some of the more notable
weather extremes recorded at Oxford are well within the range of extremes
experienced at other places in Britain.

An investigation of the occurrence of severe gales at Oxford since
1880 (Smith, 1979c) reveals that the worst events occurred in January 1881,
October 1881, November 1928 and most recently on 2nd January, 1976. On each
occasion some structural damage to buildings occurred widely in the Oxford
district, many trees were blown down, and some loss of life was attributed
to the storm. In terms of mean hourly wind speed the gale of 18th January
1881 was the most severe with a maximum hourly wind speed of 49 knots. This
storm was most unusual in that the wind was easterly and accompanied for
many hours by fine driving snow which piled into enormous drifts temporarily
isolating Oxford by road and rail. Trains from and to Paddington were stuck
for many hours in drifts between Culham and Radley. Although the strong
winds and blizzard conditions affected large areas of southern England, Oxford
was one of the areas most seriously affected. Jackson's Oxford Journal of
22nd January 1881 gives a vivid account of the effects of this blizzard. The
more recent gale of 2nd January 1976 was the second most severe in terms of
mean hourly wind speed with a maximum of 45 knots. The existence in the
Oxford district of several synoptic meteorological stations of the Meteorological Office with modern electrical cup recording anemometers furnish evidence of maximum gust speeds on this occasion. From their records it is
clear that many parts of the district experienced gusts exceeding 75 knots.
Such speeds are very rare in the Midlands and inland in southern Britain,
and this gale would seem to have reached the once-in-fifty-year or even
once-in-a-hundred-year probability level on the basis of existing anemograph
data. Such speeds are well below the maximum levels recorded at coastal
stations or in such notably windy places as the Orkney Islands.

One of the most remarkable falls of snow to have been recorded at
Oxford must have been that on 25th April 1908 when a level depth of
eighteen inches was recorded. For so much snow to have fallen so late in
the year (it was actually the weekend undergraduates arrived up for the summer term) is remarkable. On this occasion the heaviest snowfall was in
Berkshire, Oxfordshire and Cotswold area and the subsequent very rapid mel-
ting produced floods in the Thames valley around Oxford. On 13th and 14th
February 1888 during a prolonged and heavy snowstorm, which produced approximately 50 mm precipitation, snow accumulated to a level depth of between 20
and 24 inches. This appears to have been the greatest snowfall on record at
Oxford. (Radcliffe MS Observer's Notebooks). Even the recent severe snowy
winters of 1947 and 1963 did not experience more than a level depth of a
foot of snow, not all of which fell in one storm.

In one respect there does appear to be some evidence of a recent
increase in the incidence of extreme weather events at Oxford; the occurrence of large daily rainfalls. Daily falls exceeding 25 mm (approximately
one inch) occur on average thirteen times every decade and since 1860 there
does not seem to be more than a random variation in their frequency. However
the much rarer occurrence of daily falls exceeding 50 mm or 75 mm shows an

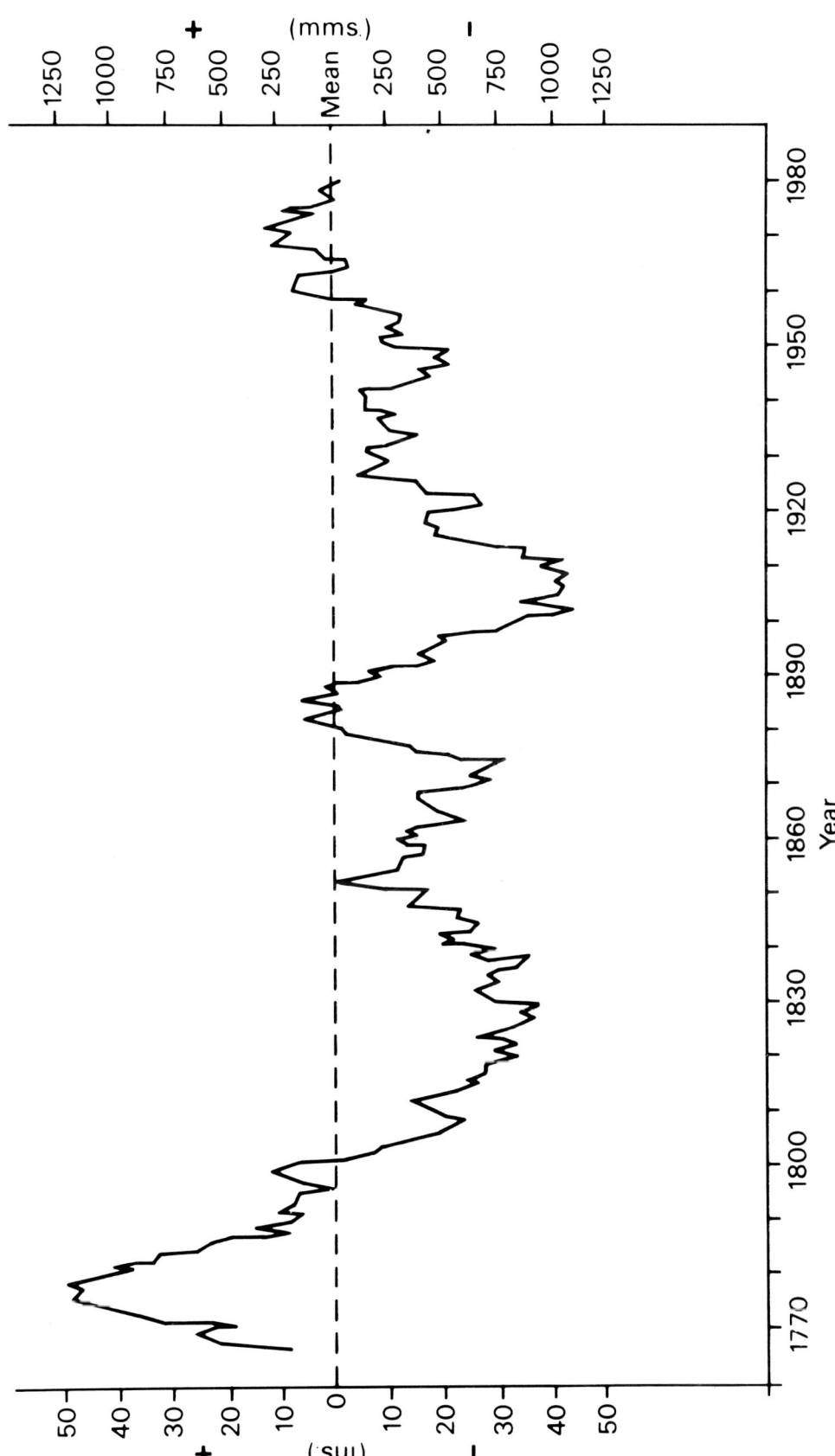

OXFORD RAINFALL: ACCUMULATED DEPARTURES FROM LONG PERIOD MEAN (645.5mm.)

Figure 6.   Annual rainfall at Oxford since 1767 shown as the accumulated departure from the long period mean.

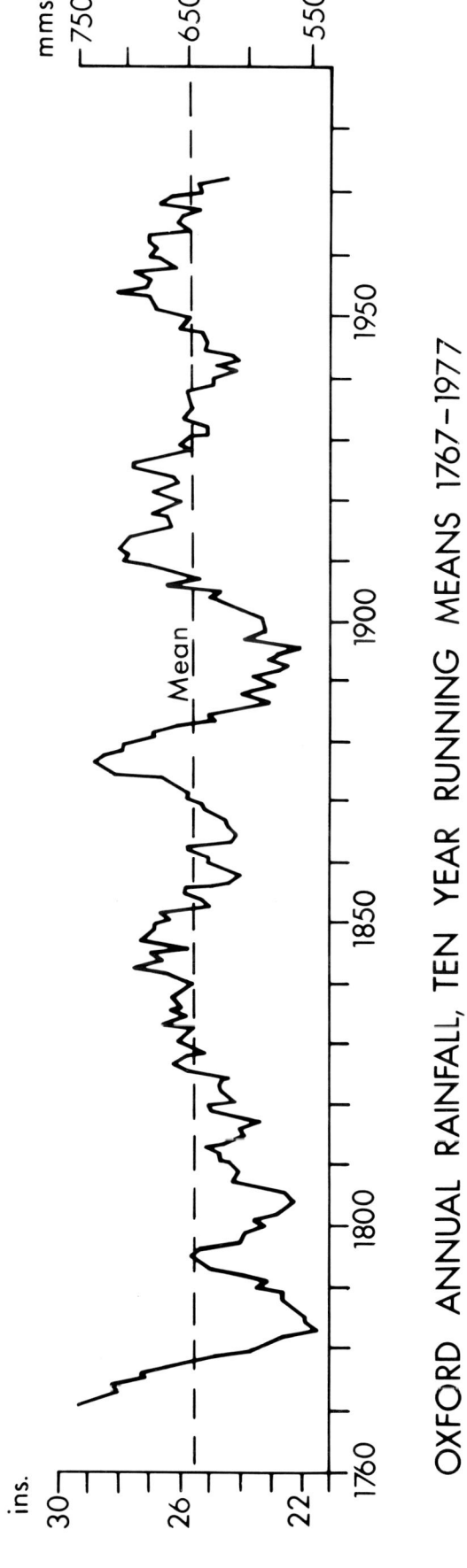

OXFORD ANNUAL RAINFALL, TEN YEAR RUNNING MEANS 1767–1977

Figure 7. Annual rainfall at Oxford since 1767 shown as ten year moving means.

interesting increase since 1950. There have been only ten falls of 50 mm or more in one day at the Radcliffe Meteorological Station since 1860, six of which have occurred since 1950. Perhaps even more significant is the fact that the three daily falls exceeding 75 mm have all occurred since 1950. Evidence of a similar trend has been noted in other places in southern Britain, particularly involving heavy thundery summer downpours. The heaviest daily fall at Oxford was on 10 July 1968 when 87 mm was recorded at the Radcliffe Meteorological Station. On this occasion falls exceeding 75 mm 75 mm occurred in a narrow belt extending from Devonshire to the Lincolnshire coast and even heavier falls in north Somerset and the Bristol region. (Bleasdale, 1974). By contrast a local downpour on 13th July 1967, during which at least 70 mm and probably 75 mm fell in exactly one hour on the Blackbird Leys estate and around the Cowley car factories, produced a mere 7 mm of rain at the Radcliffe site, (McFarlane and Smith, 1968).

SOME LONG PERIOD RAINFALL AND TEMPERATURE TRENDS

A long period meteorological record, such as that available for Oxford, provides the most reliable evidence of any short period fluctuations in the character of our climate or of any progressive trend, either for better or worse. This is a subject that has provoked much discussion in recent years when some notable extremes of weather have occurred. However, the belief that our climate is going through a period of particular instability or actually changing could be a consequence of the improvement in the meteorological reporting network and the speed with which weather disasters or extremes are now reported widely by the mass media. Similar periods in the past, when climate has been more variable and extremes more frequent, have prompted the same idea and they actually led to the more systematic collection of meteorological data. This occurred in the late eighteenth century and again in Britain around 1880.

Figures 6 and 7 show the Oxford rainfall record since 1767 in terms of the accumulated departure from the long period mean and as ten year moving averages. While the method of plotting ten year moving averages has some statistical limitations; it may over-emphasise one or two exceptional years, or be affected by natural periodicities of approximately ten years, the broad features revealed in Fig. 7 are confirmed by the graph of accumulated departures from the long period mean. In Fig. 6 a falling trend on the graph indicates a period of below average rainfall, and a rising trend a period of above average rainfall. From these two graphs it can be clearly established that there have been drier and wetter periods in the rainfall of Oxford during the last 200 years. After a very wet period around 1770 to 1780 there was a relatively dry period until about 1830. Between 1830 and 1890 there were two notably wetter periods culminating around 1852 and 1885, separated by a brief drier period around 1860. The notably wet period around 1880 was immediately succeeded by the driest period in the Oxford record which culminated around 1900 after which conditions became significantly wetter. The driest ten year period on record at Oxford was 1893-1902, with A mean annual fall of 563mm. The wettest decade was 1874-1883 with a mean annual fall of 729mm. There is a close parallel between the alternation of wet and dry periods at the end of the eighteenth and nineteenth centuries. Since the beginning of the present century there have been two wetter periods culminating around the time of the First World War and between 1950 and 1960. The increase in the frequency of heavy downpours in one day, noted above, may be one aspect of this latest wetter period. The most recent trend is towards drier conditions of which some recent dry winters and the drought of 1975-6 are characteristic. Taken together the two graphs do not appear to show any progressive trend one way or the other nor is there a regular cyclic pattern unless the similarity between the rainfall of the late eighteenth and nineteenth centuries is, perhaps rashly, taken as evidence of a hundred year cycle.

The Oxford rainfall record for the period 1767 to 1814 is less reliable than that for subsequent years because we are less certain of the site and nature of the instruments used to record rainfall at Shirburn and Oxford, while for years when readings at these places are missing the record has been constructed from available readings at places as far apart as London and Stroud which provide overlapping records with Oxford and Shirburn (Craddock and Craddock, 1977). However, the pattern is so close to that deduced for Kew (Wales-Smith,1971) and elsewhere (Craddock, 1976) that it is probably correct in its broad features.

In addition to these relatively small fluctuations in annual rainfall over the last 200 years there has also been some periodic fluctuation in the distribution of rainfall within the year and this is well illustrated by the series of histograms in Fig. 8 which show the mean decadal monthly fall for each ten year period at Oxford from 1820 to 1970. These show quite significant changes of rainfall régime. For example for much of the nineteenth century summer and early autumn were much wetter than winter and spring. At some periods September has been a very wet month, notably between 1820 and 1840; while at other times, 1891-1910, it has been very dry. Over the long period October has been the wettest month of the year and the spring months nearly always the driest. Fig. 8 suggests that during periods when annual rainfall has been well above average there has been a tendency for the wetness of the summer months and September to make the largest contribution to this.

Some indication has already been given of temperature trends since 1815 when examining the character of summers and winters at Oxford. Fig. 9 illustrates temperature trends in terms of ten year moving averages for each season at Oxford. This is more revealing than a single graph showing the variation of mean annual temperature for this shows only a relatively small fluctuation with a range of about half a degree Celsius over the period. While there have been periods, such as around 1840 and between 1870 to 1890, when the temperature of all four seasons was below the long period mean, more frequently the trends in different seasons have not been in phase. Thus the tendency to colder winters since 1940, although matched by slightly cooler summers, has been quite different to the warmer trend of both spring and autumn. Perhaps the most interesting feature of these seasonal graphs is the close similarity between the temperature trends of spring and autumn. These are sometimes in phase with either summer or winter but rarely with both. If it were not for the definite trend to cooler winters after 1920 one would be tempted to see evidence of a progressive warming of temperatures at Oxford after about 1920 and to attribute this to the "urban effect" caused by an increase in the built-up area and space heating which has been shown to have had a measurable effect on the temperature conditions of many large cities such as London this century. A careful comparison of the difference between monthly temperatures at Oxford and Rothamsted, an unaltered rural site some fifty miles away, over the last hundred years has shown no evidence for a similar man-induced amelioration of Oxford's temperatures.

CONCLUSION

There is no doubt that over the time scale of several millions, or even thousands, of years, the climate of all parts of the earth has been subject to continuous and significant changes. Geological and palaeobotanical evidence, such as are described by Dr. Goudie elsewhere in this volume, enable us to reconstruct to some extent the climate of the Oxford district at various stages of the last Ice Age. Archaeological evidence may also provide some clues as to the climate of the district in prehistoric and Roman times, but the for last few hundred years we have only the reliable evidence of instrumental meteorological records which commenced here around 1740.

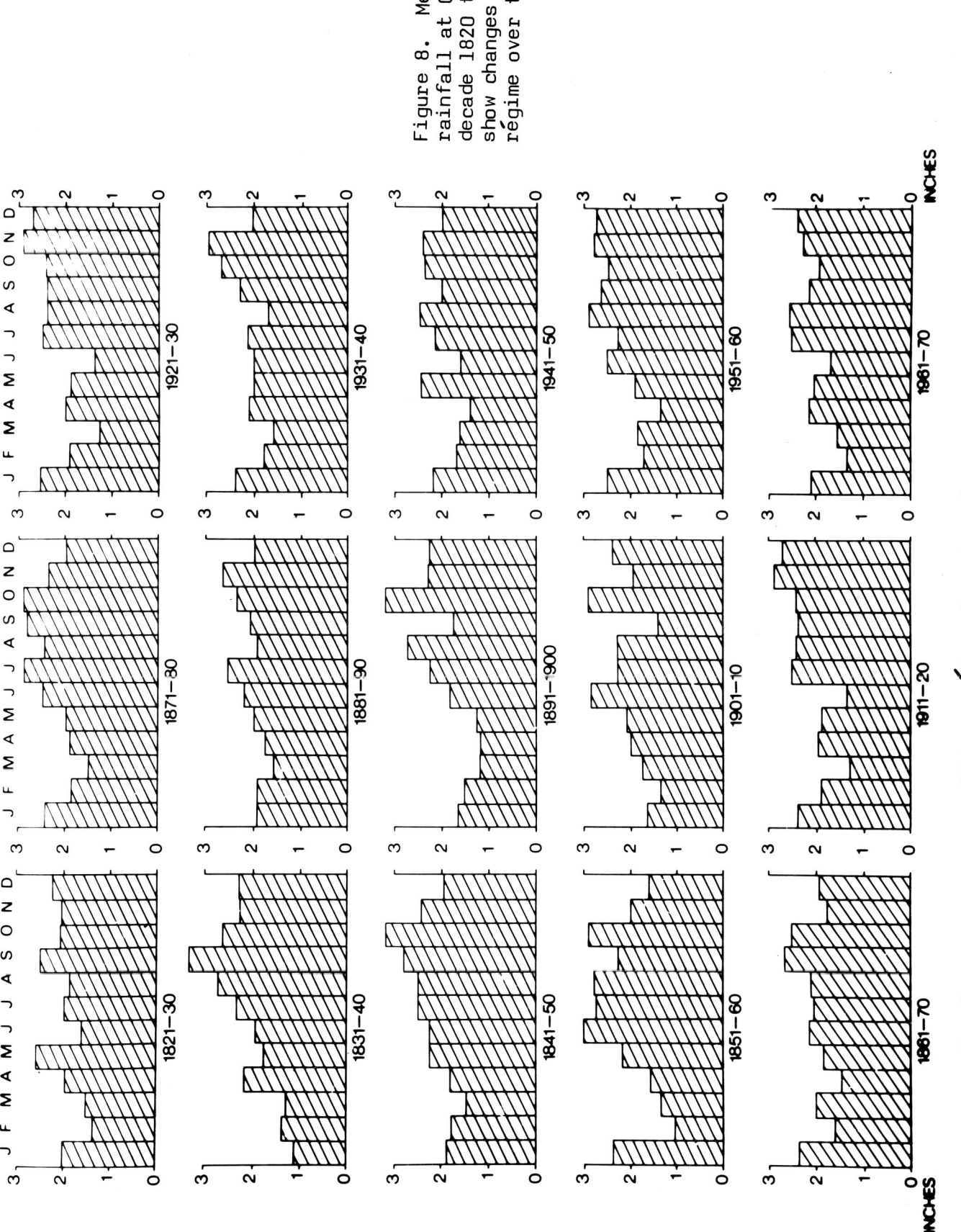

Figure 8. Mean monthly rainfall at Oxford for each decade 1820 to 1970; to show changes of seasonal régime over this period.

OXFORD RAINFALL DECADAL RÉGIMES AND MONTHLY MEANS
1821—30 TO 1961—70

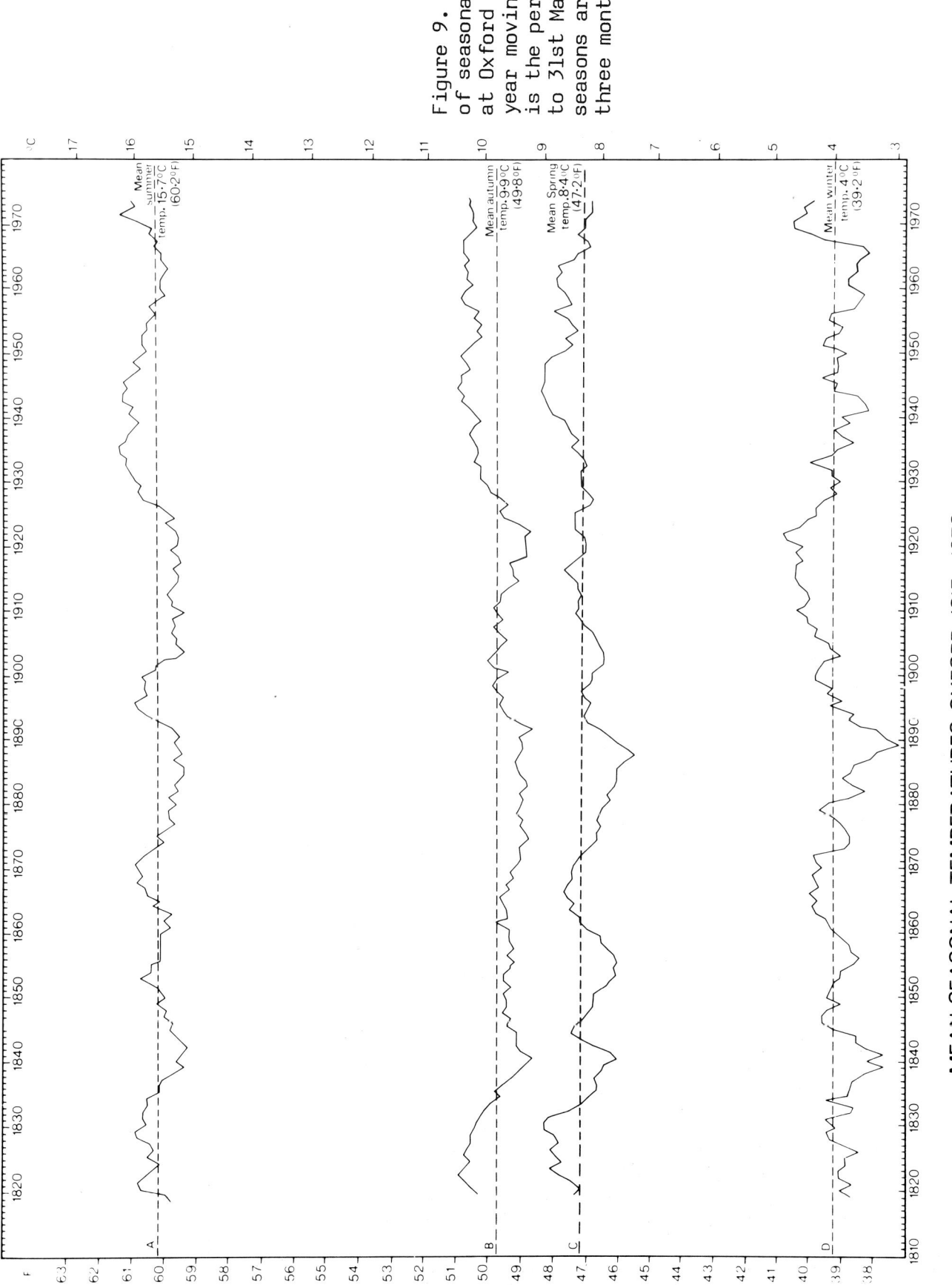

Figure 9. The fluctuation of seasonal temperatures at Oxford since 1815; ten year moving means. (Spring is the period 1st March to 31st May; the other seasons are consecutive three month periods.)

MEAN SEASONAL TEMPERATURES, OXFORD, 1815–1978
TEN YEAR RUNNING MEANS

A – JUNE – AUGUST
B – SEPTEMBER – NOVEMBER
C – MARCH – MAY
D – DECEMBER – FEBRUARY

Such records not only provide us with direct evidence of the small changes of annual and seasonal weather conditions for this period, but the range of conditions and the association of weather with wind and pressure can provide us with some understanding of the immediate causes of such fluctuations. Current work in progress which seeks to find some correlation between these known weather conditions and such other climatic indicators as tree rings (Varley, Calton, Smith and Fletcher, 1979) may enable us to extend the climatic record back into the more recent historical past before the eighteenth century. It is also important to maintain the Oxford meteorological record in conditions as close as possible to those prevailing at the present site, in order to detect any future changes or fluctuations of climate, at least until such times as automatic weather stations and meteorological satellite data render such records superfluous.

This essay has illustrated the relatively small range of variation in the Climate of the Oxford district during the last two hundred years and also drawn attention to the limitations of the notion of a "climatic average". Nevertheless a long period average has some value as a standard of comparison and, for this reason, the long period annual and monthly averages and extremes of the more important climatic elements for Oxford are listed in Table 4.

REFERENCES

Bleasdale, A. (1974), 'The year 1968, an outstanding one for multiple events with exceptionally heavy and widespread rainfall', British Rainfall, 1968 Met. Office, pp.223-31.

Craddock, J.M. (1976), 'Annual rainfall in England since 1725', Quart. J.R. Met. Soc. 102, pp.823-40.

Craddock, J.M. and Craddock, E. (1977), 'Rainfall at Oxford from 1767-1814 estimated from the records of Dr. Thomas Hornsby and others', Met. Mag. 106, pp.361-72.

Craddock, J.M. and Smith, C.G. (1978), 'An investigation into rainfall recording at Oxford', Met. Mag. 107, pp.257-71.

Frisinger, H. Howard (1977), The History of Meteorology to 1800.

Jurin, James (1923),'Invitatio ad observationes meteorlogicas communi consilio instituendas', Phil. Trans. R. Soc. 33, pp.422-27.

McFarlane, D and Smith, C.G. (1968), 'Remarkable rainfall in Oxford', Met. Mag. 97, pp.235-45.

Manley, G. (1974), 'Central England temperatures; monthly means 1659 to 1973', Quart. J.R. Met. Soc. 100, pp.389-405.

Poulter, R.M. (1962), 'The next few summers in London', Weather 17, pp.253-7.

Radcliffe Observatory, Astronomical Observations made at the Radcliffe Observatory, Oxford, 7-13 (for the years 1847-1852).

Radcliffe Observatory, Astronomical and Meteorological Observations made at the Radcliffe Observatory, Oxford, 14-47 (for the years 1853-1891).

Radcliffe Observatory, Results of the Meteorological Observations made at the Radcliffe Observatory, Oxford, 37, pp.48-52, 54-6 (for the years 1876-1879 and 1892-1935).

Royal Society (1978), <u>Scientific Aspects of the 1975-76 drought in England and Wales</u>.

Smith, C.G. (1954), 'Climate', in A.F. Martin and R.W. Steel (eds.), <u>The Oxford Region</u>, pp.37-49.

Smith, C.G. (1975a), 'The character of the summers at Oxford since 1815', in C.G. Smith and D.I. Scargill (eds.), <u>Oxford and its Region</u>, pp.14-28.

Smith, C.G. (1975b), 'Central England temperatures; monthly means of the Radcliffe Meteorological Station, Oxford', <u>Quart. J.R. Met. Soc.</u> 101, pp.385-7.

Smith, C.G. (1979a), 'An eighteenth century rainfall record at Shirburn Castle, Oxfordshire', <u>Met. Mag.</u> 108, pp.52-9.

Smith, C.G. (1979b), 'The cold winters of 1767-68, 1776 and 1814, as observed at Oxford', <u>Weather</u> 34(9), pp.346-68.

Smith, C.G. (1979c), <u>The Gale of 2nd January, 1976: its character and effects in the Oxford area as compared with some other notable gales since 1880</u>, School of Geography, University of Oxford, Research Paper 21, p.32.

Sprat, Thomas (1667), <u>History of the Royal Society</u>.

Symons, G.J. (1891), (Translation of) <u>Consideraciones temperiei pro 7 annis</u> by Rev. William Merle.

Varley, G.C., Calton, N.B.M., Smith, C.G. and Fletcher, J.M. 'Climatic signals in tree ring chronologies for British oaks', <u>Nature</u>, 278, No.5701, pp.282-3.

Altitude 63.4 m.
Lat. 51° 46' N
Long. 1° 16' W.

TABLE 4

OXFORD, RADCLIFFE METEOROLOGICAL STATION

SUMMARY OF LONG PERIOD OBSERVATIONS 1815-1975, AND EXTREME VALUES UNTIL DECEMBER 1978

ITEM	J	F	M	A	M	J	J	A	S	O	N	D	YEAR
Mean Monthly Rainfall MM. 1815-1975	53.2	41.5	41.4	44.4	50.1	54.6	61.0	61.0	60.2	66.7	60.6	55.9	650.5 MM.
Wettest Month & Year	138.7 1852	119.6 1937	133.6 1862	112.5 1818	138.7 1932	193.0 1852	183.4 1834	133.2 1971	156.1 1974	188.2 1875	186.4 1852	143.3 1914	1034.7 MM 1852
Driest Month & Year	5.3 1825	0.3 1891	1.5 1929	0.5 1817	3.6 1829	1.8 1925	0.8 1825	2.0 1940	2.5 1929	4.8 1969	4.8 1945	4.8 1835	379.5 MM 1921
Monthly Mean Dry Bulb Temp. 1815-1975	3.6	4.1	5.6	8.2	11.5	14.8	16.4	15.9	13.5	9.9	6.3	4.4	9.5°C
Highest Mean Monthly Temp. and Year	7.7 1916	7.7 1869	9.5 1938	11.2 1943	15.3 1833	18.6 1846	19.7 1921	19.2 1975	16.8 1949	13.1 1831	9.8 1818	8.2 1852	10.9°C 1949
Lowest Mean Monthly Temp. and Year	-3.2 1963	-2.6 1947	1.9 1845) 1883)	4.9 1837	9.0 1817	11.8 1909	13.8 1841) 1879)	13.3 1912	11.0 1952	6.8 1817) 1919)	2.9 1923	-1.6 1890	7.6°C 1879
Monthly Mean of Daily Max. Temp. (1881-1975)	6.6	7.3	9.9	13.0	16.7	19.8	21.4	20.9	18.4	14.0	9.7	7.3	13.8°C
Monthly Mean of Daily Min. Temp. (1881-1975)	1.2	1.3	2.1	4.1	7.0	10.0	12.0	11.7	9.6	6.5	3.6	1.9	5.9°C
Absolute Max. Temp. (1881-1975)	14.7 1930	17.7 1891	22.0 1929	27.1 1893	30.6 1947	34.3 1976	33.9 1923	35.1 1932	33.5 1911	27.3 1921	19.0 1946	15.0 1948	35.1°C 1932
Absolute Min. Temp. (1881-1975)	-14.5 1881	-16.2 1947	-10.9 1947	-4.9 1892	-1.8 1938	1.3 1892	5.1 1888	3.5 1892	-0.6 1919	-5.1 1890	-8.8 1923	-13.4 1890	-16.2°C 1947
Monthly Mean Grass Min. Temp. °C (1881-1975)	-1.0	-1.0	-0.4	1.6	4.6	7.9	10.0	9.4	6.9	3.7	1.1	-0.4	3.5°C

45

TABLE 4 (Continued)

ITEM	J	F	M	A	M	J	J	A	S	O	N	D	YEAR
Absolute Grass Min. Temp. (1881-1975) and Year	-18.8 1947	-22.2 1947	-19.1 1947	-8.7 1912	-8.2 1944	-2.8 1962	1.0 1918	-0.2 1943	-4.5 1885	-8.6 1948	-11.2 1923	-15.0 1908	-22.2°C 1947
Mean Duration of Bright Sunshine (Hours)(1881-1975)	52.1	68.6	115.5	150.1	191.1	200.1	188.0	175.5	138.7	101.3	62.7	47.6	1491.6 (HOURS)
Sunniest Month and Year (1881-1975)	94.1 1952	115.1 1949	198.4 1893	252.8 1893	293.6 1909	301.0 1975	310.4 1911	274.9 1947	222.6 1911	159.7 1921	107.9 1923	77.7 1952	1853.5 (HOURS) 1959
Dullest Month and Year (1881-1975)	14.9 1885	22.8 1940	61.9 1916	81.5 1889	112.4 1932	109.4 1909	97.4 1944	97.7 1912	64.9 1945	49.6 1894	29.7 1888	5.0 1890	1158.8 (HOURS) 1888

46

ARCHAEOLOGY IN OXFORDSHIRE, 1954-1979

Tom Hassall

Oxford and its region have long been noted as an area of exceptional archaeological activity, The tradition of an interest in local history and archaeology goes back as far as the later Middle Ages and, from the seventeenth and eighteenth centuries antiquarian studies were increasingly common. By the end of the nineteenth century the first scientific excavations were taking place.

In our own century the accumulated archaeological knowledge of Oxford and the historic county was summarised in Volume I of the Victoria County History in 1937. This survey and gazetteer was to be supplemented in 1954 by four masterly essays by Mr. H. Case, Miss M.V. Taylor, Dr. J.N.L. Myres and Professors W.G. Hoskins and E.M. Jope in the Oxford Region. These surveys still remain the most accessible overview of local archaeology. It is not, therefore, the intention of this paper to supplant these surveys, but rather to outline some of the major developments in archaeology which have taken place since they were published.

Perhaps the most striking outward development in local archaeology over the last twenty five years has been the radical change in the structure of carrying out archaeological research. The authors of the archaeological studies in the Oxford Region reflected faithfully the organisation of archaeology in 1954 and in particular the fundamental, if largely unselfconscious, role of the University. Humphrey Case, the Assistant Keeper, Department of Antiquities, Ashmolean Museum, following in the tradition of E.T. Leeds, represented the crucial role that the Ashmolean Museum and its staff have always played both by conducting their own research and by serving as a catalyst for the researches of others. The other authors were also interested local scholars all of whom were deeply knowledgeable of local archaeology but for none of whom it was their prime concern. At the same time the Oxford University Archaeological Society was the most active group in the region concerned with excavation and field work. In contrast to this undergraduate society the two senior archaeological and historical societies of the time, the Oxford Architectural and Historical Society and the Oxfordshire Archaeological Society, were not involved directly in field work, although they played a vital part in publishing the results.

H.M. Colvin faithfully captured the atmosphere of Oxford's archaeology in the 1950's when in his reviews of the Oxford Region he wrote: 'no member of the Oxford Architectural and Historical Society is likely to find fault with the scope of a book which deals so conveniently with the area which lies within coach distance of the Ashmolean Museum'.

However, within University circles even before 1954, there had been felt the need for full-time involvement in archaeology. In Oxford the work of R.L.S. Bruce-Mitford, W.A. Pantin and E.M. Jope had emphasised the critical role that a full-time field officer in Oxford attached to a City Museum could play. The need was finally answered in 1964 when enlightened members of the Oxford City and Oxfordshire County Council jointly established the Oxford City and County Museum under its first Director, Jean Cook. From its small beginnings at Fletcher's House, Woodstock the Museum has now grown into a County wide service. The Museum's first Field Officer, Don Benson created a field section, now with three full-time staff.

Parallel to the development of Local Authority interest in archaeology was the development of full-time rescue archaeology in the region. In old Oxfordshire and old north Berkshire this development arose out of the emergence of various independent excavation committees to provide an archaeological response to specific local developments. Their history has been told elsewhere and it is sufficient to note here that in 1967 the first full-time rescue archaeologist was appointed in Oxford. In 1973 the new County's rescue archaeology was reorganised with the establishment of the Oxfordshire Archaeology Unit. In 1979 there are twelve full-time staff working with the Unit.

While full-time archaeology in Oxfordshire has witnessed a spectacular growth, since 1954 the development of part-time societies and part-time involvement outside Oxford has been equally dramatic. Although the membership of the County society has remained fairly static all the new County's market towns and many of the villages now have a local historical and archaeological society, some of which are involved in active field work. This aspect will be returned to later.

Thus the organisation of local archaeology has changed radically since 1954. At the same time the numbers actively involved, both professionally and part-time, have also increased enormously. These changes have come about principally because of the explosion in our knowledge of the distribution of sites of all periods coupled with the realisation that even in the medium term only a fraction of those sites can be preserved anything like intact.

Two specific examples of our increasing awareness can be given. The richness of the archaeological sites on the gravel sub-soils of the Upper Thames was well appreciated in 1954. Pioneer aerial reconnaissance by Major Allen before the second World War, by D.N. Riley during the war and by Professor J.K.S. St. Joseph after the war had revealed the density of the sites. It was however really only the publication of The Upper Thames Valley, an archaeological survey of the river gravels that demonstrated to the local Planning Authorities, the gravel extraction companies and the informed general public that the Upper Thames gravel fields form a virtually continuous archaeological site. On a smaller scale in terms of numbers of sites, but equally significant in terms of distribution, the excavations of sites on the line of the M.40 showed how even comparatively blank areas contain past settlements. At the same time the M.40 work served as a catalyst for field work in the eastern part of the County.

The necessity of compiling a comprehensive register of both old and new sites was recognised by Don Benson and accordingly he pioneered the County Sites and Monuments Record. His system involved the use of the allocation of Primary Record Numbers to each site of each period, the plotting of these sites on record maps and the possibilities of rapid retrieval of information on sites through the use of optical coincidence cards. Benson's system has been adopted in various forms in many parts of the country. The record currently contains 11,900 items and the numbers are increasing steadily. It follows that virtually any development involving the disturbance of the ground stands a fair chance of affecting a buried site. Using the information contained within the Sites and Monuments record it is possible to demonstrate the scale of the problem posed by archaeological sites. The task of creating the Sites and Monuments record was not only undertaken to aid scholars, but also to allow rational choices to be made over the preservation or otherwise of archaeological sites. The existence of the record has meant that archaeology can be built into the planning process.

The problems of development on archaeological sites are nothing new, while the need to perserve sites intact has always been one of the main functions of the Department of the Environment (Ministry of Works in 1954). Then, as now, the Department had powers to protect sites through the process known as Scheduling. Twenty-five years ago the number of sites in the old County protected in this way was 89; the number of scheduled sites now stands at about 200 including sites in the old north Berkshire. Don Benson was, however, the first local archaeologist to realise that an equally effective way of preserving sites was to build into the planning process their preservation. At an academic level this lead to the recommendations for preservation contained in The Upper Thames Valley, an archaeological survey of the River Gravels.

On a wider level we have now seen archaeology take its place amongst the other constraints which are recognised as significant in the way the future of the region is supposed to develop. At a strategic level archaeology now features in the Structure Plan. At a more immediate level the District Councils, particularly South Oxfordshire District Council, are taking archaeology into account at Local Plan level. The recently published proposals for Wallingford and Thame show how it is intended to integrate archaeology into both towns' future development, both in terms of the preservation of archaeological features and historic topography and, where preservation is not practical or desirable, through excavation.

Even with the most careful planning, confrontation between archaeologists and the developer cannot always be avoided. Oxfordshire archaeologists, like other groups concerned with the environment, have realised that at times it is necessary to fight with logic and reason, sometimes aided by the well-timed publicity stunt, for their beliefs. Amongst a number of minor skirmishes archaeologists have been involved in two major battles. At Northfield Farm, Long Wittenham, archaeology was used - amongst other factors such as loss of agricultural land and development in the flood plain - as part of a case against gravel extraction at a planning enquiry in 1977. In this way a major prehistoric and Roman complex was successfully preserved. More spectacular was the case of Wallingford Castle where archaeology was virtually the sole criteria in resisting the proposal to build flats on the outer bailey of the great Royal Castle.

Such campaigns as these would probably have been virtually inconceivable in the 1950's or even the 1960's; for the last 25 years have seen a radical change in the approach of archaeologists and the attitude of non-archaeologists to preservation. But preservation is the exception rather than the rule. A number of examples of specific forms of development have already been mentioned: road building, gravel extraction and home building. One can add urban redevelopment and agriculture to the list. Many of the County's towns, but notably Oxford, Abingdon and Banbury, have witnessed major inner renewal schemes. All three were the subject of archaeological reports which pointed out the level of destruction, since they pre-supposed that the sites would be destroyed. But, the plough can be as destructive as the bulldozer. Plough damage is not a new phenomenon: Bronze Age barrows were ploughed out during the Iron Age, and the great henge monument, known as the Devil's Quoits, at Stanton Harcourt, was flattened by medieval ploughing; steam ploughing was perhaps even more destructive. However, throughout the region the scale and depth of ploughing since the 1950's has been dramatic as the appearance of Madmarston Camp or the Chalk downlands shows all too graphically.

When preservation is impossible, the response of the archaeologist to these and other threats has been to try to perserve, by way of rescue excavation, as much as is possible. Rescue excavations have always predominated over excavations on non-threatened sites. Rescue archaeology is not a new invention. Indeed some of the country's early pioneering rescue excavations were carried out in this region, and the dominance of rescue excavations has increased even further. Such excavations have tended to concentrate on the gravel sites because both the detail of our knowledge of sites is best and the massive proposals for gravel extraction are on a long time-scale. In addition a high level of co-operation exists between the archaeologists and the gravel companies, notably the Amey Roadstone Corporation.

It is the scale of rescue archaeology rather than the nature of rescue archaeology which has changed since 1954. But just as the scale of the developments have changed so also have methods of excavation. Probably the most obvious change has been the method of trench excavation as against open area excavation of sites. A graphic example can be given by comparing the Roman Villa at Ditchley excavated by C.A. Raleigh Radford in 1935 with its more humble counterpart at Barton Court Farm, Abingdon 1972-76, excavated by D. Miles. The latter shows clearly how large complex sites normally have the top-soil stripped off their entire area now if a full excavation is proposed. The Upper Thames Valley is an area very conducive to this 'open area' form of excavation because large-scale topsoil stripping is required by the gravel extraction companies. However the fact that such large archaeological complexes are being destroyed has meant that even within sites it is necessary to be selective. A site at Mount Farm, Berinsfield demonstrates both the problem of selectivity and the ways in which approaches are changing. The site was first excavated in 1933, by Dr. J.N.L. Myres who examined specific features within the site as revealed by air photographs. Forty four years later, G.M. Lambrick, when faced with the total excavation of the site, not only examined specific features but tested the ovarall nature of the site by random sampling.

The actual results of the last twenty five years of excavation have been commensurate with the changing structure, approach and methods of archaeology. While the simple overall picture of the region's archaeology has not perhaps changed dramatically some of the details of each period and the mechanism of continuity and change are much clearer. The earliest periods are still the least well understood because of the comparative rarity of material. The sands and gravels of the area are well-known for their lower Palaeolithic material, but much of this material was discovered during early hand gravel digging and mechanical extraction has meant a decrease in finds. However, the Highlands Farm site near Henley has continued to produce material and much of it has been described by John Wymer, while R.J. Macrae also continues to recover material from various pits including a recent find of a Lavallois flake from Berinsfield.

Mesolothic material also remains scarce. Humphrey Case pointed out the difference in distribution between the heavy tools of the Thames and small tools of the area between the Cherwell and the Evenlode. It is in precisely this area near Ascott-under-Wychwood that stratified Mesolithic material was discovered sealed beneath the later Neolithic Long Barrow. It is the long barrow which typifies the field monuments of this area during the Neolithic period. Two such sites have been fully examined at Ascott as mentioned above and at Wayland's Smithy. At Ascott, apart from the Mesolithic material, Neolithic finds were also sealed beneath the barrow whose detailed examination revealed the intricacies of its structure and the remains of at least twenty individuals in its stone cists. Wayland's Smithy, a site better known to the general public, was also extensively excavated prior to its redisplay and the excavations revealed the traces of an early barrow beneath the visible mound. Excavations have also taken place on other Neolithic sites. At the Abingdon Causewayed Camp new material has been recovered including pottery with cereal grain impressions as well as domestic animal bones. The impression is confirmed that the site was associated with domestic activity and the site can now be dated to 3000 BC to 2400 BC. Evidence from the site itself and nearby sites indicates a high level of settlement in the area. Further down river the North Stoke cursus has been examined while up river the wartime excavations of the Devil's Quoits henge monument have been greatly extended and radiocarbon dates now place the site around 2000 BC. The dense distribution of subsequent beaker sites has been confirmed. Many of the actual beakers are derived from burials, one such burial being found in Oxford itself.

In the Bronze Age the tradition of Thameside settlement continues. The most typical field monument is the round barrow in the uplands and the ring-ditch, its ploughed out version, in the river valleys. Only one settlement site has been excavated, on the chalk at Rams Hill, where three phases of settlement dating to the 11th century BC were recovered. The relationship between this site to nearby earthworks, henges and barrows was examined. Barrows themselves have still been frequently discovered and some excavated. The cropmarks of a linear barrow cemetery showed with remarkable clarity in the University Parks during the drought of 1976 while one of the major excavations of this type was of a group of barrows at a multi-period site at Stanton Harcourt.

The Iron Age in the region is the one period which has been subjected to a major review since 1954. Professor Dennis Harding has revised and studied the distribution of sites for the Thames Valley. The chronology of the period has now pushed back to the 6th century BC if not earlier and Harding has stressed the cultural divide of the river Thames and the dual influences in the area from the South East and Wessex. Harding himself excavated at Frilford and at Blewburton. The latter site with Madmarston, has been the only hillfort to see significant excavations as part of a wider study of hillforts by the Oxford University Archaeological Society. Much of Harding's synthesis depended on fragmentary excavations and unstratified material but this rather unsatisfactory evidence has now been greatly supplemented by the recent work of the Oxfordshire Archaeological Unit. The Unit has undertaken large-scale excavations at a series of Iron Age settlements of different type and status. These excavations have included a village site and a single enclosed farmstead at Abingdon; an unenclosed farm at Mount Farm, Berinsfield; and seasonally occupied sites on the flood plains of the Thames and Farmoor and of the Windrush at Hardwick.

There has been no general synthesis for the Roman evidence since 1954, though the region's pottery industry has been the subject of an intensive study by Dr. C.J. Young. His excavations at the Churchill Hospital have revealed the most complete picture of a pottery manufacturing site. Further excavations have taken place at the Roman town of Dorchester-on-Thames and two small villas have been largely excavated at Shakenoak Farm and Barton Court Farm. One of the most striking aspects of all three sites has been evidence of late Roman occupation and early pagan Saxon settlement.

The evidence for pagan Saxon settlement has continued to accumulate. At New Wintles Farm, Eynsham a seven-acre site has been examined which contains two large buildings and eleven sunken huts perhaps forming a farmstead with scattered outbuildings. Although they have not been excavated, traces of large rectangular or sub-rectangular structures, probably houses, have been found from the examination of air photographs near E.T. Leed's pioneer excavations at Sutton Courtenay. Pagan Saxon burials still predominate and the largest cemetery of this period to be excavated in recent years was at Berinsfield.

The Middle and Late Saxon archaeology of the region has tended to be dominated by Oxford where the pioneer studies of Jope in Oxford were just beginning when the Oxford Region was published. Archaeology has now revealed evidence from the eighth-century origins of the city and the development of the defences, street system and economy of the burh in the tenth and eleventh centuries.

Oxford has also dominated the medieval archaeology of the region. The Castle, the City Wall, houses within the town and in the suburbs, Churches

51

and friaries have all been examined continuing the tradition of the archaeological study of the city's past. The study of upstanding buildings has also continued. By contrast, other towns have seen less activity although domestic sites have been excavated in Abingdon and part of the Castles at Banbury and Wallingford. All the towns have been the subject of a comprehensive archaeological survey. Outside the medieval towns some of the monuments at greatest risk are the earthworks of shifted, shrunken or deserted settlements and even the County's stock of ridge and furrow is rapidly diminishing. The most substantial excavation of a village site has been that at Seacourt although the area examined lay outside the original nucleus. The only other substantial excavations have been at Tetsworth. Currently excavations at Chalgrove are providing one of the most detailed plans of a late medieval moated manorial complex anywhere in the country.

The excavations mentioned above can only give a brief glimpse of the range of activity since 1954 while the full results of many of the major excavations still await synthesis. In this respect, the scale of the excavations and the elaboration of the detail which can now be derived from excavated evidence are some of the factors which are causing an ever increasing emphasis on the protracted analysis of excavated material. In this area new methodology, particularly in the study of pottery, is enabling very detailed information to be extracted and large bodies of material to be studied. But, it is in the study of the evidence of the past environment that perhaps the greatest changes are taking place. Traditional evidence like that of domestic animal bone is now being supplemented by the study of other forms of past faunal and floral remains. Beetles and snails, waterlogged and carbonised seeds are all being collected from current excavations and are providing insights into the past ecology of the region which are having as revolutionary an effect on archaeological thinking as the now standard practice of radiocarbon dating.

While the results of these excavations will be of interest to archaeologists and historians, archaeologists themselves are now very concerned to inform the non-academic public. 'Open Days' on excavations are frequently held and well attended. Archaeology is regularly featured in the local press and local radio. Most important of all has been the interpretation of local archaeology by the Oxfordshire Department of Museum Services through its major displays at Oxford and Woodstock, and its impressive programme with school children: formally through its School Service and informally through its promotion of the club Young Rescue.

At all levels, archaeology in the region is still rapidly developing even in the recent unfavourable economic climate. But the archaeologists themselves are very much aware of the major problems which still remain to be solved. Within the profession itself is the problem of how to disseminate knowledge and to what extent the results of excavations should be fully published or simply made accessible in archives. With regard to archives the question of the long-term storage of both site records, but in particular the vast quantities of finds, remains a perpetual and growing problem. On a somewhat different plane is the problem of the looting of sites by Treasure Hunters and their relations with the world of archaeology.

However, it would be innappropriate to end on a note of gloom. Rather, in concluding, tribute should be paid to the University and above all to the Department for External Studies in fostering local archaeological studies over the last twenty five years. Mention was made at the outset of the fundamental role of the Ashmolean Museum. But other departments have also been involved, notably the Institute of Archaeology and the History of Art. More recently St. Cross College has become positively involved with local archaeology through an association with the Oxfordshire Archaeological Unit.

Individuals within the University, both senior and junior have also continued to play a vital part.

Most important of all, adult education has been fundamental in allowing the possibilities of archaeology to be appreciated by a wider audience outside the University. Archaeology has long been recognised as the perfect adult education subject embracing as it does so many disciplines and providing opportunities for students to take part in original research on primary sources.

An examination of the W.E.A. reports shows how, in the year that the Oxford Region was published, twenty courses were held in archaeology and local history, rivalling music and English literature in popularity. The old Extra-Mural Delegacy, as it then was, ran only a small proportion of these classes but one of its reports comments that it was the lack of tutors that caused the limitation of classes.

In the early sixties there was a rapid expansion in the number of classes. In 1967 the Delegacy recognised the need to appoint a Staff Tutor in archaeology. This recognition followed a memorandum from the Oxford City and County Museum in which it was suggested that a staff tutor would provide a focal point and academic leadership for the development of archaeology in the Oxford area. The memorandum was prepared by the Director of the Museum, Jean Cook, who had herself been an active tutor for the Department in Kent and by Don Benson.

The appointment of Trevor Rowley as Staff Tutor for Berkshire, Buckinghamshire and Oxfordshire followed in 1969. He immediately responded to the increasing demand for conventional courses, and introduced weekend courses both for local consumption and for a wider audience. The Department became the catalyst in organising rescue excavations on the route of the M.40 and ran a highly successful series of training excavations at its research excavation at Middleton Stoney. The Department also runs Archaeology Certificate Courses to raise the standard of local students and at the same time runs, in association with the Department of the Environment, a national archaeological in-service training scheme. Within the last year the Department has also established formal links with the Oxfordshire Archaeological Unit, thus allowing the latter organisation to fulfill its obligations as an educational charity. Thus the Department for External Studies, as it now is, has, through its Staff Tutor, become recognised as one of the leading national centres for British archaeology in all its aspects. The statistics of classes published by the Department alone bear witness to the spectacular growth in this area of activity.

This paper has attempted to summarise the growth of the study of archaeology in the region over the last twenty-five years. Even if the only development had been within the field of Adult Education there would have been reason enough for local archaeologists to congratulate the Department for External Studies.

SELECT BIBLIOGRAPHY

D. Benson, (1972), 'A sites and monuments record for the Oxford region', Oxoniensia 37, (1972) pp. 226-37.

D. Benson and J. Bond, (1975), 'Problems and Methods of Excavation', in R.T. Rowley and M. Breakell (eds.), Planning and the Historic Environment I, pp. 95-103.

D. Benson and D. Miles, (1974), The Upper Thames Valley, an archaeological survey of the river gravels.

D.W. Harding, (1972), The Iron Age in the Upper Thames Basin.

T. Hassall, (1977), 'The Battle of Wallingford Castle, 1971-1977', in R.T. Rowley and M. Breakell (eds.), Planning and the Historic Environment II, (1977), pp. 156-168.

T. Hassall, (1975), 'Archaeology and Regional Organisation', in R.T. Rowley and M. Breakell (eds.), Planning and the Historic Environment I, pp. 8-14.

A.F. Martin and R.W. Steel, (1954), The Oxford Region: A Scientific and Historical Survey.

Victoria History of the County of Oxford, I (1939).

J. Wymer, (1968), Lower Palaeolithic Archaeology in Britain as represented by the Thames Valley.

C.J. Young, (1977), Oxford Roman Pottery, BAR 43.

For detailed excavation reports and annual summaries see Oxoniensia and also, since 1970 see CBA Group 9 Newsletters, No. 1-10.

THE SMALL TOWNS OF OXFORDSHIRE IN THE NINETEENTH CENTURY

C.J. Bond

INTRODUCTION

The nineteenth century was a period of enormous urban expansion, during which certain industrial towns like Birmingham, Manchester and Leeds increased their population approximately tenfold. The old county towns of the Midlands and the South were also affected, though less dramatically. Oxford's population was just over 12,000 in 1801, when the first census was taken. By 1901 it was 49,000, an increase of over three hundred per cent, and contemporary commentators were already expressing alarm at the sea of bricks and mortar which was beginning to engulf the University city.

Developments in the smaller country market towns over the same period have, on the whole, attracted less comment. This is especially true in Oxfordshire, where the unique character of Oxford has always focussed attention upon itself to the detriment of its smaller, less glamorous neighbours. Nonetheless, the impact of the nineteenth century upon these smaller towns is still of considerable interest. It would clearly be impossible within the space available to explore all aspects of this vast topic, and no attempt can be made here to examine the political, commercial, social, literary or artistic life of Oxfordshire towns in this period. It is intended instead to concentrate on their changing physical appearance and some of the factors most closely affecting it. While the amenity value of medieval or Georgian streets and buildings is now generally acknowledged, the nineteenth-century contribution to the townscape still tends to be underestimated and undervalued, and a fuller understanding of it is highly desirable in formulating conservation policies in planning for the future.

Two points should be noted: (1) Oxford is specifically excluded from the ensuing discussion; (2) the other towns are drawn from the present county of Oxfordshire as it was redefined in 1974, though Abingdon, Faringdon, Wallingford and Wantage were still in Berkshire during the period under examination.

SOURCES OF INFORMATION

The sheer wealth of documentary sources available for the study of nineteenth-century towns amounts almost to an embarrassment. The national census listed the population of all towns at ten-yearly intervals from 1801 onwards, and the enumerators' books provide invaluable evidence for occupations, family structure and migration patterns from 1841 onwards. Quarter Sessions papers up to 1888 contain details of the condition of bridges and roads, licences for chapels, and much other material. County Council records begin following the Local Government Act of 1888. Poor Law records are available from 1834 onwards. Corporation archives include many documents relating to borough properties, bridges, markets, and the records of Improvement Commissioners and Sanitary Committees. Industrial concerns, estate agents, auctioneers, charitable organisations, firms involved with building, water supply and gas, may all have preserved company records. Directories, available from 1783 onwards, include not only volumes produced by national publishers such as Pigot's and Kelly's, but also some locally-produced series, such as Rusher's Banbury Directories (1812-1896) and Packer's Burford Almanacks (from 1860). Local newspapers are of enormous value. Oxford already had three newspapers in the eighteenth century, and many of the smaller towns subsequently acquired their own. In Banbury William Potts launched a monthly Poor Law record called simply 'The Guardian' in 1838. Re-organised five years later as the weekly 'Banbury Guardian', this is still published today. It soon had competitors: the 'Banbury Advertiser' (commenced in 1854), the 'Banbury Beacon' (1860-1905), the 'Banbury Herald' (1861-1869), the 'Banbury Evening News' (1877) and the 'Banbury Telegraph' (1893-1895). From the middle of the nineteenth century, local newspapers began to appear elsewhere. The 'Bicester Herald' and 'Bicester Advertiser' were both founded in 1855. The 'Thame Gazette' first appeared in 1856. The 'Henley Advertiser', the first of several papers published in that town, ran from 1868 to 1908. Of the larger market towns only Chipping Norton remained without its own paper throughout the nineteenth century. Few of the smaller towns ever aspired to their own newspapers, though there were a few short-lived ventures such as the 'Woodstock Herald and Charlbury Messenger', which ran only from September 1875 to February 1876.

Of even greater value topographically are the many drawings and prints by artists such as John Buckler (1770-1851) and John Chessell Buckler, his son (1793-1894), and after the 1860's the products of photographers like Henry Taunt of Oxford and Warland Andrew of Abingdon. Above all, there is a superb series of cartographic sources. The Ordnance Survey's 1:63,360 maps covered all Oxfordshire towns between 1828 and 1833, with a second edition in the 1870's and a third edition shortly after the turn of the century. Larger scale maps appeared at 1:10,560 and 1:2500 between 1866 and 1883, with a second edition of both scales published between 1897 and 1900. For Banbury, Abingdon and Henley, as well as Oxford, remarkably detailed plans at 1:500 were also published. Apart from Ordnance Survey plans, other valuable maps were produced illustrating guidebooks and directories and in connection with housing projects, railways, gasworks, water supply, sewerage and lighting undertakings.

THE SIZE OF TOWNS IN THE NINETEENTH CENTURY

Much space could be devoted to the question of definition and discussion of what constituted a town in the nineteenth century. The present selection includes places which were still functioning as market centres after the end of the Middle Ages, but excludes villages like Stratton Audley or Middleton Stoney whose medieval marketing activities were relatively short-lived. It will become apparent, however, that by the Victorian period some of the smaller medieval market towns like Eynsham or Charlbury were beginning in their turn to lose whatever urban character they once possessed.

At the beginning of the century the largest town (excluding Oxford, a qualification which applies throughout this section) was Abingdon (population 4,400), followed by Banbury (3,800) and Henley (2,900). Most of the market towns still had less than 2,500 people, down to Bampton (1,000) and Charlbury (950); but the ratio between the largest and smallest market towns in Oxfordshire was still only of the order of 4:1.

During the first two decades most towns showed an overall increase. This was most marked at Banbury, which by 1821 had already overtaken Abingdon. Burford alone amongst the smaller towns showed a decline. By mid-century the populations of many Oxfordshire towns had reached a peak which they would not achieve again before the end of Victoria's reign. A gulf was now beginning to develop between the larger and smaller towns (Fig.1). By 1851 the population of Banbury was 8,200 and still rising rapidly, and was already seven times that of Woodstock, which had reached a modest peak unusually early in 1821 and was now stagnating. Apart from Banbury and Abingdon, which remained in a class of their own, the remainder can now be seen to be dividing into two distinct groups:

(1) The more successful market towns, which continued to play an important role as local service centres, reflecting this in

56

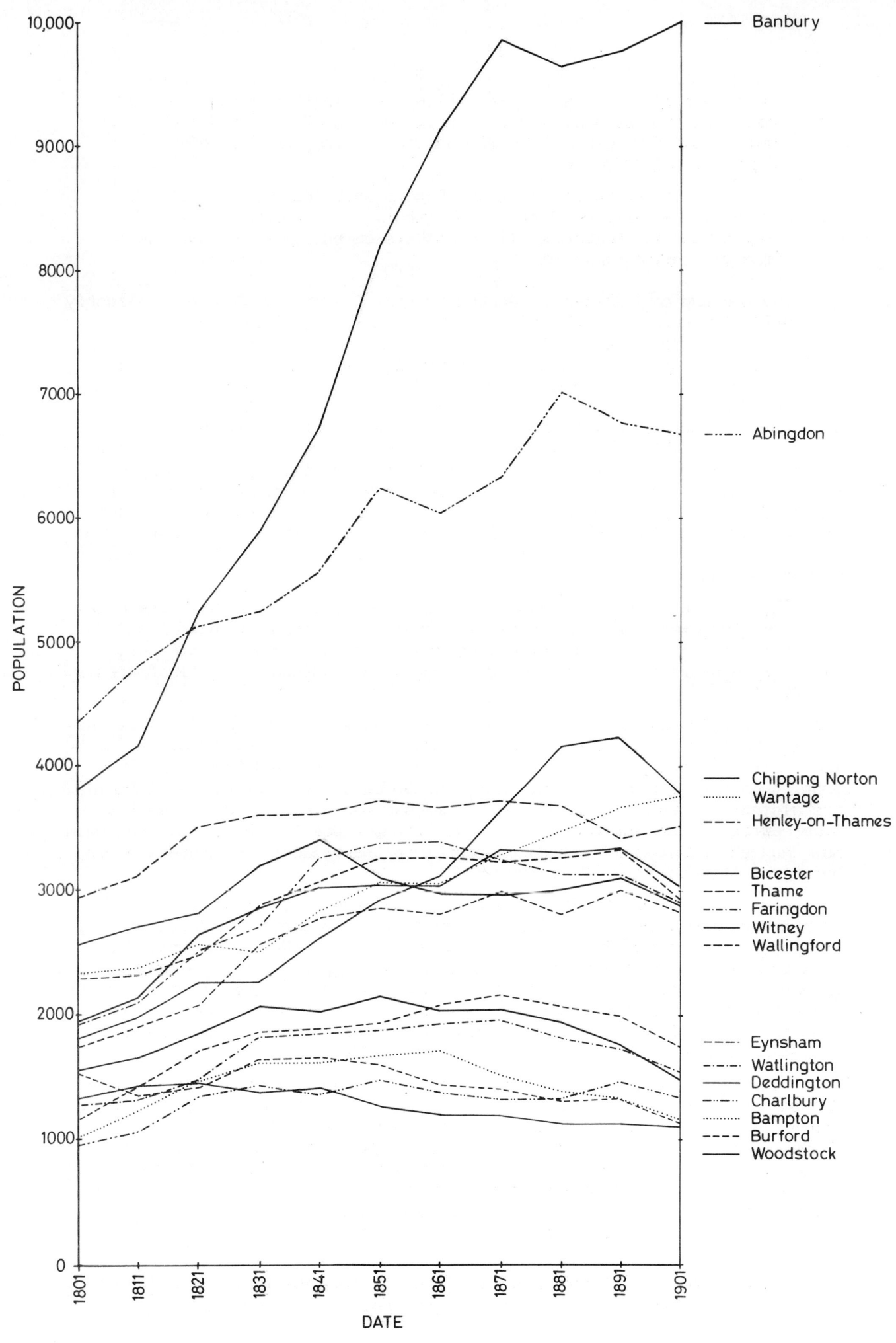

Population of Oxfordshire market towns in the 19th. century

Figure 1. Graph showing population of Oxfordshire market towns in the nineteenth century

their overall increase in population. Within this group the most spectacular expansion was experienced by Chipping Norton, which rose from ninth to third position in the county, reaching a peak of 4,200 in 1891.

(2) The lesser market towns which were entering a period of stagnation. Bampton, Burford, Charlbury, Deddington, Eynsham, Watlington and Woodstock all reveal a slow but definite decline from mid-century onwards.

By the end of the century Banbury's growth, despite faltering slightly in the 1880's, surpassed that of all other towns in Oxfordshire: in 1901 its population exceeded 10,000 for the first time. Next came Abingdon which, despite declining during the last two decades, still had 6,700 people in 1901. Banbury was about nine times and Abingdon six times the size of the smallest towns by that date. Of the remainder, the gulf between the more successful market towns and those on the brink of failure had widened until the average population of the one group was twice that of the other. The nineteenth century can thus be seen as a time of decision, when the provision of towns underwent a weeding-out process. The weaker members were losing their urban functions, while the more prosperous towns were consolidating their position and extending their spheres of influence (Figs.3 & 4).

COMMUNICATIONS

One of the keys to success or failure of a market centre in the nineteenth century was the location of each town in relation to the communication network. The superior advantages possessed by Banbury, Henley or Wallingford as route centres over Deddington or Woodstock are illustrated by Fig.2.

At the beginning of the century the transport system was still dominated by the turnpike road network. Many towns still profited from the coaching traffic. Banbury, for example, was the point of departure of no less than 54 coaches a week in 1838. Burford suffered a severe blow in 1812 when the old coach route from Oxford to Cheltenham was diverted away from the town centre to the new turnpike road along the ridge to the south. Coachmen now shunned the difficult steep descent into the valley, and a new inn was built for them on the hill in the 1820's.

Internally the street patterns remained much as they were inherited from the medieval period, though particularly troublesome obstructions were removed. The last of Banbury's town gates, the North Bar, was demolished in 1817. Paving improvements were widespread. The streets of Bicester were paved for the first time in the 1860's, though an order of the Bicester Local Board in 1864 forbidding the washing of pigs on the pavement suggests that the place still had a fairly rural air. In Abingdon paving stones had replaced cobbles in the main streets by the 1880's.

One major road re-alignment occurred in Bicester, where the coming of the railway diverted the main london road into the south-east corner of the Market Place: its earlier course survives as a row of hedges aligned on Chapel Lane, once the main entry but now a cul-de-sac. Otherwise additions to the street pattern were limited to peripheral service roads giving access to new housing developments on the urban margins. The break-up of the Calthorpe estate in Banbury, for example, opened the way for the construction of Dashwood Road and St. John's Road in 1840, while Marlborough Road was made in 1863.

Before the end of the eighteenth century only Henley, Wallingford and Abingdon had direct access to the main navigable waterway of the region,

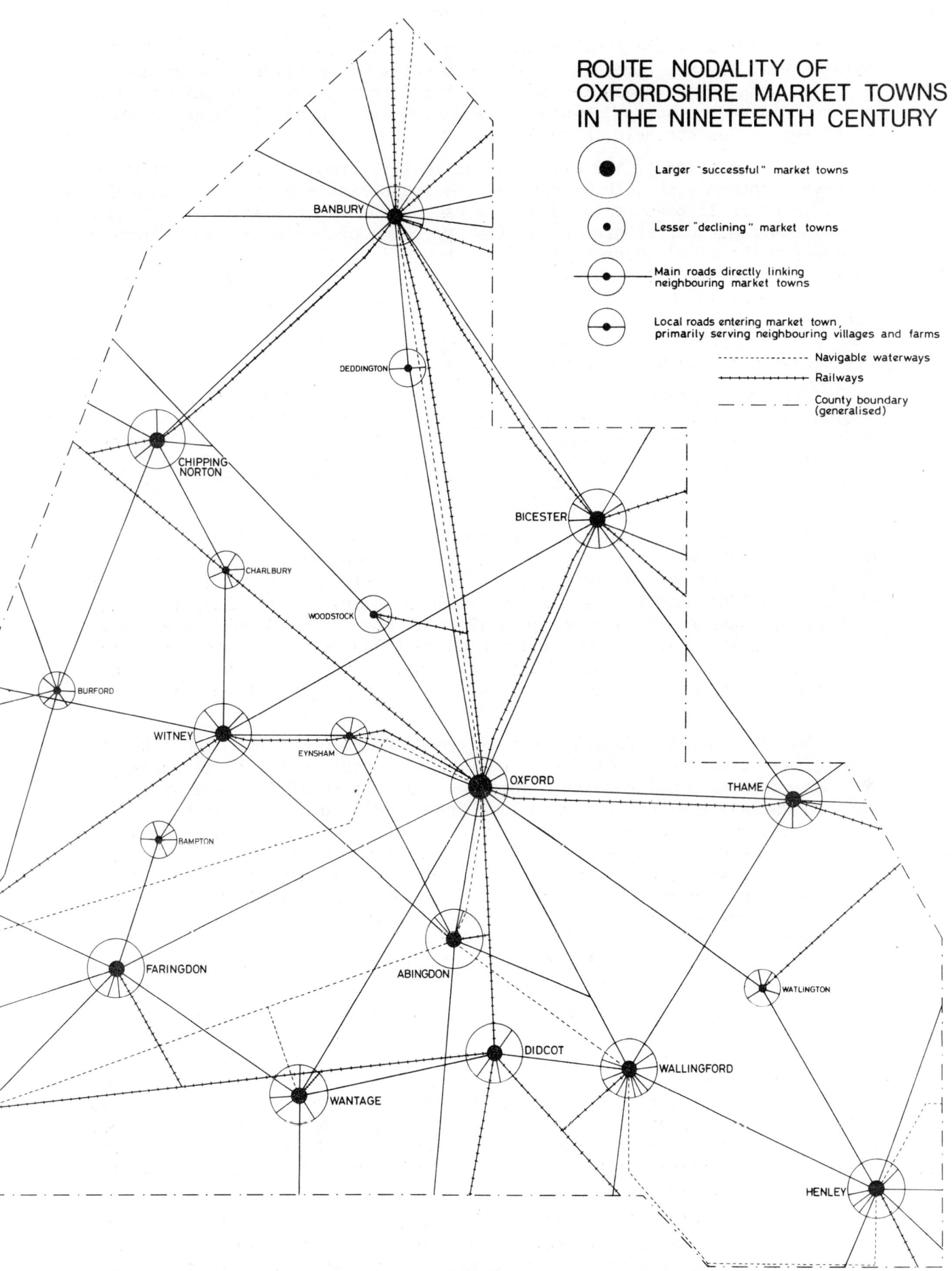

ROUTE NODALITY OF
OXFORDSHIRE MARKET TOWNS
IN THE NINETEENTH CENTURY

Larger "successful" market towns

Lesser "declining" market towns

Main roads directly linking
neighbouring market towns

Local roads entering market town,
primarily serving neighbouring villages and farms

- - - - - - Navigable waterways

+++++++++ Railways

- · - · - County boundary
(generalised)

BANBURY

DEDDINGTON

CHIPPING
NORTON

CHARLBURY

BICESTER

WOODSTOCK

BURFORD

WITNEY

EYNSHAM

OXFORD

THAME

BAMPTON

FARINGDON

ABINGDON

WATLINGTON

DIDCOT

WALLINGFORD

WANTAGE

HENLEY

Figure 2.   Diagram illustrating nodality of Oxfordshire market towns

the River Thames, while Eynsham had a wharf on the Limb Brook just off the main stream. By the time of Victoria's accession the river traffic was already changing its character and commercial traffic was beginning to lose ground to pleasure boats. Henley Rowing Club was founded in 1830 and the first Henley Regatta held in 1839.

The completion of the Oxford Canal in 1790 brought Banbury into direct waterway contact with both Oxford and the industrial midlands, and contributed in no small measure to Banbury's rapid rise in prosperity. A distinctive industrial quarter grew up on the east side of the town. From Foscote Brickworks the canal threaded its way northwards past Samuelson's Britannia Works and the Cherwell Engineering Works, past lines of wharves and warehouses (one of which is the former town hall, rebuilt here to serve a new purpose in 1860), past Tooley's Boatyard, under several swing bridges to Cobb's Girth Factory, a six-bay two-storey building of 1837 in red brick with great blank arches containing recessed windows.

The second major artifical waterway to be constructed through the region was the Wilts. and Berks. Canal, completed in 1820 and abandoned just over a century later. It joined the Thames at Abingdon, where the outline of a small basin is still partly visible and the company's name is still displayed on the iron bridge at St. Helen's Wharf built in 1824. A short branch canal led to another wharf at Wantage.

Many other canal schemes were mooted, some of which would have given other towns waterway connections. A link from Lechlade via Faringdon to Abingdon was proposed in 1784, another from Stratford-on-Avon via Witney to Abingdon in 1785, and a canal up the Evenlode valley to Charlbury in 1802. Another proposed route surveyed in 1819 would have crossed the Thames by a cast-iron aqueduct at Abingdon and run on to Aylesbury via Thame. None of these canals were built, and after a brief half-century of prosperity the canals began to suffer serious decline through competition from the railways.

In 1822 the Stratford & Moreton Tramway Company surveyed the line of a possible extension to the Thames at Eynsham, probably the first railway proposal affecting Oxfordshire. This was followed in 1833 by the Great Western Railway's plan for a main line from London to Bristol with a branch to Oxford, and in 1836-38 the proposal of the London & Birmingham Railway Company to build a branch from their main line at Tring via Thame, north Oxford, Witney and Burford to Cheltenham. The only one of these early schemes to come to fruition was the G.W.R., built in 1840-41. Like most of the original trunk lines it headed for its ultimate destination by the shortest possible route, serving the towns of the Vale of White Horse only indirectly through stations such as Wallingford Road and Wantage Road, which were often a couple of miles away.

The greatest impact of the G.W.R. was on Didcot, the site selected as the junction for the Oxford branch which opened in 1844. The railway station, half a mile east of the old village centre, soon became a nucleus of commercial growth. Three hotels were opened there, the Great Western Junction in 1846, the Royal Oak in the early 1850's and the Prince of Wales about 1860. A Corn Exchange was built in 1857 and a coal depot followed. Enormous numbers of horses were employed by the company, and the massive four-storey brick provender store built in 1885 was a familiar railway landmark until its demolition in 1976.

The influx of railway employees into Didcot created a severe housing shortage, and it was 25 years before this began to be resolved. The company did not at first accept any responsibility for housing its workers, and it was left to individual enterprise. In 1866 Stephen Dixon, an East Hagbourne farmer, purchased a hundred acres near the railway. Two years later he sold off the part fronting the Wallingford road for eight building plots. By 1872 he was undertaking building himself, and during the next fifteen years a whole series of new streets was laid out with a piecemeal development of terraces, semi-detached and detached houses. The G.W.R. did not stir itself to build any houses here until the first decade of the present century. For long this new development, the nearest thing Oxfordshire has to a railway town like Swindon or Crewe, retained a separate identity from Didcot village, being referred to as Didcot New Town, North Hagbourne or simply Northbourne. It acquired its own church, a gaunt granite building with broad lancets, in 1891.

The later developments of the railway network cannot be followed in detail here. Many new lines were laid during the next two decades, reaching Banbury (1850), Bicester (1850-51), Charlbury (1853), Chipping Norton (1855), Abingdon (1856), Henley (1857), Eynsham (1861), Witney (1861), Thame (1862), Faringdon (1864) and Wallingford (1866). The line to Watlington was opened in 1872, and Woodstock, the last Oxfordshire town of all to receive its rail connection, acquired a short branch in 1890 through the efforts of the Duke of Marlborough. A couple of cottages were demolished to make room for the new terminus, whose building survives in use as a garage.

Several towns had more than one railway station. The original 1861 terminus of the Witney Railway, a wooden building with a low hipped roof and tall chimneys, became part of the goods yard when the line was extended to Fairford by the East Gloucestershire Railway Company in 1873. A new stone station was then built with a half-hipped roof. However the original Witney terminus building has ironically outlived its successor. At Banbury the stations of two rival companies, both opened in 1850, stood side by side: Banbury General, the G.W.R. station, and Banbury Merton Street, terminus of the Buckinghamshire Railway (subsequently part of the L.N.W.R.). At Bicester the two stations stood on opposite sides of the town. Bicester London Road, the Buckinghamshire Railway station, a stone building dating from 1851 with two gables fronting the platform, is now closed, but Bicester North, a typical late G.W.R. station in red brick, opened as late as 1910, still functions.

The rail network in its final form still left Bampton, Deddington and Wantage two miles from the nearest railway and Burford four miles away. At Wantage this was remedied by the construction of a horse tramway in 1874-5 between the G.W.R's Wantage Road Station and the town centre. Originally this was intended to run into the Market Place, but the terminus was eventually sited in Mill Street, where the office building erected in 1904 still stands. By 1876 the Wantage Tramway was converting to steam power, but it continued to operate into the 1940's.

The contribution of railways to the economic life of towns was enormous, enabling the bulk import of cheap food and raw materials and the bulk export of manufactured products to and from all parts of the country. Of the seven market towns which were clearly in decline by the end of the century, it is significant that three were without convenient rail connections and two had only recently become the termini of branch lines.

MARKETS

During the medieval period few villages in Oxfordshire were more than six miles from their nearest market town, the maximum convenient distance for a man to cover on foot with goods, returning the same day. Improved transport in the nineteenth century was already making this pattern an anachronism. (Figs. 3-4)

BANBURY

ADDERBURY

DEDDINGTON

CHIPPING NORTON

STRATTON
AUDLEY

MIDDLETON
STONEY   BICESTER

BIGNELL

CHARLBURY

WOODSTOCK

ISLIP

BURFORD   WITNEY

EYNSHAM

OXFORD

THAME

BAMPTON

HINTON
WALDRIST

ABINGDON

WATLINGTON

FARINGDON

STANFORD-IN
-THE-VALE

BAULKING

SHRIVENHAM

EAST
HENDRED

WALLINGFORD

KINGSTON LISLE

WANTAGE

HENLEY

0   15km.

0   10 miles

● Towns with active markets   • Failed medieval market centres

Oxfordshire market towns in the early 19th. century

Figure 3. Spheres of influence of Oxfordshire market towns in the 19th Century

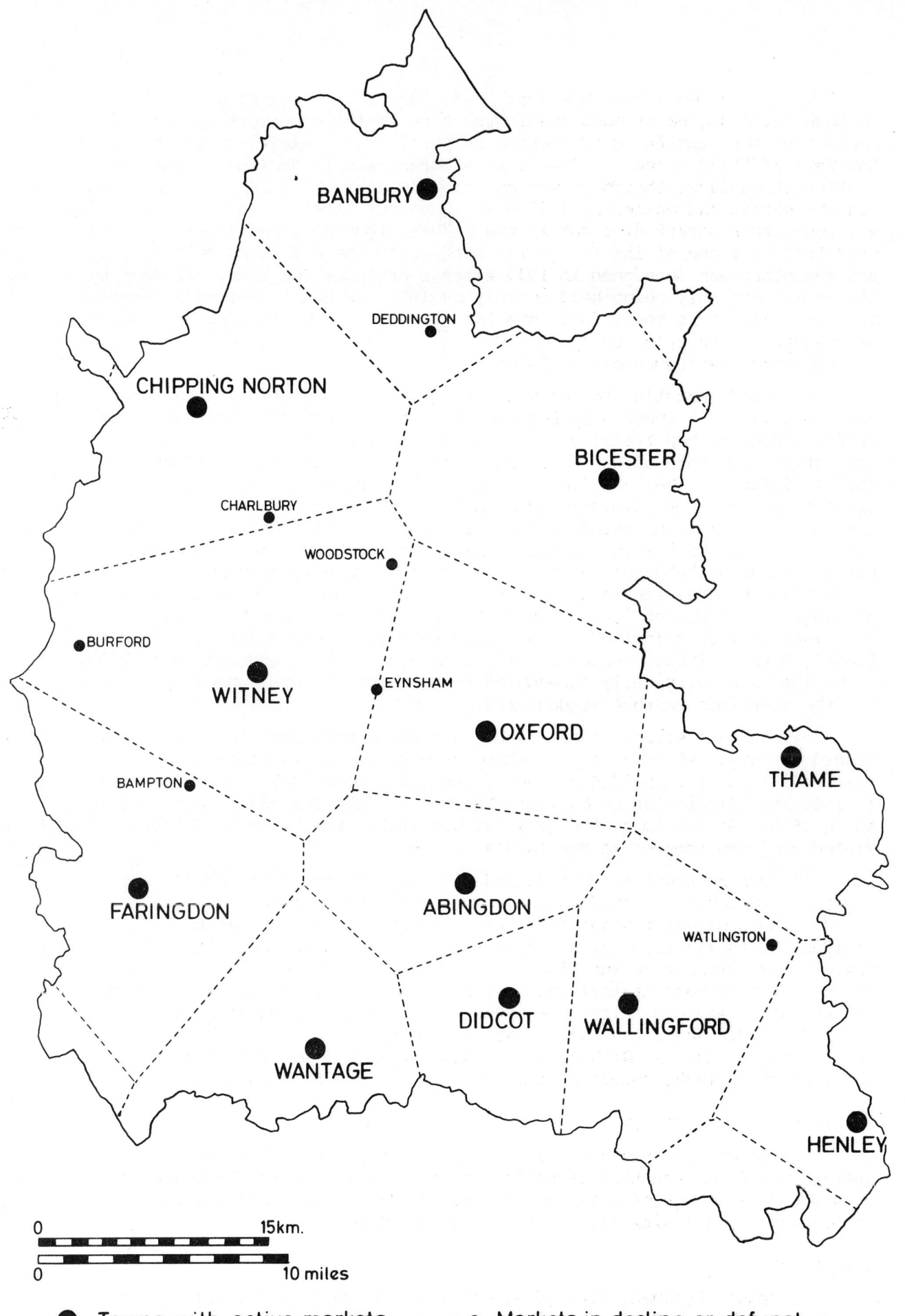

Oxfordshire market towns in the early 20th. century

Figure 4. Spheres of influence of Oxfordshire market towns in the 20th Century

We have already seen how some towns were more favoured than others through their degree of nodality in relation to the transport system. The decline of the less-favoured centres is particularly clearly seen through the fate of their markets. Charlbury's market was in decline by the mid-eighteenth century, though it was not finally lost until 1955. At Deddington the market had ceased by 1830 and subsequent attempts to revive it failed. Burford's market died out in the 1870's, though it was later revived. Woodstock lost one of its two weekly markets in the mid-nineteenth century and the other was abandoned in 1933 after a prolonged decline. At Bampton the market was only being held monthly by 1891 and had foundered altogether by 1899. All these towns fall into the lower group on the graph on Fig. 1. By contrast, Banbury's weekly Thursday market was so brisk that in 1888 a second market was commenced on Saturdays.

A second marketing tendency towards increasing specialisation was reflected in the townscape by the construction of corn exchanges after the 1850's. Banbury had two rival corn exchange companies, so eager to outdo each other that both opened their buildings in 1857 before either were actually finished. The Tory faction in the town formed the Banbury Corn Exchange Company and commissioned W. Hill of Leeds to design the classical façade with Corinthian columns, recently adapted as the entrance to the Castle Shopping Centre in Cornhill. Early photographs show its pediment surrounted by a statue of Ceres, which was subsequently destroyed in a storm. The Liberal factions's Central Corn Exchange Company built their exchange in the Market Place, where it was reconstructed with a new French Rennaissance façade in 1888. Other corn exchanges were built in Wallingford (1856), Witney (1863), Faringdon (1863), Wantage (1865) and Abingdon (1885) - the last also originally surmounted by a statue of Ceres which, curiously, met the same fate as that at Banbury.

By contrast several older market buildings were removed in the nineteenth century. At Bicester the shambles were destroyed along with the town hall in a riot in 1826 and never rebuilt. Woodstock's shambles, built in 1766 and illustrated by Buckler sketches of 1829 and 1833, were demolished in 1870. At Charlbury the tiny two-bay market hall with its hipped stone-slated roof was removed in the 1870's.

Another movement evident towards the end of the Victorian era was the increasing pressure to shift stock markets off the streets into special compounds. When Bicester proposed to pave and enclose its street market place in 1906 its application for a loan was refused following opposition from the Ministry of Agriculture and Fisheries, and in 1910 the cattle market and sheep fair were both transferred to a new site near Victoria Road. At Woodstock, cattle and pig sales were moved in 1915 from the Market Place to the yard of the Old Angel Inn, which was leased to the Corporation for an annual rent of ten pound. At Banbury a new enclosed market was established near the railway in 1925, though cattle were sold in the streets as late as 1931.

PUBLIC AND CIVIC BUILDINGS

The nineteenth century was a period of enormous social change and administrative reform, and this is reflected in the market towns by the appearance of a whole new range of buildings connected with administration, law enforcement, care for the sick and elderly, and education.

Town Halls

Abingdon, Eynsham, Faringdon, Wallingford, Watlington, Witney and Woodstock had inherited perfectly adequate civic buildings from the seventeenth and eighteenth centuries which continued in use. The lower storey of Woodstock town hall, originally an open arcade, was enclosed in 1898. The remainder of Oxfordshire's town halls were rebuilt during the nineteenth century. The earliest and plainest example is Deddington, a humble brick structure on an open arcade, which replaced a seventeenth-century predecessor in 1806. Bampton's town hall, a stone Italianate building, was designed by George Wilkinson of Witney, elder brother of the better-known William Wilkinson, in 1838. Chipping Norton has a large neo-classical town hall by G.S. Repton, built in 1842. At Banbury the seventeenth-century timber hall was replaced by a plain brick building just before 1800, and this was in turn superseded in 1854 by the present French Gothic building designed by Edward Bruton of Oxford. Thame's red brick Jacobean-style town hall by H.J. Tollitt of Oxford replaced an earlier hall in 1888, and Henley's old town hall was replaced in 1900. The old town halls of Banbury and Henley were both reconstructed elswhere, the former as a warehouse, the latter as a private house.

Law Enforcement

Several towns had lock-ups early in the century, but small town prisons were slowly being phased out. Banbury's Corporation Gaol was enlarged in 1817, but by 1833 it was being criticised as insufficient and insecure.

At Abingdon the Berkshire County Gaol was built near the bridge in 1805-11, an imposing building with octagonal central tower and radiating wings. This layout allowed the segregation of four classes of prisoners: debtors, felons, women, and those awaiting trial. When the Berkshire Assizes were transferred to Reading in 1861 the Abingdon Gaol was sold and converted to a corn store. Recently it has undergone a very successful transformation as a recreation centre.

The County and Borough Police Act of 1856 required the Justices of the Peace to establish a paid police force throughout each county wherever this had not already been done. Between 1857 and 1873 new Police Stations, which often included cells and accommodation for petty sessions, were built in all the larger market towns and some of the smaller ones, including Burford, Watlington and Woodstock. Most of the new police stations in Oxfordshire were designed by William Wilkinson, an architect better-known for his part in the North Oxford suburban development.

Poor Relief

Early in the nineteenth century employment and accommodation for the poor and needy were still being provided by parish poorhouses, which occurred in villages and towns alike. The buildings housing these institutions differed little from normal domestic buildings, and although several examples are known to survive they are not particularly distinctive or readily recognisable.

In 1834 the Poor Law Amendment Act reorganised the whole system of poor relief, combining groups of parishes into Unions which were provided with a large central workhouse. Usually located on the outskirts of the largest market town in each Union, these accomodated some 200-450 inmates apiece. Outside Oxford, Union Workhouses were built at Abingdon, Banbury, Bicester, Chipping Norton, Faringdon, Henley, Thame, Wallingford, Wantage, Witney and Woodstock. The large scale of these buildings required careful planning, and the Poor Law Commission recommended several alternative standard layouts, each providing accommodation in separate wings for different classes of pauper, who were allowed to come together only for meals and church services. The Union Workhouses at Woodstock and Wantage (Fig.5) had a plan based on rectangular courtyards; but the more usual pattern, used at Chipping Norton and Witney (both designed by George Wilkinson), consisted of a central polygonal tower with radiating wings. Chapels were often added later, those at Chipping Norton and Woodstock being designed by G.E. Street

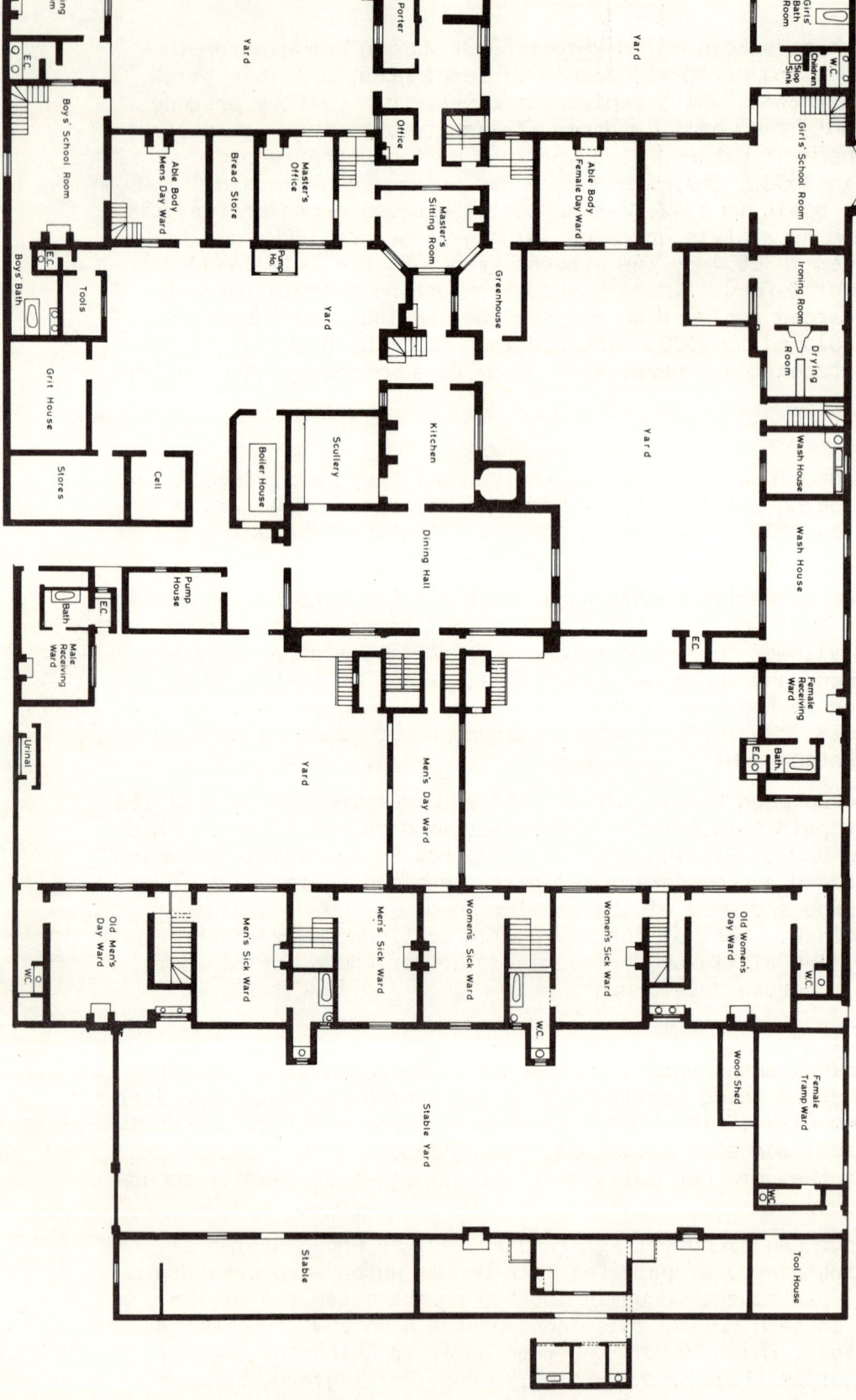

WANTAGE UNION WORKHOUSE

Based on a survey made by W. Hanson,
Engineer & Surveyor, Town Hall, Wantage,
June 1909

Figure 5. Plan of the Wantage Union Workhouse

and that at Witney by William Wilkinson.

The Chipping Norton and Henley workhouses and the administrative block of the Banbury workhouse are still used today as hospitals, while the Thame workhouse is occupied by Rycotewood College. Others have failed to find an alternative modern role. Those at Abingdon and Bicester were demolished soon after their closure in the 1930's. The Woodstock workhouse was removed in 1969, and demolition of the Witney workhouse began in 1975.

Hospitals and Almshouses

Hospital accommodation for the sick and infirm fell into two main categories: (i) Poor-Law hospitals adjoining the workhouses were built at Banbury, Wallingford and Woodstock later in the nineteenth century; (ii) charitable institutions supported by voluntary contributions included the Cottage Hospitals at Burford (1868), Wallingford (1880), Wantage (1885) and Abingdon (1887). The Horton Infirmary in Oxford Road, Banbury, was the gift of Miss Mary Horton of Middleton Cheney to the town in 1869, being completed and opened by her great-nephew four years later.

Charitable accommodation for the elderly in almshouses had been provided by wealthy benefactors since the Middle Ages. Some of the old foundations, such as Longland's and Messenger's Almshouses in Henley, had been rehoused before the mid-nineteenth century. William Wilkinson rebuilt the Holloway Trust Almshouses, a gabled stone row in Witney churchyard, in 1868. In Wantage a medieval endowment was used in 1867 to construct the Eagles Close Almshouses, a terrace of ten houses in red brick with arched doors and windows and a communal well in the front garden. Eight more almshouses in Mill Street, Wantage, were built at the same time. Townsend's Almshouses in Witney were a new foundation of 1821.

Education

Many towns acquired cultural centres, libraries and public meeting rooms during the 1870's and 1880's. As early as 1858 an old malthouse in Watlington High Street was converted to a lecture hall for 600 persons. In Banbury the Mechanics' Institute, founded in a house in Parsons Street in 1835, was transferred to new premises in Marlborough Road in 1884. The new building, a Tudor-style edifice in brick and ironstone, designed by the local architect W.E. Mills, was financed by the philanthropic Banbury industrialist and M.P., Sir Bernhard Samuelson. The original building, housing a library, public reading room, chess room, science classrooms and art school, was extended in 1893 by the addition of the Technical Institute next door. At Wallingford a Free Library and Literary Institute was built in 1871. Lord Jersey opened a free reading room for labouring men in Bicester in 1872. Abingdon acquired its free library by 1894.

The state's attitude to education remained one of laissez-faire through much of the nineteenth century, and the provision of schools was left to individual and voluntary effort. In 1800 few children received any regular schooling except for a small minority whose parents were able to afford fees or could obtain the few free places at the Grammar Schools.

Grammar Schools had been founded in Abingdon, Bampton, Burford, Charlbury, Henley, Thame, Wantage and Witney in the sixteenth and seventeenth centuries. Many of these were reorganised in the nineteenth century, and some moved into new premises. The original buildings of John Roysse's Grammar School founded in Abingdon in 1563 still survive, but in 1869 the school moved out to the western edge of the town. The imposing new red brick building designed by Edwin Dolby of Abingdon was considerably extended in 1879-80. Wantage has a particularly interesting group of Victorian schools. In addition to King Alfred's Grammar School, revived and rehoused in 1849-50, there were several important new foundations. St. Michael's Training School 'for teachers and industrial girls' operated from 1852 until new regulations about teacher training forced its closure in 1908. St. Katherine's 'middle-class boarding and day school' moved into its Ormond Road premises in 1897. St. Mary's High School 'for daughters of gentlemen' began in 1873 with fifteen boarders and was run by the Anglican Order of the Wantage Sisterhood. The School in Newbury Street partly occupies older houses, but has a range built by Butterfield in 1874-5 and a Gothic red brick chapel by Ponting built in 1898-9. The Convent is in Faringdon Road, its original buildings of 1855-61 being by G.E. Street, who began his practice in Wantage before moving first to Oxford and finally to London.

Elementary education for working-class children was developed largely through the efforts of two rival voluntary societies. The British School Society was founded in 1808 as an offshoot from the nonconformist British and Foreign Bible Society. Its Anglican counterpart, the National School Society, was founded together with the National Society for the Propagation of the Gospel in 1811. From 1833 onwards the Government made grants to both societies to aid the building of more elementary schools, at the same time strengthening their own control by appointing committees and inspectors to supervise how the money was spent.

The National School Society made the greatest contribution, building 25 new schools in the Oxfordshire market towns during the century, which provided over 7,000 places. The first appeared in Witney (1813) and Neithrop in Banbury (1817), but the peak came later, nearly half of them being erected in the 1850's and 1860's (Fig. 7). They were mostly designed in vaguely Gothic or Tudor style. The nonconformist British Schools accounted for roughly a quarter of the new schools in the market towns, the first being built at Charlbury in 1815. The largest in Oxfordshire, Cherwell British School in Banbury, was another foundation of Sir Bernhard Samuelson in 1861. The buildings of the British Schools tended to be classical in style.

Despite the efforts of these two societies it eventually became evident that school building was still failing to keep pace with the need. The Education Act of 1870 set up School Boards to remedy the deficiency by providing a further series of Board Schools, financed by a combination of local rates and government grants. The demand was increased in 1880, when it was made compulsory for all children to attend school between the ages of five and ten. School Boards controlled elementary education in Burford, Charlbury, Eynsham and Watlington by 1888, either taking over earlier National and British Schools or building new ones, which were usually in Jacobean or Queen Anne style. Because they were wealthier, could employ more trained teachers, and taught 'non-denominational' religion, Boards were seen as a threat by many clergymen, and in Chipping Norton the Anglican, Nonconformist and Catholic clergy united in an unprecedented way to oppose the foundation of a Board School in their town. Nonetheless by 1899 Board Schools provided over 1300 places in the market towns.

INDUSTRY

The increasing scale of their industrial development and specialisation in particular products is one of the features distinguishing the more successful towns like Banbury and Witney from those like Deddington and Burford which were losing ground. By 1852 Deddington was said to contain 'no staple manufacture', its population being 'almost solely agricultural'. Even in Bicester, whose urban status today is undoubted, agriculture continued to be the largest employment category throughout the nineteenth century.

Even where the industrial sector was most prominent, it remained rooted by and large in historical precedent, ultimately in the agricultural and woodland resources of the town's immediate hinterland. Witney blankets and Chipping Norton tweed can be seen as direct descendants of the medieval woollen industry of the Cotswolds, while the manufacture of leather gloves in Woodstock and Charlbury is a reminder of the medieval Forest of Wychwood, though in all cases raw materials were being imported from much further afield by the nineteenth century.

Textile Industries

Witney had been involved in the woollen industry since the middle ages, and by the seventeenth century was famous for its manufacture of white blankets, with mills along the Windrush and hand-loom weaving-shops in West End and Newland. In the early nineteenth century blanket-making was still largely a domestic industry, with wool being hand-spun by out-workers as far away as Gloucestershire: the only mill process then was fulling. The dominance of a few families, the Earlys, Marriotts and Colliers, and their co-operation during the critical first phases of mechanisation, gave Witney a considerable advantage when many other woollen manufacturers in southern England were being undercut by the Yorkshire mills. The first powered spinning mule was installed in Early's New Mill in the last decade of the eighteenth century, while the fly-shuttle was introduced soon after 1800. The arrival of the railway in 1861 brought cheaper coal and enabled Charles Early to introduce power looms in Witney Mill, with a steam engine aided by water power. Progress towards mechanisation and centralisation caused much distress amongst the village out-workers. When Edmund Wright, one of the first Witney manufacturers to employ machinery, was killed by falling into the wheel-pit at New Mill, many attributed this to divine judgement for attempting to remove their work. Despite this the mill buildings in Witney bear witness to considerable expansion in the last quarter of the century. The Witney architect William Cantwell built several new mills in the 1880's. By 1891 the blanket trade employed 500 hands and had 200 looms working, and was larger than at any previous time.

The specialisation of Chipping Norton in tweed dates from 1746 when Thomas Bliss, a Gloucestershire cloth salesman, acquired a mill in the town. When the first mill was burned down in 1872, 300 workers were laid off. A new mill was built in the valley west of the town to replace it. Its architect was George Woodhouse of Lancashire, who specialised in mills and factories. His design resembles a great house in a park, with balustraded parapet, urns on the corner towers, and a chimney rather desperately disguised as a Tuscan column rising from a domed tower. By 1891, 600 hands were employed. In 1895 the firm came under the control of the Birmingham Banking Company and the family connection receded. Nonetheless, during their time the Bliss family had contributed as much to Chipping Norton as Bernhard Samuelson did to Banbury. The results of their munificence is still evident today in the fine avenues of trees lining the principal roads into the town, planted around 1870 by William Bliss.

Banbury too had been engaged in woollen textile manufacture since the Middle Ages, and by the early nineteenth century it was concentrating on webbing and plush. The trade in webbing and horse-cloths was stimulated by increasing horse-drawn traffic on the improved roads in the eighteenth century. The principal firm, Cobb & Co., founded in 1701, established a new girth factory by the canal in 1837, where they employed 40 hands. Their works were taken over by the Banbury Tweed Company in 1870, but another firm, Mead's Girth Factory, survived till 1932. Plush-making, an industry ideally suited to hard-water areas as it does not require scouring or fulling, became important in the Banbury area in the mid-eighteenth century. Initially Banbury served mainly as the marketing centre for hand-loom weavers in the surrounding villages, but by 1831 the plush industry employed 550 people in the town. There were then three main firms, Harris's with 160 looms, Gillett, Lees & Gillett with 150 looms, and Baughan's with 120 looms. From mid-century competition from Coventry eclipsed the Banbury industry. In 1851 there were only 200 plush-weavers, a decade later half that number. Gilletts abandoned plush-making in 1850 to concentrate on their more profitable banking interests, and their business was bought by Cubbit's, who ceased in 1909. Baughan's was taken over by John Hill, who continued in production to 1899.

The smaller woollen industries present in other towns such as Burford cannot be pursued in detail here.

Leather Industries

Tanning had been a significant industry in most market towns during the medieval period. In Abingdon tanneries operated in Ock Street and Lombard Street into the late nineteenth century, and tannery buildings have been recorded at Wiggins Yard in Burford and at Hythe Croft, Tanners Lane in Eynsham. Other leather industries around the beginning of the century included parchment-making at Wallingford, saddlery at Burford, and the manufacture of leather breeches in Bampton and Woodstock.

Leather gloves had been made at Woodstock at least since 1580, and gloving was also carried out in Bampton, Banbury, Bicester, Burford, Charlbury, Chipping Norton, Henley, Watlington and Witney in the early nineteenth century. By mid-century gloving was becoming increasingly concentrated in Woodstock and Charlbury, where Somerset and Worcester firms were establishing new factories and taking over smaller businesses, though many processes were still carried out by outworkers in neighbouring villages. By the end of the century gloving employed about 2,000 women and 200 men in and around Woodstock. Most firms occupied converted domestic premises, and it was not until the 1890's that purpose-built factories such as that of R. & J. Pullman in Woodstock (1891) or Messrs. Fownes in Charlbury (1896) began to appear.

Brewing

Ale was brewed in Abingdon, Banbury, Bicester, Wallingford and Witney in medieval times, and by the sixteenth century malt was being sent down river to London from both Abingdon and Henley. By the Victorian period most Oxfordshire towns had at least one brewery, some up to six or seven. Up to the end of the century some inns, such as the Lamb in Burford and the Marlborough Arms in Woodstock, still brewed their own beer. Elsewhere, however, breweries had expanded from small beginnings to major industrial concerns, their tall gravity-fed brewhouses, pyramidal-roofed malt kilns, extensive storehouses, cooperage, offices, stabling and yards making a striking contribution to the townscape. In Banbury Thomas Hunt, a Cropredy farmer, began brewing in the Unicorn in 1807. Shortly after moving to new premises in Bridge Street in 1847 he took William Edmunds into partnership, and their business subsequently expanded, absorbing in succession Wyatt's Brewery (1879), the Sun Brewery (1884) and Dunnell & Co. (formerly Austin's Brewery) (1918), all in Banbury, in addition to Hudson's Witney Brewery and Hunt's of Burford. By 1918 Hunt Edmunds was the only brewery surviving in Banbury and its premises covered some six acres. It succumbed in its turn to a takeover in 1967 and its buildings were demolished shortly afterwards. The same fate befell Clinch's Eagle Brewery in Witney, started in a converted flour mill in 1841, taken over and closed in 1963, and its fine buildings destroyed in 1978. Others like Hitchman's in Chipping Norton and Shilling-

ford's in Bicester have also gone; but in Henley New Street is still dominated by W.H. Brakspear's brewery, founded in 1756 as a sideline of the
local banking firm of Hayward, Fisher and Brakspear, while in Abingdon,
Morland's Brewery, another concern which has absorbed several smaller businesses, still flourishes. Although now closed, the premises of some of the
smaller breweries, such as Reynold's in Sheep Street, Burford, taken over
by George Garne towards the end of the nineteenth century, can still be
identified.

Agricultural Engineering

Banbury's role as an engineering centre effectively began with James
Gardner, a High Street ironmonger, who patented machines for cutting hay
and straw in 1815, and invented a turnip-cutter in 1834 which was still
being made in Banbury a century later. Gardner died in 1846, but soon
afterwards Bernhard Samuelson arrived in Banbury and bought up his business.
Samuelson, born in Hamburg in 1820 of English descent, had originally established a railway works at Tours, but fled to England following the revolution
of 1848. He began the Britannia Engineering Works in Fish Street on a small
scale with 27 workmen. By 1859 he employed 300 people and for a time almost
cornered the world market in agricultural machinery, producing reapers,
digging and forking machines, turnip-cutters and lawn-mowers. Samuelson's
presence was felt in all aspects of Banbury's life: he was M.P. from 1865
to 1898, a member of the Board of Health and the Banbury Agricultural Association, a founder of schools and colleges and governor of the Horton Infirmary. Other engineering works in Banbury included Lampitt's Vulcan Foundry
established in 1837 and Barrow's Cherwell Works founded about 1861, but
neither rivalled the supremacy of the Britannia Works. It was largely
through Samuelson's enterprise that Banbury developed from being merely a
prosperous market town to a considerable industrial community.

The only other town to develop a comparable industry was Wantage, where
the Vale of White Horse Ironworks had been established by Charles Hart in
Foundry Lane, premises occupied later in the nineteenth century by Messrs.
Gibbons & Robinson, who had a national reputation as manufacturers of
steam threshing machinery and other agricultural implements. A mile west
of Wantage in 1866 William and Thomas Nalder started a second iron foundry
in a wharf building on the canal at East Challow, employing about 200 men by
1900.

Other Industries

The Victorian expansion stimulated all aspects of the building trade.
In particular, brickworks appeared throughout Oxfordshire wherever there
was suitable clay, and themselves provided employment in Banbury, Bicester,
Deddington, Faringdon and Thame. Many other crafts and industries carried
out in the market towns in the nineteenth century, such as Bicester sacking,
Henley silk, Woodstock polished steel, the Burford bell-foundry and the Banbury rope and furniture trade, cannot be explored in detail here. Mention
should, however, be made of lace-making. This craft had appeared in
south and east Oxfordshire in the sixteenth century, and still provided
considerable employment for women in Bicester, Thame and Banbury in the
early nineteenth century. The introduction of mechanised lace manufacture
destroyed the domestic industry, which was virtually extinct at Thame by
1884. This once important craft has left little documentary evidence and
no distinctive sites or buildings in the landscape for the industrial
archaeologist.

Services

At the beginning of the nineteenth century even the principal market
towns still relied mainly on wells for their water-supply, while sewage

71

disposal facilities were equally inadequate for growing populations. Bicester churchyard contains a memorial to 64 people who died of cholera in six weeks in 1832. Burford suffered a cholera outbreak in the same year, as did Witney and Banbury in 1854. In Banbury 73 people died in an outbreak of smallpox in 1827.

The second half of the century witnessed great improvements in the provision of water and sewerage. Banbury Water Company was formed in 1856. At Chipping Norton a spring-fed reservoir was built at Glyme Farm in 1878. In 1880 the Henley-on-Thames Water Company began pumping from a deep well to their reservoir on Badgemore Hill. This company was the first in England to adopt the Atkin's Patent for softening and purifying the water. Charlbury Water Works Company was formed through the efforts of the Albright family in 1896. However, to the end of the century Bicester and Deddington remained entirely dependent on wells. Sewerage schemes first appeared in the 1860's. Banbury's council bought Spital Farm, Grimsbury, for sewage beds in 1867. Abingdon's drainage works were designed in 1877 by Bailey Denton, one of the foremost drainage engineers of his day.

Improvements in lighting began rather earlier. The first Private Act for a gasworks in Banbury was acquired in 1825, and the Banbury Gas Company established its works at Grimsbury in 1833. Henley and Abingdon acquired gas works the following year, followed by Faringdon (1835), Wallingford (1836) and Chipping Norton (1837). Over the next twenty years the streets of all the larger towns were lit by gas, and the practice was extending to the smallest towns - Woodstock (1853), Deddington (1855), Eynsham (1858), Watlington (1866) and Charlbury (1880). Banbury was the first Oxfordshire market town to acquire an electricity company in 1901, but it was long before gas lighting was entirely superseded.

HOUSING

Despite its considerable importance and interest, the study of nineteenth-century housing in market towns has been much neglected until very recently.

Early in the century new housing was confined to the piecemeal redevelopment of individual town centre plots, building to the rear of burgage tenements and on back-lane frontages, and limited ribbon development outwards along certain main roads. The visual effect of such piecemeal development can be quite attractive, where the varied styles and details of nineteenth-century houses are intermingled with older buildings. An example is Grove Street in Wantage, where houses of this period contribute as much to the townscape as the Tudor and Georgian survivors amongst which they are interspersed. The west side includes two short terraces, Nos. 29-39 (South View), a row of late Victorian three-storey artisan cottages with attic dormers, heavy tiled porches and a tunnel rear access, and Nos. 63-69, earlier, of two storeys, in English bond brickwork with red stretchers and grey-blue headers, the central doorway of the five having a Gothic arch. Nos. 81-82 and 85-86 are semi-detached Victorian villas of two storeys and attics with heavy wooden porches and dormer windows with curved bargeboards. Just to the north Crooks Terrace is a long early nineteenth-century row aligned at right-angles to the street, of Flemish bond brickwork with paired doorways under tiled porches cantilevered on wooden brackets and a tiled mansard roof with crested ridge and catslides over the attic dormers. On the east side Nos. 64-68, a trio of two-storey red brick houses built in 1889 on a visually important corner position, display a symmetrical face towards Garston Lane with gables at either end, yellow brick lozenge motifs and dressings to the ground floor bays, and a rounded chamfered corner to the road junction. Finally at the outer end of Grove Street is a long ribbon of early nineteenth-century brick cottages in Flemish bond brickwork with vitrified headers, a rear passage separating each unit from its pantiled semi-detached privy.

The peripheries of Bampton, Deddington, Eynsham, Thame and Watlington were still under open-field cultivation at the beginning of the century, and marginal expansion did not become feasible until enclosure allowed the sale of farmland in consolidated building plots. Population pressures in the towns where this restriction applied were too modest to threaten any serious overcrowding, but even so there are occasional cases of building along closed yards and burgage tails, such as The Tchure in Deddington and Kings Head Yard in Chipping Norton. Vine Cottages in Bicester, a backland terrace south of the Causeway, have no street frontage at any point.

Enclosure removed one of the main obstacles to large-scale peripheral expansion. Even so, the spread of some towns was still restricted by inviolable private estates. Henley, hemmed in by Fawley Court, Henley Park and Friar Park to the north and west and by Remenham Park Place across the river, could only expand southward towards Harpsden and Rotherfield Greys. Woodstock's expansion was similarly one-sided, all new building being driven eastwards by the powerful constraint of Blenheim Park on the west and south. In the very centres of Bicester and Charlbury sizeable private grounds were preserved intact.

Artisan Housing

The study of working-class housing in the Oxfordshire market towns has begun only very recently, and an overall synthesis would be premature. However, a few selected examples may be useful.

In Banbury artisan terraces were still being thatched up to 1820 – an example on the Warwick Road was demolished about 1900. After 1850 Banbury's main expansion was east of the Cherwell, where a predominantly working-class suburb grew up at New Grimsbury. A typical development in this area was the series of two-storey red-brick slate-roofed terraces in The Causeway, whose history has recently been investigated by Sarah Gosling. Some 37 houses here were put up by a small local builder, William Wilkins, between 1856 and 1871. Wilkins began as a bricklayer in 1835, but advertised himself as a builder after 1850, and from 1860 also ran a timber-yard and brickworks in Duke Street nearby. The Causeway terraces, built to the minimum standard acceptable to the Banbury Board of Health, housed mainly new immigrant workers on the railway and other industries: in 1861 70% of the families occupying them had come from outside Banbury.

Building standards improved later in the century, with variations on the theme of the bylaw terrace becoming increasingly widespread. Such housing is by no means as uniform as it first appears, all sorts of social distinctions being indicated by the presence or absence of front gardens, bay windows or internal hallways. Many developments were still built on a piecemeal basis, for example the short red-brick row in London Road, Bicester, conveniently dated to 1887 by its name Jubilee Terrace. As towns expanded beyond their medieval peripheries, however, more uniform developments began to appear. In Henley at the end of the century a series of identical two-storey red-brick terraces with white bands and dressings, heavy plastered round-arched doorways, occasional midland-type tunnel accesses to the rear and Welsh slate roofs were being constructed in King's Road, Clarence Road and York Road immediately north-west of the old town. Distinctive pavements of buff Bridgwater tiles characterise this development. In Bicester at about the same time much building on the London Road and the newly-opened Priory Road was carried out by George Layton, builder and prominent townsman.

His most striking products were Bath, Newport and Manchester Terraces in Victoria Road, begun in 1890 using the imported yellow bricks which are the hallmark of much of Layton's work.

By and large throughout the nineteenth century neither employers nor local councils recognised it as any part of their function to provide accommodation. Housing tended to be left to the speculative builder who, not unnaturally, usually built to the minimum acceptable standards of his time. There were some exceptions, however. Nalder Brothers, the Wantage ironfounders, built a terrace of twelve houses for their workers called Naldertown soon after 1870. In Old Woodstock in 1869 and 1874 the Blenheim estate built a terrace and several semi-detached cottages in stone with brick dressings and slate roofs and terracotta date plaques. In Oxford Street in Woodstock shortly afterwards the Worcester gloving firm of Edmund Webley built a row of workers' cottages. In Didcot the Great Western Railway finally built a long row of houses on Station Road in 1903 and another terrace in Wessex Road in 1904.

Because of the overall dominance of the small speculative builder, few of the smaller nineteenth-century houses in the market towns achieve much in the way of architectural style, but some attempts were made. In Wantage No. 39 Newbury Street and in Neithrop in Banbury Nos. 188-190 Warwick Road are small Tudor-style cottages. In Woodstock Nos. 25-27 High Street are a Gothic pattern-book product in bright red brick, standing out boldly amidst its grey stone neighbours, with steep bargeboarded gables, pointed-arched windows, ornate lights and a band of glazed patterned tiles. In Abingdon Tesdale Terrace in Bostock Road, built in 1895, has some interesting art nouveau details. Most extraordinary of all are Nos. 23-24 Cornhill in Banbury, two exuberant polychrome turretted follies commissioned from William Wilkinson in 1866 by W.J. Douglas of Castle House, 'to present an attractive appearance when viewed from his grounds'. They contrast vividly with the restrained character of most of Wilkinson's work.

Middle-Class Housing

Even in an essentially artisan quarter like Grimsbury in Banbury, the main-road frontage along Middleton Road is lined with larger houses built in a variety of styles and materials for more prosperous families. Banbury also has some fine terraces of three-storey houses with basements in Marlborough Road, built around 1880-1890 and distinguished by their use of ornate moulded and cut bricks in bands, doorway piers, plinths and lintels.

Victorian suburbs like north Oxford, composed of large detached houses in their own grounds, are not common in the smaller towns. The wooded riverside slopes around Henley were being colonised by wealthy metropolitans even before 1800, and by the end of the nineteenth century Henley was described as 'surrounded by handsome villas and plantations'. This development was, however, essentially piecemeal and unplanned, and only in Abingdon do we find an example of a suburb planned as a unit on an ambitious scale (Fig.6). Albert Park, the centrepiece of this estate, was laid out in 1864-5 by the Governors of Christ's Hospital. Its focal point is a tall pillar with a statue commemorating Prince Albert, designed by Gibbs of Oxford and erected in 1865. Around the outer rim of Park Crescent a series of large detached villas were built in red and blue brick, timber and stone. Their styles vary greatly, but the planting of their grounds with exotic trees and shrubs acts as a unifying characteristic. No. 14, of red brick with arched doorway and windows and a timbered two-storey bay window under a timbered gable, was the home of Edwin Dolby, architect of the new Abingdon School building which it faces across the park. No. 19, also of red brick, with cusped window arches, has a tall pyramidal tower with a wrought-iron

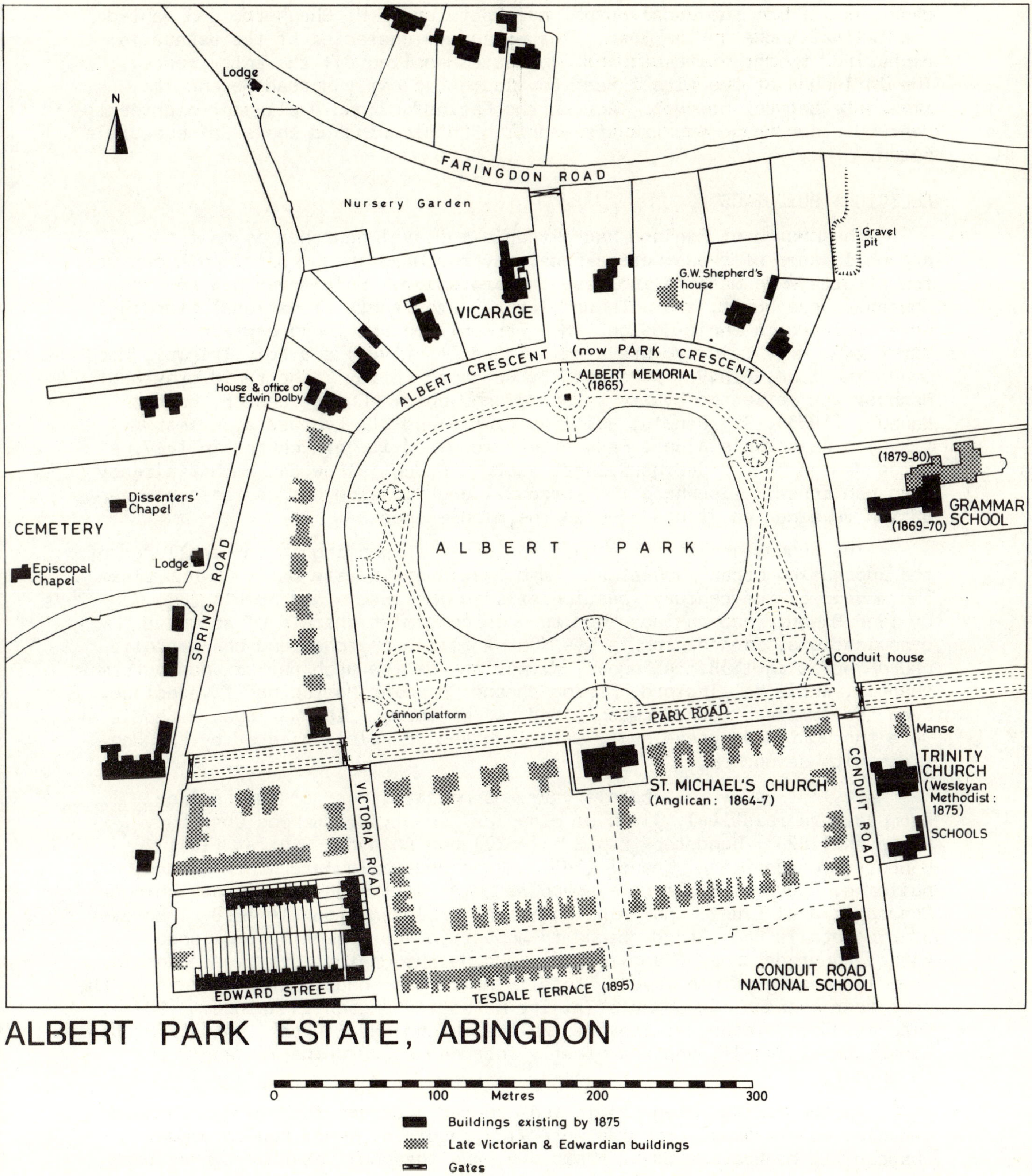

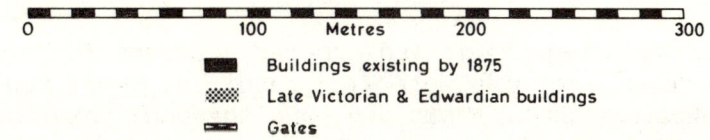

N

Lodge

FARINGDON ROAD

Nursery Garden

Gravel pit

VICARAGE

G.W. Shepherd's house

ALBERT CRESCENT (now PARK CRESCENT)

ALBERT MEMORIAL (1865)

House & office of Edwin Dolby

(1879-80)

CEMETERY

Dissenters' Chapel

ALBERT PARK

GRAMMAR SCHOOL

Episcopal Chapel

Lodge

(1869-70)

SPRING ROAD

Conduit house

Cannon platform

PARK ROAD

Manse

TRINITY CHURCH (Wesleyan Methodist: 1875)

VICTORIA ROAD

ST. MICHAEL'S CHURCH (Anglican: 1864-7)

CONDUIT ROAD

SCHOOLS

CONDUIT ROAD NATIONAL SCHOOL

EDWARD STREET

TESDALE TERRACE (1895)

ALBERT PARK ESTATE, ABINGDON

0 — 100 — Metres — 200 — 300

■ Buildings existing by 1875

▨ Late Victorian & Edwardian buildings

▭ Gates

Figure 6. Plan of the Albert Park estate, Abingdon

crest, built for the local carpet manufacturer, G.W. Shepherd, who wanted the tallest house in the town. The exclusive character of the estate is emphasised by the white-painted iron gates sealing off the entry roads. The influence of the Albert Park development clearly spread beyond its immediate bounds, however. Across the Faringdon Road a pleasant eighteenth-century stone house was transformed with Gothic windows and a Chinese-style porch.

RELIGIOUS BUILDINGS

The Church of England had sizeable medieval churches in most towns, and while some of these were expensively restored in the nineteenth century, few efforts were made to increase the provision. Only seven new Anglican churches were built, and although several architects of national standing were employed in their design, they were all modest in conception. The first two, Holy Trinity, Greys Hill in Henley (1848) and Holy Trinity, Wood Green in Witney (1849), were both by Benjamin Ferrey. The rapid growth of Banbury was reflected by its three new churches: Christ Church, South Banbury (1853), St. Paul's, Neithrop (1853) and St. Leonard's, Grimsbury (1890). Abingdon's Albert Park estate acquired its own church in 1867, a muted design by Sir George Gilbert Scott. Didcot's new church has already been mentioned. Elsewhere the parochial organisation and church accommodation remained as it had been in the middle ages.

The nonconformists were more active in responding to the challenge of the increasing urban population. Many new chapels were built in and after the middle of the century, particularly in the 1840's and 1870's (Fig.7). By 1900 Banbury had no less than ten nonconformist chapels of assorted denominations, in addition to its four Anglican churches and one Catholic church built in 1838. Abingdon, Witney and Henley each had six nonconformist chapels, while Wallingford, Faringdon and Chipping Norton had five apiece. Even the smallest towns commonly had two or three. The Wesleyan Methodists were the most widespread sect, with eighteen chapels, followed by the Baptists with seventeen.

Stylistically the chapels vary enormously. Most of the earlier examples are relatively plain or classical in style, such as Charlbury Wesleyan (1823), Woodstock Baptist (1827) and Abingdon Baptist (1841). Banbury Congregational Chapel (1857) is an unusually late Greek Revival building. Several Italianate examples built in the 1860's include Abingdon Congregational (1862) and Chipping Norton Wesleyan (rebuilt 1868). However, Gothic details had already begun to appear in the recently-demolished Witney Congregational Chapel (1828), and as the century progressed Gothic came increasingly into favour, totally dominating chapel architecture in the last four decades. Woodman's Trinity Methodist Church in Abingdon (1875), with its Gothic steeple, looks more like an Anglican church than St. Michael's, Albert Park, itself, and was clearly intended to outshine its Anglican neighbour.

As the rising urban population created a demand for new churches and chapels, so new burial grounds were also required. Many nonconformist chapels had no graveyards of their own, and the Anglican churchyards were soon under pressure. The 1852 Interment Act set up Burial Boards in towns which could either be elected and controlled by church vestries or operated directly by town councils. The Boards were given powers to acquire land, which was usually located near the contemporary edge of the built-up area. In Chipping Norton over three acres was given for a new cemetery by William Bliss in 1882. By the end of the century cemeteries with iron railings, evergreen shrubs, gravel walks, caretakers' lodges and mortuary chapels (often in pairs, one for Anglicans, one for Nonconformists), had become a characteristic feature of the Victorian townscape.

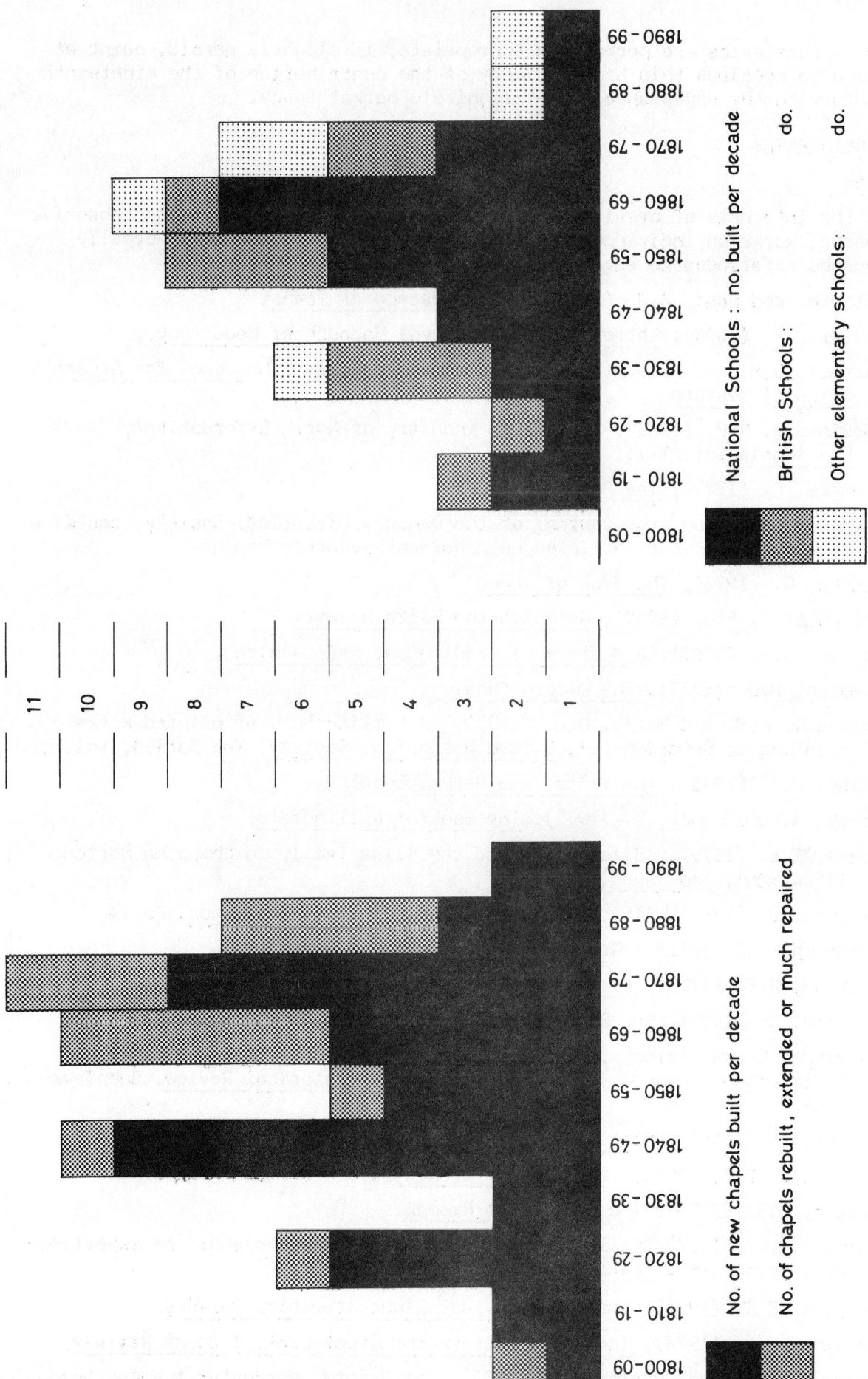

Figure 7. Histograms illustrating the chronology of construction of
elementary schools and nonconformist chapels in the Oxfordshire
market towns in the nineteenth century

Cemeteries are perhaps an appropriate, if slightly morbid, point at which to conclude this brief summary of the contribution of the nineteenth century to the appearance of Oxfordshire's market towns.

BIBLIOGRAPHY

Note

In the interests of brevity, only the most recent and/or most comprehensive general works on individual towns are listed here. These will normally include references to earlier publications.

Aston M. and Bond, C.J. (1976), The Landscape of Towns.

Ballard, A. (1896), Chronicles of the Royal Borough of Woodstock.

Barratt, D.M. and Vaisey, D.G. (1973), Oxfordshire, a Handbook for Students of Local History.

Beckinsale, R.P. (1963), 'The plush industry of North Oxfordshire', Oxoniensia Vol.XXVIII.

Bloxham, C. (1975), The Book of Banbury.

Cake and Cockhorse, the Journal of the Banbury Historical Society, contains many valuable short articles on nineteenth-century Banbury.

Clarke, G. (1978), The Book of Thame.

Clinch & Co. Ltd. (1939), Guide to the Eagle Brewery.

Colvin, H.M. (1963), A History of Deddington, Oxfordshire.

Compton, H.J. (1977), The Oxford Canal.

Cordeaux, E.H. and Merry, D.H. (1955), 'A bibliography of printed works relating to Oxfordshire', Oxford Historical Society, New Series, Vol.XI.

Dalby, J.B. (1971), The Wilts. and Berks. Canal.

Dewey, J. and Dewey, S. (1977), The Book of Wallingford.

Evans, R.L. (1975), 'Bliss Mills and the Bliss family in Chipping Norton, 1758-1920', Top. Oxon. No.20.

Everett, S. (1969). 'The Workhouse in Oxfordshire', Top. Oxon. No.14.

Goodrich, P.J. (1928), Great Faringdon Past and Present.

Gretton, M.S. (1920), Burford Past and Present.

Hammond, N. (1979), The Book of Abingdon.

Harrison, B. and Trinder, B. (1969), 'Drink and sobriety in an early Victorian Town: Banbury, 1830-1860', English Historical Review, Supplement No.4.

Hedges, S. (1968), Bicester wuz a Little Town.

Higgins, S.H.P. (1958), The Wantage Tramway.

Holden, J.S. (1974), The Watlington Branch.

Horn, P.R.L. (1972), 'Pillow Lacemaking in Victorian England: the experience of Oxfordshire', Textile History, Vol.III.

Jenkins, S.C. (1975), The Witney & East Gloucestershire Railway.

Jenkins, S.C. (1978), The Great Western and Great Central Joint Railway.

Jenkins, S.C. and Quayle, H.I. (1977), The Oxford, Worcester & Wolverhampton Railway.

Kelly's Directories of Berks., Bucks. and Oxon. (1883 onwards).

Leyland, N.L. and Troughton, J.E. (1974), Glovemaking in West Oxfordshire.

Lingard, R. (1973), The Woodstock Branch.

Lingard, R. (1978), Princes Risborough - Thame - Oxford Railway.

Lingham, B.F. and Hall, M.J. (1977), The Changing Face of Didcot.

MacDermott, E.T. (1927), History of the Great Western Railway.

Meades, E. (1949), The History of Chipping Norton.

Monk, W.J. (1894), History of Witney.

Paine, C., et. al. (1978), 'Working-class Housing in Oxfordshire', Oxoniensia Vol.XLIII.

Pevsner, N. (1966), The Buildings of England: Berkshire.

Philip, K. (1968), Victorian Wantage.

Plummer, A. & Earl R.E. (1969), The Blanket Makers, 1669-1969: A history of Charles Early & Marriott (Witney) Ltd.

Record of Witney, the Newsletter of the Witney and District Historical and Archaeological Society, contains useful notes on Witney in the nineteenth century.

Russell, J.H. (1977), The Banbury and Cheltenham Railway, 1887-1962.

Saint, A. (1970), 'Three Oxford Architects', Oxoniensia Vol.XXXV.

Schulz, T.E. (1938), 'The Woodstock Glove Industry', Oxoniensia Vol.III.

Sherwood, J. and Pevsner, N. (1974), The Buildings of England: Oxfordshire.

Taylor, A.M. (1964), Gilletts, Bankers at Banbury and Oxford.

Tomalin, G.H.J. (1975), The Book of Henley-on-Thames.

Trinder, B. (1965), History of Banbury Methodism.

Vaughan, A. (1979), A History of the Faringdon Branch and Uffington Station.

Victoria County History, Berkshire Vols. III-IV (1923-24), Oxfordshire Vols. V-X (1957-72).

THE HISTORY OF PLANNING IN OXFORDSHIRE

John Minett

I wonder how many people feel when they drive over the Chilterns or leave Aylesbury for the west or Reading for the north that they are entering another world. The sign 'Oxfordshire' by the side of the road seems to mean more than just another county. It marks the end of 'London' - the end of commuter land, of Green Line buses and parades of neo-Georgian shops. It is the beginning of the 'other England' which Geoffrey Moorhouse wrote about in the 1960's; part of the great swathe of rural England which appears so often on pictorial calendars. Oxfordshire in many ways depicts an ideal of England: at its heart a cathedral city, market town and ancient university, with surrounding acolytes of small ancient towns and villages, set in a varied and often beautiful countryside. It has been cited as the model geographical region and the model administrative unit. The history of planning in Oxfordshire is primarily concerned with preserving that character - even if it is now little more than a mask for many of the most recent aspects of 20th century technology, such as institutes for nuclear research, centres for training the armed forces or land farmed by highly advanced mechanical techniques

In considering planning in Oxfordshire it is important to distinguish between the city of Oxford and the county districts. As in many similar situations there is a conflict between pressure for outward growth from the city and resistance from the surrounding rural areas. Planning started in the county to try to reconcile these issues but, as mentioned in the paper by J.F. Barrow, they remain unresolved.

Although a study of planning history should perhaps start with the development of Oxford from its beginning as a planned defence settlement guarding Wessex against the Danes, I am going to leave you to read about that and the following millenium (1) and concentrate on statutory planning resulting from parliamentary enactment. Furthermore, I am going to spend more time discussing planning between the wars, a time when I consider most of the main principles underlying present policy evolved.

Statutory planning started in this country after 1909, when, under the Housing and Town Planning Act of that year, Boroughs and Districts were given the power to produce plans to guide and control their expansion. Planning in Oxfordshire started in the 1920's.

Following the Housing and Town Planning Act of 1919 which required all towns with a population over 20,000 to produce a plan for their future development, Oxford City Council initiated their first plan in October 1923. Then the Council passed a resolution to undertake an 'Oxford (Regional) Town Planning Scheme and Oxford (Special Area) Town Planning Scheme'. It was called 'Regional' because the plan was intended to cover not only the City of Oxford, but also the Urban District of Headington and parts of the surrounding rural districts. The term 'Special Area' referred to the historic centre of the city for which conservation measures were allowed under the Housing Act of 1923.

To implement the production of a plan the City Council formed a Housing and Town Planning Committee, and, with the other local authorities involved, established a Joint Regional Advisory Committee. Three Town Planning assistants were appointed to the City Engineer's Department to help prepare the scheme. In September 1925 a 'Preliminary Statement' of proposals for development was adopted by the City Council and submitted to the Ministry of Health for approval, which they did in 1927.

81

The scheme was presented as a single map and a short report, which set out regulations regarding land-use zones, housing densities, heights of buildings and proposed new roads or road widening. The whole of the central area of Oxford was designated for University and commercial uses. New industry was to be confined to a small area in the south east of the city around the Morris Motors factory at Cowley. Almost all the 'Regional Area' was zoned for residential development at varying densities, though mainly for eight or twelve houses per acre. The only open space to be preserved was common land such as Port Meadow and narrow strips alongside the rivers. The road proposals comprised the building of an outer ring road and some inner link roads.

Apart from being the first town planning scheme in Oxfordshire, and one of the earliest in the country, the 1927 plan is interesting for a number of reasons. First it went beyond the powers provided by Parliament in that it covered the built-up area as well as land which was intended to be developed. Secondly, because of the problems of compensation - whereby if land was not allowed for development the owner could demand compensation - almost the whole of the unbuilt-on land was designated for housing, so that even at the low densities then prevailing, the population of Oxford could have exceeded 850,000! Finally, the road proposals demonstrate the inertia that is inherent in a plan. The northern part of the outer ring was started by 1930 but the whole ring was not completed until the 1960's. The Marston Ferry section of the inner relief road was built, despite increasing doubts about its value, but not for over forty years!

Early planning schemes could, in many ways, be regarded as quite 'positive' because they were concerned with expansion and therefore strongly orientated towards public works. This was not only true of town plans but also of the 'regional plans' which were increasingly made from the beginning of the 1920's. But the late twenties and thirties saw a shift towards plans being used for conservation, as, encouraged by the Local Government Act of 1929, the Shire counties became ever more involved in co-ordinating plans for rural areas.

The first regional plan to affect Oxfordshire was in fact commissioned by a private body. In 1927 the newly formed Council for the Preservation of Rural England (CPRE) commissioned a 'planning survey' of the Thames Valley from Cricklade to Staines. In the same year, Oxfordshire County Council called a meeting of local authorities in the county and formed a Planning Advisory Committee to oversee a planning survey of the county. The same eminent consultants, the Earl of Mayo and Professors Adshead and Abercrombie, were commissioned to produce both reports.

In comparison with the planning 'schemes' of the period which had to be legalistic in their language, regional planning surveys make very interesting reading. The approach taken was that of a landscape architect - treating the whole area as a garden to be planned for a multiplicity of uses with beauty being regarded as of equal importance to function. Indeed Major Anthony Muirhead, Chairman of the Oxfordshire Regional Survey Report published in 1931 suggested that 'Regional Planning is no more than an official name for a process which aims at putting into practice an interest, I might almost say an instinct, which is inherent in the minds of most of us....' The British people, Major Muirhead asserted, are the best gardeners in the world, whether dealing with window boxes or ducal domains. They are also the best colonizers. They 'desire to apply themselves to a portion of the earth's surface, and, through the twin operations of progress and preservation, so to order it to the best advantage' (2). Thus regional planning was likened to landscape gardening.

The CPRE Report on the Thames Valley was published in 1929. It was concerned with means for preserving and enhancing the character of the riverside. Presented as a bound volume, beautifully printed on vellum with sketches and coloured maps, it provided a general description of the river and its towns before setting out a catalogue of those things that disfigured its character. Foremost among the authors' worries were petrol filling stations and advertising hoardings. The increasing proliferation of old railway carriages as holiday homes also concerned them, as did the incursion of new industry. A sugar beet factory at Eynsham appears to have been their particular bête noir.

The discription of disfigurements bring the period very much to mind - 'the typical petrol station with its row of coloured pumps and tin advertisements' (3); roofs of pink asbestos slates or corrugated iron. Commenting on the Thames Valley for recreation they approved, surprisingly, of boathouses and some villas but not of temporary huts. Orderly rows of tents, on the other hand, were quite different and often provided 'a charming feature of the scene'. Their warning of the insidious growth of huts carries a flavour of social life of the time - as camping became popular with the middle classes. First comes a simple hut between tents for cooking; then the family begin to use it for meals in wet weather; a dining room follows and possibly a bedroom is added 'for a maid or someone who does not care to sleep under canvas' (4). So gradually a rambling series of shacks are built.

The Oxfordshire Regional Survey Report took a similar approach, showing particular concern for trying to preserve the rural character of Oxfordshire and the setting for Oxford as the focus of county life. The problem was how to cope with the development pressure around Oxford, caused by the growing car industry at Cowley whilst at the same time retaining the character of the university city. In addition, the outward pressure from London along the trunk roads and railways posed a possible future threat to the character of Oxfordshire's towns and villages.

'Taken as a whole, Oxfordshire as a region required no less measures for protection than prescriptions for progress, as with the exception of the area around Oxford, there are few signs of change' (5). So wrote the authors in the preface to the County report, and most of their proposals relate to the area around Oxford which they called 'mid-Oxfordshire'. They advocated a reduction of the land designated for residential use in the area covered by the Oxford (Regional) Town Planning Scheme, this to be achieved by increasing the area preserved for floodland along the rivers. At the same time they confirmed that plan's road proposals, adding a further improvement to the Northern Bypass between Oxford and Eynsham. A major new proposal was that a series of satellite villages should be built around Oxford to take some of the pressure off the city.

The authors mention looking for a site for a satellite town for London somewhere at the base of the Chilterns. They considered expanding Thame but concluded that it was not a sensible proposal. They also had further thoughts about the use of the Thames for recreation, and suggested that it might be converted in places around Oxford into artificial lakes - 'features' they suggested 'that would not be costly to construct and that would have a wonderful aquatic interest' (6). Such an idea might be revived again as we ponder what to do today with all the old gravel workings around Oxford.

As with the Thames Valley report, petrol filling stations, advertising hoardings and cheap building materials were raised as issues. So was the need to stop housing being built as ribbon development along the new trunk roads and by-passes. At the heart of the matter was the problem of control, exacerbated in those days by the fact mentioned in connection with the Oxford plan: that any land owner precluded from developing his land could claim compensation.

To avoid claims for compensation, only land which could be defended from development because of ownership or liability to flood could be regarded as safe. Consequently most land in a planning scheme was zoned for development, though some very subtle forms of zoning resulted.

In the Thames Valley report the consultants explained that there were two ways of controlling land - by zoning, and by 'reservation'. Zoning applied to areas where building was expected to be controlled by a town planning scheme. Normally three types of character zone were adopted - residential, commercial and industrial. In addition, town planning schemes laid down the maximum density of houses per acre and the height of buildings to be allowed. In built-up areas of towns and villages densities ranged from three to twelve houses per acre. In the countryside densities varied from a maximum of one house to one acre to one house per ten acres. (Wild moorland areas were sometimes zoned at one house per 100 acres.)

'Reservation was the name given to rural areas where there was a presumption against development. To get around the issue of compensation, the Oxfordshire Survey suggested the use of a method which had been adopted for the Witney Town Planning Scheme, produced for Witney Urban and Rural Districts (7). This scheme designated a rural reservation where normally the only development allowed would be agricultural buildings, and residential development at about one house per ten acres using a 'pooling arrangement'. Under the 'pooling arrangement' landowners were permitted to put houses anywhere on their land up to a maximum of one house per ten acres. The intention and hope was that they would be grouped so that, for example, the owner of 1,000 acres might create a new village of 100 houses. Owners of less than ten acres were allowed a single house. Single houses with a curtilage attached of about ten acres were allowed anywhere 'and these may include chauffeurs' or gardeners' cottages'.

As with present day structure planning, the Oxfordshire Regional report was only intended as a guide. 'It is not intended to be a detailed index to which every person or every local authority can apply a sealed-pattern solution of particular problems. Rather it is designed to provide a framework within which local authorities and local individuals, with the particular knowledge and experience which are theirs, fill in the details for their own areas (8).

As we have seen, the detailed approach of producing a 'planning scheme' was already being pursued for Oxford City and its immediate neighbourhood, and for Witney, by 1930. In addition, schemes were being prepared for the Henley, Goring and Crowmarsh districts of South Oxfordshire and for Chipping Norton, Woodstock, Thame and Banbury. By the mid 1930's the West Oxfordshire Districts used the same consultant, T.F. Thompson, and consequently had virtually combined their planning operations. Thompson's reports for these Authorities were all very similar, containing a preamble explaining the reason for planning followed by an explanation of procedures for applying for planning permission and notes on siting, design, materials and colour considered suitable for the locality.

A similar but far more detailed planning scheme was published for Oxford City in 1939. Consisting of two enormous 1:2500 scale plans which covered the administrative area of the city, and accompanied by a report of 60 pages of close print which set out regulations and intentions for roads, zones, materials and heights of buildings, it differed greatly in style from the discursive regional reports. This was necessary because, unlike the regional reports, once a 'planning scheme' was approved by the Minister it became a legal document. In fact, as with most other schemes of the period, the Oxford plan of 1939 was never submitted for approval. Rather than face claims for compensation, local authorities preferred to keep their plans unofficial and use 'interim development control' powers.

The Banbury report of 1933 provides an example of planning control of the period when it states 'before any building, rebuilding, or external alterations - including re-roofing - can be proceeded with, plans must be submitted and approved by the Joint Regional Committee. The Committee can approve plans with or without conditions' (9). Any design which the Committee was not satisfied with would be submitted to an advisory panel consisting of an architect, a surveyor and a Justice of the Peace, whose decision would be final.

Time does not permit me to discuss the proliferation of private plans and reports for Oxford which were produced during the war. Anyone who would like to get an inkling of the debate of whether Oxford should be a single or twin city, which was conducted via the plans of Barnett House (1939/41), the Oxford Preservation Trust (1942) and Thomas Sharp (1947), should in the first instance consult Steven Hopkins' paper on 'Planning in Oxford' (1978).

From 1943 all development, whether or not on land covered by a planning scheme became subject to planning control. In 1947 the whole system was changed (10). The compensation issue was at least mitigated when the right of a landowner to develop his land was removed. At the same time county districts lost their planning powers. From then until Local Government was reorganised in 1974, planning was carried out by the County Councils and County Boroughs, so that planning in what is now Oxfordshire was split between three authorities - Oxfordshire, Berkshire (for what is now Vale of White Horse District) and Oxford City.

I do not intend to go into any detail on their plans which appear very prosaic in comparison with pre-war reports. Nor do I intend to go into any detail on their attempts at joint working which, by all accounts, were not very successful. Suffice it to say that the objective of each authority continued the aims of the pre-war plan to conserve the rural character of the area as a setting for Oxford. In 1959, under pressure from, amongst others, the Oxford Preservation Trust, they did agree to submit proposals for a Green Belt. The Minister formally approved this plan fifteen years later.

Major Muirhead had graphically stated the problem of Oxford when he wrote in 1931 'The Oxford of Matthew Arnold "whispering from her towers the last enchantments of the Middle Ages" now finds her satellite at Cowley proclaiming in the more strident tones of modern advertising the prospective advantages of the new Morris model!' (11). The Oxford City Development Plans of 1955, 1967 and 1972 all had as their prime aim the reconciliation of the multiple roles of the city as market town, industrial centre and university city. The Oxfordshire Development Plan of 1954 aimed to preserve the agricultural character of the rural areas, and the Berkshire Development Plans of 1953 and 1960 aimed to maintain the special character of Oxford, while at the same time accepting the new basic industries of 'atoms, oil and motor cars'. This policy of conservation remains essentially the same today. It has on the whole been successful, but with ever greater and proliferating pressures from research establishments, improved roads and faster trains, how long can it hold?

REFERENCES

(1)   Fasnacht, R. (1954), A History of the City of Oxford.

(2)   Mayo, Earl of, et al, (1931), Regional Planning Report on Oxfordshire p.ix.

(3)   Mayo, Earl of, et al, (1929), The Thames Valley, p.60.

(4) _ibid_, p.60.

(5) Mayo, (1931), _op.cit_ p.v.

(6) _ibid_, p.vi.

(7) _ibid_, p.37-9.

(8) _ibid_, p.xi.

(9) Banbury and District Joint Regional Planning Committee (1933), _Regional Planning of Banbury and District_.

(10) Town and Country Planning Act 1947.

(11) Mayo, (1931), _op.cit_, p.xiii.

Bibliography in addition to those mentioned above.

Barnett House Survey Committee (1939-41), _A Survey of the Social Services in the Oxford District 1938-40_.

Berkshire County Council (1955), _Development Plan_.

Chipping Norton and District Joint Town Planning Committee (1932), _Town Planning - an explanation of the Chipping Norton and District Planning Scheme_.

City of Oxford (1927), _Town Planning Scheme (Regional and Special Areas) - preliminary statement of proposals for development_.

City of Oxford (1939), _Oxford City Draft Planning Scheme_.

City of Oxford (1955), _City of Oxford Development Plan_

Hopkins, S. (1978), 'Planning in Oxford - an historical survey and bibliography', _Oxford Polytechnic Department of Town Planning Working Paper 31_.

Moorhouse, G. (1962), _The Other England_.

Oxfordshire County Council (1954), _Development Plan_.

Sharp. T. (1947), _Oxford Replanned_.

PLANNING IN THE OXFORD REGION

J.F. Barrow

THE OXFORD REGION

The role of the professional, his perception of the problem and the setting of alternatives for political choice are all necessary requisites for the study of planning in the Oxford region. The biggest issue of the region is the matter of countywide restraint, coupled with a secondary issue, that of the location of Oxfordshire's endemic growth. It seems that everyone agrees that the Oxfordshire growth rates of the past were too high. The Secretary of State for the Environment, the County Council and some of the District Councils seem to wish to restrain the countywide population growth below an agreed figure by 1991; one which would be substantially less than what the county population would be without the intervention of planning.

The County Council want to see a restrained rate of growth directed to selected country towns rather than to the Central Oxfordshire Urban Area [1]. The physical growth of Central Oxfordshire Urban area since 1919 is broadly illustrated in Figure 1 which shows the outward spread of Oxford especially in the interwar years; the peripheral additions up to 1959 and the limited expansion since 1959 as the green belt around the built-up area increasingly took effect. If market forces were to dictate the shape of the future of the county with no public authority intervention then this Central Oxfordshire Urban Area would take on the characteristics of a growth zone with consequent major urban developments in Central Oxfordshire.

Concern by the County Council that further major expansions would lead to the emergence of urban sprawl with rates of uncontrolled growth to the detriment of the conservation of Oxford has led to the selection of a strategy aimed at severe restraint in Central Oxfordshire; coupled with the growth of selected towns beyond the green belt around Oxford.

The land-use strategy submitted by the County Council and as now approved with modifications by the Secretary of State for the Environment is a clear declaration of intent to achieve a country town strategy based on steering most new development to specific locations - such as Banbury, Bicester, Didcot, and Witney, within the context of countryside restraint of growth. Figure 2 illustrates the strategy of the County Council.

The concept of the "country towns" or "market towns" strategy is to foster greater self-sufficiency in these towns in the belief that they will be better places in which to live. The country towns strategy is likely to give greater efficiency in terms of less and cheaper travel; and by that is meant all travel, not only the journey to and from work. Such a strategy would involve less demand, countywide, on Oxford, with a sufficiently large base for attractions in the country towns so that they can compete and be more efficient.

However other major proposals for the Central Oxfordshire area such as the new road intentions of the Department of Transport outside the control of the County Council could have the opposite effect to the land-use plan. These are more fully discussed later. But at this stage some conjecture would be appropriate. If it is accepted that improved accessibility to Central Oxfordshire by the construction of new roads (and by the electrification of the rail system) helps to encourage growth, then the proposals to make Central Oxfordshire more accessible and less congested will help to stimulate and encourage that growth. The consequences could be that the area grows relatively faster than most of the country towns as development takes place on the periphery of the urban area of Central Oxfordshire. The conjecture is that gradually the country towns strategy will not be achieved or countywide restraint policies will be undermined or that both will occur.

PAST GROWTH OF THE CENTRAL OXFORDSHIRE URBAN AREA (Generalised)

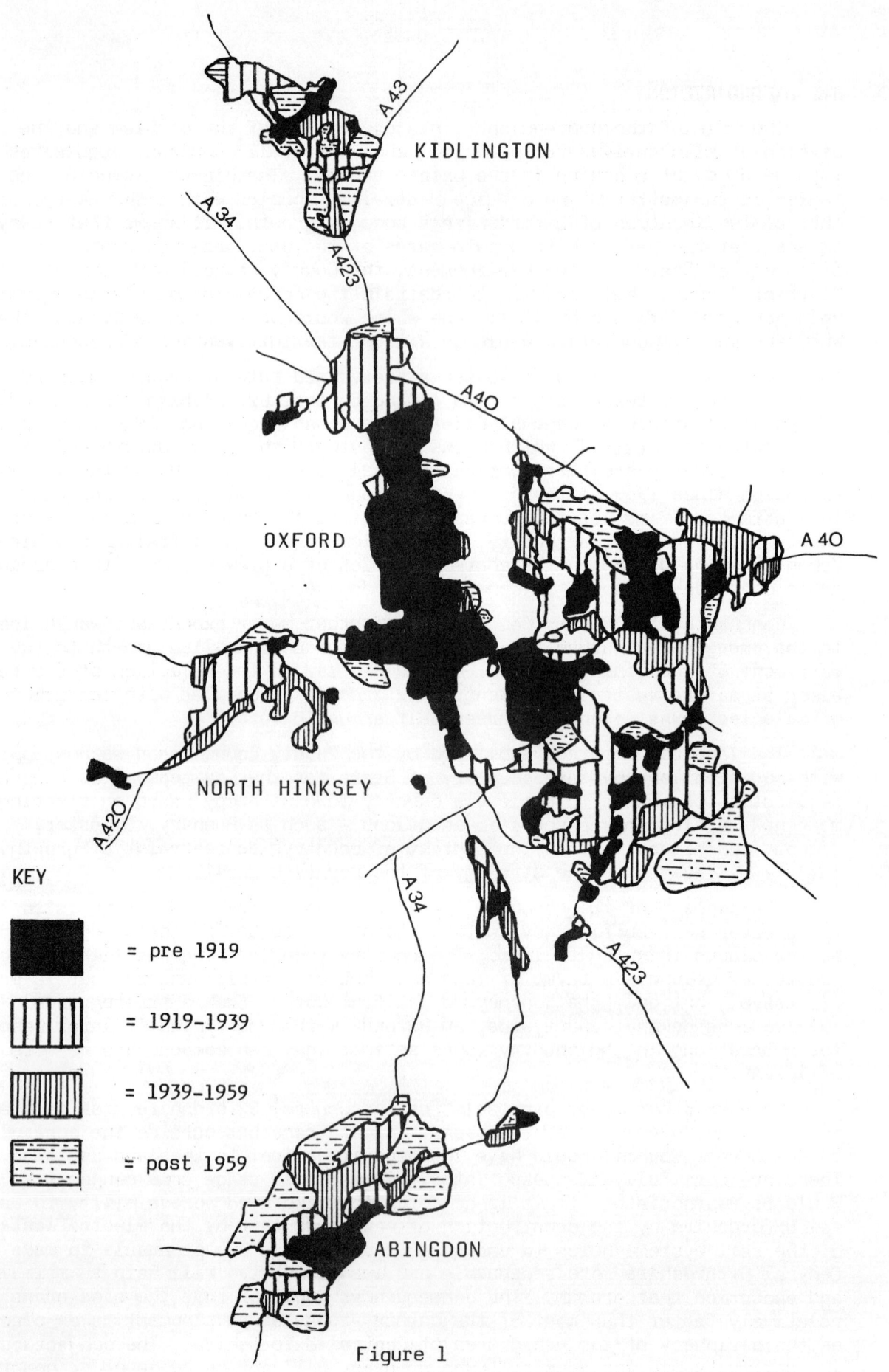

Figure 1

STRUCTURE PLAN INTENTIONS

(as submitted by the County Council to the Secretary of State for the Environment)

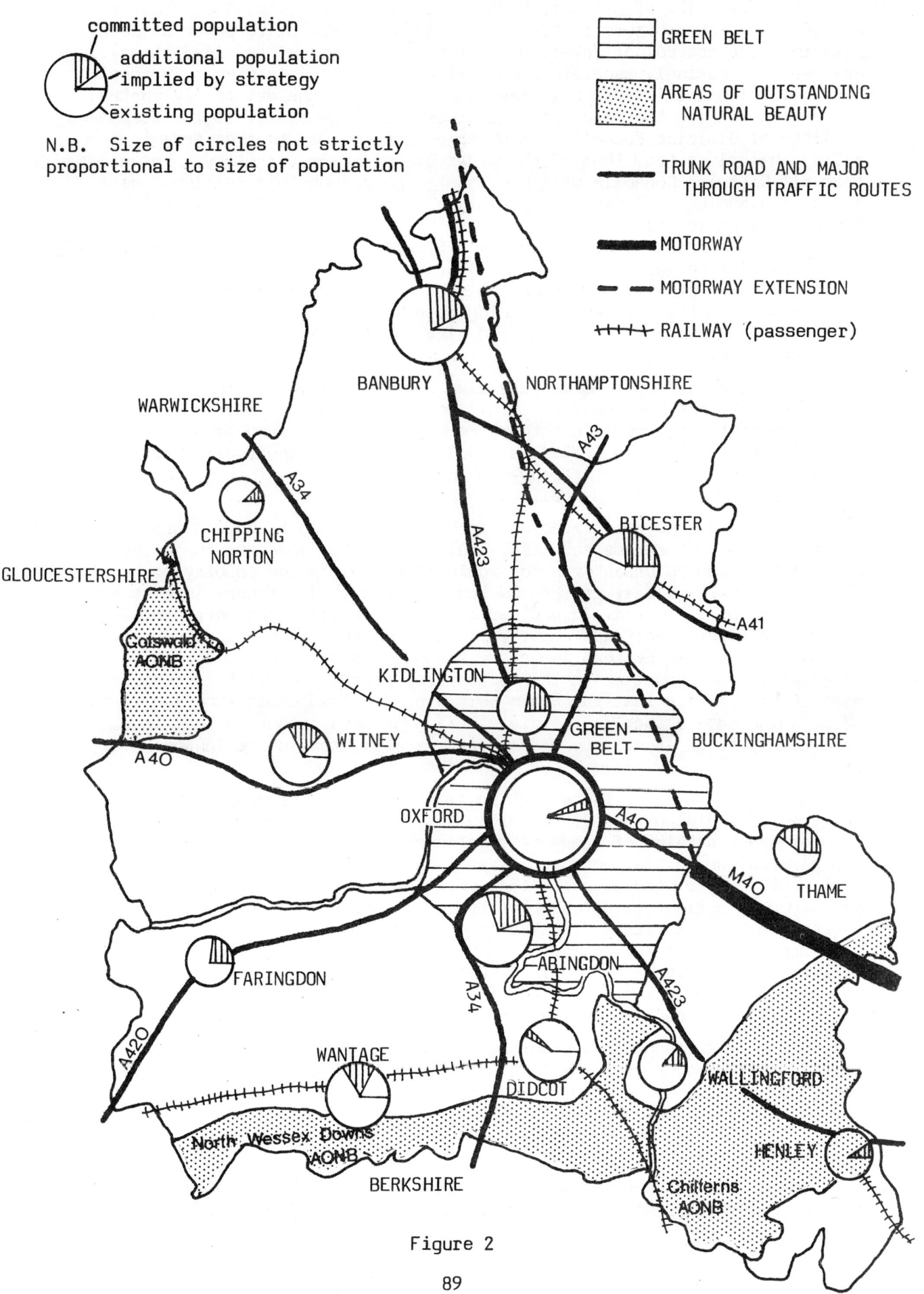

Figure 2

The activities of external bodies such as the Department of Transport are only one contributory factor. Since 1974 the executive power of local planning (the control of development, the preparation of detailed plans) has been increasingly separate from that of strategic planning. Whereas strategic planning is vested in the County Council, the day to day control of development and the preparation of local plans generally is the responsibility of District Councils. A District Council may have different policy objectives from that of the strategic planning authority. Assuming that all District Councils will continue to be responsible for local decisions on planning applications and for local plan preparation (with the County Council having to decide only whether to "certify" a local plan as being generally in accordance with a County's Structure Plan) the opportunity exists for a District Council, if it wishes to do so, to exert influence and power sufficient gradually to undermine the strategic intentions of a Structure Plan. This could mean that land-use planning powers will not by themselves suffice to limit the growth of Central Oxfordshire and at the same time reduce that of other towns.

It is ironic that the land-use plan and the transport plan which the Secretary of State has modified in his approval are mismatched. Given these expectations, should not there be consistency between land-use policies of restraint, explicitly stated, and policies for transport aimed at restraint? It is not simply a matter of land-use and roads and use of cars; exactly the same theory would apply to public transport.

If a magic wand were waved and it became possible to have a greater countywide network of bus services, would that focus more growth on the Central Oxfordshire Urban Area, or would it stimulate the country towns strategy? There are no easy answers to that question. One theory is that the less opportunity for travel, whether by road or public transport, the less the tendency for countywide growth. That seems to be logically the converse of the relationship between increased transport provision and the stimulation of growth. The reduction in the numbers for travel would, it is suggested, make it more likely that the green belt around Oxford could function, perhaps stimulating some change in the distribution of development so that it was more likely to be steered to Didcot, for example, than occur in the Oxford area.

But what chance is there that people would agree to reduce the opportunities of travel by either car or public transport as a consistent extension of the restraint of land-use development in Central Oxfordshire? In other words, would they accept the real and tangible costs of a policy of restraint? Experience suggests that the likelihood is virtually nil. Some years ago an option of restraint of travel in Oxford was postulated in order to match the restraint intentions of the land-use plan. A transport plan based on a similar policy of restraint would increase the chances of limiting countywide growth. The country towns would have a greater chance of reaching some degree of self-sufficiency because of the reduced opportunities for interaction between the country towns and Oxford.

The choice was posed and one must respect the decision to reject it. Equally, one might reject the thesis that there ought to be consistency between the policies for transport and those of land-use; but in so rejecting, one must realise that the chance of successfully achieving the objectives of one or the other is considerably reduced. The consequences must be that the land-use plan has less chance of succeeding.

The writer has seen only one example of a consistent land-use and transport poan for the Central Oxfordshire Area. This is illustrated in

Figure 3. Growth was to be focussed on and along a north-south spine passing through urban Oxford. Whilst there would have been no restriction on countywide road construction and travel by private cars, there was to be greater emphasis on public transport in Oxford and along the north-south spine, including public transport by rail.

These transport proposals would undoubtedly have assisted growth in accordance with the land-use plan, with new development proposed on the southern edges of Oxford, west of Kidlington and at Abingdon/Radley. The country towns would be likely to grow initially slower than the Central Oxfordshire Urban Area. But in the writer's opinion the resulting countywide growth would inevitably have been much greater than everyone seems to want. The development in the Central Oxfordshire Urban Area would have stimulated further and continued expansion. Furthermore it can be conjectured that the transport arrangements would have become increasingly inefficient and the subsidy requirements for the public transport networks would increase to become a very heavy county expenditure. This type of strategy was rejected by the County Council.

The Secretary of State for the Environment has now approved, with modifications, the County's submitted Structure Plan. Some have expressed the view that his amendments to the location of housing and employment are sufficiently small and spread over such a long period that they are insignificant in strategic terms. Yet the output so far available on what is actually occurring in the Central Oxfordshire Urban Area suggests that development is occurring at rates greater than envisaged by the County Council or the Secretary of State. The results still require considerable refinement but it is apparent that over the last two years both planning permissions or housing and building completions have been in excess of the maximum rate implied in the Structure Plan allocation of 6,450 dwellings in the Oxford and adjoining area (including Kidlington) up to 1986. Moreover by far the larger part of these permissions and completions have been in the existing built-up area of the City itself. It is now suspected that there is still more potential for additional dwellings than the City was assuming when the Sturcture Plan was prepared and when evidence was presented at the Examination in Public into the submitted plan. If the policy of limiting the number of new dwellings to 2,000 by 1986, over and above commitments, is to be retained - and it is yet not clear if this is what the Secretary of State is seeking - there is apparently no reason for general releases of housing land in the green belt in the near future (2).

Elsewhere in the Central Oxfordshire Urban Area, notably in Abingdon, the expansion of employment is in excess of that proposed in the submitted Structure Plan. The permissions and allocations have produced some 240 jobs over and above Structure Plan commitments between January 1976 and mid 1978, almost double the rate implied by the County Council's Plan. Morever these figures only take account of the employment changes in one part of Abingdon and so do not allow for changes in the existing firms, so could well be an underestimate (3).

Considerably more work is and will be done on monitoring and on assessing the implications for the implementation of the Structure Plan especially in the light of the Secretary of State's approval. It is sufficient to say at this stage that there are some early signs of growth in Central Oxfordshire occurring at a rate which is not in accordance with the emphasis on restraint; with consequent implications for the country towns strategy and for the desire for countywide restraint of growth.

TRANSPORT

To turn to the transport proposals, particularly the Oxford transport

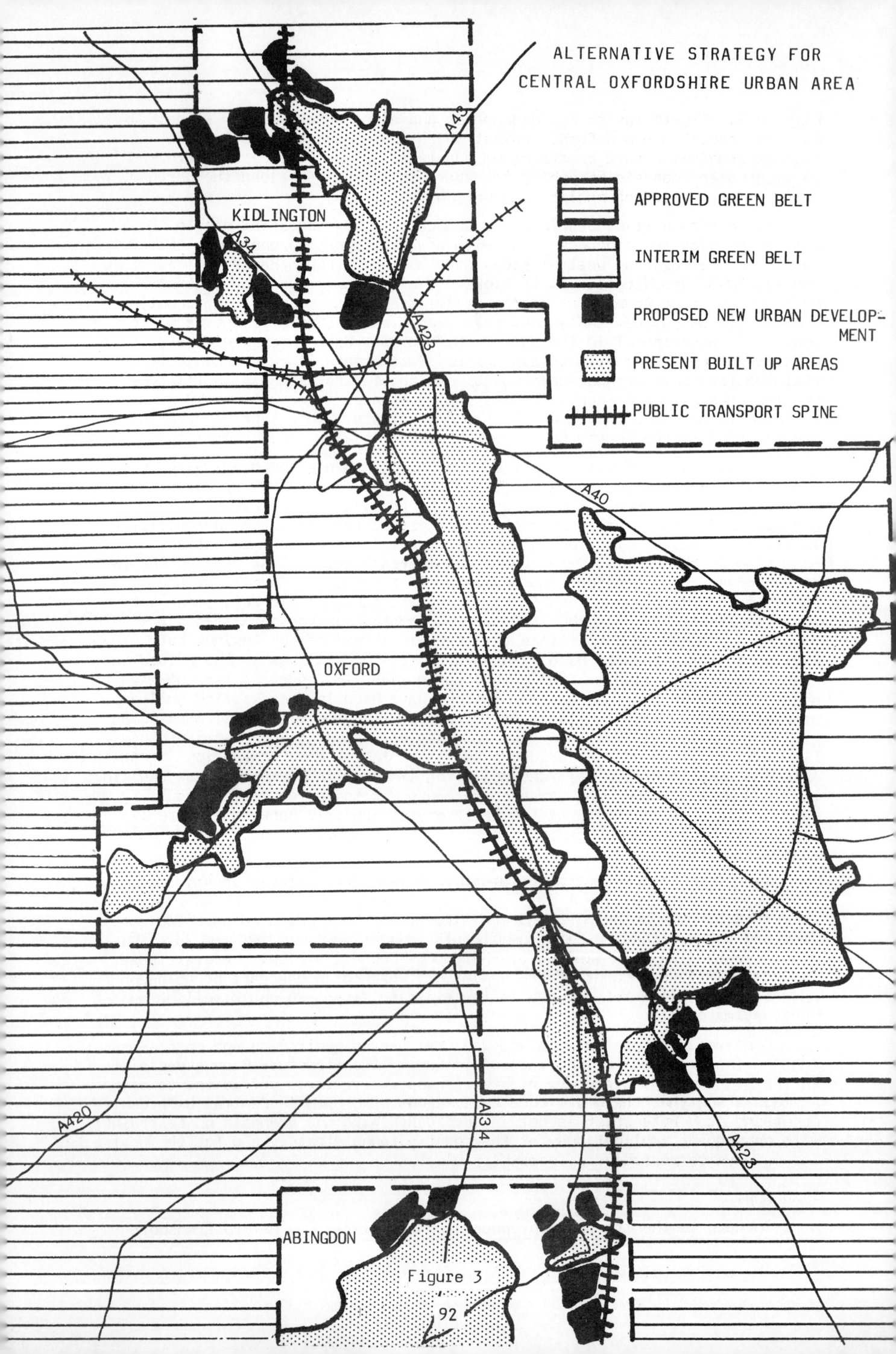

ALTERNATIVE STRATEGY FOR
CENTRAL OXFORDSHIRE URBAN AREA

KIDLINGTON

OXFORD

ABINGDON

Figure 3

92

APPROVED GREEN BELT

INTERIM GREEN BELT

PROPOSED NEW URBAN DEVELOP-
MENT

PRESENT BUILT UP AREAS

PUBLIC TRANSPORT SPINE

system it is evident that the issues have raised the greatest amount of debate.

The County Council wanted to retain parts of the existing Development Plan, the inner relief road (the County Council proposals are shown in Figure 4), as an option to bypass the heritage area of the City centre at some time in the future. A road scheme was proposed from Iffley Road westwards to the Abingdon Road and looping northwards to the Botley Road. This would not have involved the demolition of existing houses. These road proposals were seen by some in terms of trying to ease matters for motorists in Oxford. If you believe that congestion is inevitable in the future and the real options are whether to plan for it or not to plan (and therefore allow it to occur and then take palliative measures) the road proposals, if built, would simply move congestion from one place to another. In these terms, the roads could be seen as proposals which provide a route away from "the heritage area" of the City Centre and the Colleges.

Applying the same theory, the proposed access to the west of the City centre, and Botley relief road (shown in Figure 4) would move congestion from one road to another. Neither road would provide a greater capacity in terms which bring benefits to motorists at the expense of city residents. Both were environmental options and were originally designed as such. The County Council had in mind single carriageways realising that capacity constraints and junction capacity have virtually nothing to do with the issue.

In his approval of the County Council's submitted plan, the Secretary of State has deleted all road proposals. Notwithstanding the advice of the Panel who reported to him on the proposed plan, he has substituted statements providing 'a structural framework' within which new proposals may be put forward; 'to give the authorities the opportunity to consider the options open to them for ensuring the protection of the heritage area paying particular attention to the environment of the High Street and St. Aldates...' He suggested that 'measures for the management of traffic and for the development of public transport seemed a more appropriate solution to the problem with such minor improvements as might be necessary to the network'. He considered that the 'most appropriate context for this to be dealt with is the local plan for Oxford'. He invited the local authorities to consider the range of possible measures in the course of local plan preparation, including the opportunities for public comment. For the Botley relief road (or western approach) the Secretary of State has inserted a statement which provides for 'the improvement of traffic access between the junction of the A420 Cumnor Hill bypass with the A34 western bypass, the Osney Mead industrial estate and the vicinity of the Station.'

What then can be said about traffic management, and the call for a local plan to manage traffic as envisaged by the Secretary of State in his approval? The options here appear to be very small. Perhaps the commuter will be squeezed a little more but this will rebound as the parking problems increase just outside the central area on which the Secretary of State has placed a limit of 14600 car parking places. Increased pressure will be placed on the commuter to use public transport at peak hours thus requiring greater numbers of vehicles which would lie idle in off-peak periods and thereby make public transport less efficient, with the consequent demand for greater subsidy. Demands to increase park and ride operations will no doubt come forward. If a local authority is prepared to accept the additional capital and revenue expenditure and such schemes are implemented, a few cars will not enter the city but the capacity created in the urban network will be absorbed by further local traffic leading eventually to stimulation of more urban growth.

It may well be argued by others that this is speculation and conjecture. There is still a great capacity in existing road networks at many times of the day and the levels of congestion are still well below that

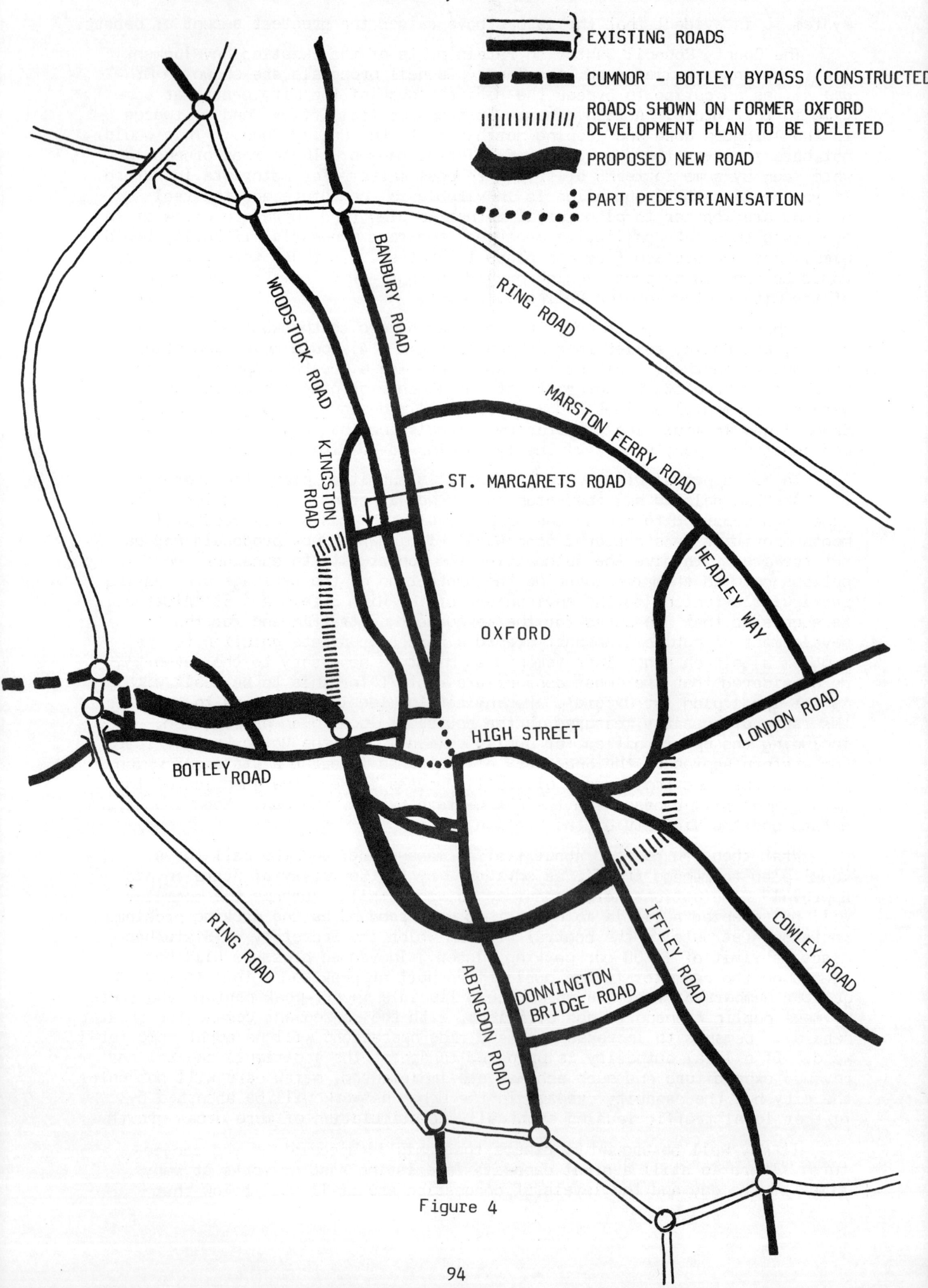

OXFORDSHIRE COUNTY COUNCIL ROAD PROPOSALS

(as submitted to the Secretary of State for the Environment)

EXISTING ROADS

CUMNOR – BOTLEY BYPASS (CONSTRUCTED

ROADS SHOWN ON FORMER OXFORD
DEVELOPMENT PLAN TO BE DELETED

PROPOSED NEW ROAD

PART PEDESTRIANISATION

WOODSTOCK ROAD

BANBURY ROAD

RING ROAD

MARSTON FERRY ROAD

KINGSTON ROAD

ST. MARGARETS ROAD

HEADLEY WAY

OXFORD

LONDON ROAD

HIGH STREET

BOTLEY ROAD

RING ROAD

ABINGDON ROAD

DONNINGTON BRIDGE ROAD

IFFLEY ROAD

COWLEY ROAD

Figure 4

experienced and tolerated in many other towns. But are not several probabilities virtually certain? Public transport will continue to decline (4).
Conversely private travel will continue to increase.

TRANSPORT AND LAND USE

To speculate about the future for the Central Oxfordshire Urban Area, as road congestion becomes less tolerable, there may well be an intensification of demands for sites on the periphery of the urban area from existing central area activities, and new development seeking a central Oxfordshire location where there is spare capacity in an improved road network. At the moment, the demands are in the form of superstores and hypermarket proposals. Other proposals will come forward as accretions, such as motels, distribution depots, warehousing and office developments to sites which are more efficient or less congested.

In terms of individial proposals these may well appear so reasonable and acceptable that they are permitted on their merits. But they must be viewed against a policy of restraint, a desire to prevent urban sprawl and a strategy of limiting the activity and urban expansion of the Central Oxfordshire Urban Area. Only time will show whether, if permitted, they gradually produce a strategy different from that which now seems desired by most people.

To return to the general theme, if restraint of land use development is desired, why, as a generalised concept, was the option of restraining traffic in Oxford unacceptable? The answer is that it was because restraint of travel amounted to a visible increase in costs to be borne locally; and the costs were too high. The public at large expect to get an improvement in the environment and restraint of growth both in the County as a whole and in the Central Oxfordshire Urban Area did not appear to have any benefits for them. Giving up some freedom over the use of the private motor car was too high a price to pay!

Oxfordshire and Oxford have so many benefits enjoyed by its residents compared to the surrounding conurbation that every strategic road proposed by Central Government and not under the control of the County Council will generate attractions and growth at a faster rate than envisaged in the Structure Plan.

The current debate on the strategic roads to the north of Oxford, A40, A34 and the links to the proposed road (X40) from Southampton to the Midlands is an example. The probability (or possibility) for urban growth if these roads are built in the way envisaged by the Department of Transport is very great. The argument in terms of severance of farm land is irrefutable. The greater issue is whether by improving accessibility of Central Oxfordshire to other parts of the country and by increasing the capacity of the local road system, such major road proposals help to stimulate urban development. If such new roads are linked into the Central Oxfordshire Urban Area then the land-use restraint policies in the Approved Structure Plan are likely to be undermined.

CONCLUSIONS

So one must come to the inevitable questions. If a town with above average amenities wishes to remain so, how can development be deterred, and restraint of growth achieved? Are land-use policies sufficient or do they need to be supplemented and supported by transport policies which are consistent with the land-use policies? If those are ineffective what other measures are within the control of the County Council as strategic planning authority?

The questions posed for the professional planner are equally taxing. Should one allow the myth to be perpetuated that the benefits of planning or restraint can be achieved at no material cost; or should the professional spell out publicly that, in order to achieve restraint on countywide growth and improvement to the physical environment, there must be some cost, bearing in mind that all the costs are intangible?

If the professional planner indicates the costs and benefits, how can the trade-off be presented in a way that conscious choice can be exercised by elected members? Will there not then come a point at which the majority will argue that the benefits are never worth the price? We might then be obliged to plan for growth in a manner that minimises the deterioration in efficiency.

NOTES

1. The Central Oxfordshire Urban Area is defined as the "on the ground" development extending from and including Kidlington, Oxford, the Oxford urban fringes and Abingdon.

2. Report to County Environmental Committee: 12 June 1978.

3. Report to County Environmental Committee: 19 September 1978.

4. TRRL Report 771. Urban Passenger Transport. Some trends and prospects F.V. Webster 1977.

THE EVOLUTION OF TRANSPORT POLICY IN OXFORD

John M. Bailey

INTRODUCTION

Since the late 1940's the issue of inner relief roads had dominated transport planning in Oxford. Much of the early controversy centred around the design and routing of the roads, rather than the more fundamental issue of their justification. In the face of growing traffic congestion the latter was apparently self-evident. But while the controversy raged during the 1950's and 1960's, the continued growth in traffic levels eventually forced the City Council into action. Parking control and pedestrianisation became the main elements in the 'Interim Traffic Management Policy' and were well advanced by 1973 when the relief road plans were officially abandoned.

The concept of traffic restraint had first appeared in the early 1960's. Following the ideas of Buchanan (1), traffic restraint within the historical centre of Oxford was an essential feature of the relief roads policy both to improve environmental standards and to direct traffic onto the new roads. However, concern began to grow over the social implications of the roads. The likely degenerating effects of large urban motorways on established communities eventually led to their abandonment by the City Council. But at the same time a new hope for the future of public transport had been sparked off by events such as the oil crisis. Measures of traffic restraint, coupled with measures to improve the effectiveness of public transport, became the hallmark of Oxford's transport policies during the middle 1970's. These included park and ride express buses and specially reserved bus lanes on the main radial roads.

Following local government re-organisation in 1974 the responsibility for transport passed to Oxfordshire County Council. At first it appeared that the policy of restraint (albeit with some change of emphasis from peak-hour to off-peak restraint) was likely to continue and indeed be extended. Proposals included further street closures and the removal of buses from existing pedestrian areas. Growing fears by city centre traders concerning the continual decrease in accessibility (and therefore attractiveness) of the shopping centre as a result of restraint, were crystallised in these proposals. Opposition began to spread within the County Council, eventually leading to a major policy reversal in June 1975. This significant change was assisted by financial pressures on the public transport aspect of the existing policy. A rapid increase in the level of demand for bus revenue support led to an equally rapid reaction from the County Council. In 1976 subsidies to the City of Oxford Motor Services were less than a quarter of the 1975 levels. Maximum freedom of movement thus became the main objective in transport policy. This meant that restraint could only be justified where a serious deterioration in environmental standards warranted it. The development of relief roads (and multi-storey car parks on a much reduced scale) reappeared in the transport plans. However, it would be inaccurate to say that policy had gone full circle since the early 1960's. The need to maintain adequate public transport, and indeed to encourage its use, was recognised; although it was less clear how this was to be achieved.

In practice, traffic restraint is still very much the cornerstone of transport policy in Oxford, but even this has failed to alleviate a rapid growth in traffic over the past two years coupled with a gradual decline in bus services.

The present paper aims to explore the changing themes that have influenced transport policy in Oxford over recent years, the effects of long-term plans on policy implementation and to provide a detailed and practical account of what has actually happened. The paper is divided into four main sections as follows:

1. The Roads Controversy: dealing with the plans, inquiries and policies of the post-war years up to 1973;

2. The Balance Transport Policy (BTP): dealing with the development of the BTP and its implementation;

3. An Assessment of the BTP: examining the effects of the BTP and some of the issues raised;

4. County Council Transport Policy: this section outlines the current policy in relation to past experience with the BTP and future developments.

1. THE ROADS CONTROVERSY

The traditional problem of through traffic in Oxford had in fact been largely overcome by the late 1940's. A by-pass for the main London-South Wales road (A40) was completed as early as the 1930's and this has subsequently been extended to form an unbroken outer ring road. A survey carried out by the City Council in 1949 (2) revealed that only 15 per cent of traffic entering the central area was, in fact, through traffic (i.e. both origin and destination outside the city); 25 per cent was moving between different parts of the city, and 60 per cent had business in the centre. It was thus the 85 per cent of 'local' traffic that was causing most of the problems at that time.

The rivers Cherwell and Thames effectively bisect the city, with most of the population living east of the river, and the city centre to the west (see Figure 1.). Until 1962 only one bridge (Magdalen Bridge at the eastern end of High Street) crossed this axis within the city, forcing a large proportion of inter-urban traffic to travel via the city centre. In 1962 the situation was eased with the opening of Donnington Bridge to the south. Subsequently (in 1971) a northern link road was also opened at Marston Ferry. But these developments still left the bulk of the traffic problem unsolved. The 60% of traffic 'legitimately' entering the central area had in some way to be accommodated, controlled and/or reduced in order to restore and preserve the unique character of Oxford's historic centre. During the 1950's, inner relief roads seemed to be the only answer, but the Council (in view of the likely environmental damage these roads would cause) remained uncommitted. The principal strategy of the City Council at that time was to '...pursue a vigorous policy of de-centralisation' (3). The Council hoped for a considerable shift of housing, shopping and business activities to the Cowley area, but subsequent re-development of the St. Ebbes area of the city centre was also planned to include commercial activities and high density housing. Inevitably the relief roads controversy continued to rage in various council meetings and ad hoc inquiries, until the Council eventually came forward with firm proposals in 1964. By then much of the development in Cowley was complete and firm proposals for city centre re-development had also been put forward. But traffic flows continued to increase.

1.1 The Meadow Road

Amendment Number One to the City Development Plan (4) (produced in 1964) set out the City Council's proposals for a relief road. The road (and indeed the whole structure of the plan) was very much an embodiment of the then contemporary views of Buchanan (5). The relief road was seen as a 'primary distributor' giving easy access to a number of proposed multi-storey car parks on the fringe of the city centre. However the report also

Figure 1. Sketch Map of Oxford

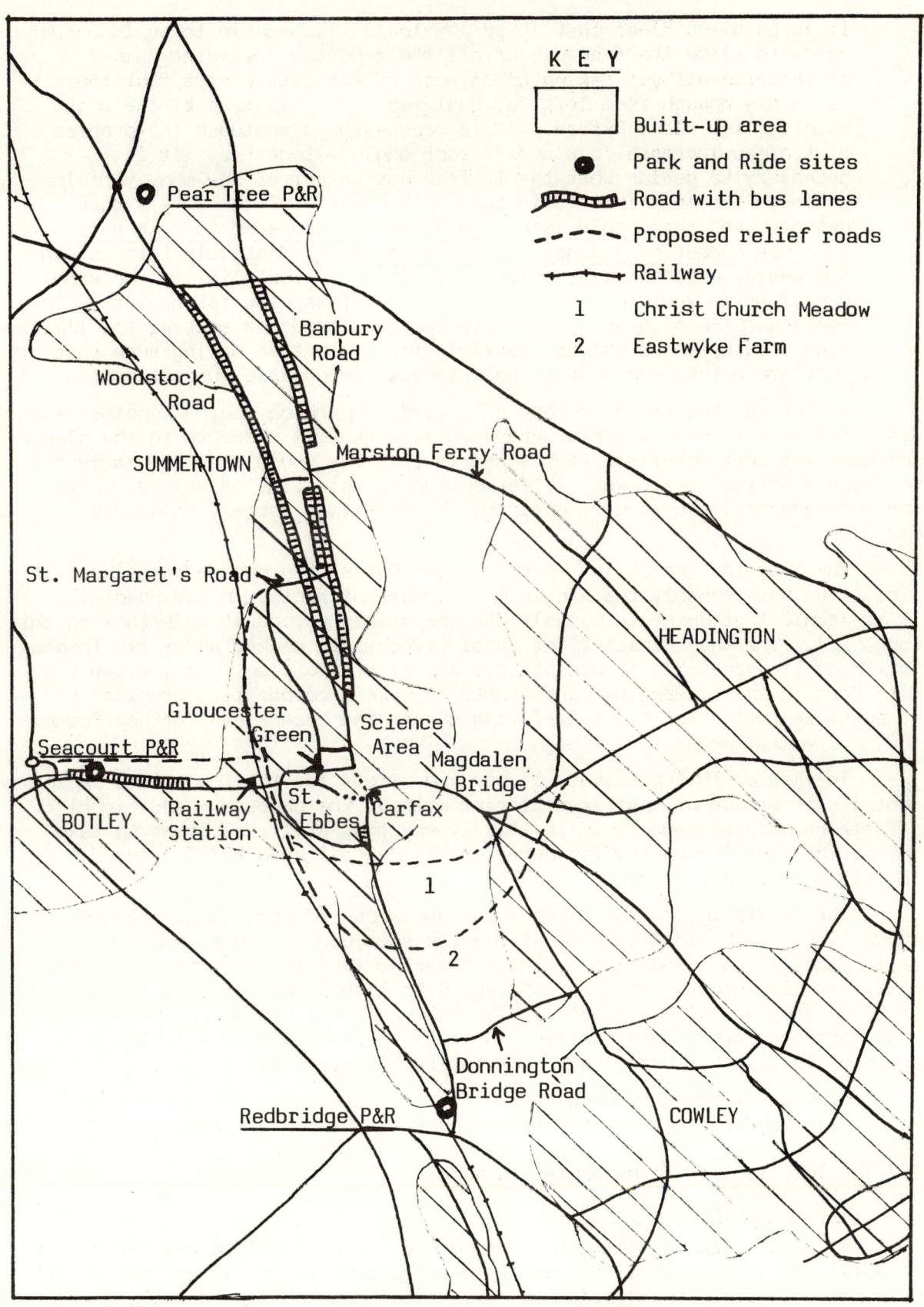

Approximate Scale: 1:50,000

emphasised the need for traffic restraint, a much less publicised aspect of the Buchanan thesis:

> 'It is becoming clear that it is physically impossible to build enough roads to allow the free use of all the expected increased number of vehicles without taking up so much of the City Centre that there is hardly enough room left for business. This is true of the whole country, let alone Oxford. It is necessary to approach the problem of traffic increase from a different angle altogether. It is necessary to decide what the traffic has to carry, how many vehicle journeys can be tolerated in the various parts of the City's road network, and then apply such regulation as is needed to make sure that this number of journeys is not exceeded. Admittedly this is, in one sense, a restrictive policy, but it is as essential to the sane use of motor vehicles as the restriction of keeping to the left. The continued functioning of the City Centre depends on setting the limits high enough, so as not to restrict trade, and then making sure that they are not exceeded so as not to cause impossible congestion.'(6)

Strict control of the number of on-street parking spaces together with limited access to many streets were seen as essential elements in the plan. The hope was that motorists restrained in this way would use the new multi-storey car parks; there was little mention at this time of any switch to public transport. Buses were envisaged as operating largely unchanged services.

The plan for the relief road to cross Christ Church Meadow (albeit in a cutting) was probably the single most important factor in its downfall. It is ironic that Buchanan himself was one of the strongest objectors on this count (7). The then Minister for Local Government, backed up by his Inspector, found it impossible to accept this aspect of the plan. He invited the City Council to '...appoint consultants to make a comparative examination of possible routes for the relief road across the Meadow and further South.' (8).

In view of this decision, it was impossible for the Council to implement its programme of traffic restraint without the necessary additional off-street parking capacity. In 1966 it was thus still reluctant to take any action even though traffic entering the central area had increased by 38% since 1957 (9).

The growth in traffic appears to have occurred largely as a result of population growth and dispersal within the surrounding county coupled with an increase in car ownership. Over the period 1951 to 1971, the population of Oxford City grew by only 10.25% (98684 to 108840) compared to a rise of 53.8% in the rest of the county (10). The number of car owning households also increased disproportionately. Over the period 1966 to 1971 this amounted to 2.3% for Oxford and 6.8% for the County (11).

Eventually the City Council was forced to adopt an 'Interim Traffic Management Scheme' prior to the full report of the consultants.

1.2 The Interim Traffic Management Scheme

1.2.1 On-Street Parking

A 'disc' parking scheme for the central area of Oxford was introduced in April 1970. A parking disc had to be displayed in the windscreen of all cars parking within the designated 'disc zone' between the hours of 08.30 and 18.30 Monday to Saturday. This indicated the motorist's time of arrival, from which he was allowed to park for up to a maximum of 2 hours.

A major feature of the scheme was that it envisaged a loss of 795 spaces within the designated zone (396 long term and 399 short term) (12). Although significantly short of the reduction of 1400 spaces proposed in 1964 (13), it clearly represented a strong discouragement to long-term commuter parking. Moreover, a further 213 short-term 'disc spaces' were planned with the conversion of two existing off-street car parks into the disc zone scheme.

The 'Disc Zone' was contained within a larger 'Controlled Zone' where all on-street parking was limited to designated spaces, with various limits on parking duration, up to a maximum of 24 hours. Peak hour loading and unloading restrictions also applied within the zones.

1.2.2. Off-street Parking

The increase in off-street parking capacity proposed in the 1964 plan (13) was not possible in the absence of the relief roads and their corresponding multi-storey car parks. However, in 1973 the total off-street parking capacity was 1768 spaces (14) compared to about 1000 in 1964 (15). Much of this increase in capacity had been achieved as a result of city centre redevelopment in the St. Ebbes area. Extensive demolition of older residential property to make way for shopping, commercial, recreational activities and some higher density modern housing had resulted in large areas of open land which were admirably suited to 'temporary' car parks. However, this concentration of car parks in St. Ebbes south-west of the city centre posed problems of access from the north and east (where the majority of the population are located). The most practicable route to the car parks for many motorists was via the city centre itself. In the 1964 Plan, a car park of 850 spaces (16) had been proposed at Gloucester Green, north-west of the city centre, in an attempt to alleviate the situation. However it attracted strong opposition on the grounds of poor access and extreme environmental damage.

Charging policy did not really become an effective tool in the City Council's control of parking until 1974, although it had been stated in 1964 that: 'charges....and length of stay allowed will be raised to suite the traffic situation as it develops.' (17) The majority of Oxford's central area car parks were subject to a 2-unit charging system based on 0-2 hours and a greater than 2 hours duration or a single fixed charge (see Table 1).

TABLE 1

Parking Charges at Central Area Car Parks since 1970

Duration of stay (hrs.)	Charge (pence)								
	1970	1971	1972	1973	1974	1975	1976	1977	1978
0-1	12½	15	15	15	10	20	15	15	15
1-2	12½	15	15	15	10	20	20	20	20
2-4	12½	15	15	15	20	30	40	40	40
4-6	12½	15	15	15	25	40	50	60	60
6	12½	15	15	15	40	50	60	80	80

The hopes of controlling private off-street spaces that had been expressed in the 1964 Plan (17) were soon shown to have been rather optimistic. The simple fact was (and still is) that no legislation exists for this and control via the planning legislation is very limited.

1.2.3. Traffic Management and Bus Priority

During the late 1960's and early 1970's the essence of traffic management policy was to enable the most efficient use of the available road-space
subject to environmental constraints. It was not seen as a means of traffic
restraint per se. One-way traffic schemes were a characteristic of the time,
but in Oxford a significant step was taken in 1970 with the closure of a
major city centre shopping street (Queen Street west of Carfax) to all
vehicles except buses, emergency vehicles and those gaining access. A new
link road through St. Ebbes was opened at about the same time to provide
an alternative route, but this did not become fully effective until the
other main shopping street (Cornmarket, north of Carfax) was closed in 1973.

It seems fair to say that at this time the effects of such policies
on public transport had not been widely appreciated. However, the policies
clearly recognised the need to maintain good access to the central area by
public transport. Significantly, Oxford's first bus lane (contra flow)
appeared in November 1969 as part of the St. Ebbes link-road scheme. This
enabled north-bound buses to avoid a circuitous one way system just south
of Carfax. It is evident from the 1964 Plan that the peaking problem in
bus operations had not been recognised, i.e. '...it is possible to imagine
a balance of convenience being struck where buses do a lot of the traffic
they are best suited for, such as the journey to work, and cars are used
for their best purposes, such as carrying a family and a heavy load of
shopping.' (18)

1.3 Relief Roads Revived

The relief roads issue swiftly became the focus of attention again with
the publication of the consultants' report in 1968 (19). The basic philosophy of the report was not significantly different from that of the 1964 Plan,
i.e. it favoured relief roads of urban motorway standard, providing access
to multi-storey car parks and backed up by traffic restraint in the city
centre. The report is however particularly notable for its depth of analysis.
Apart from an extensive land use and travel survey (including home interviews
and 1-day travel diaries with 1 in 8 households in the area), a detailed
environmental survey setting out 'acceptable' standards of traffic flows and
parking provision for each of Oxford's central area streets was carried out.
There was a very detailed analysis of the environmental effects of the
alternative relief roads. After this report there seemed little doubt that
if a relief road was to be built at all, then the Eastwyke Farm route (south
of Christ Church Meadow) was the most suitable (see Figure 1).

The report adopted an interesting 'new' line on the traffic restraint
issue, i.e. the possibility that it might result in a direct reduction in the
extent of travel by private car. However, the consultants made a rather
restrictive assumption: 'It is difficult to compare schemes that involve
varying degrees of restraint. In order to make such comparisons we have
assumed that total travel will remain constant and that travel diverted
from private transport will be carried by public transport. It is as well
to appreciate the limitations of such an assumption.' (20) Unfortunately
it appears that the consultants failed to take adequate note of their last
remark as the assumption underlies the traffic assignments in the report.

Although ostensibly recognising the need for a public transport plan
(16), in addition to relief roads and parking control, in practice the
report says little more about bus services than the 1964 Plan: i.e. the
analysis is confined to re-routing of services and the provision of limited
stop services.

The 'low capital investment' variant of the Eastwyke Farm route was accepted by the Department of the Environment in 1970 following a public inquiry (22). The relief roads were to be built as shown in Figure 1 and the city centre was to have total parking provision of 14,600 spaces (including private and residential spaces) by 1991. Multi-storey car parks of 2,500 and 1,500 spaces were planned at St. Ebbes and Gloucester Green respectively. Limitation on the number of on-street parking spaces, a reduction in the maximum permitted waiting time and restrictions on vehicular access to the city were among the main measures of traffic restraint suggested in the report, adding support to the City Council's Interim Traffic Management Policy.

1.4 Relief Roads Abandoned

Opposition to the relief roads grew rapidly during the early 1970's. Probably the most ardent protesters came from East Oxford, where the majority of the 174 houses and 19 business premises that would need to be demolished to make way for the road were located. The emphasis in the opposition had clearly changed considerably since 1966. The focus was no longer the need to preserve the 'unique' Christ Church Meadow, but to avoid the destruction of the East Oxford Community. The protesters of the 1960's had, to all intents and purposes, succeeded in their aim of stopping the Meadow Road. Some of the residents of East Oxford (and other social and political groups within the city) clearly saw the Eastwyck Farm route as a shifting of the burden from the rich to the poor; from the 'gown' (i.e. the University interests) to the 'town'; from those most able to articulate and finance their opposition to those least able. At the same time the restraint policy appeared to be gaining favour, together with the possibility of improved public transport and 'park and ride' as an alternative to massive central area car parks. The latter, especially the car park proposed at Gloucester Green had also been bitterly opposed since 1964.

In 1972, after previously accepting the consultants report and formerly approving this as Amendment No.2 to the City Development Plan (3), the City Council finally decided to abandon the relief roads and concentrate its transport policy on traffic restraint and improved public transport. The result of its recommendation was the publication in March 1973 of a report entitled 'A Balanced Transport Policy' (21).

2. THE BALANCED TRANSPORT POLICY

On paper, the Balanced Transport Policy Document looked very different from what had been seen in the previous plans; but in practice it was largely an extension of the ongoing policies already discussed. The significance of the report lay in its aims to co-ordinate these policies and assess their effects on a much wider frame of reference. The significance of public transport was recognised and dealt with more fully than in any previous City Council Plan.

Two basic themes ran throughout the report:

(i)   the desire for a more even balance of provision for
       the 'needs' of all travellers;

(ii)   an emphasis on the wider social as well as environmental
       aspects of transport policy.

The report concluded that the benefits to motorists of the proposed relief roads were likely to be small, given the extent of traffic restraint necessary, even if they were built. Apart from the social and environmental problems associated with the relief roads and the high capital costs involved in their construction, the report listed two other disadvantages which appear to have received much less attention in the past. These were:

(i) the constraints imposed on possible future transport strategies which are in turn dependent on future planning policy, land use and activity patterns;

(ii) the allied need to provide extensive parking structures on valuable city centre development sites.

The problem of traffic congestion did of course receive a lot of attention in the report. Although this was very much a problem of the morning and evening peaks, the report recognised that off-peak travel by car was growing and that policies to encourage the use of public transport at peak times were likely to worsen this trend. Moreover, excessive 'peaking' in public transport operations was likely to seriously threaten its financial viability. Therefore, while concentrating policies on peak hour traffic restraint, the report emphasised that the measures designed to increase the attractiveness of public transport should apply to both peak and off-peak services. The policies adopted clearly formed an integrated package, but for analytical purposes they can be separated as follows:

(i) traffic management; including bus, cycle and pedestrian priority measures;

(ii) control of parking and the development of 'park-and-ride';

(iii) improvements to the quality and attractiveness of public transport.

Subsequent developments have followed largely along the lines of the BTP and these will be covered where appropriate. However the change in political control after 1974 has resulted in a significant change in the underlying philosophy which we shall be discussing later, in section 4.

2.1 Traffic Management and Bus Priority

The policy of restricting access to the city centre and discouraging through traffic became fully effective in March 1974 following the introduction of a one way scheme in the University Science Area (east of the city centre, see Figure 1). This scheme was specifically designed so that through traffic would be subject to a very circuitous route. However, revision of the scheme in November 1975, largely as a result of local opposition to the high traffic flows on some internal roads, much reduced its effectiveness. A two way route was re-established through the area with much of the central core being subject to restricted access. This lead to a rapid growth in traffic using the route, although it may have also reflected a general trend to increasing traffic flows within the city as a whole (see Figure 2).

Better provision for both pedestrians and cyclists were important components of the BTP, as they had been in previous policies. Plans were put forward for a city-wide network of cycle routes. It was intended that these should utilize existing footpaths, parks and residential roads to avoid the heavily congested radial and link roads. Two such routes have been established in the south of the city, but opposition from landowners in the north has seriously restricted progress.

Apart from allowing buses to use particular streets that were otherwise subject to restrictions on access, the establishment of 'bus only lanes' on three of the main radial roads into the city was a significant measure of bus priority. These were primarily for 'inbound' buses (i.e. buses en route to the city centre) and operated from 0700 to 1900 hours daily. Extensive parking restrictions and the provision of 'peak-hour clearways' supplemented the bus lanes. Figure 1 shows their positions.

Figure 2

Average 24 hour Weekday Traffic Flows
(Monday to Friday excluding cyclists)

Note 1: Figures shown are the total 2 way flows
  2: Base lines of all graphs are at different flow levels

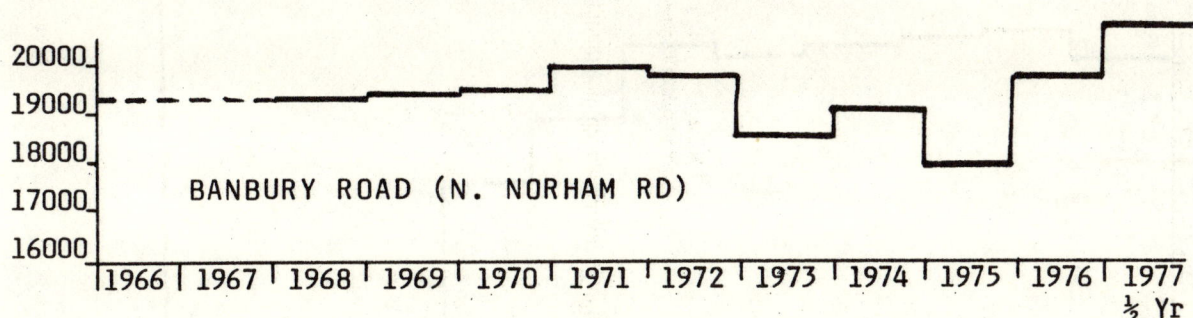

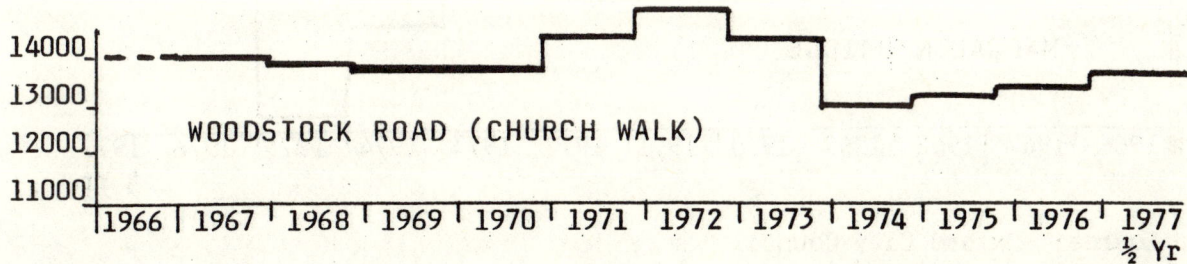

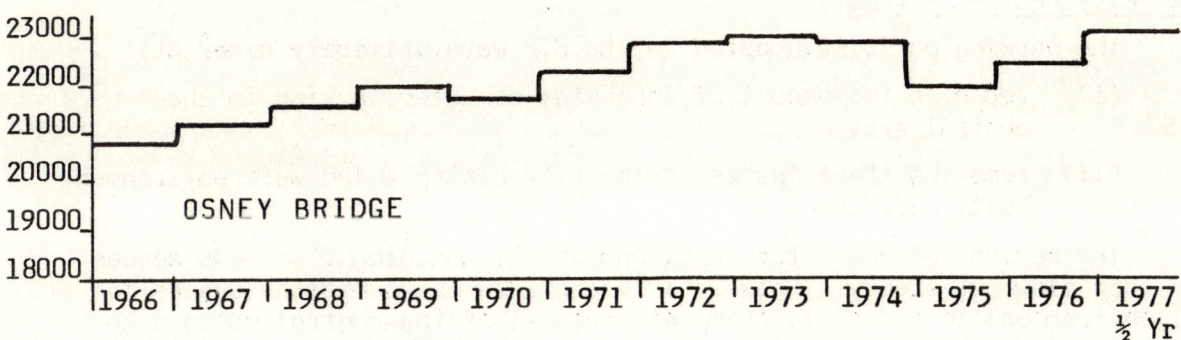

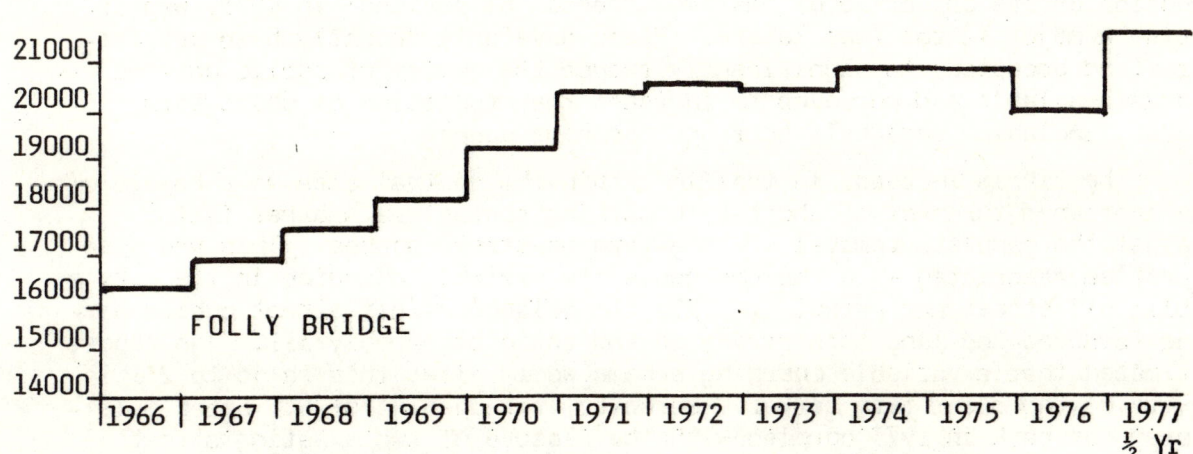

Figure 2 (continued)

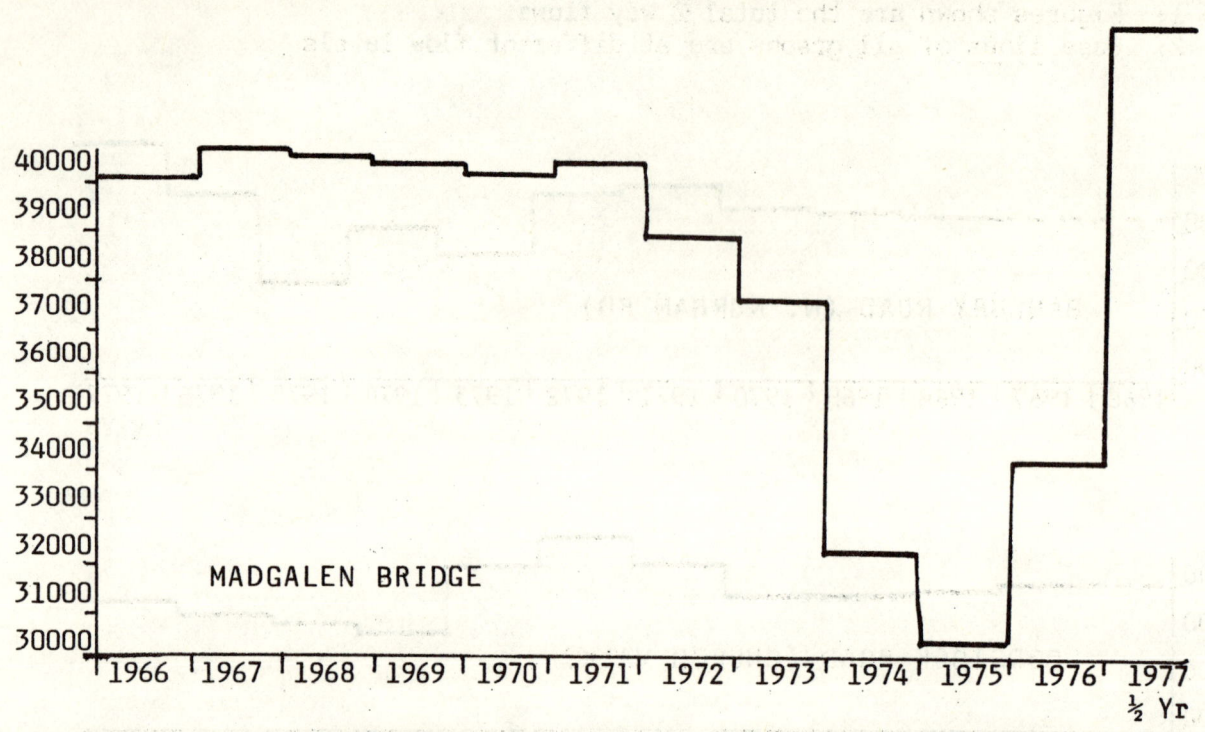

MADGALEN BRIDGE

Source: Oxford City Council

2.2 City Centre Parking

The parking policies adopted in the BTP were primarily aimed at:

(i)   reducing the amount of long-stay commuter parking in the
        central area;

(ii)   removing those spaces in the city centre which were environmen-
        tally undesirable.

The removal of short-term environmentally damaging disc zone spaces
has been slow but steady. Between 1975 and 1978 the number of spaces had
fallen from 643 to 501 (25). Complete removal of the controlled zone to
eliminate long-term spaces was suggested (26) but these proposals have met
with considerable opposition from the public and have generally been
politically unpopular. Opposition from the County Council following the
adoption of its objective of 'maximum freedom of parking' in 1975, was of
course a major factor (see later). Plans have only recently been put forward (and accepted) to significantly reduce the number of public parking
spaces available and moreover to increase the proportion of short-term
spaces, including some half hour and one hour spaces.

The likely increase in traffic within the central area as a result of
the increased turnover of short-term parking spaces was another factor
against the complete removal of long-term on-street spaces. This was also
a problem associated with the changeover to variable charging in the city's
public off-street car parks. In 1973 the balance of off-street public parking favoured the long-term parker in the ratio of roughly 3:1. The report
estimated that a variable charging scheme would alter this ratio to 2:1 in
favour of the short term parker. Moreover, the opening of St. Ebbes multi-
storey car park in 1973 coupled with the closure of two existing street

level car parks, represented a net addition of 514 spaces to the total off-street parking capacity within the city centre. The City Council was however aware that restricting parking to those able and/or willing to pay would create considerable opposition from the public. The establishment of park and ride (see later) was thus an essential element in the policy, in providing an alternative means of travel.

As with previous parking policies there seemed little scope for removing many of the 7,800 (27) private parking spaces within the city centre.

2.3 Park and Ride

There were two main objectives for park and ride:

(i)   to reduce traffic flows on the radial roads (28)

(ii)   to minimise the amount of land in the central area used for car parking, thus releasing valuable sites for re-development (29).

Since its opening in November 1973, the park and ride service has operated mainly on two principles:

(i)   car parking is provided free at car parks on the periphery of the city so that users pay a specified fare on the park and ride buses;

(ii)   buses are provided as a limited stop service originally operated under contract to the city council, but subsequently operated by the bus company as a stage service.

There were three P and R car parks in the city (see Figure 1); the northern and southern car parks were linked by a cross city bus service on a 12-minute frequency which operated Monday to Saturday (excluding evenings). The western car park was served entirely by the regular stopping buses at a frequency of 7-8 minutes. Return fares from the car parks varied from 25p to 30p (with a 5p reduction after 1500 hours) and accompanied children under 16 travelled free (see Table 2).

TABLE 2

Bus Fares on Park and Ride Buses, to City Centre

R = Redbridge,   S = Seacourt,   P = Pear Tree

		Charge (pence)						
	1973[1]	1974[1] R/S	1975[2] R/S	1976[2] R/S	1977[2,3] R/S	1977 P	1978[2,3] R	1978 S	1978 P
Single: adult	5	5	10	10	10	15	15	15	21
child	2	2	5	5	5	5	5	8	5
Return: adult	10	10	15	15	20	25	25	25	30
child	4	4	5	5	–	–	–	–	–
off-peak	–	–	–	–	15	20	20	–	25

[1]children up to 3 years travel free

[2]children up to 5 years travel free

[3]accompanied children over 5 and up to 16 travel free

2.4 Parking Control in the Suburbs

It was essential in achieving maximum use of P and R to avoid environmental deterioration in residential areas on the periphery of the centre, that adequate control of suburban parking was also achieved. The residential areas adjacent to the disc and controlled zones have comprehensive residents parking schemes, carefully controlling the number and time limit of non-residential on-street spaces and giving residents exclusive use of the remainder. Suburban off-street car parks have also been subject to a flat rate charge since 1971, currently at 15p, or a variable charging system set slightly lower than the charges for the city centre. An exception is the Botley Shopping Centre car park which lies about ½ a mile west of the Seacourt P and R site. This is outside the City boundary and is controlled by the Vale of the White Horse District Council. At present car parking here is free.

2.5 Public Transport

With congestion being seen as the main problem for public transport, the measures of traffic management and bus priority were regarded as most significant. However a number of supplementary policies designed to improve the attractiveness of public transport have also been implemented.

Improvements in bus services carried out by the bus company, in consultation with the City Council, since 1973 included:

(i) A simplified fare structure (5p units) to allow fast boarding times and an increase in the maximum age at which a child can travel free (from 3 to 5 years). (Note: the 5p unit fare structure was abandoned after a fares increase in January 1977).

(ii) The introduction of off-peak shoppers' return tickets and multi-trip tickets giving unlimited travel within the city for a day ('City Clearway') or one, two or four weeks ('City Master').

(iii) The provision of new bus stop signs (those in the centre showing service numbers), additional bus shelters and standardised destination displays on vehicles.

(iv) Increased evening frequency (compared to 1970-1973 period) from 30 to 15 minutes on the important Headington-Summertown (via city centre) service in June 1975).

(v) Increased frequency on Botley and Iffley Roads (from 10 to 7½ minutes) in July 1976 and additional services to the Railway Station.

(vi) The introduction of limited stop services between Bicester and Oxford, Witney and Oxford, and Abingdon and Oxford; these being primarily for peak users, but in the case of the Abingdon service, operating a half-hourly frequency during the day since July 1976.

3. AN ASSESSMENT OF THE BTP

The Balanced Transport Policy clearly represented the first major attempt at implementing transport policy since the war. The aim of this section is therefore to assess what the practical effects have been. It is, however, important to remember that the BTP is an integrated package and although surveys have been conducted on particular components the causes and effects go beyond the particular policy under consideration (e.g. Park and Ride). The problem of assessment is aggravated by a general lack of 'before' data.

3.1 Traffic Flows and Environmental Improvements

Automatic traffic counts taken by the City Council on each of the main radial roads showed a marked decline in the amount of traffic entering the central area over the period 1971-75 (see Figure 2). This was of the order of 11 per cent. The number of serious and fatal accidents had also declined over the period 1971-73 (30). City Centre street closures, parking controls, improved traffic management measures and better pedestrian crossing facilities are probably the main contributory factors here. However, since 1975 the trend has been reversed. Between February 1975 and February 1978 comparable traffic flows increased by an average of almost 10 per cent (see Figure 2). The effective re-opening of the science area to through traffic in 1975 was likely to have been a major cause of this. But growth has not been confined to the radials affected by this. Perhaps it reflects a gradual acceptance of, or adaptation on the part of motorists, to the traffic restraint policy.

Whether the city centre environment has improved is, of course, a highly subjective judgement. However 2-way traffic flows in Cornmarket (limited to buses, ambulances and taxis) amounted to only about 1000 vehicles (60 per cent of which are buses) for the period 8 am to 6 pm (31). Accidents have been more or less eliminated in these streets and pedestrian flows appear to have increased near the Queen Street end. Pedestrian flows in Queen Street itself have increased appreciably (32). Many other city centre streets with restricted access and parking, can probably be said to have a substantially improved invironmental quality.

3.2 Evidence of the Bus Lane Surveys

Surveys of travellers on two of the main bus lane routes were carried out in November 1974 (car users and bus users) and February 1975 (cyclists), to investigate the effects of the bus lanes (33). Bearing in mind the problems already mentioned, it is useful to summarise some of the results.

A total of 1436 questionnaires were returned in the car users survey representing a response rate of 40%. Less than a third of respondents considered that their own travel by car had been affected at all. The only measured characteristic amongst car users that bore any relationship to impacts upon their own travel, for better or worse, was the nature of the most probable alternative mode; drivers who might 'otherwise' cycle felt benefitted, those who would walk, dis-benefitted. Twenty-one per cent of all reported impacts concerned benefits. Of these, 19% were gained from the perceived improvements to non-car modes, 63% were outright reports that car use was now more attractive than before (principally due to 'smoother' driving conditions), and only 9% of benefits derived from the undertaking of trips apparently being generated and not transferred. The nature of perceived dis-benefits to car use fell into categories with the following decreasing rank order of apparent importance: Hazard increase, (Benefits of all types), Delays, Nuisances or Frustrations, Congestion and "Forced" Change in travel arrangements. The single most frequently reported impact was that of increased journey time by car. This could clearly also represent the effect of traffic management measures in the city centre.

The suggested benefits to cyclists were borne out by the survey of cycle users. A clear majority (65%) within a group consisting largely of 'captive' mode users benefitted from the scheme. The percentage of those disapproving of the scheme - mainly for reasons of hazards associated with it - was low, at 7%. It was suggested that cyclists using the lanes at peak hours, although predominantly in favour of the scheme as a group, were more likely to report disapproval than others.

In the bus users survey the response rate was much lower (24%), but the third bus lane road (Botley) was also included in the survey. About 6% of the respondents reported a transfer from car or cycle to bus. That an improvement in the bus service had been perceived by car users is clear from the car-users survey, but in many cases it seemed such benefits were insufficient to result in a change of mode. However, a further 15% of bus patrons responding reported making increased use of the service, but the effect on patronage is difficult to determine without a knowledge of the extent of increased use, (e.g. if use increased by an average of 10% then patronage would rise by about 1.5%) (34). Even a small percentage change can however result in a large absolute effect. The evidence from this survey clearly supports the view that bus service patronage has increased by a small amount.

3.3 The Effects on Public Transport

Continued integration of Oxford's City and County bus services since 1970 has made it impossible to obtain patronage figures for Oxford City separate to the rest of the City of Oxford Motor Services (COMS) network. Figure 3 therefore refers to the whole network. The increase in 1974/5 does not appear to have been maintained, although patronage figures based on ticket counts fail to take full account of the use of multi-trip tickets and the free travel concession to children under 5, they may therefore be an understatement.

Figures on modal split are difficult to obtain other than those given in the Central Area Study for 1966 (35). In that year 38.4 per cent of trips to the central area were by bus. In 1974 the City Centre Activities Survey put the figure at 40 per cent for shoppers and workers (36). In view of the evidence we already have of both declining bus patronage and decreasing traffic flows, if the modal split going to bus has increased then it must have been due to a greater relative decline in the number of trips by car. In very broad terms it seems fair to conclude on this evidence that modal split has not changed significantly since 1966.

The bus lanes have certainly brought some savings in bus journey times (37) as has the reduction in congestion resulting from the moves towards greater pedestrianisation. However, reliability of services does not appear to have consistently improved, if we use miles lost as a proxy measure (see Figure 4), although miles lost is still only about 1 per cent of total mileage. Problems of vehicle failures are of course common to bus operators throughout the country, and beyond the control of individual operators. These problems have been exacerbated by recent shortages of both new vehicles and spare parts. Staff shortages have been another common problem; but COMS would argue that measures adopted by the City Council to improve public transport have resulted in improved staff morale. The root of the problem appears to have been delays in the introduction of revised services (notably in 1976 and 1978), given that the requisite reductions in staffing levels have gone ahead as planned, to minimise costs. The 'other' category in Fig. 4 corresponds largely to congestion. This appears to have been on an increasing trend since 1975. Moreover taking miles lost as a measure of the effects of congestion is likely to understate its true importance, since only extreme congestion, when buses are turned short of their destinations, is recorded. The effect on lost time is likely to be much higher. Surveys of lost time were carried out by the company as part of its Market Analysis Project and particular problem areas identified (38).

Fears of 'overpeaking' as a result of the BTP (i.e. a considerable increase in public transport demand at the peaks when the costs of operation are highest) appear to have been unfounded, simply because off-peak and peak schedules are not vastly different. However, bus company costs have been rising in real terms over the period both as a result of wage increases and

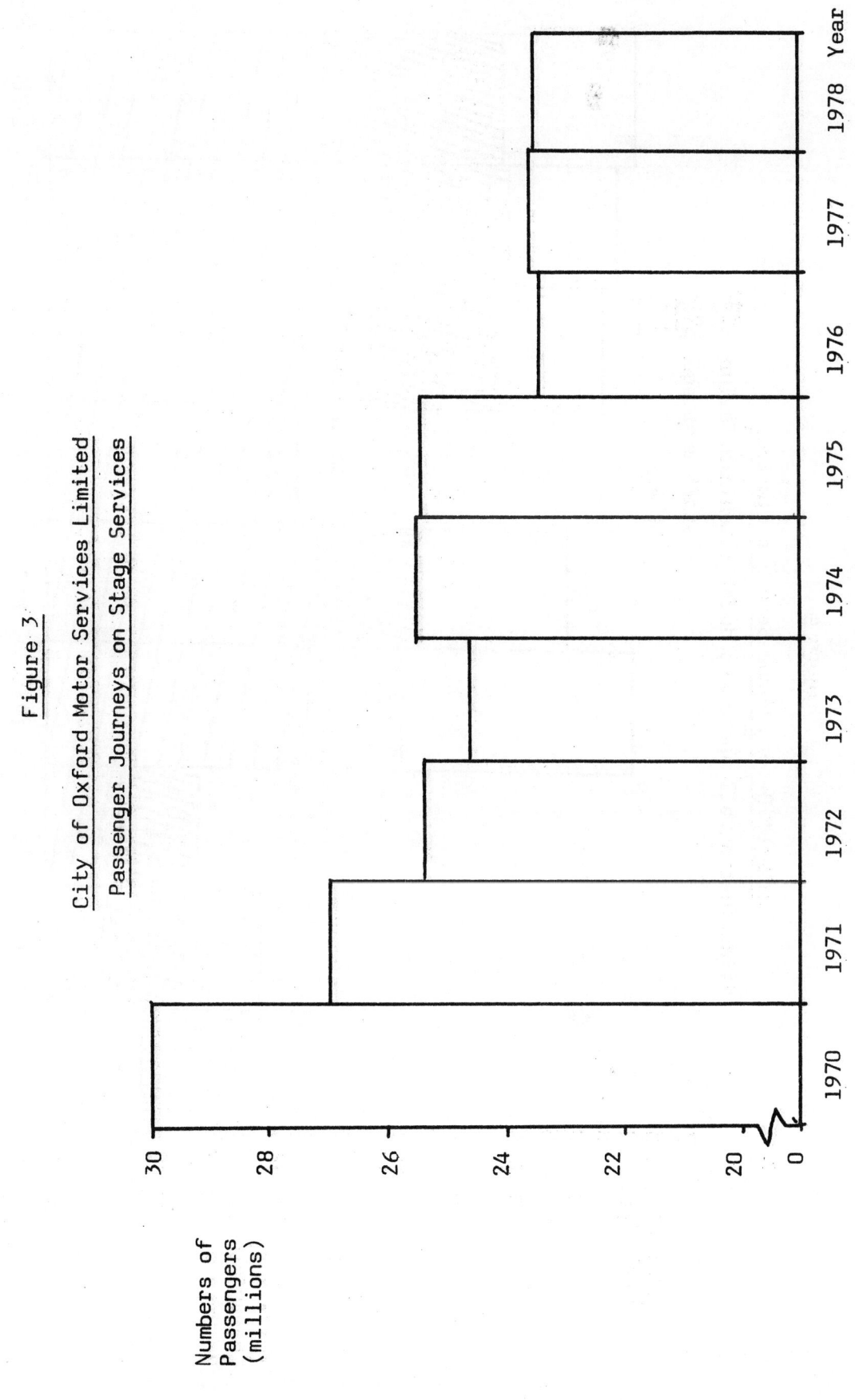

Figure 3

City of Oxford Motor Services Limited

Passenger Journeys on Stage Services

Numbers of
Passengers
(millions)

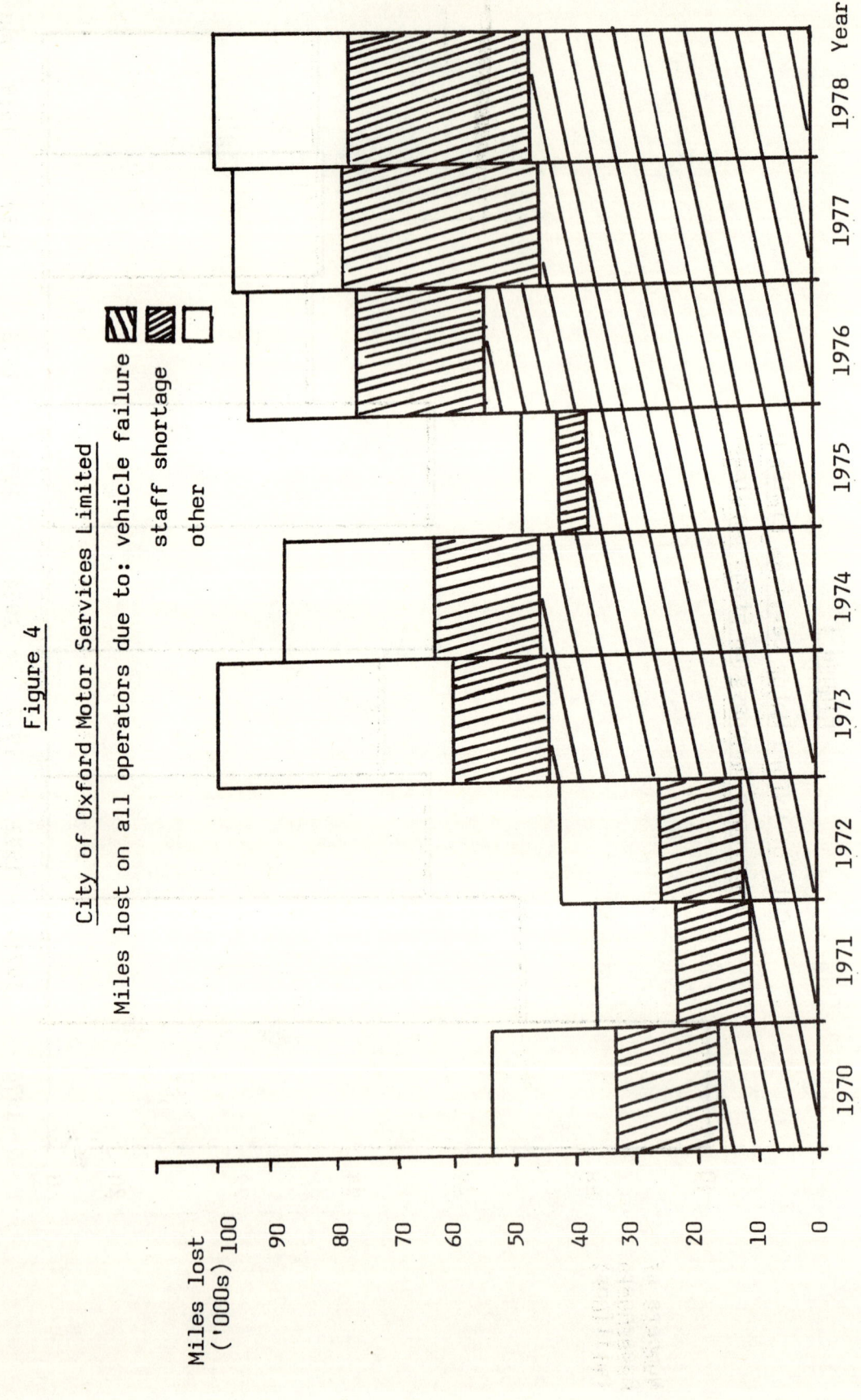

Figure 4

City of Oxford Motor Services Limited

Miles lost on all operators due to: vehicle failure

staff shortage

other

Source: Data supplied by the company

112

rising costs of vehicles. Inevitably fares have also risen in real terms
and this has probably outweighed some of the favourable effects of the
BTP. An index of average revenue per passenger together with a separate
index showing average parking charge per car is given in Figure 5. It is
important to stress that the revenue index will also include the effects of
changing journey length, that the two indices are not comparable in
absolute terms due to the difference in base and that the availability of
free off-street parking spaces is ignored. The two indices are consistent
from 1974 to 1976 and then diverge again. Clearly parking charges are still
relatively low for a family (see Table 1) whereas the fare for a typical trip
within the city of about 3 miles rose from 5p in 1970 to 21p in 1978 and
23p in 1979.

3.4 The Problem of Parking Control

Nature of Demand

In Oxford the demand for parking spaces has consistently shown a marked
difference between weekdays and Saturdays. The latter tends to cater
primarily for shoppers and shows a peak in the early afternoon (39). This
has changed little as a result of the BTP; but there has been an appreciable
change in the Monday to Friday parking pattern.

Table 3 shows parking duration for 1972, 1976 and 1978 in central area
off-street car parks. There has clearly been a shift from long-term to short-
term parking over the period of the BTP with little change subsequently.
This obviously reflects the change to a variable charging system designed
to discourage long-term parkers. There does not appear to have been a
marked increase in the utilization of spaces as may have been expected as
a result of the BTP. But Table 3 does show a general increase in utilization
recently which perhaps lends further support to the idea of motorists coming
to accept the policies and being prepared to pay (or perhaps it reflects the
declining cost of parking in real terms over the past 2 years). It is also
worth remembering that the capacity of public off-street car parks in central
Oxford increased from 1768 spaces in 1972 to 2282 in 1976.

TABLE 3

Parking Duration at City Centre Car Parks

Sample weekday (not Saturday): (per cent)

Duration of stay (hrs)	Oct 1972	Jan 1976	Feb 1978
0 - 1	16	24	21
1 - 2	18	33	27
2 - 4	14	32	26
4 - 6	10	8	9
6	42	3	17
	100	100	100

Utilization
Average turnover
per available space   2.16[1]   1.91[2]   2.05[2]

[1] 12 hour sample period   [2] 10 hour sample period

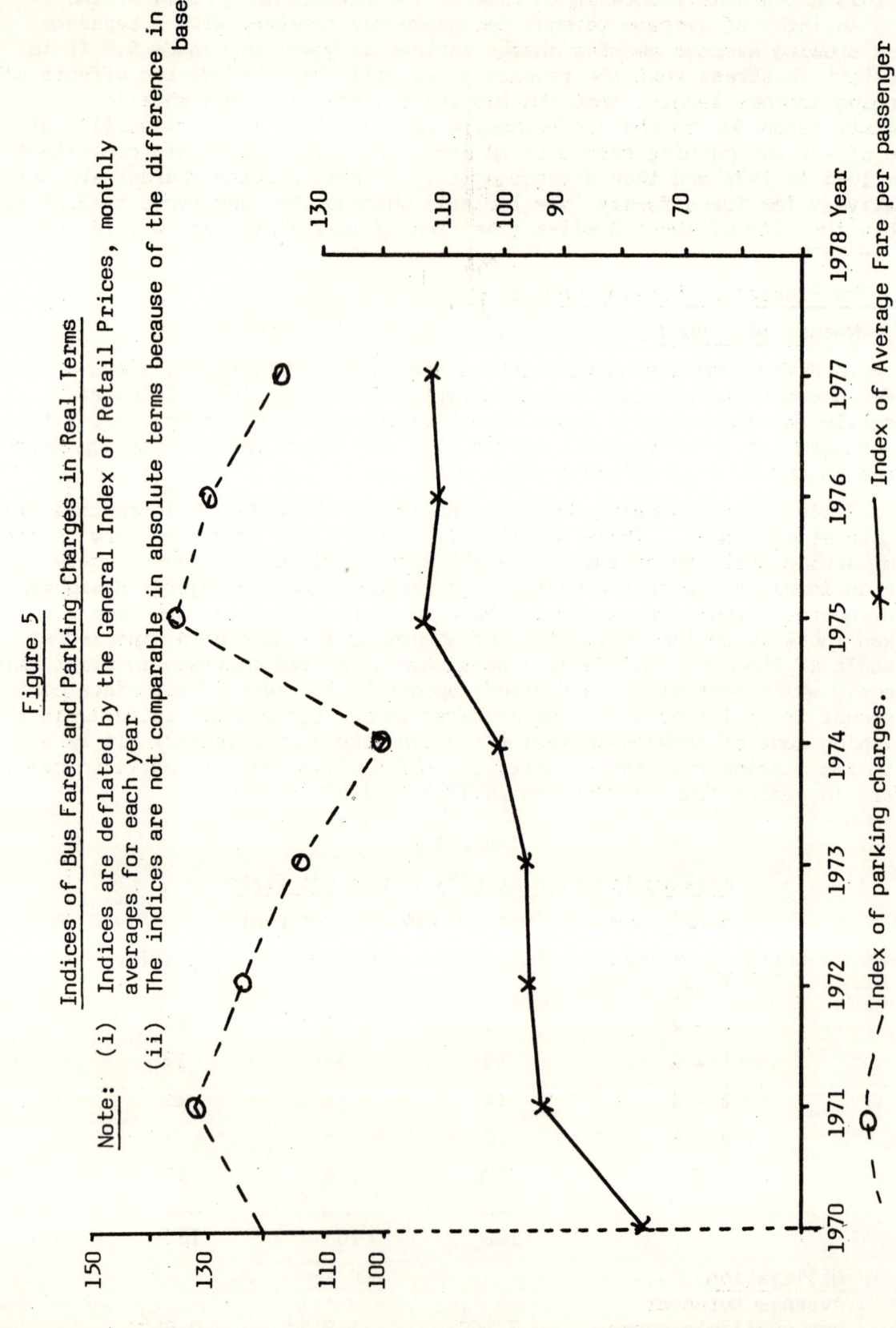

Figure 5

Indices of Bus Fares and Parking Charges in Real Terms

Note: (i) Indices are deflated by the General Index of Retail Prices, monthly
averages for each year

(ii) The indices are not comparable in absolute terms because of the difference in
base.

— — — Index of parking charges.

———— Index of Average Fare per passenger

Park and Ride has certainly attracted some of the longer-term parkers, as evidenced by the percentage of cars parked for longer than 6 hours (40). The extensive surveys that were carried out into the Park and Ride scheme for both the TSU and the City Council, give considerable insight into the nature of demand for parking in Oxford. Surveys of both users and non-users (i.e. motorists travelling past the P and R car parks towards the city centre, as potential users) were carried out.

In a survey carried out on a Tuesday, at Seacourt P and R car park, it was found that the majority of users would have previously parked in a public off-street space (44%) or on-street space (33%), whereas the majority of non-users (56% parked in private spaces, and some on street (24%). Eighty per cent of the non-users incurred no parking charge (41). Forty-nine per cent of users claimed that the difficulty of parking in the city centre was an important reason for using P and R, together with another 23% who stressed its low cost (42). Although 23% of non-users claimed the alternative free parking in the city was an important reason for their non-use and 26% emphasised the inconvenience of P and R, a further 50% said they were effectively constrained to use of the car because of its importance for other trips during the day (mainly business) (43). In both cases the majority of respondents were travelling to work (64% users, 70% non-users). It may be that shoppers were under-represented in that their use of the service is less frequent and the incentive for a positive response is less pressing.

Not surprisingly, the evidence would suggest city centre parking to be the first choice for many motorists and use of park and ride is conditioned by this. The considerable price disincentive for long-term city centre parkers and the decreasing availibility of long-term on-street spaces has certainly forced some workers to use P and R, except for the lucky ones with their own free private space. Preliminary evidence from household surveys conducted by TSU shows that there has been a considerable growth in the use of private off-street spaces (44). The main disincentive to the use of P and R (especially for shoppers) seems to be the prospect of gaining a free on-street space in the city centre. Motorists who might otherwise have used P and R from the outset are thus encouraged to travel to the city centre and often spend considerable time obtaining a space (45).

The Significance of Park and Ride

During the morning peak (0800 to 0900) about 15% of traffic on Abingdon Road and 9% on Botley Road was transferred to Park and Ride (46); which is reasonably in line with what was expected in the original BTP report (47). Off-peak rates of interception were much lower. On Abingdon Road the average hourly rate (0900-1700) was about 3.3%. A total of about 270 cars were replaced by 12 buses during the morning peak (both sides combined) compared to 180 cars entering the city between 1000 and 1600 being replaced by 72 bus journeys. Thus, in the peak one bus replaced about 23 cars, compared to an average figure of 2½ for the off-peak. It is particularly important to consider the low rate of off-peak interception when one remembers that P and R buses used city centre streets which were primarily intended for pedestrian use, causing additional environmental disbenefits. On Saturdays the demand was of course much less and an average rate of interception throughout the day was about 1 bus for 8 cars.

Given the above figures, it is obvious that use of the special bus will display the same peaks and low off-peak loadings. However, it is interesting to note that of those P and R users surveyed on the Botley Road, 14% would have previously parked on the outskirts and used a regular bus, and 8% would have used a bus for the whole of their journey, representing a clear displacement from existing public transport. For those who parked in the suburbs, the detrimental effect on public transport was at least partly offset by a reduction in parking nuisance. Furthermore, when the buses were surveyed, it was found that 15% of users did not use the P and R car park at all; they had in fact walked to the P and R site or had been driven there by car('Kiss and Ride'). It is likely that most of the former group would have used conventional bus; but in the latter case it is impossible to tell whether they would previously have driven all the way to town, used a conventional bus, or perhaps not even made the journey at all. Such effects are very difficult to quantify, but must be borne in mind when assessing P and R. Certainly the potential for 'walk and ride' is much less at Pear Tree P and R car park due to its isolated position, and the problem of transferral from existing public transport has been eliminated, at least at Seacourt by the withdrawal of contract buses.

It thus seems that although there are benefits from P and R at peak times, its operation at off-peak times is far less significant. The latter has resulted largely as an offshoot of the peak service given its relatively low marginal costs. Certainly a peak only service imposes an additional time constraint on users. Existing peak demand is likely to include some users who travel at one of the peaks (morning or evening) but not at both. These people would clearly be discouraged by a peak only service. Although off-peak use of P and R is very low at the moment, if this could be appreciably increased, then the benefits, in terms of reduced traffic flows could be considerable. More direct routing and a new image for P and R buses (separate livery) coupled with more advertising may have gone some way to increasing patronage.

Financial Implications

The introduction of variable charges and their gradual increase since 1973 (see Table 1) was important not only as a policy strategy within the BTP, but to maintain a self financing parking policy in line with government policy. In January 1976 the City Council was anticipating a deficit of £140,000 (48) on car parking and park and ride. Increased charges since then (coupled with higher utilization mentioned earlier) has brought a surplus on central area car parks of about £17,000 in 1976/7 and £9,000 in 1977/8 (49).

Similar problems were experienced with Park and Ride bus services running a deficit of £40,768 in 1976/7 and £55,687 in 1977/8. Since the bus company has taken over operation of P and R the City has agreed to pay a much smaller sum in subsidy for additional services at Christmas (estimated) to be £9,800 for 1977/8) (50). The financing of park and ride and indeed public transport in general has been a major issue between City and County Councils since 1974. We shall be returning to this in the next section.

3.5 Accessibility and Traffic Restraint

The likely effect of greater off-peak car restraint in Oxford is complex. Many off-peak trips (e.g. for shopping) are relatively unconstrained with regard to location. Therefore, restraining such travel by car to central Oxford could just as likely result in a change of location (e.g. to some other town that is more accessible) as it could in a change to Park and Ride or existing bus services. Recent surveys have shown that access by car to a shopping facility is considered essential to many mothers with children (51). These arguments do not of course apply to work trips, where timing and location are only variable over a much longer period. The potential for success of car restraint in this respect is much higher, and indeed this has been shown in Oxford. However, encouraging a greater use of public transport at the peak, only accentuates its economic problem, if corresponding (or ideally even greater) increased use at the off-peak is not also achieved.

In Oxford the BTP has been much criticised, notably by the Chamber of Commerce, for the restriction it places on accessibility to the centre by car and the detrimental effects this is likely to have on trade. Little quantitative evidence has, however, been put forward to support these arguments. On the contrary, the City Council points to the bouyant demand for shopping space in the city and especially the heavy commitment by Marks and Spencer in the construction of a larger new department store (52). There can be little doubt that Oxford is growing as a shopping centre and that the population in the county as a whole is also growing (53). These effects may have outweighed any shift away from Oxford as a result of traffic restraint.

3.6 The Immediate Problems

The BTP had its roots in policies that were designed primarily to control the mounting traffic congestion in the City during the early 1970's; and there can be little doubt that it has achieved some appreciable success. Given this objective, the facts that the volume of traffic entering the central area is again on the increase, surely poses the most immediate problem. Moreover, in 1976 there were estimated to be over 13,500 parking spaces in the city centre (54), which is not far short of the 14,600 accepted in the Development Plan for 1991 (55), on the assumption that the relief roads would have been completed. The majority of these are private spaces, so that the estimate is likely to be appreciably short of the true figure. In the short-term it thus seems essential to achieve some reduction in parking provision and inevitably this will mean public spaces. In view of what has been said above a reduction in on-street spaces could favour both park and ride and off-street car parks. The average parking duration at many disc zone spaces is little more than an hour (56), so a reduction in permitted parking time (at present 2 hours) would have to be less than this if it is to be considered an effective alternative policy. As we have already mentioned this is in fact planned, together with a 'pay and display' charging system. Provision for a car park on the north of the city centre is also likely to reduce unnecessary travel to the St. Ebbes car parks, for traffic entering the city from the north. However, it would be unwise at the moment to increase the total off-street capacity, so that any new car parks should be offset by a reduction in spaces elsewhere.

4. COUNTY COUNCIL TRANSPORT POLICY

The main issues that have evolved during the BTP seem to have centred on the differential effects of peak and off-peak traffic restraint, particularly the consequences for public transport, and accessibility and commercial prosperity of the central area. They have been taken up by the County Council in its own approach to transport policy, resulting in a significant difference in emphasis (if not objectives) from that put forward by the City Council in the BTP.

4.1 Peak versus Off-Peak Restraint

The BTP was aimed mainly (but not exclusively) at achieving a reduction in commuting by car. Congestion off-peak was not considered so great as to warrant specific controls; although travel by bus at off-peak times was to be encouraged. The likely transfer from car to bus at peak times (as evidenced by the Park and Ride Service) was a major cause for concern to the County Council because of its likely adverse effects on public transport costs, although this does not appear to have been significant so far. The importance of minimising bus operating costs and maintaining services without subsidy had been strongly emphasised in the County Council's

Consultative document on Transport Policy (51). Moreover, peak restraint in many cases left the car available for off-peak travel by other members of the household when otherwise it would have been parked all day in the city centre. But the document re-iterated the need for traffic restraint to allow environmental improvements and to ensure the city centre did not decline as a result of uncontrolled congestion. The solution thus seemed to lie in concentrating restraint at off-peak times and allowing maximum use of the road capacity and car parks at peak times when, it was stated, environmental considerations were less important.

The measures suggested illustrated another significant change of emphasis in policy. Restraint was to be achieved by physical controls (i.e. road closures) and not limited to parking and traffic management. The street closures would of course apply only at off-peak times (10 am to 4 pm). It was however hoped to achieve a greater degree of pedestrianisation in the two main city centre shopping streets, by providing an alternative buses - and commercial vehicles - only route.

We have already seen that off-peak restraint is likely to cause as many problems in maintaining accessibility to the central area as it solves. These seem to have been overlooked in the Consultative Document, which foresaw a transfer from car to bus. In an article broadly supporting the County Council's approach, Heggie (58) recognised this oversight and suggested that peripheral car parks, possibly linked to Park and Ride services would be needed. He foresaw little hope of increasing the use of public transport off-peak, although there would obviously be cost advantages from a more even pattern of demand throughout the day. If the demand for public transport was to continue to decline, then on Heggie's view we should accept this and plan for a gradual reduction in supply.

An important objective in County policy (and indeed crucial to the BTP) has been that of achieving a more balanced provision of transport facilities for those without cars. The City Council had hoped that the public transport system would have been strengthened by at least some transfer by city residents from car to bus. The P and R car parks had been located on the outskirts of the city to provide facilities for those travelling from rural areas by car, i.e. those areas not already (adequately' served by public transport. Rising bus fares have probably been a major reason why public transport has not reached a greater degree of absolute importance. Given the above objective it is difficult to see how one can allow a major reduction in urban public transport. In rural areas cheaper, more unconventional schemes can be encouraged where existing services are inadequate or expensive (which the County Council are doing); but in urban areas such as Oxford the bus is likely to remain the major form of public transport. As yet the County Council have provided no real answers to the problem, although admittedly in Oxford it has probably not reached a sufficient degree of urgency.

4.2 The Structure Plan Transport Strategy

Shortly after the publication of the Consultative Document, the County Council, being faced with the immense problems of off-peak restraint and considerable opposition to the idea of restraint by physical restriction, abandoned the whole idea. This was a major political reversal, fundamental to the future development of transport policy in Oxford. The policy adopted was determined by the elected members of the Council and not the professional officers. The stated objective was 'maximum freedom of movement' subject to the four constraints:

(i)   an acceptable quality of environment;

(ii)   convenient conditions for those without cars;

(iii) limitations on expenditure;

(iv) maintaining the viability and prosperity of Central Oxford.

In the Structure Plan (59) the aim is to maximise freedom of movement 'and parking', emphasising the Council's desire not to restrict parking for other than financial or environmental reasons. Although the emphasis of policy had changed, the measures to be adopted still involved a large degree of traffic restraint. This was necessitated by the significance of the constraints.

The policies to be adopted included:

(i)   the retention and development of bus lanes and bus priority measures to encourage the use of public transport;

(ii)   to retain and develop Park and Ride services subject to careful monitoring of the benefits and costs;

(iii) to improve the city centre environment by excluding buses (where possible) from otherwise pedestrianised streets;

(iv)   to build two additional multi-storey car parks, at Gloucester Green and the Railway Station;

(v)   to retain the relief road lines as amended in 1970.

4.3 City Council Reaction

The relationship between County and City Councils has been somewhat strained since local government re-organisation in 1974. All traffic orders proposed by the City Council have to be submitted to the County for approval. This has meant that a considerable amount of City Council staff time and effort can be spent on preparing policies which subsequently fail to gain approval. Naturally this will occur to some extent as a result of the democratic process, but there seems little justification in subjecting all proposals to that process twice. With the advent of the County's transport strategy, the organisational strains have been worsened by a conflict on policy. The City Council have stated that: '...the greatest difficulty in implementing the Balanced Transport Policy has been the emergence of an alternative County Council policy in the 'new Oxfordshire'" (60). But as Munby emphasised in an article (61), the two Councils do not differ very much in their stated objectives. The difference comes in the degrees of emphasis given to the objectives and the constraints. Subsidy policy in general, and particularly for the Park and Ride Service is an example of such conflict.

In line with its aim of maximising freedom of movement, the County Council had adopted a so-called market approach to public transport co-ordination. The basic network of bus services is expected to run on a break-even basis. It is then up to the District Councils and local transport groups, which have been set up in rural areas, to consider these services and suggest improvements if necessary. The County Council will then consider these for financial support. However, it is the County Council's policy to minimise subsidies, and indeed it has set a cash limit of £150,000 for each of the next five years from 1979 (62). The Council envisages a gradual decline in the established NBC newtowk within the County, initially being replaced by smaller local operators with lower overheads and then by more specialist 'self-help' schemes at local level (e.g. car sharing and community members).   In Oxford City the stage bus network is likely to provide the mainstay of public transport for many years yet, but the City Council has been conscious of its gradual decline. At the moment the county is subsidising a service for hospital visitors, and may find it necessary to subsidise more services when the new John Radcliffe Hospital

119

is opened in 1979. The Park and Ride service was subsidised entirely from City Council rates until its takeover by the bus company. The city thought this to be unfair to the city rate payers as the service was intended mainly for people living outside Oxford. But the County Council refused to allocate any of its bus revenue support fund, even though money was available, on the grounds that park and ride at that time was not good value for money. It has now agreed to pay the estimated £9,500 for supplementing Park and Ride over the Christmas period.

Parking policy is another area of disagreement. The County's refusal to restrict parking capacities goes completely against the BTP approach, although there is some difference in objectives on this point. The county unlike the city do not see the need to reduce traffic on the main radial roads, arguing that "...those living there have either remained there or acquired properties there, knowing that the roads would be very heavily trafficked", (63). The County's plan to build additional multi-storey car parks, particularly the one at the Railway Station has met with opposition from the City in concordance with their opposition to the relief roads. It is difficult to see how such a car park can provide adequate access to the city centre without a shuttle bus for example. It is certainly not on the periphery.

The proposal to retain the relief road lines does of course strike right at the heart of the BTP. Although there is no chance of their being built in the foreseeable future due to financial constraints, they undoubtedly blight a considerable area within the city which is of high development potential.

Although the county have agreed to release land for housing development within the city subject to careful monitoring of the transport consequences and to allow an increase in the city centre shopping provision after 1981, the basic growth strategy accepted in the Structure Plan is in favour of the small county towns and not Oxford City. The City Council (64) have argued that more concentrated development (based on the Oxford area) is appropriate to encouraging use of public transport. The County however favour decentralisation coupled with its local transport schemes preferably unsubsidised. But clearly Oxford is going to remain an important regional centre, indeed it is somewhat ironic that the County Council's decentralisation policy actually allows for an increase in population of Oxford and its immediate area greater than would have occurred under its 'centralisation' strategy (65).

CONCLUSION

Transport policy in Oxford (as opposed to Transport planning) has been characterised by a pragmatic approach. The authorities have reacted to pressures resulting from increasing traffic levels, environmental deterioration, declining public transport, maintaining accessibility, and financial stringency; many of which are in conflict. In practice, policies have tended to be palliatives, when the underlying causes were changing land use patterns and population growth.

The latter were certainly recognised in the plans of the 1950's and 1960's, where inner relief roads and multi-storey car parks appeared to provide the answers. The social and environmental problems caused by such roads have been the subject of debate throughout the period, culminating in the early 1970's in a new hope for public transport as an alternative. Today it is recognised that such an alternative does not exist, but neither do we want vast urban motorways.

Irrespective of which structure plan policy alternative is accepted,
there seems little doubt that population in the Oxford Area and within the
market towns of the county, is likely to increase. Oxford is going to continue to grow as a commercial and (to a lesser extent) industrial centre.
The essential problems are (i) to ensure accessibility for both private and
public transport whilst maintaining the historical character of the city,
(ii) not only to face up to the inevitable decline of public transport as
the County Council have done, but to plan for appropriate levels and types
of future provision and to attempt to stem this decline if the alternatives
are less attractive.

There is clearly no answer, but there is scope for pursuing new policies.

NOTES

1. Ministry of Transport. Traffic in Towns (Buchanan Report), 1964.

2. City of Oxford. Development Plan, written analysis 1953, 15.

3. Ibid, 16.

4. City of Oxford Development Plan Amendment Number One, written analysis
    1964.

5. Note 1, op cit.

6. Note 4, op cit.

7. Buchanan, C.D., Evidence to the Oxford City Development Plan Inquiry,
    1965.

8. Hansard 26.1.2966.

9. Note 4, op cit and Scott, Wilson, Kirkpatrick and Partners, Oxford
    Central Area Study 1968.

10. Oxfordshire County Council, First Structure Plan for Oxfordshire, Report
    of Survey, 1977.

11. Ibid.

12. Oxford Times 18.11.1966.

13. Note 4, op cit, 170.

14. Oxford City Council. A Balanced Transport Policy, 1973,28.

15. Note 4, op cit, 169.

16. Ibid, 171.

17. Ibid, 170.

18. Ibid, 161.

19. Scott, Wilson, Kirkpatrick and Partners, Oxford Central Area Study 1968.

20. Ibid, 42.

21. Ibid, 6.

22. City of Oxford, Development Plan; Amendment Number Two, written
    Statement 1970.

23. Ibid.

24. Note 14, op cit.

25. Oxford City Council. Highways and Traffic Committee Minutes, June 1978.

26. Oxford City Council. A Balanced Transport Policy 1976.

27. Note 14, op cit, 23.

28. Ibid, 13.

29. Oxford City Council, Report on Central Area Parking and Park and Ride, Highways and Traffic Committee minutes, October 1976, 25.

30. Note 26, op cit.

31. Oxford City Council. Vehicular Use of Cornmarket Street and Queen Street. Report to Highways and Traffic Committee June 1977.

32. Ibid.

33. Papoulias D. and Dix M.C., Results of Surveys to Investigate the Nature and Impacts of Bus Lane Schemes in Oxford, Traffic Engineering and Control, Vol. 19, No.1, 1978.

34. Ibid.

35. Note 19, op cit.

36. Oxford City Council - Comments on the "Consultative Document on a County Transport Strategy" 1975.

37. Oxford City Council. Highways and Traffic Committee Minutes June 1978.

38. City of Oxford Motor Services Ltd., Market Analysis Project 1978. Unpublished Report.

39. Note 36, op cit.

40. Parking duration (per cent of cars parked) at Redbridge P and R car park, weekday February 1975: 0-1 hrs, 1%; 1-2 hrs, 6%; 2-4 hrs, 20%; 4-6 hrs, 14%; 6-8 hrs, 17%; 8 hrs, 43%. Source: Note 41, op cit, Table IV.

41. Papoulias, D. and Heggie, I.G., A Comparative Evaluation of Forecast and Use of Park and Ride in Oxford. Traffic Engineering and Control Vol. 17, No. 4 1976 Table IV.

42. Ibid, Table IV.

43. Ibid, Table VII.

44. Bailey, J.M., Traffic Restraint in Oxford. Preliminary report on analysis of household data. Unpublished.

45. Oxford City Council, A Balanced Transport Policy 1976, p.20 and Heggie, I.G., A Pilot Survey of Urban Travel Behaviour in Oxford, Transport Studies Unit Working Paper 21, 1976.

46. Heggie, I.G. and Papoulias D., Operational Performance of Park and Ride: Objectives and Achievements in Oxford, Transport Studies Unit Working Paper no.13 1976.

47. Note 14, op cit, 35.

48. Ibid, 29.

49. Oxford City Council, Highways and Traffic Committee, Financial Estimates, 1977/8 and 1978/9.

50. Ibid.

51. Heggie, I.G., A Pilot Survey of Urban Travel Behaviour in Oxford, Transport Studies Unit Working Paper 21, 1976.

52. Note 26 op cit.

53. Note 10, op cit.

54. Oxfordshire County Council. Transport Policies and Programme 1976.

55. Note 19, op cit.

56. Oxford City Council Surveys.

57. Oxfordshire County Council, Consultative Document on a County Transport Strategy 1975.

58. Heggie, I.G., The Decline and Fall of Public Transport, Surveyor 12.3. 12.3.1976.

59. Oxfordshire County Council, First Structure Plan for Oxfordshire 1976.

60. Note 26, op cit 21.

61. Oxford Mail, 19.9.1975.

62. Oxfordshire County Council, Draft Public Transport Plan 1979/84, p.10.

63. Ibid 59.

64. Ibid 26.

65. Note 59, op cit, Tables 4.1 and 4.2.

CONSERVATION AND THE OXFORD GREEN BELT

D.I. Scargill

In 1975, and fourteen years after the public enquiry was held, the Secretary of State for the Environment gave his formal approval to the outer boundary of the Oxford Green Belt. The inner boundary was not approved, although the hope was expressed that this inner portion of the Green Belt would continue to enjoy the same level of protection from development as before. The Secretary of State's decision may have been a concession to those who had been pressing for the Green Belt's formal recognition, but it is difficult to avoid the conclusion that, by making any kind of distinction between its inner and outer parts and notwithstanding his statement about protection, he was exposing the inner Green Belt to development pressures and to the demands of those who sought to change its boundary. Some would go further and see in the Minister's action a clear invitation to the local authorities concerned to propose changes in the inner boundary of the Green Belt in the course of preparing their local plans.

Discussions about a Green Belt for Oxford had taken place in the mid-'fifties and the boundaries were agreed by the local authorities in 1956. Plans were submitted to the Minister and from 1958 the Green Belt became operational in the sense that it was taken into account in planning decisions and was included in development plans. Three authorities were involved, the County Borough of Oxford and the Counties of Oxfordshire and Berkshire.

When it was defined, the inner boundary of the Green Belt followed fairly closely the limits of the built-up area of Oxford although a number of pieces of land where development was expected to take place were excluded from it. One such tract was that on which the Osney Mead industrial estate was subsequently built. Like that of the Green Belt, the administrative boundary of the City of Oxford also follows quite closely the edge of the built-up area; the two boundaries are not, however, coincident except over relatively short distances. Port Meadow constitutes the largest single portion of Green Belt within the boundary of the City; others coincide with the Thames and Cherwell valleys. These aside, there are only small patches of the Green Belt within the City boundary at Barton, Horspath and Osney (Fig.1). This administrative boundary of Oxford was not altered when, in 1974, the old County Borough became a District of the new County of Oxfordshire. The City District thus continues to be responsible for development control in those same portions of the Green Belt. Responsibility for day-to-day planning control in the remainder of the Oxford Green Belt rests with the other four District Councils which make up the new County. Three of them, in fact, share a common boundary with the City whereas the fourth, West Oxfordshire, comes within a single parish of the City limits. The significance of this division of responsibility for the protection of the Green Belt will be considered in more detail below.

THE ROLE OF THE GREEN BELT

In 1955 the then Minister of Housing and Local Government, Mr Duncan Sandys, issued a ministry circular (CMND 42/55) setting out the purposes of a Green Belt. These were:

(i)   to check the growth of a large built-up area,

(ii)   to prevent neighbouring towns merging,

(iii)   to preserve the special character of a town.

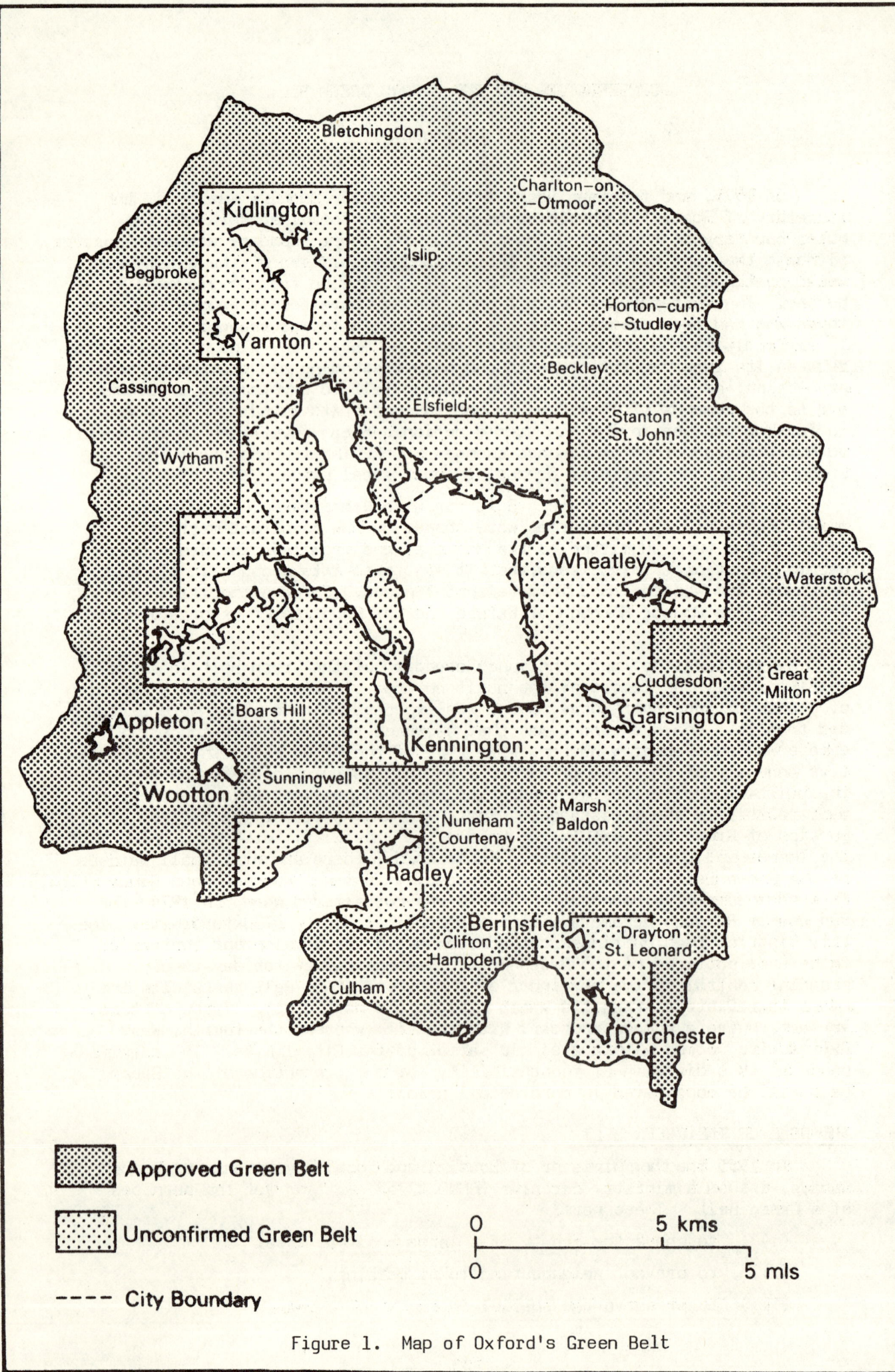

Figure 1. Map of Oxford's Green Belt

Legend:
- Approved Green Belt
- Unconfirmed Green Belt
- City Boundary

0 — 5 kms
0 — 5 mls

The same document also referred to forms of development that would be acceptable in a Green Belt. These were listed as: buildings for sport and recreation, hospitals and similar institutions standing in extensive grounds, cemeteries and mineral workings. The circular thus established guidelines, both as to the circumstances making it appropriate to designate a Green Belt, and also on land uses that could be regarded as permissible or non-permissible. Backed up by a number of later publications - Circulars 50/57, 38/60 and a Ministry Pamphlet, The Green Belts (1962) - it has been the standard reference on Green Belts in planning offices and at public enquiries ever since. What, one may then ask, were the purposes of designating a Green Belt for Oxford?

(i) To check growth

On the face of it, this objective seems more appropriate to a large city such as London than to Oxford. It must be recalled, however, that the City Council has had a policy aimed at restraining growth in employment in Oxford ever since 1946 and the Green Belt may be said to complement that policy.

In 1946 the Morris and Pressed Steel companies agreed to limit growth in the number of their employees to a combined total of 16,000. As a policy it has not been wholly successful; employment at Cowley has exceeded 25,000. Nevertheless some of the car industry's growth has been diverted elsewhere, for example to Pressed Steel's factory at Swindon. The City has also confined the use of its industrial estates at Horspath and Osney Mead to firms relocated from unsuitable sites in the inner city. Where failure has been more obvious has been in the authorities' unwillingness or inability to curb the growth of service industries in the City resulting in a continued expansion in the number of those employed (Table 1). Not until 1972 was a policy of restraint on the expansion of these forms of employment adopted. Meanwhile rapid growth had been taking place, particularly in administration, education and medical services. The University has imposed limits on the growth of its student population but there has been expansion elsewhere, for example at the Polytechnic and in many 'fringe' educational establishments such as language schools. Oxford's important role as a centre for medical care and research is likely to be enhanced when the new John Radcliffe hospital is in full use. The J.E.T. nuclear research project at Culham (below) has also brought European scientists to Oxford, competing in the housing market.

TABLE 1

Population and Employment in the City of Oxford

	Population Total	Numbers Employed
1951	98,684	62,430
1961	106,291	74,230
1971	108,805	81,300
1976	*	84,900

* The Structure Plan gives a population total for 'Oxford and nearby areas' of 137,500.

Employment growth has taken place in Oxford in spite of a thirty-year-old policy intended to curb growth. If some of the employees have to travel further to work than they might wish, it is the failure of the policy, not of the Green Belt - intended to assist the policy - that is to blame. Oxford, furthermore, has not been without its prophets who have pointed to the problems likely to follow from uncontrolled growth. As early as 1931 a Regional Planning Report on Oxfordshire (Mayo, Adshead and

127

Abercrombie) called for limits to growth within a 6-mile radius of the
City. Thomas Sharp went further in 1948, suggesting a policy aimed at
reducing the numbers then employed in Oxford and a ban on all forms of
growth within a radius of ten miles. It is interesting to speculate on
whether Sharp's objectives could have been achieved if advantage had been
taken at that time of the New Towns or Town Development Acts to establish
a satellite town for Oxford, just as satellite towns were built beyond
London's Green Belt. The choice of Bicester would have offered many
advantages: a good rail link with London and the Midlands, plenty of land
then used by the military, and a fast road to Oxford that could have been
made dual carriageway at low cost, enabling business contacts with Oxford
to be readily maintained. In 1979 the town would have had the prospect of
a motorway link with London. It is idle to dwell on lost opportunities,
but tempting nevertheless to see some justification for the idea in the
'country towns strategy' proposed in the County Structure Plan of 1976.

(ii) To prevent merging

The role of a Green Belt in preventing the merging of settlements is
most obvious in the case of a conurbation of closely associated towns like
that of West Yorkshire, or where a couple of towns have grown up in close
proximity, for example Gloucester and Cheltenham. Oxford's situation is
quite different: of the 'country towns' of the Oxford region only Abingdon
is close enough to justify separation by means of a Green Belt. Yet a
closer examination of the map reveals a number of inflated 'villages' on
the fringe of Oxford - Kennington, Kidlington, Yarnton and Horspath, for
example - which in post war years have absorbed large overspill populations from Oxford. Unlike such old village nuclei as Headington,
Cowley or Wolvercote, however, which were engulfed in the interwar expansion
of Oxford, these former villages have retained a measure of physical separation from the main built-up area of the City and a correspondingly greater
degree of identity. In most cases it is only a field or two which separates
them from Oxford, but these narrow strips of Green Belt afford a psychological
as much as a physical break and serve to maintain a sense of community within
them. In this way the role of a Green Belt in preventing nearby settlements
merging is fulfilled in a most valuable social manner. Even Sandford and
Old Marston, though tenuously linked by development to the City, are
sufficiently surrounded by Green Belt to feel that they are still distinct
villages. Both have fought to retain their separate local government status
and the contribution of the Green Belt to the preservation of their semi-
rural character is widely appreciated, witness Sandford's opposition to the
proposed superstore and Marston's to the relocation of the 'gypsy' camp.
Opposition in South Hinksey to the siting of the rubbish crusher provides
a similar example.

(iii) To preserve a town's special character

To Oxford's many visitors the special character of the City resides
in its unique assemblage of university and college buildings. Mellow
walls, elegant quadrangles, intricate stonework and beautiful gardens
are all a part of this international image of Oxford. To this image the
Green Belt may be thought to contribute little directly except, as in the
case of Christ Church Meadow, where it constitutes a kind of backcloth to
the range of college buildings beyond. Yet indirectly, by preventing this
historic core from being swamped by twentieth century sprawl, it has contributed immeasurably to the preservation of Oxford's special character.

Then there are the views from the surrounding hills. Oxford is in
a 'bowl', flanked to the east and west by hills which rise no more than a
hundred metres above the general level of the City but which are high

enough to afford those famous views of the 'dreaming spires'. Despite some early post war suburbanization, the hills have been kept remarkably free from development and, electricity transmission wires apart, the classic views from Boars Hill or Elsfield are not so very different from what they were in Matthew Arnold's time. The views are dramatic because, when the sun shines on its old buildings, the historic city appears to rise out of the surrounding meadowland, like 'a jewel set in a sea of green' according to Sir Michael Sadler, founder of the Oxford Preservation Trust. These meadows, all a part of the Green Belt, almost encircle the ancient city, extending in tongues to its very centre. No greater proof can be found of the contribution of a Green Belt to the preservation of the special character of a town. Looking outwards from the centre there is the great advantage, available to most of Oxford's citizens, of being able to walk into open country within ten or fifteen minutes. Few cities of this size have more public footpaths extending outwards from their built-up limits than Oxford.

PRESSURES ON THE GREEN BELT: FROM THE CITY

In an age of mass car ownership cities exhibit a strong tendency to turn themselves inside out. Town centres are beset by problems of traffic congestion, parking, high rents and rates, physical decay and the stresses of redevelopment. As a result, people and activities move out to the urban fringe where there is space and relative freedom of movement. This is a universal tendency, most evident in the largest cities where government action is now being taken to offset the decline of the 'inner city', but not absent even in smaller cities with historic cores such as Oxford. Indeed the tendency for functions to decentralize may be exaggerated in Oxford where the presence of so many university buildings reduces the amount of space available in the centre for other activities and restricts the opportunity for providing vehicular access to the rear of shops.

Throughout the 1950s_ and much of the 1960s, decentralization was actively encouraged by planning policies which favoured the comprehensive redevelopment of run-down areas of the inner city. Oxford did not escape this vogue for slum clearance and much of St. Ebbe's was swept away, people being rehoused on edge-of-town council estates at Cutteslowe, Barton, Rose Hill and Blackbird Leys. Sadly the rebuilding of St. Ebbe's has been long delayed, in part due to uncertainties over the line of an inner relief road, so that even in 1979 several sites remained under-used as temporary car parks.

Slum clearance is no longer fashionable and local authorities no longer compete to destroy as many homes as possible. The current planning ethos favours rehabilitation of existing dwellings and the preservation in situ of the local community. The City Council has had considerable success with this policy in Jericho and it is being extended to parts of east and south Oxford with the designation of General Improvement Areas. Commercial redevelopment has also taken place with the building of the Westgate Centre. By such means the authorities are doing something to arrest the decline of the centre and the flight to the periphery. The pressures to decentralize nevertheless remain strong and their effect on the Green Belt must be considered next.

One of the most obvious effects of outward urban expansion is to be seen in the demand for housing. This demand was anticipated when the Green Belt was defined in the 1950s and no fewer than ten settlements - the so-called 'inset villages' - were designated for growth (Fig. 1). In these places development would be permitted provided it did not spill

out beyond an 'urban fence' which was drawn around them on the map. Elsew:
where growth was not to be allowed except in the form of 'infilling' or
the 'rounding-off' of existing settlements. The success of the inset
village policy in directing growth may be judged from the fact that in the
1960s the population of the ten parishes which included these settlements
grew by some 27 per cent. Particularly high rates of increase were recorded in Garsington (85.6 per cent) and Wheatley (46.5 per cent), villages
attractively situated on low hills to the east of Oxford, and at Radley
(61.6 per cent) in the Thames valley. In twenty-three other parishes
lying wholly within the Green Belt the rate of population increase in the
1960's was only 4.6 per cent, although this overall figure obscures high
rates of growth in a number of favoured dormitory settlements: Horton-cum-
Studley (52.5 per cent), Beckley (25.1 per cent) and Sunningwell parish
which includes a part of Boars Hill as well as the fringes of Abingdon
(29.7 per cent).

The intention of restricting growth to selected settlements confirmed
the 'key village' policy of Oxfordshire and Berkshire County Councils as
set out in their development plans in the early 1950s, although the lists
of 'inset' and 'key' villages are not perfectly coincident. There were, for
example, eight 'key' villages in what became the Green Belt, five of which
were designated as 'inset' villages (Berinsfield, Dorchester, Kennington,
Radley and Wheatley) whilst three were not (Bletchingdon, Great Milton and
Islip). In 1966 a Guide to Planning in Oxfordshire was published and this
became the basis of planning policy in the county for the next ten years.
The strategy as set out in this Guide was to concentrate expansion in
fewer, 'specified' villages, directing growth so far as possible to the more
distant 'country towns'. It was thus a forerunner of the strategy
elaborated in the Structure Plan for the new county (1976). Even so,
five of the old County's 'specified' villages were in the Green Belt
(Berinsfield, Dorchester, Garsington, Wheatley and Yarnton).

It is apparent from the above that planning strategies evolved over
the last twenty-five years have anticipated and made provision for substantial growth of population and housing within the Green Belt, albeit confining
this expansion so far as possible to selected settlements. The directional
element in these policies appears to have had some success as suggested
above; population growth in the 'specified' villages of the Green Belt
being 19.9 per cent in the 1960s against 4.9 per cent in the rest of the
Green Belt. Green Belt policy, some would suggest, has acted as a general
deterrent to development - the corresponding figures for the 1950s were
47.9 per cent and 8.9 per cent - but in assessing any such differences account
must also be taken of such matters as the fall in the birth rate which took
place in the mid-1960s and the increase in personal car ownership, encouraging residence further from place of work. The counter argument to this is
that, by allowing growth to take place in so many 'key', 'inset' or 'specified' villages, the local authorities have pursued a policy inconsistent
with the whole idea of a Green Belt, which is to inhibit growth. Enlargement
of these places as dormitory settlements has increased their dependence on
Oxford for work and services, adding to congestion in the City and the dominance of the latter within its region (Uzzell, 1977). What is more, growth
has not been prevented in the non-designated settlements, especially those
closest to Oxford. Of these, Horspath presents the best example, where
various appeals have been allowed by the Secretary of State. Expansion
has also been permitted beyond the 'urban fence' of designated villages, for
example at Yarnton where, in 1977, an appeal was allowed for 212 houses to
be built in the Green Belt.

It may be argued that there is a need for housing which it is socially
unjust to oppose. The Structure Plan recognized a need for 2,000 more

dwellings for the City, over and above existing commitments, by 1986. These will require about 150 acres of land, and in 1978 some was taken from the Green Belt for housing at Barton. But care must be taken to distinguish between the need for public and private housing. The former may have to be satisfied by the release of a certain amount of Green Belt land at carefully selected sites, though the demand for council housing might also be met in part by purchase of dwellings in 'Improvement Areas' and by curbs on the conversion of existing property to student use. There can be less sympathy with the demand for private housing. Within an hour's rail journey of London and with the M.40 close by, Oxford is now a commuter settlement for the Capital, whilst it remains a favoured place of retirement for alumni of the University. The demand for private housing will never be satisfied however many houses or flats are built, though it must be tempting for the City Council, drawing less income than most cities from its central area because of the presence of so many colleges (charities), to increase its revenue from the rates by allowing high class residential developments where possible. The Blackhall allotment site, on the edge of, but with implications for, the Green Belt, affords an interesting test case.

Pressure on the Green Belt arises not only from the demand for housing but also from the needs of industry and services. Modern industry demands spacious plant layout and also land for car parking, canteens, storage etc. These needs, most easily met on the edge of a city, reinforce a natural tendency for firms which originate in backroom premises near the centre to move outwards as they expand their business. This was the experience of William Morris, whose car manufacturing business had outgrown its Longwall Garage site by 1912 when a move was made to the old military college at Cowley. In 1926 the Pressed Steel Company was set up on a site close to the Morris assembly works and the two companies,now combined in British Leyland, have made considerable extensions to their original plants. Despite attempts at reorganization on site, the need for more space has inevitably added to pressures on the Green Belt over the last twenty years or so. The first major incursion into the Green Belt took place in 1961 when permission was given, at ministerial level, to build a spare parts depot on 44 acres of land. The most recent application has been for some 30 acres of land on which to park finished cars prior to despatch. If permission had been obtained it would have closed the narrow gap which at present separates the motor works from the village of Horspath. The issue raises two important considerations: can cars be stored in a manner less wasteful of land, and can the sending out of cars by road be justified when a rail link exists to the freight terminal at Didcot?

Reference has already been made to the City Council's wish to relocate 'non-conforming' industries on industrial estates. One of these, the Horspath Road estate was the subject of a public enquiry in 1973 when the City sought permission to extend it along the by-pass where a small portion of the Green Belt lies within the City boundary. Permission was refused. The City's application to build another industrial estate on land, not in but adjacent to, the Green Belt at Littlemore was likewise refused in 1978. Attention is thus being given to the possibility of moving firms to an industrial estate at Abingdon, a policy that would be consistent with the 'country towns' strategy of the Structure Plan.

There is generally less pressure on office-based activities to decentralize than on manufacturing industry, the former relying to a greater extent for their business on the network of contacts that exist within city centres. Some enterprises are less dependent than others on such linkages, however, and for them the attractions of an urban fringe location may be as strong as they are for industry. A good example can be found in the siting of the local offices of the Electricity Board between Oxford and Yarnton.

Out-of-town shopping has become a part of the American way of life, and in many of the countries of continental Europe the hypermarket or superstore is a common sight on the approach road to major cities. This is not the case in Britain where planning permission for these large shopping centres on the edge of cities has usually been refused. The demand for them remains strong, however, and as habits change, with more car-borne shopping and bulk purchases to fill deep freezers, the pressure on local authorities to allow superstores to be built is bound to grow. Four sites in the Oxford Green Belt, all on the edge of the City, have so far been the subject of failed planning applications, but all of them (at Pear Tree and Red Barn on the Woodstock Road, at Sandford and at Botley) have continued to be the subject of public enquiries following appeals. Only one superstore application has so far succeeded, the SOLO store at Wheatley opening in 1978, but the war of attrition between commercial interests and the planning authorities is certain to continue. Meanwhile it is interesting to observe the subtler ways by which retailing invades the Green Belt, making use of existing enterprises such as car sales and filling stations as outlets for goods as diverse as motor boats and wine.

It has been suggested that cities are turning themselves inside out. Oxford grew up in the first place around a crossroads formed by two main routeways, one running east to west from London to Gloucester and South Wales, the other north to south from the Midlands to the Solent ports. For centuries the life of Oxford was centred on the crossroads (Carfax) formed by the intersection of these two roads. Following the completion of the city ringroad in the mid-'sixties, however, the intersection of the A.40 and and A.34 has been moved some three miles north of its historic position and now centres on the road junctions formed by the Woodstock Road and Pear Tree roundabouts. To this focus of routeways - this modern Carfax - have been attracted in recent years two motels, extensive car sales and servicing, a telephone station and vehicle park, a park-and-ride car park and bus terminal, plus applications for the two superstores. That this can happen, even when the sites in question are in the Green Belt, is proof of the attraction which such urban fringe locations now offer to a wide range of urban activities. There are, in fact, twelve of these major road junctions on the Oxford ring road, all of them in, or very close to the edge of, the Green Belt and all equally attractive to a variety of urban land uses because of the high degree of accessibility they offer to the motor vehicle. It is here that the greatest pressure for development arises, and the biggest test for the Green Belt in the years immediately ahead.

PRESSURES ON THE GREEN BELT: FROM OUTSIDE THE CITY

In 1967 the author wrote, 'There seems little doubt that in the next ten or twenty years the Oxford region is going to acquire a good deal more industry and many more people' (Scargill, 1967). That view was based on the rate of population increase then taking place - the population of Oxfordshire rose by 23.4 per cent between 1961 and 1971 - and on the attraction which the Oxford region has for firms seeking to move from overcrowded sites in London and Birmingham.

Oxford has a central position in southern England. Eight A-class roads radiate from the City; it is within a few miles of the M.40 and has fast rail connections with London and the Midlands. The Oxford area offers an ideal location from which to distribute goods throughout the southern half of the country. This is evidenced by the rapidity with which sites on the Milton trading estate were taken up a few years ago and by the success of town expansion schemes like those of Banbury and Bicester. Official planning policy is nevertheless to restrain growth. In the Strategy for the South East (1967) the Oxford region is shown as an area

132

of minimal growth, and this is broadly echoed in the Structure Plan which stresses the need for continued restraint on employment growth in Oxford itself. Consistent with its 'country towns' strategy, the Structure Plan does, however, anticipate a certain amount of industrial and commercial expansion in the small towns of the region 'in order that the industrial and commercial prosperity of the County is not impaired' (page 57). It is thought that the number of people employed in the county could rise from the total of 220,000 in 1971 to 266,000 in 1991, the total population from 505,000 to 612,000 over the same period.

With a falling birth rate and various factors inhibiting industrial expansion, the indications in the late 1970s, have been that growth may not exceed these relatively modest expectations. Yet the fact remains that any growth is bound to increase the pressures on Oxford since, notwithstanding efforts to boost the 'country towns', the City will continue to draw the population of the whole county to it for a wide range of higher order services. This drawing power of the City has implications for the Green Belt, not least as the approach roads are improved in various ways and additions made to the park-and-ride facilities on the urban fringe. Threats to the Green Belt from road-building proposals are particularly serious. In 1978 the Eastern Road Construction Unit of the Department of Transport published plans for three alternative routes to by-pass the A.40 where that road passes through north Oxford. Any of these would effectively close the gap between Oxford and Kidlington because of the development pressures that would certainly follow. A by-pass of the A.43 at Gosford was also proposed. Other plans affecting the Green Belt are for an extension of the M.40 towards Banbury and Birmingham, the Ministry's favoured route threatening to destroy forever the unique solitude of Otmoor.

The 'pull' of Oxford is felt in other ways, not least because of the City's reputation as a centre of learning. In 1964 the Lady Spencer-Churchill College moved from Bletchley to a site in the Green Belt at Wheatley. So extensive are the buildings of the college - now a part of Oxford Polytechnic - that it can hardly be described as an 'institution standing in extensive grounds', and its tower block is an intrusive landmark visible from far afield. The Oxford area is very attractive to research laboratories, partly because of the presence of the University and partly also because of the siting at Harwell in 1946 of the Atomic Energy Research Establishment. The latter has since spawned a number of related institutions including the Plasma Physics and Nuclear Fusion Laboratory at Culham, built in the Green Belt south of Oxford on a site that had served as a Royal Naval station in the war. Recently Culham was chosen as the location for the J.E.T. (Joint European Taurus) nuclear research project, a prestigious European Community establishment that is expected to have 400 scientists working on the site within a year or two. Many of them are from member countries of the E.E.C., bringing their families with them for a period of years and thus adding to demands for housing and services.

A different kind of pressure on the Green Belt arises from the need for gravel and sand for the construction industry and other purposes. The Thames valley is rich in these resources and the Green Belt is already scarred with former gravel workings, some of them flooded. A County Policy Statement published in 1974 pointed to the valuable resources of gravel that lay between Yarnton and Cassington and this portion of the Green Belt must therefore be considered vulnerable to strong mineral-working pressures.

PRESSURES ARISING FROM THE DECLINE OF TRADITIONAL LAND USES

Change in the Green Belt is brought about, not only by the demands made upon it for housing, industry and so forth, but by the permissive factor of an increasingly unprofitable agriculture. Farming on the urban fringe is subject to the depredations of vandals and to the behaviour of an indifferent public who drop litter, leave gates open, walk over crops and allow their dogs to interfere with farm animals. It is also affected by road improvement schemes and other forms of development which break up farm units, leaving a patchwork of ill-shaped fields that are difficult to work. Faced with these problems it is hardly surprising that some farmers are tempted to make what profit they can in the short term and then to sell for urban development when a suitable offer is made, 'farming to quit' as it is often called. Meanwhile hedges and fences are neglected, barns left to decay, and there is progressive deterioration in the aesthetic quality of the landscape. Designation of an urban fringe as Green Belt may serve to check this process of decay leading to change but it is unlikely wholly to prevent it.

The most recent study of agriculture in the Oxford Green Belt is one commissioned by the Oxford Preservation Trust and published in 1979. This study found that, overall, the agricultural pattern of the Green Belt was not very dissimilar from that of the wider surrounding area. Statistics published by the Ministry of Agriculture hide a number of more localized differences, however, and closer investigation of the inner portion of the Green Belt, closest to the City, revealed some distinctive aspects of urban fringe land use and farm structure. One of these is the predominance of part-time farming. Within the inner portion of the Green Belt, for example - that part to which ministerial approval has not been given - the proportion of farm holdings classified as part-time is as high as 62.5 per cent. A part-time holding for these purposes is considered to be one which demands fewer than the equivalent of 275 man/days of work per year. This percentage in the interim Green Belt, almost two-thirds of the total, compares with 48 per cent in the County as a whole (Table 2).

TABLE 2

Part-time and Full-time Holdings (percentage of the total)

	Oxfordshire	Green Belt as a Whole	Inner Green Belt
Full-time	51.9	47.1	37.5
Part-time	48.1	52.9	62.5

With so much part-time farming it is not surprising that nearly 60 per cent of the land in the inner Green Belt is rented as opposed to being farmed by owner-occupiers. The corresponding figure for Oxfordshire is under 45 per cent (Table 3). In the Oxford Green Belt much of the land is rented from institutions, especially from colleges of the University. In a section of the inner Green Belt picked out for detailed study (below), the proportion of land rented from institutions of this kind reaches 80 per cent of the total.

TABLE 3

Land Occupance (percentage of the total)

	Oxfordshire	Green Belt as a Whole	Inner Green Belt
Land rented	44.9	51.1	59.1
Land owned	55.1	48.9	40.9

Another characteristic of the inner Green Belt is an emphasis on cropland with a correspondingly lower proportion of land under permanent grass than elsewhere in the County. There is more horticulture, a traditional urban fringe activity, but there is also a greater interest in cereals and other forms of cropping. This may be related partly to the difficulties involved in keeping livestock close to a city, but it can also be explained by the tendency for farmers who live elsewhere and rent a field or two close to the City to sow and harvest a crop which only requires their presence on those particular fields for a few days in the year (Table 4).

TABLE 4

Land Use (percentage of the total)

	Oxfordshire	Green Belt as a Whole	Inner Green Belt
Temporary grass	15.7	15.8	15.1
Permanent grass	27.2	28.5	22.0
Cropland	53.0	51.0	58.7
Other *	4.1	6.7	4.2

(* rough grazing, woodland, roads etc.)

In addition to looking at the Green Belt in these broad terms, the Study also investigated the nature of the problems faced by farmers in a particular portion of the inner Green Belt on the eastern fringe of Oxford. Several of these arose as a result of the paucity of effective barriers between farmland and urban land uses. In a few places the ring road provides a good barrier, as does the security fence around the British Leyland works. But in general barriers were poor, an example being that adjoining Blackbird Leys, Oxford's largest housing estate, which consists of nothing more than a stream gully (often dry) and insubstantial fencing. It is in such places that the possibility of conflicts arising as a result of trespass and vandalism are most likely, and indeed a good deal of vandalism was reported from the farms close to Blackbird Leys. Quite substantial amounts of time and money were having to be devoted to 'protecting' holdings, strengthening gates etc. Animal enterprises were not popular because of the degree of interference with all kinds of beasts, and crops such as potatoes and vegetables had to be grown as far away as possible from potential thieves. This interfered with rotations. Other problems arose from development pressures of the kind discussed above. In this particular area they included uncertainties over Leyland's search for car storage space, the plan for a Country Park at Shotover, one of the superstore proposals, and the possibility of a gypsy camp being sited alongside the Watlington Road. Threats of this kind have a blighting effect which reduces farm morale and creates resentment.

It may be possible to afford the farmers rather greater protection from trespass by strengthening fences and other barriers. But fences can easily be broken and it will be recalled that there are many footpaths encouraging movement from Oxford into surrounding farmland. The Study noted that the 'spacing of radial foot routes into and out of the city fringe hardly anywhere exceeds one mile, and in many cases is less than half a mile'. Where barriers are ineffective the answer may lie in the creation of buffer zones between housing and agricultural land. It has been suggested that this could be done by planting trees on unwanted strips of land, but the likely damage to young trees from vandals makes one doubt whether this is a realistic proposition.

Alternatively, where agriculture is under intolerable pressures, the answer might be to purchase farmland for recreational purposes, creating a buffer of playing fields and other forms of open space between houses and farms. It could be argued that such a change of land use is quite consistent with the aims of a Green Belt as set out in the 1955 Circular and has the great merit of retaining the 'green' appearance of much of the land in question. In places it has already happened, as at Cutteslowe Park on Oxford's northern fringe. Elsewhere there has been an extension of playing fields into the Green Belt, a recent example being the purchase by Wadham College of a site in the Cherwell valley at Summertown following the sale of its old field nearer the city centre for housing. There is certainly no shortage of demand for recreational open space whether it be for rugby, as a golf driving range or for horse jumping. To help satisfy the less formal needs of ramblers and others there is a proposal to create a Country Park at Shotover. This demand also comes from visitors and the City's Recreation Committee, encouraged by the Thames and Chilterns Tourist Board, are now looking for caravan and camping sites on the edge of the City.

The principal argument against the spread of recreational land use lies in the degree of 'urbanization' that inevitably accompanies such change. Country Parks have car parks and lavatories and may attract ice cream stalls; playing fields have pavilions where it is tempting to hold discos to defray expenses; parks for the general public cannot be run without administrative offices; whilst caravan parks can scarcely be described as 'rural' in appearance. There is still some greenery about, but it is far from having that timelessness and rusticity that survives, however tenuously, along the Cherwell or the Hinksey stream. There is no guarantee, either, that a recreational area will actually serve the purpose of a buffer, indeed it may have the opposite effect. This appears to be the case at Cutteslowe where a small stream forms something of a natural barrier but a footbridge that is part of the footpath to Water Eaton gives ready access to fields where every year there is damage to standing corn from trampling.

FUTURE OF THE GREEN BELT

It is evident that the Oxford Green Belt is under pressure and that there is no easy or obvious solution to the problem. As a planning policy it has had some success over the last twenty years but it has also been subject to progressive erosion, especially along its inner boundary where the local authorities have been unable or unwilling to resist change. Indeed they have themselves contributed to it, most evidently in connection with schools (Iffley Fields). Pressure on the Green Belt has also built up as a result of failure to contain the growth of Oxford, particularly as a centre of employment, and of an over-generous policy of permitting expansion in selected villages close to Oxford.

There is a school of thought that believes the Green Belt concept is out-of-date, that the aesthetic as well as the agricultural value of land around a city is never uniform, and that the most valuable portions of existing Green Belts could be preserved as wedges extending from the centre outwards with corridors of growth between them. It is certainly true that Oxford's Green Belt is of varied aesthetic character, and the spires are not to be seen from all directions, but then the views of the spires are not the only forms of visual pleasure that can be derived from maintaining the present Green Belt. As the Preservation Trust's Study states, 'Views of Collegiate Oxford are not the only ones of note in the Interim Green Belt area: there are others, different, but nonetheless part of the Image'. Furthermore, to permit corridors of development would conflict with the containment policy which the City Council has been attempting to exercise for over thirty years now and which has become accepted strategy in the newly-approved Structure Plan.

It may be necessary to release small portions of Green Belt land for council housing, and agreement on suitable sites should be reached as quickly as possible so that the inner boundary of the Green Belt can be formally approved, removing uncertainty over its future. Housing pressure from commuters must be resisted, however, and it should be made clear that applications for industrial estates, superstores, or for more garages and motels will not be permitted on the urban fringe. Responsibility for maintaining a strict policy on the Green Belt rests with both landowners and local authorities. Prominent amongst the former, as we have seen, are institutions, especially colleges of the University. In the past these institutions have acted as guardians of Oxford's open spaces - think of Christ Church Meadow - but faced with large bills for the restoration of old buildings or the addition of new ones, the temptation to sell a field or two on the edge of the City is very great. Speedy confirmation of the inner boundary of the Green Belt is necessary in order to prevent speculation.

The role of the local authorities is not beyond doubt. Three important issues are, in fact, raised: (i) the division of responsibility for the Green Belt between two tiers of local government, County and District, (ii) the purpose which the local authorities see the Green Belt serving, and (iii) whether or not the boundary of the Green Belt is 'for all time'. On the first of these matters, a certain amount of confusion appears to have arisen as a result of the translation of Green Belts from 1962 Act Development Plans to 1971 Act Structure and Local Plans (Hebbert and Gault, 1978). In some parts of the country a Green Belt Subject Plan has been prepared by the Counties as a framework within which the Districts will draw up their Local Plans; elsewhere a greater measure of responsibility for the Green Belt has been left with the Districts. Where such a field of uncertainty exists the possibility of conflict is increased, especially as in Oxford where the preparation of fringe Local Plans is bound to get caught up in the argument for the extension of the City boundary. Given the present structure of local government it is difficult to avoid the conclusion that Oxford's Green Belt would profit from as strong a lead as possible from the County.

Differences of opinion exist between local authorities on the purpose of a Green Belt. Some prefer to stand by the objectives set out in the 1955 Circular, the emphasis here being on restraint, whilst others seek to adopt management policies towards the Green Belt, particularly with regard to the extension of recreational land use but also towards landscape conservation and enhancement. There is obvious danger of inconsistency where such differences of approach exist and where, as in Oxford's case, the Green Belt is shared between several Districts. The hope must be that the local authorities will consult at all stages over their policy-making for the Green Belt.

Uncertainty as to whether Green Belts could, or should, be treated as permanent has in the past hindered their formal approval. Some authorities have called for flexibility which would allow for adjustment of the boundary as housing or other needs arose. But such flexibility is seen by others as little less than an invitation to the speculator, this in spite of legislation like that of the Community Land Act. Land and property prices are raised, setting off a chain reaction which it is beyond the powers of the local authorities to control. It is difficult to see how a serious Green Belt policy can be formulated and maintained without giving to the Green Belt the maximum degree of permanence that is consistent with structure planning.

Finally the responsibility of the general public should be noted, and especially of sports clubs, ramblers associations and the many other organizations that make demands on the Green Belt. The work of conservation groups is also important, monitoring changes and acting as watchdogs, but seeking as well to improve the aesthetic qualities of the Green Belt by lobbying for the removal of eyesores such as pylons and overhead wires, and by constructive work such as tree-planting. The Oxford Green Belt offers plenty of scope for improvements of this sort, and where the benefits of this positive kind of conservation can be demonstrated the moral argument for resisting development pressures is all the greater.

REFERENCES

Berkshire County Council (1953), Development Plan, Written Statement and Map.

Hebbert, M. and Gault, I. (eds.) (1978), Green Belt Issues in Local Plan Preparation, Oxford Polytechnic Department of Town Planning, Working Paper No. 34.

Mayo, Earl of, Adshead, S.D. and Abercrombie, P. (1931), Regional Planning Report on Oxfordshire.

Ministry of Housing and Local Government (1955), Circular CMND 42/55.

Ibid. (1957), Circular CMND 50/57.

Ibid. (1960), Circular CMND 38/60.

Ibid. (1962), The Green Belts.

Oxford Preservation Trust (1979), The Oxford Green Belt, A Study for the Oxford Preservation Trust by Rural Planning Services Limited.

Oxfordshire County Council (1954), Development Plan, Written Statement and Map.

Oxfordshire County Council (1966), Guide to Planning in Oxfordshire.

Ibid. (1976), First Structure Plan for Oxfordshire.

Sadler, Sir Michael (1951), in 24th Annual Report of the Oxford Preservation Trust.

Scargill, D.I. (1967), 'Metropolitan influences in the Oxford region', Geography, vol.62, pp.157-65.

Sharp, Thomas (1948), Oxford Replanned.

South East Economic Development Council (1967), Strategy for the South East.

Uzzell, P.C. (1977), The Oxford Green Belt - Success or Failure?, in Oxford Polytechnic Library.

TOURISM IN THE OXFORD REGION

M.J. Breakell

INTRODUCTION

'Oxford - one of the city names known to the far ends of the earth, an unmatched concentration of lovely buildings set between placid rivers in a pleasant countryside; a place teeming with famous associations - with all these advantages Oxford should surely be one of the greatest tourist centres of the world. It is nothing of the kind. It does of course attract many visitors. But it treats them so discouragingly in the matter of mere comfort that few who come can enthusiastically recommend others to follow their example. It has most of the qualities which the tourist seeks but little of the equipment to enable him to enjoy them.' [1]

So wrote Thomas Sharp in 'Oxford Replanned in 1948. Thirty years later the same comment would still be appropriate yet the number of visitors has increased considerably and only now are we beginning to see new attitudes developing towards tourism.

The Oxford Region, extending from the Cotswolds to the Chilterns and incorporating the meandering River Thames, has long been considered one of the most attractive parts of lowland Britain.

In early times, ancient man avoided the thickly-forested valleys by utilising well-trodden tracks like the Ridgeway running along the chalk escarpments. In medieval times royalty and nobility besported themselves in forests like Wychwood or Bernwood retiring in the evenings to pleasant retreats nearby, some of which have survived in the form of castles and manor houses until the present day. The 18th and 19th Centuries saw the development of even more grandiose estates, such as Rousham or Blenheim, throughout the region. All these developments have produced a heritage of which we are justifiably proud today. Stage coaches introduced many early travellers to Oxfordshire, and many of today's pleasant hostelries in small towns like Thame, Woodstock, Burford and Dorchester are derived from this era. Throughout the centuries, the valley of the Thames itself remained one of the region's most significant routes, with travellers like Jerome K. Jerome or William Morris waxing lyrical over its pleasantries.

During the 19th Century, it was the turn of the railways, initially opposed for fear of despoiling the City of Oxford, but which subsequently brought thousands of visitors from undreamt of distances to enjoy the city and region, whilst the 20th Century has seen increasing numbers of visitors coming by coach and motor car. The Oxford Region is at the heart of one of the most popular trips of all, that from London to Stratford on Avon, which incorporates fleeting glimpses of both the Chilterns and the Cotswolds, as well as a short visit to the ancient City of Oxford, and has inevitably proved attractive in an era when time is at a premium.

THE ATTRACTION OF THE OXFORD REGION

The location of the region, only an hour from the heart of a metropolis and even closer to one of the world's great international airports, has produced more than its fair share of tourists from abroad.

The number of tourists visiting Britain has increased every year since 1947, climbing steadily to some 5 million in 1969 (the year when the Development of Tourism Act came into force) and to over 11 million in 1977. The increase has been particularly marked between 1974 and 1977 when numbers rose from under 8 to over 11 million visitors from overseas and when tourist expenditure rose from £837 million to £2,175 million. (2)

OVERSEAS VISITOR TRIPS TO THE UNITED KINGDOM 1947-1977

(Excluding citizens of Eire)

Figure 1.

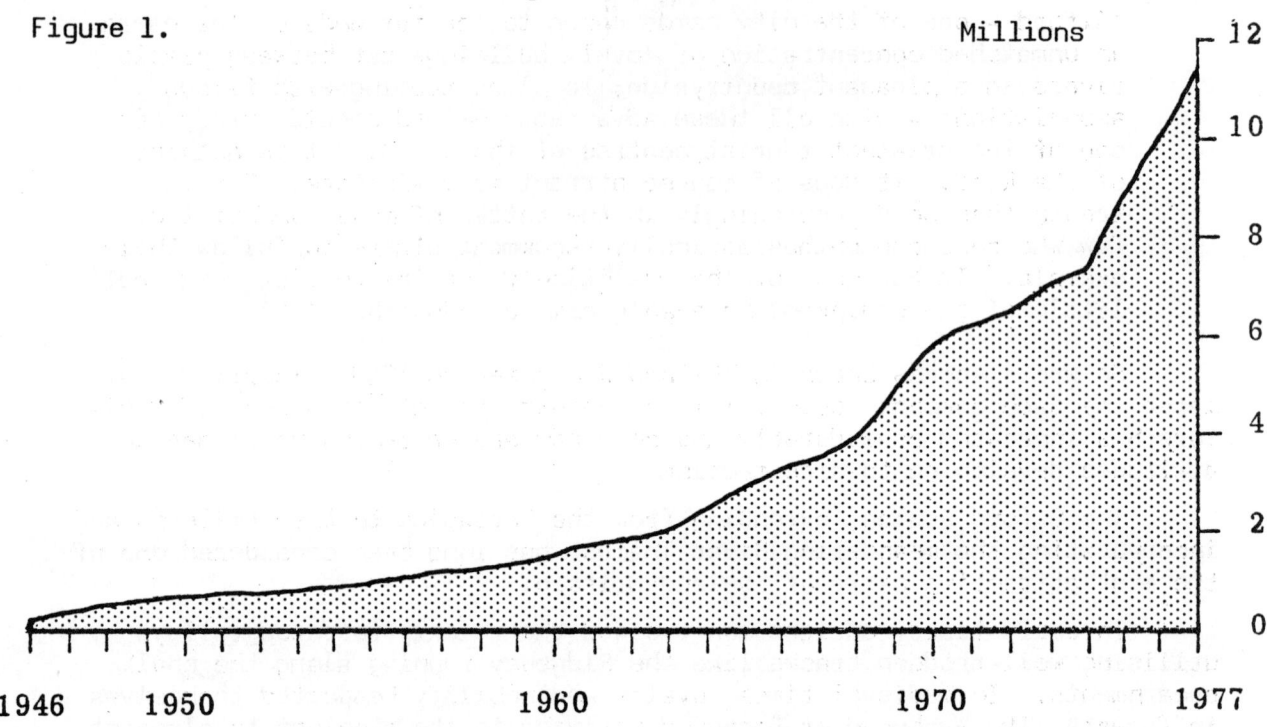

Source: International Passenger Survey, Planning for Tourism in England

This increased spending by overseas visitors to Britain now amounts to 4.5% of total export earnings, and tourism is presently our most important invisible export.

It is more difficult to determine the number of visitors to the Oxford region, as Oxfordshire lies within the Thames and Chilterns Tourist Board area, which also covers Bedfordshire, Hertfordshire, Buckinghamshire and Berkshire. The Board's recent study produced for them in 1977 by Tourism Planning and Research Ltd., divided the region into seven sub-regions, and Oxfordshire extends into five of these , referred to as Cotswolds, Downs, Chilterns, Thames Valley, and Otmoor and the Vale of Aylesbury.

In the Thames and Chilterns in 1976, approximately £1 was earned from overseas tourists for every £2 earned from British tourists. This contribution from the overseas market is higher than all other regions except for London and the South East. It should also be noted that the overseas market has been growing during the past five years, whilst the British market has remained fairly static. Surveys produced in conjunction with the Regional Tourism Study indicated the popularity of the Thames Valley with both British and foreign visitors, particularly en route to Stratford on Avon and the Heart of England. The Oxfordshire Cotswolds also interests many visitors, with Blenheim Palace and Woodstock pre-eminent, whilst the Chilterns and Downs were less sought after, particularly by foreigners.

Within the Oxford region the city of Oxford with its dreaming spires and interesting heritage was of particular interest to visitors, especially those from overseas, and no fewer than 35% of all visitors to the region came to see the colleges and the city.

Visitors to Oxford as measured by the number of enquiries at the City Information Centre have increased dramatically from 135,000 in 1970 to well over half a million in 1978, and visits to other measurable locations like Carfax Tower, Christ Church Picture Gallery, and the Various Museums have all increased substantially over the same period. [3]

FUTURE PREDICTIONS

To predict the growth pattern of tourism into the future is difficult, for there are signs that the economic advantages to be gained from visiting Britain in the mid-seventies are becoming less apparent as the exchange rate hardens, and as the economy of the world is increasingly threatened by rising oil prices.

Forecasts have been prepared for the various National Tourist Boards, and their best estimate suggests an increase in some 170 million bednights between 1975 and 1985, with expenditure rising from £2,724 million to £4,655 million over the same period. Domestic tourism is expected to grow relatively slowly, but overseas visits are expected to show a much higher rate of growth, so that by 1985 the expenditure of overseas visitors is expected to exceed that of British tourists within England.

These growth rates are particularly significant to the London, Thames and Chilterns, and Heart of England. These tourist regions are likely to continue to attract a high proportion of overseas visitors and/or businessmen. Accordingly, the total number of tourist nights spent in the Thames and Chiltern region could rise from 21 million to some 30 million over the ten year period between 1975 and 1985.

One should, of course, view the estimates of the various Tourist authorities with caution, bearing in mind that these predictions are those relating to demand (as distinct from supply) and that the various Boards do have a duty to promote the development of tourism in England.

PROBLEMS OF TOURIST DEVELOPMENT

Despite the trends of the past few years and the prognostications of the Tourist Boards for the future, many fundamental problems arise if facilities are to be provided to meet the envisaged growth in tourism within the region.

The recent Thames and Chilterns Tourism Study indicated that the pressure on services and facilities was greatest in the City of Oxford itself, where traffic and parking problems were exacerbated, where academic life was disturbed and local residents felt pressured, and where residential properties were likely to be lost to tourist uses.

Already there is evidence of conflict and congestion, as well as escalating costs in many areas of tourist provision, whilst the benefits to the community are not always so obvious. Conservation may be added as another area of concern. One can look at parking provision in the City of Oxford or in the picturesque villages and towns like Woodstock, where conflict arises between local people and visitors, particularly at certain peak periods as a result of the limited facilities that are available. One should also consider competition for accommodation, for instance the debate over the provision of hotels or housing as evidenced by the infamous Churchill Hotel site near Oxford's Folly Bridge, and the arguments for and against additional facilities for language schools, particularly within Oxford at the expense of residential accommodation.

The rapid growth of language schools in and around Oxford in recent years has particularly caused concern, especially regarding those schools which add to already overloaded facilities in the peak season.

The cost of providing the extra facilities to meet peak demand, whether it be parking space or overnight accommodation, is a debatable issue, when one tries to assess the real costs and benefits to the community.

Even though the City of Oxford currently attracts the bulk of the visitors, and many of the problems of conflict and congestion, other parts of the region are increasingly coming under pressure. Traffic on the River Thames, for example, has increased considerably in the past decade, until today, when there are some 12,000 private cruisers as well as 900 boats for hire, which, incidentally are proving increasingly popular with overseas visitors. Currently there is considerable disquiet over the provision of moorings and the tolls being levied by the Thames Water Authority.

The recent River Thames Leisure Policy Study has brought many of the problems and prospects into perspective, and indicates that many riverside locations are now undergoing severe pressure from the sheer number of visitors.

For years there has been debate over riverside sites in and around the City of Oxford, and yet the river banks which should be one of Oxford's assets still detract from the city. However, it is not only a question of cost, but also one of conservation, for development, unless carefully conceived and executed, can simply destroy the heritage which provides the basis of so much of our tourist trade.

The debate between conservation and development appears to be unending. How can we conserve our assets and yet ensure maximum enjoyment of them? In the City of Oxford in recent years one has seen considerable strides made towards the conservation of a priceless heritage: the cleaning and restoration of many buildings with both public and private funds have restored much of the fabric, whilst the increasing employment of skilled sculptors and stone masons has introduced a new element into the city's heritage.

Other schemes like the introduction of traffic wardens, the implementation of traffic management schemes and the management of coaches, as well as the individual visitor (as at Christ Church) has brought into focus the whole question of the capacity of our heritage to absorb both tourists and their vehicles in hitherto unknown quantities.

The question of environmental capacity is a difficult one. Should we be concerned with overcrowdedness expressed in physical or psychological terms, and if so who is to measure or determine the alleged degree of overcrowdedness, and how much of a role is there for market mechanisms?

Oxford may bear the brunt of the visitors, and yet as we have said, other parts of the region are increasingly coming under pressure. Within Oxfordshire certain country towns like Woodstock and Burford are showing increasing concern over the loss of basic commodity shops to tourist facilities like antique or tea shops. At the same time these towns are also under increasing pressure from vehicles both from through traffic and for parking and the whole question of conservation and the effect on the physical environment, or of retaining the fabric of the village, but also the quality of the services contained there requires more detailed analysis. Burford and Woodstock may possess a variety of attractive pubs and tea shops, but if the supply of basic food-stuffs or medical facilities are threatened, then the local population are losing at the expense of the visitor.

Somehow the benefits of tourism must be turned to the advantage
of each and every community which is at present suffering from tourism
pollution. To quote Sir George Young:

> 'For the shopkeeper an annual influx of visitors must be awaited
> with the same sense of excited anticipation as the monsoon in hotter
> climes. The colleges, however, may find an analogy with a swarm of
> locusts more appropriate. The average citizen stands somewhare
> between these poles. He may resent sharing a crowded pavement
> with a mass of foreigners, while enjoying the pretty sun-tanned
> faces as they pass, the cosmopolitan atmosphere and appreciating
> that their spending boosts his income. The truth is that tourism
> is a blessing and a blight to the City as a whole. It is also true
> to say that the individuals and organisations who receive most of
> the benefit from tourism are not those which have to bear most of
> the problems. The blessing should be appreciated and used to the
> maximum advantage, the blight should be reduced wherever possible'.
>   (4)

ADVANTAGES OF TOURISM

Perhaps we should begin this controversial discussion by looking at
the current advantages claimd for tourism, when compared with the situation
in the past.

In the case of Oxford, tourists arrive when spending power of some
10,000 students, together with that of considerable numbers of residents
who are away during 'Works Weeks' or college vacations, has been removed.
One can compare this with earlier centuries when college servants were reduced to being paupers during the long vacation, or even in 1924 when a Visitors Committee was established with the aim of relieving seasonal unemployment.

Tourism can help boost the image of the city and the region, and
thereby support its industries: in the inter-war years Oxford was advertised in a brochure supplied with every new car that left the works. Today
perhaps we should endeavour to sell our cars to individual visitors by providing attractive test-drive facilities in the region.

The contribution to other goods and services, for example course fees,
admission fees and expenditure on guide books etc. makes a substantial contribution to maintaining Oxford's educational facilities, and tourist income
not only helps retain and restore some historic buildings, but can help
create new visitor attractions like the Oxford Museum or the new Cogges
Farm Museum near Witney.

Even though the rapid growth of language schools has given rise for
some concern, research indicates that a contribution of over £5 million per
annum is currently made to the Oxford economy by eight schools recently surveyed by the Tourist Board and there are a further twenty in and around the
city.

Not only do the colleges and their staffs benefit from language students, but the advantages to shop-keepers and other supporting facilities like
transport operators are indisputable, if difficult to quantify. The pecuniary advantages to householders who accommodate such students, (currently
at rates of up to £27 per week) are also considerable, although these are
seldom disclosed for rent or tax rating purposes. Nevertheless, judging by
its recent growth it is anticipated that this sector of the economy will
continue to thrive into the forseeable future.

Cambridge has estimated that tourists spent some £20 m. in 1971 (at

1971 prices) and £40 m. in 1976 (at 1976 prices) in total. Using multi-
pliers developed elsewhere (The Tayside Region) it has been estimated for
the Cambridge sub-region that some 200 jobs would be created for every £1 m.
of tourist expenditure at 1976 prices - in other words, some 8,000 jobs
(or 5% of total employment) are generated by tourism. This figure is, incidentally, well in excess of all those employed by the Pye Group, which is
the largest employer in Cambridge. The Cambridge situation compares with
that in Oxford, where some 24,000 persons are currently employed in
vehicle building alone. Only some 4,400 work within catering and hotel
industries in the Oxford region, and even when one takes account of the
multiplier effect the city estimates 1350 jobs (840 only being full-time)
in tourist-related activities. One suspects however that this figure would
be substantially enlarged if all part-time earnings (including pin money) were
taken into consideration.. One also suspects that the trend over the past six
or seven years must bear some relationship to the rapid growth of tourism
within the city.

Clearly it depends on what weighting one attaches to the jobs created -
many of which are part-time or seasonal and not well-paid. Many, by their
very nature are in the service sector and hence often unattractive to the
unskilled or semi-skilled manual worker, as long as alternative employment
is available, and here one begins to speculate about the future of British
Leyland.

Additional economic activity caused by tourism means a further indirect contribution to rate income, and a recent study undertaken in South-
west England suggests that such income considerably outweighs the additional
expenditure on traffic, policing, health, water, sewerage and drainage, and
so on. In general though, while it is obviously difficult to quantify the
economic advantages of tourism, it is abundantly clear that facilities are
available to local residents which could not be maintained at their present
level without tourist income. These include not only those theatres, shops
and restaurants which provide a higher level of service as a result of the
additional tourist demand, but also the contribution to petrol and parking
fees, as well as to bus and taxi fares within the region, and even beyond
the boundaries of the region such as the maintenance of the express bus and
rail linkage between London and Oxford.

The impact of tourism clearly extends beyond the Oxford region and one which
clearly the many benefits to the region's inhabitants are difficult to calculate with any degree of certainty.

TOWARDS A BALANCED TOURIST POLICY

What we should be seeking is a balanced tourist policy for the region,
a policy that will be satisfactory both to resident and visitor, and
will provide a suitable compromise for developer and conservationist. How
is this to be achieved?

Clearly the British Tourist Authority, the English Tourist Board and
the Thames and Chilterns Tourist Board feel that more should be done to
cater for the needs of the tourist, and yet equally clearly local authorities
have to begin by considering the attitude of their electors to the additional
spending that may be required.

The Regional Tourist Board argues, admittedly following a very small
sample, that 81% of the residents of their area would vote to encourage
tourism if they were members of a local council, and although the local authorities would not accept that conclusion without question, they have collabor-
ated on a working party to frame a draft for a regional tourist strategy which
was produced in November 1978. The strategy for tourism in Oxfordshire

suggests:-

1. making adequate provision for current and future business tourism;

2. encouraging weekend and short stay packages to improve utilisation of existing accommodation where desirable;

3. participating in planning and implementing of appropriate policies for tourism on the River Thames;

4. planning and implementing appropriate visitor management measures for the City of Oxford and facilitating growth of those types of tourism which the City can accommodate. Close collaboration between local authorities, private sector interests, transport operators and tourist boards will be needed. Special study of the visitor management problems will be required;

5. encouraging existing visitor attractions with spare capacity in their role of providing a day out for tourists, day visitors and residents;

6. encouraging Chipping Norton and Witney as tourist centres, the former in particular as a centre for the Cotswolds.

It also suggests the provision of additional serviced accommodation together with more camping and caravanning facilities. The County and District councils are currently considering the working party's proposals, and in some cases producing local policies on tourism, which will endeavour to implement those proposals deemed acceptable.

In the case of Oxford City a special study of visitor management will be required if the City is to survive the deluge of increasing numbers of visitors. For despite policies encouraging the spread of tourism, it seems likely that most visitors to the region will still regard the city as their main objective, at least on their first visit.

The Council feels that tourist policies must seek to:

(a) maintain an attractive and satisfactory environment in which visitors and residents alike will take pleasure both now and in the future;

(b) increase the benefits and minimise the costs of tourism;

(c) solve where possible the day-to-day problems which visitors create and encounter, which should also prove advantageous to the local resident.

Managing the environment of Oxford City for the benefit of tourists could produce results of benefit to the rest of the region, and hence I shall now consider Oxford in more detail.

THE OXFORD CITY CASE STUDY

Initially we considered the question of congestion caused by visitors and particularly their vehicles within the Oxford region. Within Oxford it is largely a question of traffic flow and traffic management particularly at peak periods and at key locations. Car drivers trying to reach the Ashmolean Museum or the Randolph Hotel cannot go down Cornmarket, and coach drivers cannot use the High Street, yet tourists are notoriously difficult to control in this respect. Explaining the complex traffic and parking rules and regulations that vary so remarkably throughout Britain is confusing even to the locals - particularly Oxford's multi-storey car park ticket system - so who helps the tourist! We need to explain our rules and regulations more clearly if we are to expect our visitors to respond favourably. One way may be to provide information before entering the city and I am not suggesting that we want to emanate the Americans or Spaniards with their conspicuous billboards advertising our city or county, but one or two skilfully-located and well-designed maps and information boards (like those to be found at the entrance to many French towns) would clearly be beneficial, and would avoid the frustration of the visiting car driver or tour guide desperately trying to park near Oxford's Information Centre.

One location is the lay-by between Wheatley and Oxford, a lay-by which contains the first public conveniences on the 50-mile stretch of road between Uxbridge and Oxford and hence a popular stopping point, would be a key location for information on the region. Such a site could initially be supplied with a mobile information unit but this could subsequently be provided with an information and interpretation centre perhaps in conjunction with the proposed Shotover Country Park.

Another way to alleviate congestion would be to facilitate Park and Ride for visitors to Oxford. At present there is no Park and Ride system operating along the London Road (where most tourists enter Oxford), although if one was tried experimentally from the Polytechnic car park operating on a daily basis from mid-July to mid-September and at weekends throughout the rest of the year could prove beneficial to both visitors and local residents without inconviencing the work of the Polytechnic. Naturally such a scheme would need advertising, using for example the afore-mentioned mobile information unit in the Shotover lay-by or a mobile unit located in a conspicuous part of the Polytechnic car park. A route could easily be devised down Morrell Avenue - a double decker would provide a grandstand view of the Oxford skyline from the top of South Parks - then via St. Clements and High Street, along Cornmarket past the Randolph Hotel, connecting at the bus station and train station with other public transport services, then returning via Queen Street, the High and Headington Hill to the Polytechnic. I suspect that such a service if sufficiently advertised and properly equipped (taped descriptions or student guides) for example could prove very popular. Not only would such a service provide an interesting sight-seeing tour for visitors travelling by both private car and public transport, but it could also usefully augment existing services used by local residents. For example, it would provide a direct line to the railway station while helping to alleviate traffic congestion at busy periods.

HOSTELS AND HOTELS, CAMPING AND CARAVANNING

Accommodation in Oxford for visitors is a severe problem and the saga of the proposed Churchill Hotel has understandably caused considerable unhappiness within the council.

The restricted scope of Bed and Breakfast facilities and lower quality hotels should similarly cause concern and the current debate over the Youth Hostel simply cannot be ignored. The Youth Hostel which is located within a conservation area has been on its present site for 40 years and hence pre-dates conservation, even planning legislation by some considerable period, and has recently had its attempt to expand refused. The arguments against expansion may be valid as Headington is undeniably a pleasant retreat for those who live there. Despite youth hostelling having changed in recent years with the relaxation of rules for those travelling by car or coach, a location in Jack Straws Lane, far from the city and away from a bus route, is hardly ideal. Yet young visitors to our city are increasing in number and we simply provide no alternative other than occasional rooms loaned as an overflow, if these can be found. Those who have travelled around Europe, possibly with a rucksack on your back can compare this situation with Copenhagen where 'Use It' was actually established by the City Council to help visiting young people. People could be despatched to the country towns as we try to do with the Youth Hostellers by despatching them to Charlbury, but the real problem is that they come to visit Oxford, and surely we must be prepared for them to expect to stay locally.

IN CONCLUSION

Some would view tourism as a form of environmental pollution requiring treatment at a national level, and while that may appear an extreme line to take it would seem reasonable to aid those local authorities which seek to provide the necessary facilities, either by direct payment from the Exchequer or by establishing the machinery for levying a local tourist tax.

Local tax differentials have never been a popular proposition partly because of the difficulties in producing a workable scheme. The government does however currently provide support for tourism in development areas and, as a result of a recent dictate, in the intermediate areas too. It could well be that such assistance needs to be offered to those areas where tourism also requires careful management.

The Oxford region is no exception, and it seems to me that there is a distinct case for more Government support to rural areas to aid the additional employment generated by tourism, and for the support of services which could be coupled with the development of tourism.

The principle of promoting the country towns of Oxfordshire has now been accepted, but it will doubtless prove difficult to implement in the present economic situation. It could well be that tourism could provide the economic support for the employment and service regeneration that we need in rural parts of the Oxford region.

I am reminded of James Hilton's words in Lost Horizon, 'When the High Lama asked him whether Shangri-La was not unique in his experience, and if the Western World could offer anything in the least like it, he answered with a smile - Well, yes ... to be quite frank it reminds me very slightly of Oxford'. I feel that those of us who are privileged to live in or near our Shangri-La should show our respect and gratitude by protecting it from despoliation but simultaneously allowing others to share its pleasures, both now and in the future.

REFERENCES

1. Sharp, T., Oxford Replanned (1948).

2. 'Planning for Tourism in England', English Tourist Board (1977).

3. The Impact of Tourism in a Historic University City, paper by P.G. Robottom delivered to a Brighton conference (1979).

4. Tourism Blessing or Blight, Pelican, Sir George Young (1973).

OXFORD BETWEEN THE WARS: LABOUR AND THE MOTOR INDUSTRY

R.C. Whiting

Since the 1920's Oxford has had two identities, one as a university town, the other as a producer of motor cars. Before 1914 the local economy was inwardly directed towards meeting the needs of the University, and fluctuations in employment reflected the pattern of collegiate demand (1). By 1939 the major employers were two car firms at Cowley, Morris Motors and Pressed Steel, with nearly 10,000 workers between them, the next largest firm being the University Press (with 840 workers) which was part of the traditional Oxford world (2). As a consequence, Oxford's economy was far more influenced by national patterns of demand than it had been before 1914, and in this respect the City had become part of the wider industrial society. For the working-class the car factories ushered in a different world. Instead of the face-to-face conditions of non-factory employment, where union organisation (except in printing) had been uncertain and precarious, there came large-scale factory production methods which, because they high-light divisions between employers and employed, have tended to encourage militancy and collective action.

This paper tries to assess the social aspects of this transformation by looking at the response of labour to the developing motor industry (3). The particular focus will be on the determinants of working-class militancy in a period of economic change which involved the adoption of high output, assembly line methods of production. The puzzle as far as Oxford is concerned is why firms in which employment conditions appeared to be broadly similar differed so markedly in their industrial relations during the inter-war period: Morris Motors remained virtually free of strikes and untroubled by union organisation, whereas Pressed Steel had more recorded strikes than any other car firm, and had to concede recognition of trade unions.

This problem throws light on the wider social aspects of industrial change since strikes and trade union organisation were the products not only of working conditions and the immediate problems of shop floor life, but also of the nature of the working-class groups recruited to the car factories. This is particularly true in the case of trade union organisation in the 'new industry' areas in the 1920's and 1930's, within which Oxford was situated. Unions were slow to devote resources to areas of new industrial growth, at least in part because they already carried heavy administrative costs on memberships reduced by unemployment. In addition, where managements were hostile to unions, recruitment drives by outsiders also required reciprocal gestures from workers within the factories. The burden of pressing for union organisation therefore fell heavily on local working-class groups, at least in the first instance. Hence, in areas of new industrial growth like Oxford, where unions had no established strength, their growth was to be dependent on the prior commitment of workers to trade unions and to the Labour Movement.

With strikes, proximate factors - in particular pay - tend to compli-cate the issue, but they do not remove the relevance of wider social attitudes. It has often been stressed that material conditions of employment do not exist for workers as 'objective' realities, but can be perceived and inter-preted in different ways (4). It is therefore important to devote attention to the effect on their attitudes of the wider social lives of workers, in order to explain satisfactorily patterns of collective action. The specific interest here will be in the extent to which variations in outlook and behaviour (such as occurred in the Oxford car factories) derive from the historical background and experience of the working-class groups concerned.

One of the features of the growth of the motor industry at Cowley was the diverse sources from which it recruited labour. While the majority came from the immediate area, and had therefore been drawn from largely non-industrial occupations, prospects of work also attracted a smaller number from the traditional, longer-established industrial areas of the North and the West, then suffering from depression. It will be relevant to consider whether the latter, coming from areas where the Labour Movement was an established part of working-class life, reacted differently to the new employment conditions compared to those from the immediate locality where trade union organisation was at best a somewhat marginal phenomenon. It is important, too, to establish how such factors related to other aspects of factory life - managerial policy and pay, for example - in shaping working class militancy, and how far the differences in outlook produced by historical experience persisted in the new conditions of employment introduced by the car factories.

These themes have more than local interest. If Oxford was changing in the inter-war period, so were the Midlands and South more generally, as Hobsbawm has pointed out:

'What was new was the visible contrast between the flourishing home market industries and despairing exporters, symbolised in the contrast between an expanding Midlands and South-East, and a depressed North and West. In a broad belt stretching between the Birmingham and London regions, industry grew: the new motor manufacture was virtually confined to this zone'. (5)

Nor was the contrast in industrial relations between Morris Motors and Pressed Steel merely a 'quirk' of Oxford's transition. If Pressed Steel's strikes were being matched by disputes at Ford's and Austin's, the quiet life at Morris Motors was also being enjoyed at Vauxhall's in Luton (6). Although one town's experience cannot encourage confident generalisation, if the social and economic changes affecting Oxford were being experienced elsewhere in the Midlands and South, and were meeting a similarly uneven response from workers, the explanations for the Oxford case may well have wider relevance. This paper falls into two main parts: the first outlines working conditions in the Oxford motor industry and the attitudes of employers to labour; the second considers the workers' response, and the reasons for the contrast between the two firms.

I

In the years before 1920, the motor industry was in the main organised on a small workshop basis with many firms each being responsible for a small number of cars, reflecting its antecedents in cycle and motor cycle production (7). This state of affairs continued in the immediate post-war boom, with the entry into the industry of many small firms. However, during the expansion of output after 1923, in the context of falling prices, the advantage fell to those firms able to make cost savings through high output, rather than to small, specialist producers. By the end of the 1920's the production of private cars was concentrated in five major firms, of which Morris's was the leading producer, followed by Austin's, most of which had adopted assembly-line methods of mass production.

Both the Cowley car factories, Morris Motors and Pressed Steel, fit into the 'emerging modern' sector of the industry rather than that of the declining small firm. Lord Nuffield had begun making cars in 1912, and just before the First World War was employing 80-100 men (8). It was after the war that he moved from batch to line production, and employment increased. The development of production techniques at Morris's took place in two stages.

In the first, soon after the First World War, a rudimentary assembly line was set up, the chassis being pushed from one operation to the next, instead of remaining stationary. The new system permitted sub-division of work, and, with the use of conveyors to carry materials to the assembly line, a continuous flow of production (9). The second major change was the mechanisation of the assembly lines in 1934 (10). Production had doubled compared with the previous system, while the size of the labour force increased by about 62%. For the workers, mechanisation of the line meant a loss of control over the pace of work, and for the management, the possibility of more intensive use of labour within the working day. It was pointed out in 1934:

> 'at the present time the output from the five lines is about 3-400 chassis per day, though if necessary this can be considerably increased while still maintaining the eight-hour shift.' (11)

One engineer described the benefits of the 'flow line layout' as lying in the fact that 'it helps us to take control over the time we are buying' (12). Developments in the organisation of assembly work also involved a real advance for management in the tight control over labour provided by the conditions of work, and not by the variable strength of personal supervision. Vic Feather made this point in a description of working conditions at Ford's:

> 'There is constant supervision, although to a great extent the belt sees to it that the men are kept constantly at work, and there is not much chance to slack.' (13)

Pressed Steel also relied upon sub-division of work and mechanised assembly lines. The firm was set up by two American companies, Budd's of Philadelphia and J. Henry Schroeder, and Nuffield had an interest in it until 1930. The production of pressings, and the assembly of body panels were tasks for semi-skilled rather than skilled men (14).

What were the common features of work at the two factories, apart from the potential for the more intensive use of labour, provided by the mechanically driven assembly line? In comparison with car production in the pre-First World War engineering workshop, the assembly of cars in the 1930's demanded an increasing proportion of semi-skilled workers to operate single purpose machines on a task of short duration, and not all-round skills with machines of universal application (15). The skills which were required were no longer at the point of production but with the toolmakers and designers, a more highly skilled group than the traditional fitter or machinist (16). As with the determination of the pace of work, the sub-division of tasks tended to increase the power of management within the factory. The protection provided by skill was no longer available at the high output car factory, as an A.E.U. worker discovered who arrived at Morris Motors in 1921, and found that

> 'the firm seemed to prefer semi-skilled labour and had subdivided operations in the assembly shops so that men who were quite unskilled could learn their portion in a day or two.' (17)

Recruitment of labour for assembly line work was therefore in the main unaffected by any demand for engineering skills at Morris Motors and Pressed Steel. The struggle to reserve certain tasks for the skilled man was fought out not in the assembly line, high output factories, but in the smaller, specialised firms, particularly those making car bodies, where machinery for shaping or rapidly jointing timber was economising on skilled labour (18). A number of strikes in body-building firms and departments were aimed at preventing the introduction of semi-skilled workers (sometimes women) (19), problems which did not affect the 'emerging modern' sector of the industry where the division between the skilled and semi-skilled was firmly established.

The condition of the labour market outside the particular factories should also be considered. It has frequently been suggested that the high unemployment of the inter-war period gave managements some freedom in their treatment of workers, for two reasons: first, with surplus labour, managers could 'hire and fire' with relative ease (thus making shop stewards particularly vulnerable); second, because the insecurity induced by pervasive unemployment heightened the sense of dependence of workers on employers. It might seem perverse to apply this argument to the 'new industry' towns, for they enjoyed a lower rate of unemployment throughout the inter-war period, compared to what was being suffered elsewhere.

However, although the yearly averages put towns like Oxford in a favourable light, the motor industry did suffer from cyclical fluctuations in employment, particularly from 1930 onwards. Firms were affected most acutely during the summer months, after the spring sales period was finished and before new models were in production for the October Motor Show. Fluctuations in employment during the year could be quite severe: in 1934, for example, unemployment reached its lowest in March at 2%, and its highest in July at 28.8% (20). It was frequently alleged that managers would use these lay-offs as a means of shedding militant workers from the labour force (21). The effect of irregular employment on workers probably depended on the strength of their organisation within the factory. In the post-Second World War period irregular employment was a serious grievance for workers, since it produced high but uncertain earnings, and was an important cause of strikes (22). Whether it had the same effect in the inter-war period is another matter, since workers were generally less well organised, and trade unions weaker. In these circumstances it probably induced insecurity rather than provoking collective unrest.

In matters of trade union organisation, the Labour Movement was not well placed to meet the growth of a new industry within the engineering sector, using predominantly semi-skilled workers. Up to 1933 the inapplicability of a multi-union approach based upon specific occupational skills (e.g. iron founders, electricians, mechanics, vehicle builders) for assembly line production methods (as opposed to the specialist firms) had not been replaced by a union willing to recruit among semi-skilled engineering workers. The Workers' Union, based in the Midlands, was in severe difficulties for most of the 1920's, and although the T.& G.W.U. nominally took over its interest in the semi-skilled engineering sector, it was not financially strong enough to devote much attention to the motor industry in towns like Oxford until 1933.

But while firms like Pressed Steel and Morris Motors had some freedom in their use of labour, the developments in production technology did not operate entirely to managements' advantage. As a consequence of the sub-division of work, different sections in a factory became far more interdependent; a stoppage on one assembly line could disrupt the entire output. During a strike at Austin's plant in Birmingham in 1936 by 58 metal workers (which brought out a further 5,500 workers) a local report commented:

'the seriousness of the stoppage lies on the fact that each section of the factory is dependent on the others. In the West works virtually the entire body building activity is concentrated, and the hold-up in that section will inevitably affect the stream of finished cars normally issuing from the factory.' (23)

This was not true of the smaller firms, where groups of workers could not exert leverage over the rest of the labour force.

Since the car factories using assembly lines were therefore vulnerable to disruption by even quite small groups, labour had to be treated

152

with some sensitivity. An additional factor was the use of piecework payment systems which, because of the frequent negotiation for rates over
particular jobs, served as foci for grievances over pay, and perhaps for more
general discontents. In the 1920's 'advanced' management was giving some
thought to the necessity of winning the commitment and loyalty of workers to
the large scale enterprise. Attention was given to welfare, and to bringing
social activities within the ambit of the firm. Even where labour had very
little discretion over how work was done (as in the car factories), it was
still felt that a committed and loyal worker was an asset to the enterprise
(24). As Cole described the effort:

> 'Canteens and sports clubs are multiplied and improved; and everything
> is tried to arouse in the worker's mind a sense of loyalty to the
> factory, and get his mind to connect it with the pleasant associations
> of social activities as well as the irksomeness of toil.' (25)

Morris Motors appeared heavily involved in this type of activity, according
to the <u>Works Manager</u>:

> 'Tennis, cricket, swimming, hockey, rugger, soccer, rifle and other
> clubs, which are all under the supervision of the welfare department,
> are well patronised, while the Morris Band recruited entirely from
> employees, is one of the most successful bands in the country.' (26)

This multi-faceted relationship between management and workers had
been developed in the 1920's, and yet Nuffield, somewhat ironically, held
a qualified view of its importance. 'I do not believe in overdoing it. You
cannot intermingle work and pleasure,' (27) and his main theme was that the
level of wages was crucial:

'A low wage is the most expensive way of producing. A moderately
high wage, particularly if it depends on effort, gives a man an interest in
life. Men will only work if they know they are going to earn more home com-
forts, hobbies and amusements.' (28)

His attitude towards trade unions was equally straightforward: 'I never
allow trade unions to interfere with me', (29) and he proved this in 1925
by dismissing a group of members of the National Union of Vehicle Builders
who were trying to recruit within the factory (30).

Outwardly, the approach of the Pressed Steel management to its labour
force was similar to Nuffield's: welfare provision, high wages and anti-
unionism. The firm patronised sporting and social activity to encourage
'team spirit', and it was 'not opposed to paying out more money, but was
very decidedly opposed to any appearance of falling in line with trade union
practices in any way.' (31) In 1931 the firm joined the League of Industry,
an organisation set up by Nuffield in 1930 to encourage co-operation between
employers and employed, and workers from both firms took part in activities
organised by the league (32). However, although the methods of production
at the two firms were generically similar, and both employers pursued similar strategies in dealing with their workers, industrial relations within
the two firms differed sharply. At Morris Motors throughout the inter-war
period, the tendency for large-scale units of production to emphasise the
divisions between employer and worker, and so provoke conflict and encourage
support for trade unions, was held in abeyance. The success of Nuffield's
autocracy was shown by the inability of trade unions to recruit at all
extensively in his Cowley factory (or for that matter at his radiator factory in North Oxford), and in the absence of any significant strike activity. The firm passed through a difficult adjustment from large to small
horse power car production during the Depression without any deterioration in labour relations, and withstood the growing strength of general and
engineering unions after 1933 when they made some effort to recruit in the
'new' industries. (33)

Life turned out very differently for managers at Pressed Steel. In the years soon after its opening in 1926 the firm was affected by four disputes over reductions in pay under the piecework system. These strikes were small scale affairs, only one lasted longer than a day and none involved more than 100 workers out of a labour force of 2,000. They hardly compare with the big strikes at Austin's in 1929 (10 days long, involving 7,000 workers) and the four day strike at Ford's at Dagenham in 1933, which also involved about 7,000 workers. The Pressed Steel strikes of 1929-31 betray their origins in grievances over piecework, problems which concerned only a small number of workers and about which those in other departments might have known or cared very little.

The decisive change came with a strike in the summer of 1934 which began, like the previous disputes, as a grievance over piecework payments, but which developed into a fight for trade union recognition and ended with the T.& G.W.U. recruiting over 600 workers into their organisation (34). Thereafter things got worse rather than better; whereas the four strikes which took place before 1934 cost the firm 231 working days, the five that followed cost 66,162. Recognition of the workers' organisation lead to an intensification rather than a diminution of conflict, in part at least because the Pressed Steel shop stewards did not encourage the observance of the disputes procedure to which both union and management had become committed following the 1934 strike. The shop stewards did not see themselves as officials of the T.& G.W.U. but as the representatives of the workers in a context in which, they argued, there was little faith in the union. Andrew Dalgleish, national officer of the T.& G.W.U. for the engineering industry, complained during a strike in 1936 that

> 'there was constitutional machinery which the union had to observe, and these men who came out on strike without observing the machinery were strangling any efforts which the union could make on their behalf.' (35)

The formal rights of shop stewards under the procedure agreement were limited. Although they could deal with problems in the departments in which they worked with departmental foremen, they had no right of access to higher management, which was restricted to the full-time union officials (36). At Pressed Steel the shop stewards did manage to expand on their role as laid down in the procedure agreement, and frequently negotiated with management, thus increasing their power as representatives of the rank and file (37). However, the de facto abrogation of the disputes procedure was only accepted by management as long as the shop stewards performed the same function as union officials, namely to prevent disruption of work while grievances were discussed. But the derivation of their power from the shop floor as negotiators for the rank and file was not always compatible with this role, and the conflicts arising over rate fixing and manning levels on the assembly lines, for example, led to a series of unofficial disputes which in turn pushed management into clamping down on the activities of shop stewards (38). One of the chief shop stewards was eventually dismissed in October 1938, because of his refusal to restrict his involvement to the particular department in which he was working. The unsuccessful strike by the entire workforce to re-instate him ended a turbulent period of industrial relations at the plant. The bitter disagreements about pay, and the inability of both management and union to achieve relatively stable industrial relations, broke sharply with the situation before 1934, when opposition to management had been small-scale and fragmented, and also contrasted starkly with industrial peace at the factory next door, Morris Motors. The rest of this paper will try to account for this divergence, and will concentrate upon the different patterns of labour recruitment to the two firms, and so emphasise the importance of historical experience in accounting for the behaviour of workers in the new locale.

II

It might be objected that observed behaviour is an imprecise guide to attitudes. The absence of strikes, or the failure of attempts to establish union organisation, might have reflected two conditions. Either workers supported Nuffield in his opposition to trade unions, or, even if their commitment to their employer was weak, they were ready to accept, in a more calculating way, that to try to challenge Nuffield's outlook would do more harm than good.

For Morris Motors in the 1920's there is evidence that both these facets of the deferential - the voluntary and the coerced - worked in the firm's favour. There were public displays of support for his arguments to retain the protective McKenna duties for the motor industry, and appreciation of various of his welfare schemes, for example free life insurance (39). In addition, the level of wages paid tended to be above union rates, and it was feared that if union recognition was achieved, Nuffield would reduce earnings to union levels (40). Even when disagreements did arise there was little opportunity for pursuing them, since existing unions were weak and militants liable to dismissal. Either unions did not have branches in Oxford in the 1920's, or they were so small that they were swamped by the increase in working population demanded by industrial growth. Because they had yet to adapt to the 'emerging modern' sector of the industry, unions could not offer an alternative focus of loyalty to the Morris firm. The benefits of union membership were unclear (given relatively high earnings), while the costs (dismissal) were immediately visible.

These factors might explain the failure of union organisation, but they do not necessarily account for the apparent absence of conflict. As the small-scale, unsuccessful disputes of 1929-31 at Pressed Steel indicate, workers went on strike even when the odds were against a successful outcome. But labour was not a uniform mass; its assessment of conditions of work did not depend solely on their 'objective' consideration, but also on workers' historically conditioned perceptions and attitudes. Part of the reason for Nuffield's success in maintaining peaceful industrial relations was his ability to recruit local workers who had no background or experience of factory employment, or of labour organisation.

The social base of Nuffield's paternalism was a heterogeneous first generation labour force which had had little prior involvement in trade unions. In 1927 a N.U.V.B. member

> 'spoke of his experience at the Cowley works, and stated that all
> kinds of tradesmen and unskilled men were working there assembling
> bodies, who seemed to lack any of the principles of the trade
> union spirit.' (41)

Common working conditions did not automatically break down these differences: the close timing of assembly operations kept workers closely tied to their particular tasks (42).

Rural labour was one group within this mixture (43). The number of agricultural workers in Oxfordshire declined more rapidly over the decade 1921-31 than was the case in England and Wales as a whole, falling by 32% compared to 17%. The decline was more marked in the area nearer the city than in the outer parishes of the county. It was not always the case that labourers shifted residence as a consequence of moving to the town; many stayed in the surrounding villages to take advantage of lower rents and cycled to work (44). The incentives to make the journey were twofold. In the early 1920's the position of the agricultural worker in Oxfordshire was becoming precarious, the sharp drop in agricultural prices after 1921 leading to de-control of wages (45). The recruitment of farm workers by the Workers' Union following the establishment of the Agricultural Wages Board after the First World War, was matched by a rapid decline in membership after 1921 (46). While the labourer might have been pushed towards the town in search of alternative work because of the uncertain conditions on the farm, there were positive incentives too, shorter working hours and higher pay. In 1936 the average wage paid to a farm worker in Oxfordshire was 32-36 shillings a week for 50 hours work in the summer and 48 in winter (47). In the car factories, the earnings were irregular, but averaged 70-80 shillings a week for between 44 and 47 hours a week. The farm worker was unlikely to cause much trouble at the car factories: earnings were a distinct improvement on past experience, and even if he had been a member of the Workers' Union, the strength of that organisation had been highly erratic and had offered only slight protection against the cost-cutting activities of the farmers. The value of trade union membership, if it threatened the continuation of highly paid work (as it did at Morris's) might well have appeared uncertain. Local employers were certainly keen to employ farm workers; according to a Ministry of Agriculture inspector 'a very definite preference exists among contractors and others for local workers off farms rather than for travellers from a distance' (48).

The main consequence of Nuffield's recruitment of local labour in the 1920's (of which the farm workers were one group) was to preserve the exclusive and inward-looking nature of working class society, even though the conditions of large-scale factory employment broke sharply from local traditions. This is indicated by the way the Morris workers assessed the fairness of their wages. They tended to choose local agricultural workers as their reference group, and this was an obstacle to trade unions organisation. According to an organiser of the A.E.U.:

> 'A comparison of their standards with rural workers outside
> their district created a sense of satisfaction which reflected
> itself in an attitude of disregard for trade union organisation! (49)

This choice of reference group makes the obvious point that we are considering labour in an industry which was still in its infancy. Wage comparisons were still made across occupations, usually with the industry from which workers had been drawn and not between car plants over a geographically wide-ranging area, probably because of lack on information and inadequate communication between workers in car factories. The continuing accommodation with labour at Morris's in the 1930's, when conditions both inside and outside the factory changed quite markedly, underline the importance of the social characteristics of labour in explaining the nature of industrial relations, and reinforce the suggestion that such 'accommodation' was voluntarily accepted by labour rather than being the product of coercion by management.

The successful strike for trade union recognition, the support of a major trade union, and continuing recruitment at Pressed Steel after 1934 clearly improved the status of trade unions in local working-class society. Their power was visibly much greater, and they were no longer the vulnerable institutions to which workers might have been wary of committing themselves. The place of the union in any calculative assessment of collective action had changed markedly. Yet trade unions could derive no advantage from this in their attempts to recruit at Morris Motors. Although in the aftermath of the Pressed Steel strike the T.& G.W.U. recruited about 100 members at Morris's, neither it nor any other union was able to achieve a more solid position, and recognition did not come until 1941. It also proved difficult for activists to exploit the weakening of Nuffield's personal link with the Cowley factory. With the growth of the firm and the expansion of his interests elsewhere, Nuffield devoted less time to the running of the Cowley factory than he had done in the past, and responsibility for the revival of the firm around the smaller horse power car lay with L.P. Lord, managing director in 1933-36 (50).But Nuffield's close identification with the firm remained, and a superficially trivial incident supplies some evidence of it. In August 1937 the Ministry of Labour refused to pay the Morris workers unemployment benefit for the three weeks in the summer when they were laid off and for which, as a result of a scheme introduced in May 1936, they were given holiday pay (51). The significant point is that the workers appealed to Nuffield to redress the grievance and not, as would have been more appropriate, to the trade union representatives on the Court of Referees which had to arbitrate over the dispute. Their belief in Nuffield as a fair employer, and their reliance upon him for their standard of living, rather than on the trade unions, had remained unimpaired.

The development of formal fringe benefit schemes by management in the 1930's - a profit-sharing scheme, savings club and pension provision - meant that the firm kept ahead of union demands on a broader front than wages alone (52). But perhaps of equal importance, there had been no significant addition to the labour force after the peak of growth at the end of the 1920's (in 1930 Morris Motors employed 4,420 at Cowley, and in 1939, 4,670) so that the social base of paternalism had not been significantly disturbed. The only strike which took place in the 1930's, a one day affair in August 1935, involved a group of younger workers (aged between seventeen and twenty one), but this was not a curtain raiser for a much more widely based dispute, as had been the case at Pressed Steel (53).

Why was Pressed Steel unable to match the success of this anti-trade union policy? Despite the outward similarities in management, policy and type of work régime between the two factories, there were obvious factors working against Pressed Steel in their handling of labour. In the first place, although they were committed to welfare and social provision on the lines favoured by 'advanced' management, they lacked Nuffield's standing in the local community. While the managing director, Otto Mueller, acted the part by attending works dances and presenting prizes at sports meetings, (54) he and his colleagues could not match Nuffield's place in the local society. While Nuffield's financial support for local hospitals, football clubs and churches emphasised his benevolence to the wider community, the newcomers at Pressed Steel tended, by comparison, to be faceless men (55). They had to rely far more on organisations to convey their 'commitment' to the workers, than on personal example.

But the extent to which a sense of grievance at work could be allayed by the limp handshake of managerial benevolence was bound to be limited, particularly when working conditions were noticeably worse than at Morris's. Because steel panels were covered in grease, and also produced a fine iron dust when being hammered into shape, work was dirtier than with the assembling of cars. In the street it was quite clear who worked for which firm: Morris workers wore jacket and tie, Pressed Steel men greasy overalls, a straight division between the 'rough' and the 'respectable' (56). It was also more dangerous, particularly the pressing out of the steel sheets into body panels. In 1930 the Factory Inspectorate successfully prosecuted the firm for failing to fence off power presses (57). The firm also appear to have driven their workers at crucial periods. Again in 1930 the firm was prosecuted for employing women between a Saturday afternoon and a Monday morning, because of the need to produce car bodies in time for the October motor show (58). There is no evidence that there were any such incidents at Morris Motors, but these were specific incidents which reflected the relative newness of the methods of producing the all-steel car body in large numbers. Nuffield, who had originally intended to use Pressed Steel as the sole supplier of bodies for his cars, was disappointed at the early performance of the company. According to Miles Thomas, then sales manager at Cowley:

> 'The actual delay in the production of bodies from Pressed Steel was nothing like so troublesome as the appallingly low standard of quality when the first output began to come off the line.' (59)

An important aspect of such a difficult beginning was the necessary employment of American technicians to operate the imported technology, and these were reportedly highly unpopular with the workforce (60). Outward similarities in managerial aims and methods of production therefore hid sharp differences in work experiences and employer attitudes which explain in part why accommodation of labour of the sort achieved by Morris was never possible at Pressed Steel.

While these differences might account for the strikes that appeared during 1929 and 1931, they do not fully explain the much bigger strike of 1934, which began as a small-scale dispute, but which was widened into a strike involving the whole workforce in a demand for union recognition. It might be suggested that the appearance of unofficial strikes from 1934 onwards merely reflected the cyclical upturn in the economy which made workers impatient to increase earnings, and willing to resort to unofficial strikes to do so (61). But this is not the whole of the explanation. The development of the 1934 strike depended on the initiatives from within the workforce, which in turn were related to a particular pattern of labour recruitment. The responsibility for turning the strike from a limited piece-work dispute into a more broadly based movement for union recognition did not lie with the T. & G.W.U., but with the strike committee recruited from within the plant, who initially wanted the strikers to become members of the A.E.U. (62). The interesting feature of the strike committee is that its membership was made up of outsiders, those who had migrated to Oxford from some distance, and who had a very different historical experience from those recruited locally (63).

In coming to Oxford second, Pressed Steel were unable to meet their demand for labour from local sources. Although they required more skilled workers than Morris Motors, for the toolroom, for example, it was not this aspect of recruitment which seriously affected their anti-union strategy. The number of skilled men was relatively small (200 out of a total workforce of 2,000 in 1930), and although their skill gave them a common occupational identity, it was one likely to benefit their own terms with management, rather than to assist the unionisation of the semi-skilled, whose enthusiasm for piecework was taken as an indication of an improvident and irresponsible nature, unsuited to collective action (64).

For semi-skilled labour, Pressed Steel also had to rely on workers from outside the area. In the local motor industry in 1936 half the workers had moved to Oxford from outside the area, and nearly half of those migrating to Oxford went into the motor industry (65). Since Morris Motors recruited most heavily in the 1920's it was able to draw on local workers, including those who moved the relatively short distance from the region in a fifty-mile radius around Oxford. Not local by either background or experience were the second largest group, the 1,195 who came from South Wales. Trade unions were firmly embedded in their communities, and when they moved to more prosperous areas of the country in search for work, many employers were unwilling to take them on for fear of the disruption which they might have caused, This applied in particular to the unemployed miners. The Ministry of

Labour, reporting on their transference scheme, noted 'some apprehension that these workers will import into areas to which they may be transferred elements of unrest and disturbance.' (66)

The Welsh first appeared in Oxford in 1927, the local employment committee reporting that:

'The industrial prospects in the City had attracted large numbers of unskilled workers who had transferred their claims to Oxford, and who had remained here until employment was available. In this connection quite considerable numbers of miners and other workers from South Wales had come to Oxford.' (67)

It is important to underline that, according to trade union organisers, many of these 'immigrants' went to Pressed Steel (68).

Between 1927 and 1933 they were probably not a settled section of the local population, because depression encouraged movement elsewhere in search of work, or a return to Wales, where unemployment benefit could be stretched a little further (69). The net transfer of labour back into coal mining from the engineering and motor vehicle industries during the depression year of 1932 would tend to support this (70). Those who had migrated to Oxford between 1927 and 1933 tended to be the most mobile of the unemployed workers: young, single men, able to move on if work became scarce in Oxford. Local societies catering for the Welsh suffered accordingly; the Pressed Steel Rugby Club (which relied on Welsh members) and the Welsh Glee singers complained about losing members who were leaving the district to find work (71). It also frustrated attempts at trade union recruitment. One organiser visiting Oxford in 1930 found that

'our would be helper had been discharged along with a number of others, who were possibly also similarly interested, and had departed for his native woods and hills, not to say colliery refuse heaps.' (72)

By 1933 the prospects of employment in Oxford had improved, and more migrated from Wales. Since inter-regional movements were dependent on the level of employment in the receiving town, rather than the intensity of depression in the place of origin, migration from other depressed areas probably increased after 1933. To return to an earlier point, it was these groups who provided the leadership in the strike committee in 1934, and of the subsequently established union organisation. Tom Harris and Dai Huish, both ex-members of the South Wales Miners' Federation, sat on the strike committee, and became secretary and chairman respectively of the local T.& G.W.U. branch, as well as being members of the militant shop stewards' group (73). The contribution of the migrants from the depressed areas was out of proportion to their numbers in the factory. In 1936, 1,260 workers from the depressed areas were employed in the local motor industry, and if the majority of these had gone to Pressed Steel they would still have made up less than half the workforce. The strike committee itself should not, of course, assume sole responsibility for explaining the contrast between the behaviour of the workers at the two factories. The larger number of 'outsiders' among the rank and file at Pressed Steel, and their grievances with management are necessary to account for the failure of the apparently smaller number of activists who arrived at Morris Motors (and the radiator factory) from the North and Wales to have a similar impact there (74). Nonetheless, it remains important that the leadership within the Pressed Steel factory during the years 1934-38 was drawn from established working-class communities in the older industrial districts, where trade unions were a customary form of labour organisation.

III

This paper has therefore been concerned with contrasting styles of industrial relations at two Oxford car factories where conditions of employment and managerial strategy were broadly similar. At Morris Motors, 'tradition' persisted, in the form of a reluctance to press for union organisation from within, and in the virtual absence of conflict. At Pressed Steel there was unrest over a wide range of issues, and successful unionisation against the firm's wishes. To a significant extent the source of variation was the heterogeneous background of labour recruited to the new industry. This explanation has to be related to other factors, such as the shrewd managerial policies at Morris Motors, otherwise the argument becomes too crude and akin to the 'agitator' theory of militancy belaboured by industrial sociologists (75).

Two further points might be made by way of conclusion. First, the view of the Oxford working-class gained through a study of strikes and labour organisation has necessarily been a partial one, and the extent to which the fragmentation noted here was replicated in other apsects of social life is at present an unanswered question. Second, and more seriously, it might be argued that all we are observing in the Morris case is the inevitable time-lag between the development of a new industry and technology, and the organisation of a working-class response. After all, the firm did recognise unions in 1941 when it joined the engineering employers' organisation, and since the 1950's the assembly plant has had a strike-prone history. While this argument has some force, it should be emphasised by way of reply that the 'lag effect' was not produced by problems of organisation, nor by the powerlessness of unions in the wider world in the 1930's. While these had existed earlier, the 1934 strike at Pressed Steel and the firm's subsequent history showed that such problems could be resolved locally in the workers' favour. Rather, the lag was induced by workers' attitudes, themselves inheritances from a non-industrial past. The persistence of these attitudes is impressive in working conditions which, whatever the managerial strategy adopted, made explicit the intensive use of labour and the lack of discretion over the way work was done.

The extension of the line of argument advanced here is that as the background and experience of the industrial working class becomes more homogeneous (that is, recruitment takes place from within its ranks and not from, say, the service or agricultural sectors) so the community will contribute less to the determination of industrial relations (76). Such a development would also mean that the possibility of accommodation with labour, as was achieved at Morris Motors in the inter-war period, receded by the 1950's, as workers moved into employment from a background in which trade unions had been a customary form for defending interests. Turner, Clack and Roberts, when investigating the hypothesis that the strike-proneness of the motor industry in the 1950's and 1960's arose from the intake of workers unused to industrial discipline, found on the contrary that firms recruited those with industrial experience and involvement in trade unions. As they put it, the 'problem, in fact, may well often be, not that labour is "green", but that it is far from it.' (77) This indicates that in the post-war period social bases of militancy have lost their local particularity which the discussion of background and experience has emphasised here for the inter-war period. These are speculative remarks, but they do suggest that, if further research confirms the Oxford case, the inter-war period saw not only a further stage in the integration of the national manufacturing economy, but also one of the last occasions when the background and historical experience of workers served to fragment rather than unify the industrial working-class.

NOTES

1. C.V. Butler, Social Conditions in Oxford, (1912), pp.81 ff. On this book see B. Harrison, 'Miss Butler's Oxford Survey' in A.H. Halsey (ed.), Traditions of Social Policy, (1976).

2. For numbers employed by Oxford firms in 1939 see T. Sharp, Oxford Replanned (1947), p.57.

3. Attention is given here to collective action. The absence of company records for Morris Motors, and their inaccessibility at the body plant of British Leyland (formerly Pressed Steel) makes it impossible to consider individual forms of protest such as absenteeism or labour turnover. There is no mention in other sources that these were high at either factory. The absence of such records means that precision about other matters, for example the fluctuations in earnings under the piecework system, is also unobtainable. Information about strikes comes from the dispute books of the Ministry of Labour at the Public Record Office (P.R.O. LAB 34) and local newspapers. The dispute books in particular tend to miss the short-lived disruptions of work, that is the walk-out rather than the strike.

4. J.R. Cronin, 'Theories of Strikes: Why Can't They Explain the British Experience?' Jnl. of Social History 12, 1978, p.203.

5. E.J. Hobsbawm, Industry and Empire, (pbk. edn. 1969), pp.218-9.

6. The information on strikes provides no real clue as to the 'norm' for the motor industry. The 118 recorded strikes at 59 firms 1921-38 covers firms suffering several major strikes (9 at Pressed Steel), but also 37 firms which experienced only one. Nor is it apparent that these variations were related to different types of firm within the industry, whether components' manufacturers, specialist producers or larger high-output firms. Rather, the variations operated between different types of firm.

7. This description draws heavily on G. Maxcy's chapter 'The Motor Industry' in P.L. Cook (ed.), The Effects of Mergers, (1958). Throughout the paper I will refer to William Morris by the title bestowed upon him in 1934 of Lord Nuffield, in order to distinguish him from the company which bore his name.

8. Oxford Chronicle, 3 July 1914. This paper does not deal with the radiator factory in north Oxford, acquired by Nuffield from a Coventry firm in 1923, and which outwardly did not differ in the nature of its industrial relations from the Cowley assembly plant. For reminiscences of working life at the radiator factory see A. Exell, 'Morris Motors in the 1930's', History Workshop 6, (1978).

9. P.W.S. Andrews and E. Brunner, The Life of Lord Nuffield, (1954), pp.87-8, and Automobile Engineer, September 1926.

10. Automobile Engineer, October 1934.

11. ibid.

12. F. Woollard, Principles of Mass and Flow Production, (1954), p.180.

13. In file on Dagenham, T.U.C. Organisation Dept., T.604 57.4D.

14. For a description of the Pressed Steel Factory see Automobile Engineer, September 1931.

15. E.W. Hancock, 'Trends in Modern Production Methods' Journal of Production Engineering, 1928.

16. 'Notes on Mass Production' in A.E.U. Monthly Journal, March 1939. For comparison, see Alain Touraine, L'Evolution du Travail aux Usines Renault, (1955), esp. p.40.

17. A.E.U. District Committee Minute Book, March 10 1921. I am grateful to Mr. Young, District secretary of the A.U.E.W. for granting me access to this source.

18. See the description of the Vickers factory in Motor Body Building and Vehicle Construction, March 1924.

19. Strikes at the Motor Body and Sheet Metal Co., Coventry, Sept. 1925, and at Rover Cars, February 1926. Details in P.R.O. LAB 34.

20. Figures in Barnett House, Survey of Social Services in the Oxford District (2 Vols., 1938-40), Vol. 1 p.104. It was also a case of short-time working during the week. See the factory newspaper of Morris Motors 'The Spark' Vol. 2, No. 1 (produced by members of the Communist Party).

21. See Vic Feather's comments in T.U.C. file on Dagenham, op.cit.

22. H. Turner, G. Clack, G. Roberts, Labour Relations in the Motor Industry, (1967), pp.331-2.

23. Midland Daily Telegraph, 13 November 1936.

24. 'Why Welfare Matters', Works Manager, August 1935; 'Human Problems of Management', Works Manager, March 1938.

25. G.D.H. Cole, The Next Ten Years in British Economic and Social Policy (1929) p.162.

26. Vol.1, No. 1, 1934.

27. Oxford Times, 28 January, 1927.

28. System, February, 1924. The similarity of the views of Morris and Ford on wages is quite striking. According to Ford: 'Cutting wages does not reduce costs, it increases them' Ford, Today and Tomorrow, (1926), p.43.

29. Oxford Times, 1 July 1927.

30. Oxford Trades Council Minute Book, 21 April 1926.

31. A.E.U. District Committee Minute Book, 31 May 1928.

32. Oxford Times, 20 June 1931, 22 July 1932.

33. This period of the firm's history is discussed by R.A. Church and M. Miller, 'The British Motor Industry, 1922-39' in B. Supple (ed.), Essays in British Business History, (1978), esp. pp.175-8.

34. The strike was reported in the Oxford Mail, 17-27 July 1934, and discussed in T.& G.W.U. Finance and General Purposes Committee, 10 August 1934, Minute 669.

35. Oxford Mail, 30 June 1936.

36. A. Marsh, Industrial Relations in Engineering, (1965), p.266.

37. Interview with Jack Thomas, former District Secretary of the T.& G.W.U. 15 May 1975.

38. See the disputes reported in the <u>Oxford Mail</u>, 26 June 1936, 22 April 1937.

39. <u>Oxford Chronicle</u>, 9 May 1924, <u>Oxford Mail</u>, 5 March 1930, <u>Oxford Chronicle</u>, 2 April 1926.

40. National Union of Vehicle Builders' minute book (Oxford branch), 19 November 1924.

41. N.U.V.B. minute book, 6 August 1927.

42. A.E.U. <u>Monthly Journal</u>, November 1924, report from organiser for Division 18.

43. Interview with M. Kean, Morris Motors foreman, by P.W.S. Andrews and E. Brunner, in their Nuffield Biography Archive. I am most grateful to Professor Elizabeth Brunner for granting me access to this source.

44. R. Samuel, <u>Village Life and Labour</u>, (1975), p.243. The Ministry of Labour also reported similar mobility by younger workers: 'considerable numbers of boys come daily into Oxford from outlying country districts and smaller towns in the vicinity to work in the motor trade' Annual Report for 1927, Cmd 4044 p.61.

45. E.H. Whetham, <u>Agrarian History of England and Wales, 1914-39</u>, (1978), p.156.

46. R. Hyman, 'The Workers' Union' (Oxford D.Phil thesis, 1968, subsequently published under same title in 1971) p.274.

47. Barnett House <u>Survey</u> Vol. 1, p.89, 149.

48. Ministry of Agriculture Report on Labour Scarcity, P.R.O. MAF 47/3.

49. A.E.U. <u>Monthly Journal</u>, May 1931. A contemporary on factory organisation made a similar point about labour in non-industrial areas, in connection with factory location: 'Workers in country centres, or in small towns and villages have less of what one might call an industrial sense. In some respects this is an undoubted advantage. They are less obsessed by socially inherited prejudices and more inclined to give full effort and full co-operation. The wages offered will be much beyond what they have previously earned, and thus act as an additional incentive to output and effort.' Northcott, Sheldon, Wardropper and Urwick, <u>Factory Organisation</u>, (1928), p.4.

50. Church and Miller, <u>op.cit</u>, p.178.

51. <u>Oxford Mail</u>, 12-13 August 1937.

52. Dividends paid according to length of service, to a maximum of £10. H.A. Goddard, 'Profit-sharing and the Amenities of the Nuffield Factories' in Catherwood and Gannett (eds.) <u>Industrial Relations in Great Britain</u> (New York), 1939), p.267. Wages averaged £5 per week as they did at Pressed Steel.

53. <u>Oxford Mail</u>, 27 August 1935.

54. <u>Pressings</u> (company magazine) January 1928; <u>Oxford Times</u>, 9 May 1930.

55. Oxford Times 19 July 1929, 11 August 1933. For a full list of benefactions see Andrews and Brunner, <u>The Life of Lord Nuffield</u>, pp.259-65.

56. Interview with J.B. Clarke, Pressed Steel worker, 11 November 1974.

57. <u>Oxford Times</u>, 13 February 1930.

58. <u>Oxford Times</u>, 21 November 1930.

59. M. Thomas, <u>Out on a Wing</u>, (1964), pp.152-3.

60. Interview with F. Cairns, Andrews and Brunner, Nuffield Biography Archive.

61. As the Ministry of Labour noted in its report for 1936: 'The usual desire of workpeople to obtain higher wages as soon as there is an upturn in industrial conditions furnishes an opportunity for irresponsible elements to encourage unconstitutional action', p.67. However, the timing of strikes at Pressed Steel did not always reflect a calculative approach, those in July 1934, July 1936 and April 1937 occuring when unemployment in the industry locally was relatively high. The level of unemployment tended to be related directly to the duration of strikes.

62. Interviews with two participants, Donovan Brown, 17 August 1974; Harry Jones, 19 November 1974. The role of the T.& G.W.U. and the local Communist Party are discussed in my Oxford D.Phil. thesis 'The Working Class in the "New Industry" Towns between the Wars: the case of Oxford' (1978) pp.245-60. See also the Communist Review, Sept. 1934, pp.146 ff.

63. Precise information on the composition of the strike committee is hard to find. Its secretary supplied the following list in 1976: J. Milchreest (Scotland), R. Garrett (Darlington), H. Crooks (Sunderland), M. Murphy (Manchester), J. Welsh (Scotland), H. Hamilton (Wallingford, Oxon), M. Cone, T. Harris, J. George, T. Harris, D. Huish (all South Wales). This list might understate the presence of the Welsh. According to G.H. Daniel sixteen out of the 23 on the committee came from South Wales. 'Some Factors Affecting the Movement of Labour' Oxford Economic Papers, (1940), 3, p.157n.

64. According to the national organiser of the A.E.U. 'Overtime and payment by results with this class has the effect of minimising the importance of recognising and holding out for a "district rate" and produces an indifferent type of individual'. Monthly Journal, June 1934.

65. The only reliable figures are those in the Barnett House Survey, based upon the exchange of insurance books in 1936. The 1931 census did not include birthplace details.

Region of origin	No.	% of total No. of 'immigrants'
South-West (includes Oxfordshire)	4,058	36.7
North and Scotland	1,305	11.9
Wales	1,195	10.8
London	1,178	10.7

This table gives those regions contributing 10% or more of 'immigrants', with an aggregate for the North and Scotland. For the full table see Barnett House Survey Vol. 1, pp.54-5. With regard to Wales it is worth noting that one-sixth of all the migrants to Oxford from Wales had come from a small mining village, Pontycymmer, which reflects the reliance on kin and friends of those who move over long distances to look for work. Barnett House Survey Vol. 1, p.59.

66. Ministry of Labour, Industrial Transference Board Report, (1928) p.10 It is relevant to point out here that Knowles has calculated for 1911-47 that of the regions of Great Britain South Wales was the most strike prone, as was mining of all the industries. See K.G.J.C. Knowles, Strikes, (1952) pp.197,210.

67. <u>Oxford Times</u>, 18 March 1927.

68. N.U.V.B. <u>Journal</u>, Midlands' organiser's report, January 1929.

69. G.H. Daniel, 'A Sample Analysis of Labour Migration into the Oxford District', (Oxford Univ. D. Phil. 1939) xix.

70. Ministry of Labour <u>Gazette</u>, November 1932.

71. <u>Oxford Times</u>, 4 May 1929, 20 March 1931.

72. N.U.V.B. <u>Journal</u>, January 1930.

73. On Tom Harris, see by-election report in <u>Oxford Mail</u>, 16 September 1935, and note on file (uncat.) in Abe Lazarus Memorial Library, Ruskin Hall, Oxford. On Huish, interviews with D. Brown, R. Garrett, H. Jones.

74. See for example note on J.F. Ida in municipal election report, <u>Oxford Times</u>, 20 October 1933, J. Kincaid and A. Exell (see A. Exell's essays on Oxford working-class politics, held in the Abe Lazarus Library), for 'outsiders' at Morris Motors and the radiator factory.

75. R. Hyman, <u>Strikes</u>, (1972), p.57.

76. H.A. Turner, G. Clack and G. Roberts, when discussing community-based theories of strike-proneness for the 1950's and 1960's comment that 'more refined, though less neat, explanations look first at jobs rather than at communities or places', <u>Labour Relations in the Motor Industry</u>, (1967), p.165.

77. <u>ibid</u>., p.175.

THE UNIVERSITY IN THE CITY

Sir Norman Chester

Oxford is a peculiar place - at least it was more so fifty years ago.
Then it was known all over the world - for one thing - as the home of one of
the world's oldest and most distinguished Universities. Perhaps its only
other claim to fame was to produce a special kind of marmalade. Now it is
also known as a place which makes motor cars, formerly the kingdom of
William Richard Morris, now part of the empire of British Leyland. It now
even has a football club in the League and so many who do the Pools weekly,
and are only dimly aware of the University, know there is an Oxford United.
Nevertheless even now it is the University and Colleges which make Oxford
different from the other towns, with the exception of Cambridge.

Moreover the University and Colleges differ markedly from other English
Universities, again with the exception of Cambridge. In the first place
their buildings and facilities occupy the major part of the centre of the
city. They are not swallowed up in a vast urban area as is the case with
say Manchester, Liverpool and London. Nor are they placed in some park-
land or rural spot on the edge of the town. This, of course, is another
feature which distinguishes them from the British Leyland Factories. Nobody
who comes to Oxford can fail to notice the numerous College and University
buildings. Second, many of these buildings are of great architectural merit
and beauty, so much so that they attract tourists from all over the world.
Finally, the University is internationally, not locally, oriented. Its
members are more inclined to write to the London rather than the Oxford Times
even about local matters.

Against this background I wish now to look at the relations between
the City and the University, from two different angles. First, in terms of
the arrangement which only ended in 1974 whereby the University was entitled
to elect a certain number of Councillors and second, in more general, contemporary terms.

UNIVERSITY REPRESENTATION 1889 - 1974

The Colleges and University of Oxford were among the first places of
higher education in the world. There is little doubt that by the twelfth
century Oxford was a centre for teaching. Though this gives the University
an ancient pedigree, the town itself is even more ancient. It is referred
to in the Anglo-Saxon Chronicle for 912, and in 1015 an Anglo-Saxon 'parliament' was held at Oxford. The town did not develop out of the University, nor
did the University develop out of the town. They developed separately in the
same locality.

Before long, however, the University came to dominate the town. The
scholars had ready access to the King and his court. (Several Colleges of
course owe their origin to princely benefactions.) Attacks by townspeople on
the teachers and students led to the University being given various rights.
In 1248, for example, following the murder of a student, the Mayor and certain
other officers were compelled by law to take an annual oath to keep and cause
to be kept the liberties and customs of the University, a ceremony which
remained until 1858. On St. Scholastica's Day in 1355 (10 February) many
scholars were killed and Edward III required the City to resign into his
hands the charters recording its ancient privileges and customs. The charters
were restored shortly afterwards but with changes which strengthened the role
and powers of the University.

167

The increasing domination of the University was not by any means due merely to its legal status and privileges. Increasingly it became the main industry, the main source of employment and the main source of profit to the traders and shopkeepers. It became a self-governing institution responsible for the well being and discipline of its members. If the College and University buildings still look impressive they must have appeared phenomenal when first built having regard to the size of the buildings and houses occupied by the townspeople.

It was natural, therefore, that the University should be involved in the Oxford Mileways and Improvement Act, 1771 (1) (Geo. III C19) which established a large body of Commissioners to improve the City. These included the Mayor and Aldermen, the Town Clerk and other representatives of the City; the Vice-Chancellor, the Heads of Houses, Professors, the Proctors and other representatives of the University and Colleges and a number of local inhabitants named in the Act. The Commissioners were empowered to rebuild Magdalen Bridge, widen a number of the main streets including the High, the Broad, Cornmarket and St. Aldates, to demolish the East and the North Gates; and to undertake other activities: street paving and lighting, street sweeping and certain environmental health functions.

In the legislation, which both reformed and developed local government from 1835 onwards, Oxford was treated differently from other towns. The University and Colleges remained important partners in the provision and management of local services. It was the Mileway Commissioners not the City Council which became the Local Board of Health in 1865 but with a modified constitution. The Local Board consisted of the Vice-Chancellor and the Mayor and 45 other members: sixteen appointed by the Town Council, fourteen by the ratepayers in the several Parishes and fifteen by the University. Of the last, four were elected by Convocation and eleven by Heads and Senior Bursars. This form of University representation is to be found in the Oxford Poor Rate Act of 1854 whereby the Vice-Chancellor plus eight elected by Heads and Senior Bursars and two elected by Convocation were made members of the Board of Guardians. Until the Oxford Police Act of 1868 responsibility for the Night Watch was exercised by the University and the Day Watch by the City. In that year a united police force was established under a Committee consisting of the Vice-Chancellor and the Mayor, five members appointed by Convocation and eight by the City Council.

When the City became a County Borough under the Local Government Act of 1888 it had to wait until 9th November 1889 to acquire the powers possessed by other County Boroughs. On that day the Local Board of Health and the Police Committee were abolished and their property and powers, which included the City Library and the Market, were transferred to the Council. The Board of Guardians and the School Board, on both of which the University and Colleges were represented remained in being. The Provisional Order which made the transfer retained the right of the University to be directly represented on the main local government body for the area. The new City Council was to be composed of 45 Councillors and fifteen Aldermen. Six (ie. two each year) of the Councillors were to be appointed by the Heads and Senior resident Bursars of the Colleges and three (ie. one each year) were to be elected by Convocation. These nine University Councillors were entitled to elect three of the fifteen Aldermen. (2)

In May 1952, when A.M. Caccia was elevated from Councillor to Alderman, I was appointed a Councillor to replace him and remained on the Council until the end of March 1974, becoming an Alderman in May 1965. I therefore saw the system in operation for 21 years and three features impressed me.

First, those appointed, whether by Heads and Bursars or by Convocation, were in no sense mouthpieces or representatives of the University or the Colleges. We were never instructed how to vote nor even made aware of any policy which those who appointed us wished to see pursued. We never met together as a group to agree a common "University" policy. We did not have a 'leader' like the political groups who could stand up in the Council Chamber and announce the policy of their group on some issue. We were never formally consulted by our electors nor did any of us feel an obligation to find out the views of those who put us there or to do anything to please them.

One reason for this was that we spent most of our time on matters of little or no peculiar interest to the University or Colleges. We served on Committees concerned with housing, water, sewage disposal, markets, children, public health and allotments. Even the work of the Committees concerned with Education, Roads and Town Planning only occasionally impinged on the direct interests of the University and Colleges. In other words we were not there to deal solely with business which directly affected the University. We were not an interest or pressure group implanted in the Council Chamber. Our purpose was to help to govern the city to the best of our abilities and in the best interests of the city; the same purposes as those of the other Councillors and Aldermen. (3)

It was only occasionally that the activities of the City Council had a special interest to the University, or threatened it in some direct manner. The most important such issue during my time was that of the relief roads. This issue rose out of the steady growth of traffic which turned the High from being one of the most beautiful highways in Europe to being just a motor-way and threatened the peace and beauty of the ancient University environment. In a sense there was no University solution which was bound to differ from the City's solution. A great many dons felt strongly against a road across Christ Church Meadow but this was not because any academic interest was threatened. Nor did they all come from the Colleges adjacent to the proposed road whose amenities were in danger. Such alternatives as the Lamb and Flag road, whilst retaining the peace of the Meadow, affected a new lot of Colleges and the Science area of the University. There was no single simple University solution which the University representatives on the Council might have been asked to support or being members of the University might naturally have supported. When in the last plan my own College was threatened by a fantastic flyover from the multi-lane trunk road to Gloucester Green I was naturally against that part of it. But I voted in principal for the plan. I am now ashamed to admit this because the later Park and Ride plan looks to be a successful and much cheaper alternative. The point is that I doubt whether even on this major issue there was a clear University view which could have been conveyed precisely to the twelve University members of the Council.

I remember speaking and voting against the proposed use of the Banbury Road-Bradmore Road site for a new Pitt-Rivers Museum even though it had been successfully steered through Congregation by Hebdomodal Council. I thought it was wrongly sited and would have been better placed nearer the ring road. In any case it aroused a good deal of opposition even in University circles and was carried in Congregation (4) only by 127 votes to 74.

It should be noted that the University, usually in the form of Hebdomadal Council, appoints representatives to quite a long list of bodies: Universities (eg Birmingham and Liverpool); Schools (eg St. Pauls and the Oxford Girls' High School) and Local Education Authorities, including Oxfordshire (and for that matter Oxford City until the education service passed to the former). It would be unthinkable that the University should instruct any of these representatives how to vote.

It is also worth noticing that neither of the appointing bodies was central to the University. There are two important University executive bodies - Hebdomadal Council for general policy and the General Board of Faculties for academic affairs. The body of Heads and Senior Bursars was brought into being only for the purpose of electing Councillors to the City Council. In so far as it represented, or could speak on behalf of, any interest it would be for the Colleges. In contrast, Convocation - in theory the most representative and democratic institution of the University - is the most impractical. It consists of all M.A.'s of the University whether or not teaching in Oxford or indeed, whether or not resident in the area. Until 1918 it was Convocation which elected the two University Members of Parliament. In that year the franchise was widened to include B.A.'s. It is Convocation which elects the Chancellor and the Professor of Poetry and on both occasions M.A.'s come from far and wide to cast their votes. It was hardly in a position to instruct anybody. The only thing it could do would be to vote for one candidate in preference to another.

The second and third characteristics of the University Aldermen and Councillors I will take together because both contrasted sharply with those of the other members of Council: University members were likely to remain so much longer than other members and they were not party political, nor was their appointment usually the result of a conflict between the political parties.

There is always a fairly high turnover among town councillors. Some find the work too time consuming or not to their liking and do not stand again. Others leave the district and cease to be eligible. And there are many willing to serve but who fail to get re-elected. The Oxford Wards were fairly volatile politically. Some were likely to vote regularly for one Party but in years when there was a swing even these could fall to another party. The only way to remain for very long on the Council was to remain a Councillor long enough to qualify by seniority in your party for election to the now abolished Aldermanic bench. (5)

In contrast, once elected, a University Councillor could expect to be re-elected every three years as long as he was willing to serve. I do not know of one case during the period 1945-74 when the retiring candidate was not re-elected assuming he was willing to continue. University members did, of course, die, resign or cease to seek re-election but most of these had served for a good many years.

When I first went on the Council in May 1952 I noted that most Councillors had served for three years or less. Of the 42 non-University Councillors, nine had just been elected, seven had served for one year, five for two years, and eight for three years. Only seven had served for longer than five years. No doubt the war accounted for much of this, for many potential Councillors would have been in the armed forces or busily engaged on war work. Even so seven of the other eight University Councillors had been members for five or more years and three had been members for more than ten years. To find equally long serving members one had to turn to the Aldermanic benches, where six of the seventeen had served for over twenty years, including two of the three University Aldermen and another six, including the other University Aldermen, had served for between fifteen and twenty years.

Ten years later the pattern was not dissimilar. Of the 42 non-University Councillors twenty had served for two years or less and only seven had served for seven or more years. In contrast only three of the nine University Councillors had served for less than seven years, and five had served for ten or more years. It should be noted that the two elements in the Council kept quite distinct so far as Aldermen were concerned. The University

Councillors had the right to elect three (two after 1966) and they always chose them from among themselves. The other members had the right to elect fourteen (fifteen after 1966) and they also did not go outside their circle. Mrs. Prichard was however, still a University Alderman with almost 40 years' service followed in length of service by Lady Townsend, the leader of the Conservative group, with over 36 years. (Both were granted that rare honour: the Freedom of the City.)

Towards the end of the period the pattern changed due to the death or retirement of most of the long serving members. As a result in the last year (1973-4) only Alderman Michael Maclagan (over 26 years) and myself (21 years) had particularly long service.

The long service of the University members had two consequences for the working of the Council. First, during the period when seniority was a significant element in the choice of Committee Chairman they came to hold a good many of these important offices. Second, as the balance of political advantage swung between the Conservative and Labour groups the permanent University dozen became an awkward anomaly.

To understand these two points one must first be aware of the changing political composition of the Council. During the whole of the period 1945-1974 the Liberals were never significant numerically. Between 1949 amd 1952 they had one member, then none for the next ten elections. They achieved four seats at the election of May 1962, another in 1963, only to lose four in 1965 and the remaining one in 1966. Politically, therefore, it was a battle between the Conservative and the Labour groups. Between 1945 and 1957 the Conservatives had a majority of the non-University members - as many as 50 of the 56 in 1950-51 and 1951-52. During this phase of Conservative domination the University members could act without much fear of running into political criticism. It was not until 1957-58 that the Conservatives found themselves marginally in an overall minority - with 32 out of the 68 members.

In these earlier years there was a strong tendency, indeed an understanding, for each Committee to seek its Chairman from among its most long serving members. This was subject to the limitation laid down in the Council's Standing Orders; "No member of a Standing Committee shall be Chairman of it for more than five years in succession." Chairmen who wished to stand again were usually re-elected annually for the full five years. They were then quite often succeeded by the Vice-Chairman, if available. There could however be a political element in the choice certainly for one or two of the major policy committees.

Thus when I went on the Council in May 1952, of the twenty Standing Committees thirteen were chaired by Conservative and seven by University members. Of the Vice Chairmen fourteen were Conservative with Labour and University having three each. By 1957-58 more of the Labour members had worked their way up through the system so by now they had six of the nineteen Standing Committees including Education, Establishment, Highways and Watch held respectively by Marcus Lower, Arthur Kinchen (Establishments and Highways) and Bob Knight.

The election of May 1958 gave Labour 24 Councillors and at the subsequent Aldermanic election they secured all four places giving them eight, and so providing them with 32 of the 68 members. As a result they decided to take the Chairmanship of what they regarded as the most important Committees: Finance, Estates, Housing, Parliamentary and Planning. They already had the chairs of quite significant committees. Even so this still left the Conservatives with seven chairmen and seven vice-chairmen but the University now provided only one and four respectively.

The Labour domination was short-lived. By May 1960 the Conservatives were back to 31 members, and by May 1961 to 34 members. This enabled them to reduce the number of Labour Chairmen so that in 1962-3 the Conservatives provided ten and the University members nine of the Chairmen of the nineteen Standing Committees. The high proportion of University Chairmen was due only partly to the desire of the Conservative group to pay back the Labour group for how they had been treated in 1958. The Conservatives had lost some of their more able and experienced members and were rather short of people of chairmanship calibre. In contrast there were several University members who not only had long service but also were generally respected and regarded as good men of business. Councillor Baker (over sixteen years service) was Chairman of both the Finance and Planning Committees; Alderman Brewer (over seventeen years) was Chairman of the Watch and the Water Committees; Councillor Maclagan (over fifteen years) was Chairman of the Estates Committee, Councillor Mrs. Penelope Thompson (seven years) was Chairman of the Education Committee and Councillor Keith-Lucas (twelve years) was Chairman of the Housing Committee. Among the ten Committees chaired by Conservatives were such comparatively minor ones as Allotments, Baths, Catering and Markets. In the post-war years, this was the peak period of the influence of University members on the Council.

The struggle between the Conservative and Labour groups for dominance was not conducive to the continuance of the role of University members, indeed of any members, who were not active participants, in that struggle. So long as the Conservatives had a clear majority overall it was arguable that the existence of twelve University members was immaterial even if they all voted the same way. But the situation which emerged after the election of May 1958 while giving Labour a clear majority over the Conservatives still left them in a minority overall. At this point the charge was made that the University members were a "built-in House of Lords." According to an article in the Oxford Magazine, (6) one experienced observer "believed that nine out of the twelve University members could usually be relied upon to vote with the Conservatives when it came to a party vote." If this were true the gap between the two parties would be very narrow for the Labour group only had 32 of the 68 members.

I doubt whether, during the two municipal years 1958-9 and 1959-60, any major policy proposal of the Labour group was thwarted by the University members. The fact is that a large number of municipal decisions can be and indeed are decided without reference to any particular political creed.

It was not until the success of the Liberals at the election of May 1962 that the issue of University representation came active again. The Liberals gained four seats from the Conservatives and in May 1963 they added a further gain. Labour also gained four seats in 1963 so that Liberals and Labour together now had 23 Councillors as against nineteen Conservatives. In May 1964 the Labour group used its majority of Councillors (the Liberals abstaining) to take over two Aldermanic seats held by the Conservatives and then won both the subsequent by-elections. They now had 29 members which, with the Liberal five, gave them just half the Council. Again the University members were put in the position of appearing to hold the balance of power.

The Liberal group appeared to be very much concerned about machinery and believed in the purest principles of representative democracy. They favoured evening meetings so that people who were busy during the day could participate more. They wished to abolish the office of Alderman and refused to vote in their election. (One of their small number refused to allow himself to be elected to the Aldermanic bench even though that would have given him a much more certain and longer period on the Council.) And naturally they agreed with the Labour view that the existence of appointed University members was not consistent with a proper system of representative government.

There was, however, another factor which came to weigh with the Labour group and no doubt generally in the Council. The rapid growth in the population of the city had so far been accommodated within the old ward boundaries, substantially unchanged since 1928 when the population was some 30,000 less. The development of the motor industry had led to some wards having electorates far in excess of the other Wards. The Cowley and Iffley Ward had some 18,000 voters, and the Headington and Marston Ward had over 16,000 as against the 5,000 odd in the North, South and West Wards. A redistribution or a revision of boundaries was therefore needed, and was indeed only being delayed because of the possibility of changes in the City's boundary. If the number of University representatives could be reduced, then, providing the size of the Council was not correspondingly reduced, these seats would be available for the under-represented areas of the City. The Labour Party thought that such a change would favour them. It was their view, therefore, that any reduction in University representation should be accompanied by a corresponding increase in the Councillors and Aldermen elected in the usual way. The Conservatives also came to accept this view as making easier any change in the number and size of wards.

On 17 June 1963 the City Council debated a motion of the Labour group moved by Councillor Roger Dudman and seconded by Alderman Marcus Lower the leader of the group. It read:

"That:-

(i)   Council adopt the principle that University representation on the Council be reduced to three Councillors elected by Convocation and one Alderman elected by such Councillors;

(ii)   the Parliamentary Committee be instructed to report to Council not later than September 16, 1963, on the steps necessary to bring this into operation."

An amendment was moved by Councillors Ann Spokes and Fred Ingram (both Conservatives) (a) to omit paragraph (i) and (b) to ask the Parliamentary Committee to consult the University and the Colleges before reporting to Council. It was defeated by twenty votes to 26. The substantive motion was then carried by 26 votes to 19. (7) If I remember correctly the University members abstained.

The Parliamentary Committee were advised by the Departments concerned that the most appropriate way of making the change would be by way of Section 25 of the Local Government Act, 1933, which dealt with alterations in the number of Councillors. This would involve the Council passing a resolution by a clear majority, ie at least 35 members would have to vote for it. The resolution would support a petition to Her Majesty praying for a reduction in the number of members but not specifically dealing with University representation. Before any Order in Council would be made the Home Secretary might appoint a Commissioner to hold a local inquiry. Such a local inquiry would be unlikely to present much difficulty, providing the proposal was not seriously contested. The Council would, however, have to explain and be prepared to defend their objective of reducing University representation. It would emerge that the University had not been consulted and indeed that their attitude to the proposal was not known. The Parliamentary Committee therefore recommended that as a next step consultations with the University should be put in hand. (8)

The recommendation was opposed by Councillors Dudman and Edmund Gibbs and defeated by 22 votes to eighteen on July 29. The Parliamentary Committee were required to report on all possible methods of giving effect to the earlier Council decision "including the retention of the present total number of members of Council." (9)

The Parliamentary Committee reported to the Council at a meeting of 18 November, 1963, (an interim report had explained the impossibility of meeting the deadline set by the motion). The new factor which had emerged during the second debate was that the Labour group wished the total size of the Council to remain the same. This could only be brought about by the creation of an additional ward or wards. Having sketched the three possible methods of securing the changes the Parliamentary Committee, in order to facilitate a discussion, recommended that the Town Clerk should prepare a petition under Section 25 of the Local Government Act, 1933, asking for both the reduction in the number of University representatives and an alteration in the number of wards. They also recommended that this action should not be put in hand unless it were supported by a clear majority, ie 35 votes as required by the 1933 Act. However, should the recommendation not receive the requisite 35 votes and be therefore of no avail for practical purposes, consultation with the University on the whole question of University representation should be sought. (10)

At the Council meeting of 18 November 1963 the Conservative group moved an amendment to the effect that a petition should not be prepared which was defeated by 26 votes to 27. Only two University representatives - Aldermen A.B. Brown and Mrs. Prichard - voted and were for the amendment. It was clear, however, that the proposal had no chance of securing the necessary 35 votes. The City Council, therefore, agreed unanimously (59 votes to none) to enter into consultations with the University.

The meeting between representatives of the City and of the Hebdomadal Council of the University took place on 27 February 1964. The City representatives, composed of two Conservatives, two Labour and one Liberal, learnt that there was unlikely to be much difficulty in securing the elimination of the Heads and Bursars method of election but it would not be easy to obtain agreement about the size of the reduction in University representation. A letter from the Registrar dated 11 March 1964 said that it would be necessary for the Hebdomadal Council to consult Congregation, and possibly Convocation, but in the light of discussions which it had already had with the Colleges it believed that Congregation would be willing to see representatives elected by Congregation rather than by Convocation and 'Heads and Bursars'. If, however, University representation were to continue it could hardly be on the basis of less than that then appropriate for one ward, ie six Councillors and two Aldermen. Hedbomadal Council asked that the City should consider this alternative. It would also welcome the views of the City Council on the suggestion that members of Congregation should be entitled to vote either in the "University Ward" or in an ordinary ward, but not in both. (11)

Thus two new points had emerged. All along the method of election by Heads and Bursars had been thought to be less democratic than election by Convocation. The latter vote was by public ballot by a potentially large electorate. (12) Any M.A., B.C.L., Bachelor of Medicine or holder of any higher degree of the University could be nominated as a candidate. In contrast the meeting of Heads and Bursars, though representing considerable power was quite small, some 60 votes in theory but a much smaller number in practice. The voting took place in secret and the candidates were not publicly announced. Convocation was, however, very unsuitable for the election of Oxford City Councillors for the major part of it consisted of M.A.'s who no longer lived in the city. Congregation composed of the teachers and senior administrative staff was the general electorate of the University. Hebdomadal Council was elected by Congregation.

The proposal that members of Congregation might be constituted a ward, and dons should have a choice of voting in it or in the ward in which they lived, could not stand up to serious examination. In part it was used as an answer to those who argued that, under the present arrangement, University teachers who lived within the City had two votes whereas other citizens had only one. In part by equating the University with a ward the figure of six Councillors and two Aldermen could be justified. It also had a parallel in the arrangement whereby professional and businessmen and shopkeepers entitled to a vote for business premises could use it in that ward or use their residential vote but not both. Had the University representatives been there to represent the interests of the University, it might have made more sense. But in any case a large part of the work of a Councillor is concerned with the problems of his own ward - traffic, planning, schools, street lighting etc. The Councillors for a University ward would be able effectively to represent neither the interests of the University nor of local residents. The Parliamentary Committee therefore dealt with this suggestion very briefly: they would not wish to curtail the voting rights of members of Congregation.(13)

The Parliamentary Committee split on the question of the future number. The Committee was composed of twelve members: five were Conservatives, five Labour, one Liberal and one University. The Committee by a bare majority recommended that the Council should stick to its view that the University should have only three Councillors and one Alderman. Normally a Committee's recommendations are put in Council by the Chairman, or if absent, by the Vice-Chairman. But the Chairman of the Parliamentary Committee (Lady Townsend) was the leader of the Conservative group and the Vice-Chairman (Robert, later Lord Blake) was also a Conservative and had also voted against the recommendation. It was, therefore, left to Alderman Marcus Lower, the leader of the Labour group, to move the Committee's report. (14)

At the meeting of Council on 6 April 1964 Councillor Blake moved that the words "six Councillors and two Aldermen" should be substituted for the Committees recommendation. This was carried by 31 votes to 28. It will be noticed that the Labour-Liberal vote was one more than that of November 18 - Alderman Pickstock being available to vote on this occasion. This was one below their potential voting strength. The Conservatives were supported by three University Aldermen and five University Councillors (I was present but abstained). When the amended version of the recommendation was put as a substantive motion it was carried by 30 votes to 29. As names were not taken for this vote it is not possible to say who changed his or her mind. (15)

When Hebdomadal Council was informed of the Council's decision it moved a resolution in Congregation on 19 May 1964 asking the House to agree in principle that University Councillors on the City Council should in future be elected by Congregation and that the proposal of the City Council that University representation should be reduced to six Councillors and two Aldermen should be accepted. There was quite a spirited debate on an amendment to reduce the number to three and one. This was moved by Mr. G. Fowler, a Fellow of Hertford College and a Labour Councillor for the Cowley and Iffley Ward. It was defeated by 53 votes to 28

It now looked as though agreement had been reached. However at its meeting on 27 July 1964 the Council rejected by 29 votes to nineteen the recommendation of the Parliamentary Committee that the legal formalities should be put in hand for securing the agreed reduction. (16) Allowing for holidays the vote reflected the result of the election of May 1964 whereby the Conservatives lost three Councillors and two Aldermen. In November, therefore, the Parliamentary Committee instructed the Town Clerk to inform the University that the Council now favoured a reduction to three Councillors and one Alderman. The Registrar replied that Hebdomadal Council felt that the vote taken in Congregation on May 19 should be regarded as the considered view of the University.

The City Council were now faced with a difficult situation. If they
went ahead and petitioned the Queen for a reduction of University representation to three Councillors and one Alderman they would meet opposition at the
local enquiry which would increase its cost and reduce the chance of success.
Of more immediate importance the Labour and Liberal groups could not of themselves muster the 35 votes necessary to meet the requirements of the Local
Government Act of 1933. If, however, they accepted the smaller reduction they
would have the general support of the Council and would be likely to achieve
speedy results. Nevertheless before that situation was reached they made a
further attempt to secure the larger reduction.

Council at its meeting of 5 April 1965 debated another report of the
Parliamentary Committee. This recommended that a petition be prepared to
secure the reduction to three and one but if that did not secure at least 35
votes the petition should ask for a reduction to six Councillors and two Aldermen. A separate petition would be needed to enable the number lost by the
University to be made available for a newly created ward but a report on this
would be made when a decision had been taken on the size of the reduction.
After several amendments had failed the first recommendation was carried by 31
votes to 24. (The latter figure included three University members.) As this
was insufficient Council voted by 48 to none that the petition should ask for
the larger number of University representatives. (17)

The course of the controversy about University representation needs to
be seen in the light of two other factors. First at its meeting on 18 March
1965 the City Council agreed to propose an extension of the City boundary to
the Local Government Commission set up to review such matters. Until this
application had been settled it would be difficult to make changes in the wards
of the City. This might complicate the timing of the reduction in the number
of University representatives.

Second, at its meeting on 21 September 1964 the Council took the view
by 25 votes to fourteen that the office of Alderman "as at present constituted"
was "outmoded and undemocratic" and asked the Parliamentary Committee to consider the steps that could be taken to end it. A similar motion had been
defeated by 31 votes to 23 at a meeting on 1 July 1963. (18) Both motions were
moved by the leader of the Liberal group (Councillor Ivor Davies). Although
there was some cross-voting, those who carried the second motion were largely
the same as those who voted for the larger reduction in University representation. To most of them both arrangements stood condemned as offending the
basic principle that democracy meant decisions being taken by those who had
successfully faced the electorate at regular intervals. The Council subsequently submitted a memorandum to the Maud Committee on Management of Local
Authorities. (19)

The vote of April 1965 settled the matter. The drafting of the two
petitions was put in hand. Formal resolutions were agreed by the Council on
1 November 1965. The proposals included an increase of the wards from seven
to eight, the additional ward to be formed out of part of the Cowley and Iffley
Ward. The Ministry of Housing and Local Government held an inquiry in the
Town Hall on 18 January 1966 to deal with the proposed transfer of the right
of election to Congregation. Ward changes were a matter for the Home Office.
On 18 November 1966 the Privy Council agreed the necessary Statutory Instruments. (20)

The City of Oxford (University Representation) Order 1966 fixed the
new number of University representatives and settled the transitional arrangements. The four most recently elected University Councillors were deemed to
have been re-elected and the two other places were filled at the election of
May 1967. Four of the five Councillors due to come up for election in May
1967 and May 1968 did not seek re-election. The reduction from three to two

Aldermen was left to be settled by agreement or, in default, "by lot cast", at the annual meeting of the Council. In the event Alderman J.N.L. Baker decided to retire, otherwise, as the junior Alderman, I would have resigned. This decision was fortunate for me but less fortunate for the Council. During his 22 years he had been one of the leading policy makers. Chairman of the very important Finance and Planning Committees and Lord Mayor in 1964 to 1965 he was a powerful expositor and debater and added stature to the Council. He was an excellent example of the values and virtues of the system of University representation.

The change to election by Congregation resulted in more contests. In May 1967 there were three candidates for the two places. The winners secured 347 and 310 votes. There were four candidates for two places in May 1970 and three for two places in May 1972, the last election to be held. The Ward carved out of the overlarge Cowley and Iffley Ward was called Blackbird Leys. At the first election held in May 1967 three seats were available and they were all won by the Labour Party.

The new arrangements did not last very long. Late in 1971 the Secretary of State for the Environment (Mr. Peter Walker) produced a Bill for the re-organisation of English and Welsh Local Government. Among other things it abolished County Boroughs and it also abolished Aldermen. The Minister wrote to the Vice-Chancellor on 20 January 1972 saying that after careful thought the Government had come to the conclusion that the system of direct University representation should lapse when the present Oxford City Council ceased to exist. The same decision had been taken with regard to Cambridge and to Aldershot, where three presentatives of the Borough Council were appointed by the Secretary of State for Defence. Having, he said, "taken a general stand in favour of vesting responsibility in directly elected members...we feel it would be impossible to re-create the special arrangements which were originally introduced in the very different circumstances of the last century". The decision was "entirely acceptable" to the University which had indeed already issued a statement that "it would not be appropriate for the University to seek to elect councillors to serve" on the new authorities. (21) So on the 31 March 1974 the system of direct University representation on the City Council came to an end.

What conclusions and lessons emerge from this history?

First, anyone who believes that it was a case of the University versus the rest is very far off the mark. Quite a number of Council members, even excluding the University representatives were connected in some way with the University. Marcus Lower, the leader of the Labour Group and Frank Pickstock, another leading Labour member, were both engaged on the Extra-mural side of the University. Also for a time John Briscoe and Gerry Fowler held Labour seats whilst ellows or lecturers of Corpus and Hertford respectively. On the Conservative side Robert (later Lord) Blake was a Fellow of Queen's, Peter Spokes was on the staff of Bodley Library; Lewis Wilcher was head of Queen Elizabeth House and Tom Meadows was a Laboratory Technician. The husband of Lady Townsend had been a Professor and the husband of the Liberal, Sylvia Chilver, a Fellow of Queen's. Janet Young and Ann Spokes and indeed several others had been undergraduates and Janet (now Lady) Young's father was Alderman Baker.

As for the University representatives, few were members of the Hebdomadal Council or of the General Board of Faculties. Alan Brock Brown may be singled out as a rare figure bestriding the several worlds: Bursar of Worcester, Member of Hebdomadal Council, University representative and Mayor (22) all at the same time. (Sir) Kenneth Wheare, was a member of Hebdomadal Council, University Councillor and Chairman of the Education

Committee, Professor of Government and Public Administration and Fellow of
All Souls at the same time. Norman Whatley, Mrs. Prichard and Mrs. Penelope
Thompson were not tutors nor Fellows. The University of course is a highly
decentralised institution. On many issues there was room for several opinions -
within the University proper, within the group of University representatives
and within the two main political groups.

In passing it was noticeable that though Morris and Pressed Steel had
now replaced the University as chief employer I cannot recall one member of
the management side of either company serving on the Council. The industries
of Cowley and the problems they created were represented mainly by trade
unionists in the Labour group.

Secondly, though many of the University representatives showed an apti-
tude for Council work and enjoyed it, I doubt whether many would have become
Councillors had they had to face the normal election. It was not merely that
they would not have liked to engage in a public political election every three
years, nor was it that not being representatives of a Ward they did not have
the load of ward business which other Councillors had. Both these counted,
but far more significant was that they would not have been happy confined
within the discipline of a political party.

During my 21 years on the Council party politics came to be increasingly
significant. At first the Conservative groups had a fairly relaxed attitude
towards the actions of their individual members. On a few issues the leader
of the group would expect members to vote in accordance with party policy,
particularly that embodied in election addresses. The leader - for most of
the early years the charmingly formidable Lady Townsend - could normally
expect her supporters, when in doubt, to follow the line she was taking in
Council. But it was recognised that there was no particular party policy in
respect of a great deal of Council business. The interests of one's Ward
might cause one to take a line different from other Conservative Councillors,
and there was room for differences of opinion and public expression of them
on most items of business. The University representatives fitted readily
into such a political atmosphere.

The situation changed when electoral successes in the late 50's brought
the Labour group near to a majority. They believed that they had a general
policy which, if put into operation, would benefit the City. They disliked
therefore, any factor which might stand in the way of their success. One
such factor could be members of the Group not voting in accordance with the
line agreed by the group at one of its regular meetings. They believed
strongly in majority rule not only in the Council chamber but also within
their own private meetings. It was therefore incumbent on their members to
vote in Council in accordance with that internal party vote. In other words,
they believed in party discipline. In the Council their more militant
speakers were inclined to imply that there was something rather nasty and
sinister in the make-up of their opponents. The atmosphere in the chamber
could on occasion be quite bitter.

My impression is that this more politically-charged atmosphere caused
the Conservative group to react in the same way. Moreover, now that they no
longer had a clear majority and indeed at times had fewer members than Labour,
party differences in public only helped the other side. Certainly I was
acutely aware of the tenseness and discipline of the two major political
groups during my last ten years on the Council. And this was not only in
respect of major issues such as relief roads or the sale of council houses
but even in respect of some planning applications and the detailed recommendations of Committees. In such disciplined battles the University representatives were rather like fish out of water. To their personal judgement of
the merits of a particular policy they now had to add a consideration of the

political implications of their vote. A good many of the University representatives, particularly those who had served in the earlier period disliked the new atmosphere. They were not happy at being caught up in slanging matches or to see debate rendered useless by party positions taken up before the Council had even met.

It was claimed, particularly in Labour quarters, that the University representatives were predominantly Conservative. One or two were obviously so, one or two were obviously pro Labour and there were at least a couple of Liberals; but my general impression is that none was prepared to toe a party line. Academics are individualists and do not take readily to being told how to vote. Most votes in Council were taken by a show of hands but Standing Orders allowed any ten members to rise and demand that names be recorded. This was done only on issues which for one reason or other a party or both parties wanted to be able to point to the way particular persons had voted. I believe it was used by the Labour group on occasion to reveal the vote of the University members. These named voters show a good deal of cross voting. Let me take one example - the issue of the sale of council houses, which the Conservatives believed in and Labour were against.

In August 1964 the Housing Committee recommended that the existing scheme for the sale of council houses should cease. A motion for its rejection was moved by Ivor Davies, the Liberal leader, and was carried by 28 to 27. On that occasion four University representatives voted for, two voted against and two abstained. The Labour vote was lower than its membership because several of their members were held to be disqualified from voting because they had an interest, being council tenants. In November 1964 the Labour group brought forward a motion to ask the Minister of Housing and Local Government to remove the disability of these members for this purpose. The motion was carried by 39 votes to 21 with five University members voting for it and none against. The Minister removed the disability and a motion to stop the sale of council houses was debated in December 1964. This time it was carried by 32 votes to 29. Three University members voted for it (including two who had voted against in August), four voted against, and two, including the Lord Mayor, abstained.

It can also be said that the University members did not consider it their function to keep the rates down - a policy which would have been generally helpful to the University and the Colleges. On the whole they were expansionist and believed that the City should provide a high standard of service. Between 1950 and 1962 the City's expenditure on rate fund services, excluding Housing and loan charges, trebled and even after allowing for price increases, was up by some 55%. Yet during much of this period the Conservatives and the University members were in a majority. In 1963/4 Oxford levied a rate per head higher than the average for all County Boroughs for all but two out of thirteen services.

GENERAL RELATIONS OF CITY AND UNIVERSITY

As we have seen, University representation did not provide a working link between City and University on such planning matters as student numbers and new building. The City, in its evidence to the Franks Commission in April 1965, said that had these representatives been in receipt of a mandate from the University and had voted as a University block they would have been even less acceptable to the Council. Though many University members had given distinguished service to the City Council and, as individuals, had often paved the way to co-operation, this was not enough. The City envisaged the appointment of a permanent planning staff by the University and the Colleges to work closely and continuously with the City's Planning Department.

The University had already begun to be concerned about the problems created by the continual expansion of numbers. In the early 1920's there were some 4,000 students, 350 academic staff and 25 Colleges. By 1964/5 the number had grown to about 9,500 students, over 1,100 academic staff and 31 Colleges with three new ones being planned. Now the figures are around 12,000-12,500 with some 1,500 academic staff.

The problem created by the growth in size of the University has been exacerbated by three other developments. First, by the emergence of the Oxford Polytechnic with its new buildings and residential quarters on Headington Hill. Second, by the commercial attraction of an Oxford address for an increasing number of private teaching institutions, eg St. Clare's and the several language schools. Third, by the use of Oxford as a regional hospital centre. A large part of the Headington area is taken over by the John Radcliffe, Churchill, Nuffield Orthopaedic and Warnford Hospitals. But even without them the expansion of the University would have posed problems for the City.

Had all these developments taken place in a town as large as Birming-ham or Manchester, or had they taken place on the City outskirts, as was the case with the new Universities, the problems presented would have been very different and easier to handle. But the University and Colleges occupy the City centre and their expansion has taken the form of a spreading of this centre.

Even so this expansion would not in itself have created such serious problems had it not been for the City's agreement with the County Council to impose a green belt around its boundary and, in some parts, within it. For, as a result, each expansion of the University means a contraction of the land available for other purposes within the City. People in search of houses are thus increasingly driven to leapfrog the green belt and to buy or build houses in the surrounding villages and towns - eg Abingdon, Cassing-ton, Kidlington, Wheatley, Witney and Woodstock.

This in-filling is valuable to the County for its increases the via-bility of the smaller villages and rural communities. But it has created several problems for the City. For one thing it has meant that a larger and larger core of the City is denuded of permanent residents. This core has little communal life except that based on the Colleges during Term. The counterpart of this is that more and more of those who work in the City are commuters. They come in between 8 and 9 am. and leave between 4.45 and 5.45 pm. judging from the continuous crawl of cars at these times along the Ban-bury, Botley, Iffley and Woodstock Roads. Another consequence is that the level of house prices within the City is abnormally high, which puts it out of reach of the ordinary citizen.

The consequences for the core of the City can be seen in the changes that have occurred in quite recent years along the Banbury and Woodstock Roads. Each year has seen the accommodation available for the ordinary citizen pushed further and further north. In the case of the Banbury Road there is now not a great deal of ordinary private accommodation until one gets past the Summertown shopping centre, in other words, until under a mile from the City boundary. This is not solely a main road phenomenon - it is steadily affecting the side roads. Much of it, but by no means all, is due to College expansion, eg the development of St. Antony's, the graduate accommodation built by Jesus and University Colleges, and the increasing number of houses acquired by Colleges to provide accommodation for the fairly recent big increase in post-graduates, many of whom are married. But St. Clare's, a private institution, has steadily been acquiring houses in the Lathbury Road area to house not married graduates, who might live in the area for two or three years, but transient students mainly from overseas. The

City Council seems unwilling or unable to curb this last kind of development.

I believe that if the City is to remain a viable and real community it has got to put a stop to the encroachment of all other uses on the land and accommodation available for the ordinary long term resident. Such a policy would seem to carry at least three important implications.

First, there is little or no scope for an increase in University numbers or of new research institutes or centres unless these mainly take place outside the core of the City traditionally the home of the University. I can see no reason why a limited University development could not take place on suitable sites adjacent to the ring road. The Oxford Centre for Management Studies sited at Kennington is an interesting development of this kind. Had the scheme for a magnificent new Pitt-Rivers Museum succeeded, I am convinced that it would have been much better sited say at the end of the Abingdon Road than in the Banbury Road-Norham Gardens area. Many in the University are still obsessed with the idea that every academic facility should be within a short walk from Carfax - notwithstanding the fact that in order to get near Carfax some of them have made a five to eight mile car journey, some of it rather tedious. Activities not concerned with the everyday teaching of undergraduates could with advantage be sited three or four miles from, rather than within one mile of, Carfax.

Second, something must be done quickly to make better use of the land in the St. Ebbe's - St. Thomas's area. I am sure there is scope there for a mixture of good flats and more modest living accommodation. It would bring life back to the centre of the City and relieve the pressure on the other residential parts. This is very much a matter for the City which I understand owns much of the land. But it ought to secure the collaboration of private developers and encourage those who own land in the area to use it mainly for housing.

Third, unless measures of this kind are actively pursued during the next decade, the whole policy of the green belt will be brought into question.

The University cannot avoid being involved in the longer term planning of Oxford. The car industry is very important in terms of the numbers it employs. Its decline would seriously affect the prosperity of a large number of citizens and the shopkeepers who depend on them. But its existence does not pose serious planning problems, unless it were to wish to expand, which would now appear most unlikely. The growth of the Polytechnic, the hospitals and the numerous non University teaching schools have exacerbated the problem and any plans for their expansion need critical examination. But the greatest single factor is likely to remain the size and character of the University.

It now appears to be generally accepted that the number of undergraduates and graduates should be stabilised at around 12,500. Certainly there is no prospect of doubling or trebling of numbers that has occurred since the 1920's. Indeed there is good reason to believe that the size of the University in terms of number of students is unlikely to change much in the next ten years. Nevertheless it is difficult to believe that the University and the Colleges will be exactly the same in the year 2000 as they are now. Any changes that do occur will not, I feel sure, include an increase in the undergraduate members, if only because of the decline in the number of school leavers. They are much more likely to occur on the post-graduate research side. Governments, Foundations and private benefactors will continue to be attracted to Oxford by reason of its international reputation. They will continue to press the University to take an active interest in this or that new field of study and research. Developments of this kind would not necessarily be reflected in the number of students, but they would involve more building and more academic staff. I do not favour an ever expanding University but it would be unfortunate if the University's choice was restricted by a lack of suitable sites.

The University has had a City Questions Committee since the early 1960's. At present it is composed of five members appointed by Hebdomadal Council and five elected by the Colleges. It is primarily a body within the University for discussing general planning, traffic and similar issues. In 1967, when Lady (Janet) Young became leader of the Conservative Group, it was given a wider significance: it began to provide a vehicle for the exchange of information and ideas with the City Council. There is an understanding between the City and the University that either side can ask for a joint meeting. My general impression is that such meetings and the existence of such machinery have gone a good way to meet the complaint of the City Council in 1965 that it was very difficult to obtain an authoritative view of the longer term needs and plans of the University and Colleges. The machinery does not, however, seem to be much in use at the moment. It was most active when the City was drawing up its Development Plan. There does not appear to have been a joint meeting for getting on for two years.

The term City Questions, and indeed the title of my paper - the University in the City - are both rather dated. For the City Council is no longer in complete control of planning and highways as it was before the Local Government Act of 1972. The County Council now has a significant role to play. There is, however, no formal arrangement between the University and the County for the discussion of common problems, though there has been at least an informal get together.

CONCLUSION

There is clearly a big difference between the system of University representation as it existed until March 1974 and the present arrangement whereby representatives of the City and University consult with each other from time to time on matters of direct concern. Under the former arrangement members of the University were engaged in furthering the well-being of the town as a whole. Mrs. Prichard did a very great deal for the welfare services and Freddie Brewer played a major role in the development of the Polytechnic to take but two obvious examples. But none of the University members could speak authoritatively for the University and Colleges on such important planning matters as size and building.

The current arrangements, including the existence of a City Questions Committee enable the City Council to get the authoritative information and answers which it needs for planning purposes. That is a gain. But it puts the University in very little different position from any other major interest group which needs to deal with the City or County Councils, eg British Leyland or Oxford United. What has been lost in the change has been the active interest of a number of University people in the general welfare of the city and the progress of the services it provides.

In his letter announcing the end of University representation the Secretary of State for the Environment said he hoped that close links would nevertheless be maintained between the University and the Civic government. He pointed out that the Council would have wide powers to co-opt persons on to its committees. He trusted that this and other means of collaboration would be fully explored. The Vice-Chancellor said that Hebdomadal Council shared that hope. It seems unlikely, however, that either the City or County will make use of co-optation. There remains, therefore, only the normal electoral process. It is to be hoped that some dons will adopt this course. I suspect, however, that not many will be attracted, if only because few will accept for long the domination of party voting and discipline which now prevails in the City and County.

FOOTNOTES

(1) The 1771 Act was the first of five Local Improvement Acts commonly known as The Mileway Acts.

(2) The texts of most of these statutes and orders are contained in L.L. Shadwell, Enactments in Parliament, see also A History of The City of Oxford by Ruth Fasnacht, pp. 151-4 and 161-73. For the working of local government in the Oxford area in the inter-war years see Social Services in The Oxford District, Vol. 1, Chapter IX.

(3) At one time it was usual for the University representatives to wear M.A. gowns instead of Council robes on ceremonial occasions. It was, however, increasingly felt that this was an undesirable demarcation and so the custom changed.

(4) Oxford University Gazette 1965-6, p.953.

(5) At least that was true until 1964 when the convention that Aldermen seeking re-election had all party support ceased to be accepted by the Labour group.

(6) 1 May 1958, p.388.

(7) Council Book 1963-4, Minute 168.

(8) Council Book 1963-4, Paragraph 458.

(9) Council Book 1963-4, Paragraph 472 (6).

(10) Council Book 1963-4, Paragraph 867 (4).

(11) Council Book 1963-4, Paragraph 1574.

(12) Contests were rare. There was one in October 1964 no doubt stimulated by the current discussion the previous one being in November 1944. Very few voted on either occasion.

(13) Had it ever come into operation it would have almost certainly resulted in splitting the University on party lines.

(14) Council Book 1963-4, Paragraph 1574.

(15) Council Book 1963-4, Minute 1603 (3).

(16) Council Book 1964-5, Paragraph 292 and Minute 411 (1).

(17) Council Book 1964-5, Paragraph 1476 and Minute 1515 (13).

(18) Council Book 1963-4, Minute 287 and 1964-5, Minute 674.

(19) Council Book 1964-5, pp. 1118-1120.

(20) The City of Oxford Order, 1966, confirmed by the Ministry of Housing and Local Government Provisional Order Confirmation (City of Oxford) Act 1966 transferred the election of City Councillors from Heads and Bursars and Convocation to Congregation. The City of Oxford (University Representation) Order 1966, fixed the number of University representatives on the Council. For texts see University Gazette Vol. XCVII, pp. 764-5.

(21) Oxford University Gazette, 2 March 1972.

(22) During the period 1945-74 the University representatives provided five Mayors: N. Whatley (1949-50); A.B. Brown (1953-54); F.M. Brewer (1959-60); J.N.L. Baker (1964-5) and M. Mclagan (1970-71).

HARWELL AND ITS IMPACT ON THE OXFORD REGION

E.J.S. Clarke

PART I

The first part of this paper about Harwell and the Oxford region tells how the Atomic Energy Research Establishment came to be and a little about what has gone on there; the rest discusses the impact on the surrounding population.

Figure 1 shows the Harwell site in relation to Harwell village and to the local road network.

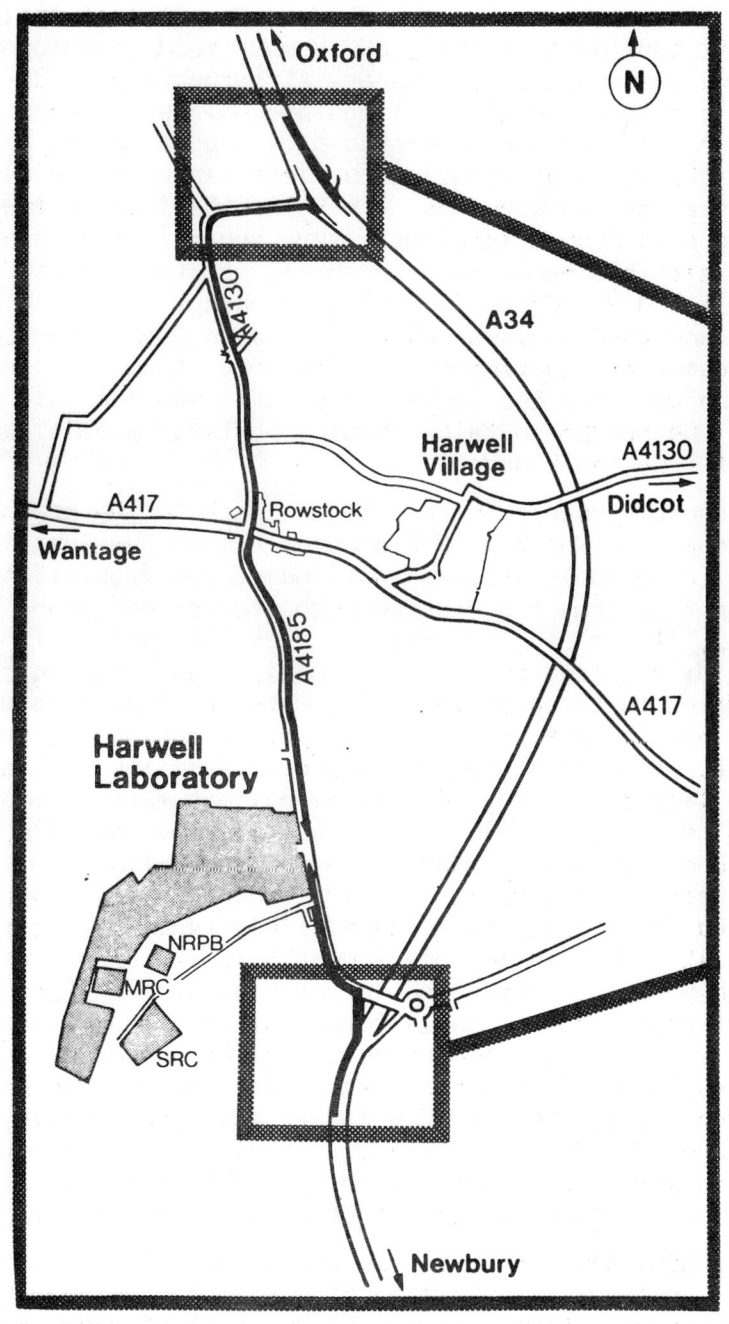

Figure 1

Harwell village lies on a band of green sand which has made the soil fertile and favourable for fruit farming particularly since, after the railway came to Didcot, produce could be sent to London quickly and easily. To the south and west is an area historically known as Harwell Field. This lies upon the relatively poor soil of the upper chalk: here a few farms once eked out a modest existence. Immediately after the first world war a horse racing establishment came there; then the Air Ministry made a temporary landing ground and then finally in 1935, a few years before the outbreak of the second world war, a permanent airfield was built as part of the first major measure of rearmament to meet Hitler's preparations in Germany.

At this time the population of Harwell village was only about 1000. The airfield was commissioned in April 1935 and came into operation on the first of April, 1939. At the beginning of the war it was a home of the luckless Fairey Battle, which was no match for the fighters of the Luftwaffe. After the fall of France the airfield housed an Operational Training Unit from which aircraft took part in the 1,000 bomber raid on Cologne. Later the airfield became the headquarters of the 6th Airborne Corps. On the night of 5th-6th June 1944 a huge force of Sterlings and Halifaxes took the paratroops and glider-borne forces who were to play a part in the invasion of Europe (Operation OVERLORD) by securing the left flank of the allied army's landing on the River Orne in Normandy. Three months later Harwell was a base for the less successful Arnhem landings. Very shortly after Arnhem the post-war future of the airfield began to take shape. At the end of September, President Roosevelt and Mr. Churchill met in Quebec to discuss the final stages of the war and make post-war plans. Also in Quebec was Lord Cherwell, the Dr. Lees Professor of Experimental Philosophy, at the Clarendon Laboratory in Oxford, who was then the Paymaster-General and the scientific adviser to Mr. Churchill; he now began talks about a post-war atomic experimental establishment in the United Kingdom.

The atomic energy project in the UK goes back to two groups of refugees from Hitler's Europe. In March 1940 Professor Frisch (an Austrian) and Professor Peierls (a German), wrote an outline of the feasibility of an atomic bomb. From that time the British bomb project developed until, by the end of 1942, it was decided that the necessary scale of production was too large for the United Kingdom in war conditions and under air attack; so the British agreed to throw in their lot with the Americans who, by then convinced that an atomic bomb was possible, were planning the Manhattan Project to produce it. So most of our key scientists in the nuclear field were sent over to America. Among the few exceptions were a second refugee group, the French team led by Halban and Kowarski, who had managed to escape from Bordeaux to England in June 1940. They brought with them, almost under the noses of the Germans, the world's entire stock of heavy water which had just been delivered from Norway in 26 cans. This team was primarily interested not in the military but in the civil possibilities of nuclear science. There was not much effort at that time to spare in Britain for such a long-range project, but room was eventually found for it at the Cavendish Laboratory in Cambridge and a small group of people gathered there, engaged in thinking about a nuclear pile moderated with heavy water. There was a similar interest in Canada, and the Canadians were ready to receive this group, so that an Anglo-Canadian-French team was established in Montreal University by 1944. This team had some common ground with the bomb project in the United States, but was virtually cut off from it by the American security wall.

So it was natural that at Quebec in the autumn of 1944 we should begin to think about the post-war organisation of atomic energy and the future of this Anglo-French-Canadian team, along with the host of other much greater post-war anxieties which crowded in upon us as Hitler's Germany began at last to collapse. The Canadians would have liked to maintain an Anglo-French-

Canadian project, but the French team were already pining to go home to liberated France. The British still hoped to play a significant part in the military and perhaps in the supporting production effort in the United States. Given that such a large part of our effort might be in North America, it was unthinkable to have the UK experimental base there too. So we needed an experimental establishment in Britain. Where was it to be?

It rapidly became clear that the only practicable site for such an establishment would be on an airfield. In bomb-damaged Britain, hungry for housing and new factories, we could only get a flying start if we went for an airfield with its engineering workshops, its roads, its water supply, its housing and, above all, the hangars which could house large nuclear machines. To go anywhere other than a major airfield would put the project back some two years. Then, the establishment had to be near Oxford or Cambridge. The papers of the time specified a site near a "major University", but in reality it had to be near either the Clarendon or the Cavendish Laboratories to be acceptable to the few scientists who mattered.

The Air Ministry put up a list of seventeen airfields, but the inspecting team soon realised that this contained many temporary sites that had few of the facilities they sought. They wanted good brick structures, not Nissen huts; solid roads not dirt tracks; concrete runways rather than grass fields. Thus the specification became a permanent airfield near Oxford or Cambridge that the Air Ministry would be prepared to release. Most of the cards were stacked in favour of Cambridge: John Cockcroft, the Director at Montreal, who had already been designated Director of the UK establishment-to-be, came from the Cavendish, so did several of his Montreal team. Other senior staff who were to come from the Malvern Telecommunications Research Establishment were mostly oriented towards Cambridge. However, the Air Ministry was biased towards Oxfordshire. At the beginning of 1945 when the Germans were about to collapse, the front of the future - if there was to be a front - would be somewhere near where the Iron Curtain now lies. Therefore the Air Ministry were not happy to release any East Anglian airfields, though they did offer, under pressure, Duxford and Deben. Other requirements for the airfield were now defined - a low water table (as it was thought that radioactive scrap might be buried on the site) and a large water supply (because a water-cooled pile like the American reactors at Hanford[1] would need 100,000 gallons a day). Then the site must not be too near a town because the nuclear hazards were not at that time well-defined; yet it must not be too far from attractive housing and schools and shops or too many scientists would refuse to be posted there.

Deben was soon rejected because of its high water table. Cockcroft was strongly in favour of Duxford, conveniently sixteen miles down the road from Cambridge. But this site was ruled out because of poor water supply and because it was far from anywhere except Cambridge: Sixteen miles would be a long way for most of the staff at a time of petrol rationing. The inspection team then went to Benson in Oxfordshire, to which they were immediately attracted; it offered all the permanent buildings and other facilities they sought. The diplomatic station commander was very sympathetic; he fully understood what they were after and realised that Benson would meet the team's needs but "perhaps the countryside round Benson was rather populous for an experimental station handling such dangerous things?" Harwell airfield, not far away, had all Benson's facilities but with open country around it; would it not be better to go there? One of the team did indeed go there the next day, looked from without over the Harwell field, and fell in love with it. So despite the team's icy reception on their official visit, Cockcroft and his colleagues soon took what was the effective though not yet the authoritative decision one evening in the nearby "Horse and Jockey".

187

Harwell had the advantage over all the other places seen of being near schools - such as the Girls' High School at Oxford and Royce's at Abingdon - where the sort of staff which Harwell hoped to attract would wish to send their children. Abingdon and Wantage were suitably distant yet near enough to be considered for housing. There was a good rail service to London and to Birmingham, where the University housed one of the nuclear projects which had not gone to America. So the choice fell on Harwell. There were last-minute hitches: from the Air Ministry, because Harwell's very long runways were wanted for the new Barbazon aircraft, and from the Thames Conservancy which was anxious about the discharge of effluent to the Thames. These objections were overcome; on 31st December 1945, the RAF pulled down their flag and next day the atomic energy project took possession of the airfield. (Plate 1: Site Aerial Photo 1946 - RAF Photograph Crown Copyright reserved.)

Harwell must be the only large establishment in the history of the United Kingdom which was set up with no terms of rererence and under hardly any chain of command. Cockcroft could carry out whatever programme he thought fit and had only the Permanent Secretary of the Ministry of Supply to whom to report. Although within a month an atomic energy production organisation was set up in the Ministry of Supply, under Lord Portal of Hungerford (the wartime Chief of the Air Staff), Harwell was not then brought under his control. The whole blueprint of the place was in Cockcroft's mind. His plan was to cover atomic energy from particle physics to the functioning of major reactors. The entire fuel cycle was to be studied - prospecting for uranium; mining; processing imported ore concentrate; production of uranium metal, and of the gaseous uranium hexafluoride required for producing enriched uranium; the manufacture of fuel elements; the operation of reactors; and the handling of the spent reactor fuel. The electronic and analytical requirements were to be covered; so was the production of isotopes for industrial and medical purposes. Cockcroft's view was that some 50% of Harwell's effort should be self-initiated research and 50% should support the production programmes which would be carried out elsewhere. This approach was to give Harwell its strength in the long term. Scientists were afforded the opportunity to do what they thought was important and in the long run what they thought was important proved to be so for the country. But, in the short term, this approach did not always fit the needs of the moment and proved an embarrassment when problems multiplied as the factories and production reactors were being designed, built and operated in the north of England.

By the middle 1950's, Harwell had 94 buildings of which 34, with 375,000 sq. ft. of accommodation, were inherited from the RAF. A huge laboratory had grown up inside a security fence. In some ways Harwell was still recognisably an old airfield. The hub of the establishment was still the four RAF hangars clustered along the perimeter track. These hangars, disembowelled, built on and bricked over, now housed most of the bigger nuclear machines, though some had been built at the western extremity of the site. The RAF pre-war housing was still in use as were the NAAFI, the messes, and the RAF sewerage plant, now combined with a complicated effluent disposal installation. The old runway pattern and dispersal points were clearly visible from the air, but on the ground the laboratory looked like a University campus interspersed with bits of factory; and a very attractive campus it was at that, for the former military bleakness had disappeared forever under an extensive tree planting and garden-scaping programme.

Then, by the late 1950's, it became clear that Harwell was growing too big. The Atomic Energy Authority, which took over responsibility for the atomic energy project in 1954, found that the administrative problems of such

R.A.F. PHOTOGRAPH.

PLATE 1   Aerial view of A.E.R.E. Harwell, 1946

an intensely complex site were unwieldy and that the local labour market was in danger of running dry. These difficulties mounted when, with the Suez incident of November 1956 and the first oil crisis, a struggle began to meet the Government's nuclear requirements as quickly as possible.

So a series of decisions was taken to disperse the Harwell facilities. The first step, in 1957, was to split off all fundamental atomic particle research to the newly created National Institute for Research in Nuclear Sciences (NIRNS). This was an administrative reorganisation; the Institute used the original Harwell buildings, and expanded on a closely adjacent site when it became the Rutherford Laboratory under the aegis of the Science Research Council (SRC). Secondly, in 1959, a new site was set up at Winfrith in Dorset where pilot reactors could be built to explore the many different avenues towards large scale power reactors; thus that side of the business disappeared out of the Oxford region. Thirdly, fusion research - the attempt to release power not by splitting atoms but by fusing light ones - was removed, in 1960, to a new laboratory at Culham eight miles away. Lastly, also in 1960, a special unit was set up at Wantage to research into the industrial uses of radioisotopes. The first three of these decisions each split off several hundred workers so a considerable devolution of Harwell's responsibilities was achieved.

The Isotope Unit was reabsorbed into Harwell in 1970; the other devolutions were permanent. On the Harwell site there are, in addition to the AERE and the SRC, two much smaller administrative units. An off-shoot had been established there by the Medical Research Council (MRC) in the early days for research into the protection of human tissue from radiation. Then there was to be established in 1970, the National Radiological Protection Board (the NRPB) which was an offspring of the Authority, the Department of Health and Social Security, and the MRC. This Board was set up as a national point of authoritative reference in radiological protection, both for radiation workers and the public. The NRPB took over many of the functions, and most of the staff, of the Radiological Protection Division of the Authority Health and Safety Branch, which was located at Harwell. The Board's new buildings are just outside the AERE fence. In the remainder of this paper the term 'Harwell' includes all four of these establishments on the Harwell site as well as the Atomic Energy Research Establishment. AERE, however, still employ about three-quarters of the total manpower on the site. Away from the site the influence of Harwell has been responsible for the establishment at Letcombe of an Agricultural Research Council laboratory looking at the effect of radiation on plant life. Much later, in the middle 1970's, two non-Government organisations were to settle in the area because of the advantages of being near to Harwell. These were the British Non-Ferrous Metals Association (BNF) at Wantage and the Research Establishment of the Metal Box Company.

The effect of these changes on the Atomic Energy Research Establishment's manpower can be seen in the following table. The column labelled "Cat. A" refers broadly to qualified scientists and engineers.

TABLE I AERE STRENGTHS AT 31 MARCH 1947-80

	Cat. A	Total	
1947	(279)		Take-over from RAF Jan 1, 1946
1948	(656)	(2372)	Total on site incl. contractors 4166
1953	811	(3200)	
1956	1265	(5782)	Suez; decision to split off NIRNS
1959	1714	6275	Decision to split off Culham, Winfrith, Wantage

190

TABLE I (cont.)

	Cat. A	Total	
1962	1374	6013	
1965	1370	6067	Science and Technology Act
1968	1282	5534	Wantage re-absorbed
1971	1164	4829	Public Expenditure White Paper
1974	1082	4091	Oil Crisis
1977	1155	4236	Windscale Inquiry
1980	1205	4418	Estimated

After the peak in 1959 there was a steady fall in manpower due at first to the transfers but then to a period of slight decline in the importance attached to atomic energy research. The nation now seemed to have over-reacted to Suez, and perhaps the first nuclear power programme had been over-done. Moreover, the production factories were beginning to say that little more basic science was needed and that all that was wanted was applied re-search (which their own laboratories could do) and engineering skill; so their demands on Harwell went down and, despite the rundown of manpower, there seemed some threat of unemployment there.

In 1965, the Science and Technology Act allowed Harwell to diversify into some non-nuclear research, but nevertheless the establishment's work-load still fell. In 1970 the incoming Conservative government published a White Paper on public expenditure which proposed drastic cuts in several categories of public finance, including that on research. Harwell was thus faced with a choice: either it could shrink drastically over the next few years, or it could earn substantial sums of money from sources other than the Atomic Energy Vote. Under the then Director, Walter Marshall, it took the decision to do the latter and to sell research to other Government Departments and to industry, both at home and abroad. At first the sales targets seemed impossible, but by 1974/5, which was the Government's dead-line, Harwell had fulfilled the requirements of the 1970 White Paper. There had been very little further reduction of manpower, and once achieved the sales success was maintained year by year.

The following Fig. 2 shows that in 1977/8 AERE was getting 50% of its revenue from the Atomic Energy Vote and 50% from other sources. This was a very different 50/50 from that aimed at by Cockcroft: his decision, it will be remembered, was 50% self-initiated research and 50% applied to the produc-tion problems of the Atomic Energy Project. Figure 3 shows the distribu-tion of scientists and engineers in 1977/8 which was necessary to achieve that financial result. The self-initiated research, now called the under-lying programme, accounts for only 19% of the effort. The nuclear power programme takes 36% but this is now an area where AERE has to respond to guidelines laid down by the project directors of the Authority's northern reactor development establishments. The remainder shows the proportion of scientists engaged in revenue earning activities.

The most recent phase of AERE's history stems from the oil crisis following the Arab/Israeli war of late 1973. The new urgency in solving the UK's energy needs has not, as in 1956/9, concentrated on the more rapid progress of atomic energy. It has, nevertheless, made considerable demands on Harwell. One development has been to harness AERE's experience to the exploitation of North Sea oil. Techniques of "remote handling" inside the

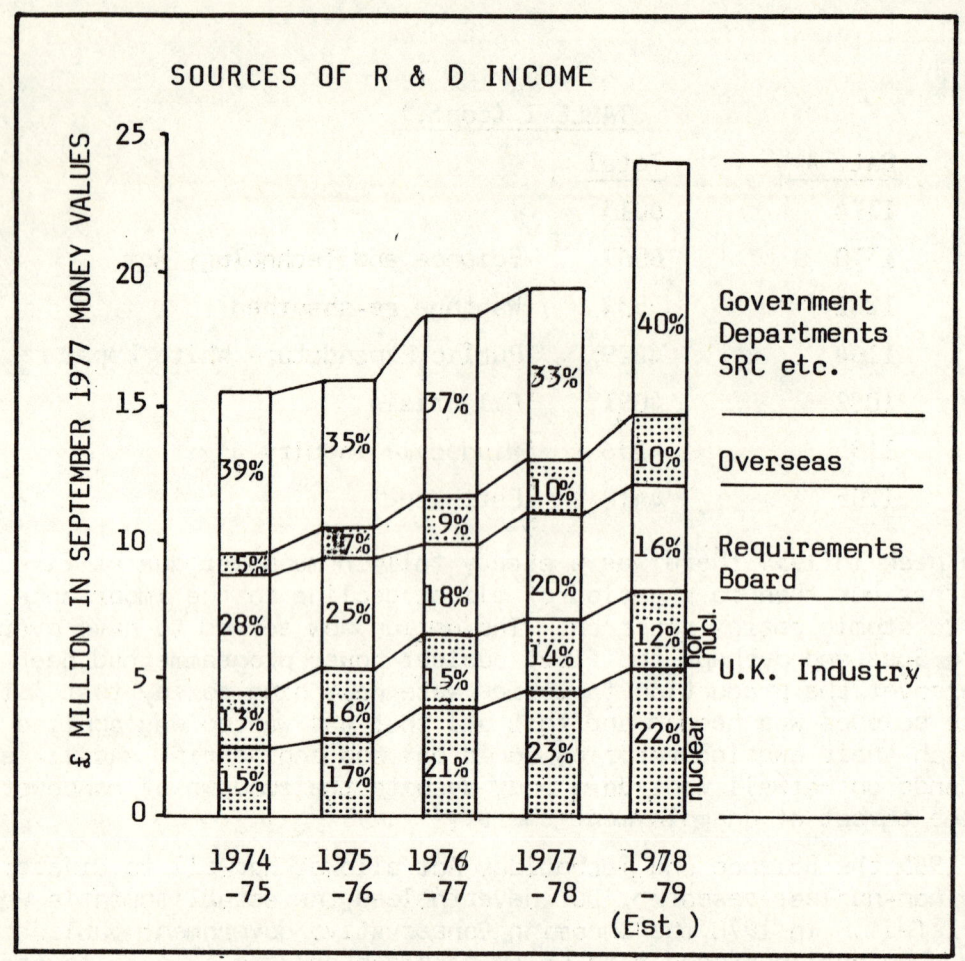

Figure 2

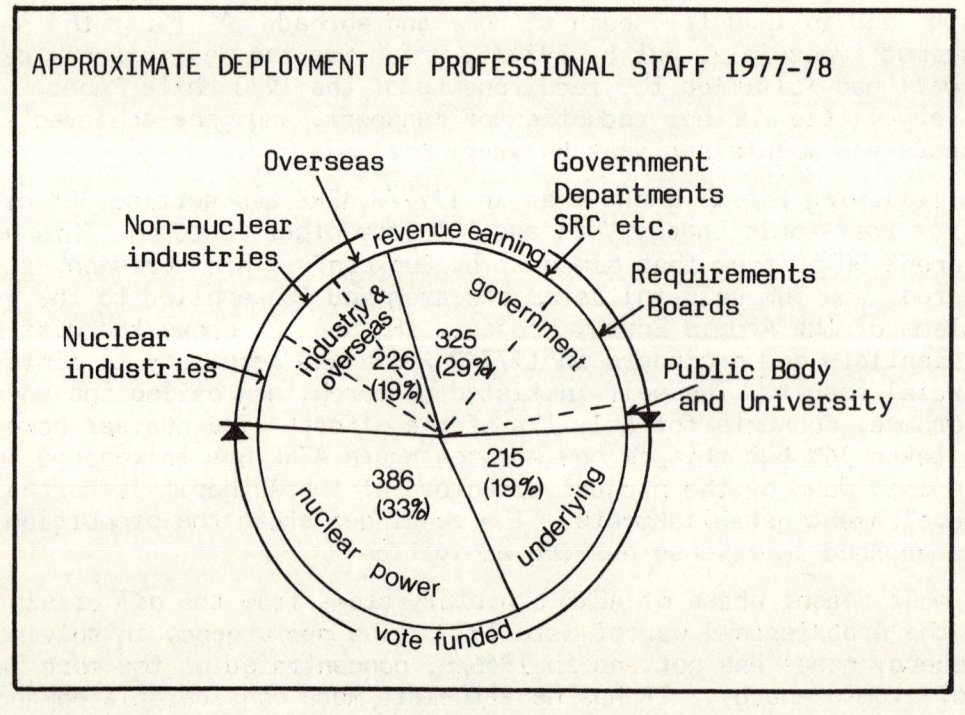

Figure 3

hostile environment of a nuclear reactor have been applied to operating problems in the hostile environment of the North Sea. Other pressures on Harwell have arisen from the development of new non-nuclear sources of energy, for instance, in trying to generate electricity from the motion of the waves. Much of this non-nuclear energy work is not justified by its economic prospects, but by the implicit assumption that Governments in the future may greatly restrict the use of nuclear power. Demands for absolute safety have been made which have never been applied to other industries and there has been an emphasis on dangers which do not arise from new knowledge about atomic energy but from new assumptions about society. This has imposed considerable burdens on AERE: for instance, in devising methods of storing nuclear waste which would be 'fail-safe' in a society even more prone to violence than our own and perhaps incapable of responsible monitoring.

PART II

So much for the history. We then come to the second major part of this paper which is the impact of Harwell on the Oxford region. If one examines the impact of a normal business one asks: how does what it sells affect society or its environment? One cannot think of Harwell's effect on Oxfordshire in that way. Harwell has had less impact on Oxfordshire than on Hong Kong in the desalination of its water supply and the application of isotopes to its harbours! Only in the sale of isotopes and perhaps in the Hazardous Materials Service have Oxfordshire's citizens been significantly affected directly by Harwell. The Radcliffe Infirmary bought £16,000 worth of isotopes from the Radiochemical Centre at Amersham last year and most of them were produced in Harwell's reactors; that could mean something well over about 200/300 diagnoses or treatments in a year. The Hazardous Materials Service is AERE's work in cleaning up the nasty chemical messes which industry occasionally makes, e.g. in the overturning of a lorry filled with chlorine.

So Harwell's effects come mainly from the population and the money which it has brought into the area. If one compares the years 1931 and 1951, one finds a doubling of the population in the villages and parishes near to Harwell and actual depopulation in other areas of North Berkshire. The 100% increase applies very nearly to both Abingdon and Wantage. Then from 1951 to 1961 the areas close to Harwell show only a small expansion: with the increasing use of the family motor car the workers at Harwell spread over a wide area. Wantage and Abingdon had only a 25% growth and the biggest increases were in Didcot and those southern parts more affected by London than Harwell. It is difficult to isolate the effect of Harwell because once transport was freely available one also has to take into account the pressure of the University and Nuffield works to the north and London to the south-east. One effect, however, which is mainly attributable to Harwell is that in 1961 Abingdon, Wantage and Wallingford had 8,000 children under four years of age, whereas on the standard distribution of the nation's population one would expect only 6,500 children. The early Harwell generation was quite prolific! The following table compares population and employment in 1968. Wantage and Grove had a population of 11,431 but only provided 2,760 jobs. Abingdon had 14,863 people but only 4,732 jobs; but Harwell village and site with a population of 3,273 men, women and children employed 6,948 people. The table also shows the predictions which the planners made in 1970 for 1981: some of which, particularly those for Wantage and Grove, are clearly not going to be realised.

TABLE II. POPULATION AND EMPLOYMENT

| | 1968 | | 1981 | |
	Population	Employment	Population	Employment
WANTAGE	8,145	1,290	9,405	1,620
GROVE	3,286	470	15,846	2,910
ABINGDON	14,863	4,732	18,888	4,982
ST. HELEN WITHOUT	2,550	1,740	2,550	1,740
CALDECOTT	3,490	253	5,450	593
DRAYTON	2,378	176	2,378	176
DIDCOT	14,030	2,044	14,875	2,379
NEW DIDCOT	1,141	83	4,501	153
HARWELL VILLAGE	2,376	165	2,796	190
THE SITE	897	6,883	897	6,883

SOURCE: Didcot, Abingdon, Wantage Transportation Study. December 1970

Housing and Transport

Now let us look at the geographical distribution of the population working at Harwell. The following table shows the spread of Authority housing in 1960 and totals of subsequent sales to sitting tenants.

TABLE III. HOUSING AND TRANSPORT

| | Houses | | | Daily Bus Passengers |
	Built	Sold		
ABINGDON	326	219	570	(Abingdon to Rowstock)
WANTAGE	366	114	550	(Grove/Wantage to Rowstock)
DIDCOT	30	6	400	
WALLINGFORD	100	12	120	
CLIFTON HAMPDEN	12	–		
FARINGDON	–	–	200	(Faringdon to Wantage)
GORING	–	–	30	
OXFORD	–	–	170	
AERE				
(ex RAF	86)	–		
PREFABS	200	–		
TOTAL HOUSES	1,110	351		
HOSTEL PLACES				
AERE		194		
ABINGDON		290		

325	ROUTES TO READING
470	ROUTES TO NEWBURY
2835	TOTAL DAILY LIFT

All the above are Authority-owned houses or hostel places. In addition 500 Local Authority houses were allotted initially to AERE employees.

The RAF left 203 houses on the site. 200 aluminium bungalows were
added in 1947/8: these "temporary" prefabs are still giving excellent
service, and those who canvass the area at election time know that, whenever
there is a rumour that the prefabs are to be replaced by permanent housing,
there are fierce protests. But the site houses only a small proportion of
Harwell's workers. In the account of the choice of the Harwell site we
noted that the nearness of Abingdon and Wantage was one of the attractions.
Talks about housing began with the Borough of Abingdon and with the Urban
District Council of Wantage soon thereafter. From the first, Abingdon and
Wantage did everything possible to help. Elsewhere there were difficulties,
partly stemming from the attraction which employment at Harwell had for
agricultural workers (just as Harwell was in turn to suffer later from the
employment pull of the much more highly paid motor car industry in Oxford).
The Chairman of the Harwell Parish Council said in 1946 'there is sure to
be a percentage of the residents who will leave the district. The number
of workers entering the village will intensify the housing problem.
Whether the government is prepared to supply accommodation or not, these
workers must have no priority in the Wantage rural housing scheme'.
Relatively few houses also were built in Didcot - not because of hostility
but because Didcot was governed from Wallingford and it was difficult to
get through to Wallingford about problems in Didcot. Most of these houses
were built in traditional brick but there was a group of permanent prefab-
ricated British Iron and Steel Federation houses which date from the late
40's when everything was being done to save bricks and timber. Many of the
houses have the type of 'open fronted' gardens which have since become more
usual in this country but of which the pattern was brought over from the
Canadian Deep River housing scheme pioneered originally by the Professor
of Planning at McGill University.

The total Authority and council housing staff only provided for some
2,000 out of the 6,000-odd employees. Of the remainder a large proportion
is brought into work by Authority transport. Excluding those living in
Authority houses who use Authority buses, it is roughly true to say that of
the site employees one-third live in Authority houses and hostels and of
the remaining two-thirds in private houses one half are brought into work
in Authority transport and one half come in private cars. The Authority
transport system has 41 different bus routes and 400 daily pick-up points.
The geographical distribution is set out in Table III and illustrated in
Figure 4. Nine percent of bus passengers are SRC, MRC, NRPB employees or
attached staff.

Now let us look at the total manpower on the site today and the total
cash flow:

TABLE IV. MANPOWER (AVERAGE) AND EXPENDITURE - 1977/8
THE "SITE"

	Total Manpower on Site	Staff	Expenditure - £m. less VAT		
			Other Current	Capital	Total
AERE	4214	21.3	17.5	3.4	42.2
UKAEA (HQ)	100	0.8			0.8
SRC	1176	7.2	9.3	4.0	20.5
NRPB	290	1.5	1.2		2.7
MRC	130	0.6	0.3	0.1	1.0
TOTAL	5910	31.4			67.2

The total manpower at Culham 820; that of the Agricultural Research Council
at Letcombe 114. The Culham expenditure was £14.3 m.

195

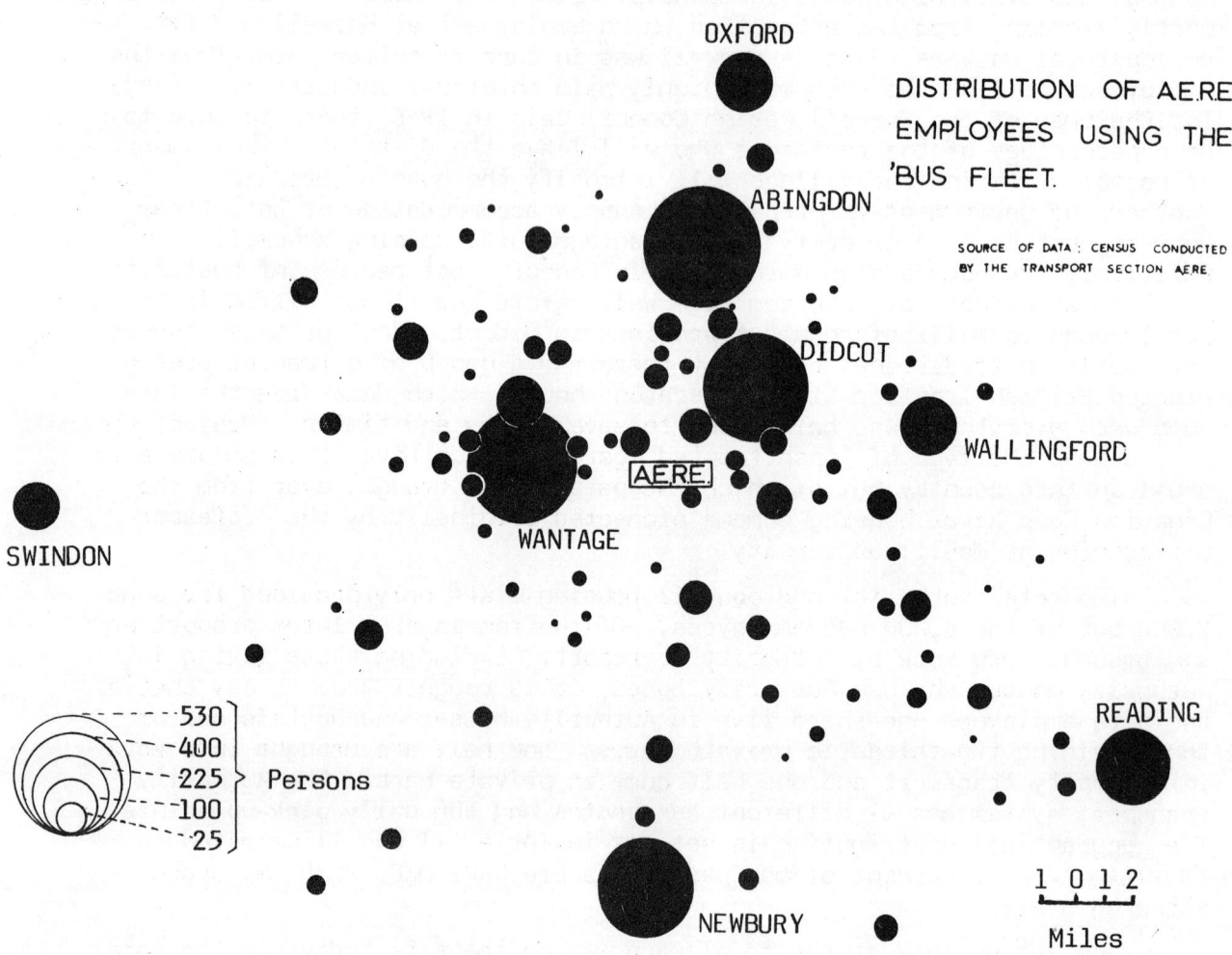

Source of Data: Census conducted by the Transport section A.E.R.E.

Figure 4

£31M per annum is paid out for salaries and wages by all the establishments on the site. The total expenditure including that for contracts, stores and capital was £67M. What effect did this expenditure have on Oxfordshire? There is a large literature about what economists call the "multiplier": the factor used to multiply the population directly employed in any activity in order to estimate the total population for which that activity creates a livelihood. A reasonable estimate might be that, after allowing for the secondary employment which its demand generates locally, Harwell is responsible for some 10,000 jobs, i.e. between 5 and 6% of the total Oxfordshire employment. The multiplier in money terms might be a little larger, for of the £7M on capital expenditure - more than half of which was by the SRC - some £3M was placed in the Oxford area. On the other hand, of the "other current" expenditure relatively little is spent locally. The largest element of this lies in the purchase of stores and materials, where only about £1½M came from the Oxford area - over one-third in engineering work, one-third on transport - mainly the hire and maintenance of the transport fleet already referred to - and one-fifth for books and stationery. This figure is low because Oxfordshire is, the car industry apart, not a major manufacturing area and much of Harwell's demand for instrument work goes to lower wage areas further afield, e.g. to cottage industries in Wales and the Isle of Wight.

Rates

One other element of "current expenditure" deserves special mention: the rates paid to local government. The site covers three parishes and there is a pumping and effluent installation at Sutton Courtenay and hostels and housing in local towns (see Table III above).

TABLE V. RATEABLE VALUES AND RATES
SITE PROPERTIES 1977/8

Parish	Rateable Value £	Rates £
ABINGDON	19,000	16,745
CHILTON	9,800	8,490
EAST HENDRED	219,000	188,340
HARWELL	369,000	317,598
SUTTON COURTENAY	5,500	4,708
CHILTON (SRC)	305,000	262,910
HARWELL (MRC)	24,000	21,000
HARWELL (NRPB)	21,500	18,500
HOUSES IN HARWELL EAST HENDRED) CHILTON) ABINGDON) WANTAGE) DIDCOT)	140,000	120,000
TOTAL	1,112,800	958,291

The rates for the houses are approximate.

The parishes of Harwell and East Hendred each get two-thirds of their rates from the site and Chilton get over four-fifths.

	Product of IP Rate	Of Which from Site
HARWELL PARISH	6,110	4,140
CHILTON PARISH	3,805	3,150
EAST HENDRED PARISH	3,305	2,190

197

East Hendred thus has a rateable value of £2.6 per head of population, whereas the nearby Blewbury, which is about the same in housing values, has only 90p per head. But the rentable (and therefore rateable) value of installations for research and development is not high and the total contribution from the site in rates is less than £1M. This represents only 1.8% of Oxfordshire's rate income in 1977/78 compared with over 4% from Didcot power station. Even if account were taken of the domestic rates paid by the much more numerous Harwell employees, compared with those from the power station, Harwell would still provide less than two-thirds of the Didcot station rates.

Harwell's direct effect on the infrastructure of the local countryside has not been large. The establishments are self-contained in most respects. The site has its own sewage plant, its own fire service and police. Formerly there was a responsibility for responding to local fire calls and for snow clearance on the local stretch of the A34. This has now come to an end. Harwell has had a history of total failure to secure a modification to the road pattern in order to ease its problems at in- and out-muster at the beginning and end of the working day. When the A34 was eventually re-routed, Harwell's needs were not prominent in the solution: the Harwell traffic was not held to justify a full roundabout near Chilton, and Rowstock remained a pressure point until very recently. Harwell's biggest social impact has probably been on schools - a nursery and a primary school has been established on the site. The existence of the Oxford High School for Girls and Royce's at Abingdon, St. Edmunds and others, was an important factor in the choice of Harwell (see page 188) and close links with these schools have indeed developed. A special bus was run to Oxford High School for nearly 25 years and a grant was made to Royce's by Harwell to expand the science laboratories there. Interesting research could indeed be done on the effects on the schools through inheritance of the IQ level of Harwell parents.

Social Impact

The only detailed study of social impact was carried out in relation to Abingdon in 1959. The population of Abingdon at the time was 13,000 of which almost one quarter came from families where one or more parent was working on the site. The following table derives entirely from the work of Miss Heather Poulsford and shows the large percentage of Harwell's support enjoyed by the main clubs in Abingdon and the even greater extent to which Harwell people volunteered for Committee work.

TABLE VI. SOCIAL IMPACT OF SITE ON ABINGDON

<u>1959</u>

POPULATION OF ABINGDON	13,110	
SITE POPULATION (644 HOUSEHOLDS) IN ABINGDON (510 SINGLE)	3,100	

	% Members	% Committee
SPORTS CLUBS		
TENNIS	40	75
ROWING	39	50
ANGLING	1	-
BOWLS	-	-
ARTS		
MUSIC	50	33
OPERATIC	80	100
BELL RINGERS	3	-
UNICORN THEATRE	16	20

TABLE VI. SOCIAL IMPACT OF SITE ON ABINGDON (cont.)

SOCIAL	% Members	% Committee
TOWNSWOMENS GUILD		
AFTERNOON	5	-
EVENING	56	64
WOMENS INSTITUTE	5	-
ROUND TABLE	5	25
CHURCHES		
ST. HELENS	13	13
ST. NICHOLAS	50	44
METHODIST	30	16
FITZHARRIES		
SUNDAY SCHOOL	80	100

Bowls, bell ringing and angling probably appealed to higher age
groups than those represented by most of the Harwell population at the
time. There was tremendous interest in arts, music and opera and the percentage of church population explodes the idea that scientists are not
religious. Unfortunately, no figures were secured from the political parties
of the relative political allegiances of the Harwell workers as none of the
parties released any detailed records.

Effluent

In talking of the various social and environmental impacts, we come
to the water-borne and airborne discharges from the establishment. Water-
borne effluent goes into the Thames. The formula, prescribed for Harwell
when it was being planned, was that a person must be able to swallow 2.9
pints of crude water every day of his life from the discharge point of the
pipeline into the Thames and not get more than 1% of the recommended permitted concentration of any radioisotope. The problem of how long a person would live who actually tried to drink 2.9 pints of crude river water
at Sutton Courtenay, has never been solved. It is sometimes thought that
the formula was devised in order to ensure that the Harwell site could not
be selected, for the formula required the river water at the discharge
point to be more than twice as pure as that on which the population of
greater New York has survived for many years; and made no allowance for the
mixing of the effluent into the great body of Thames water: the Harwell
discharge is one part in 4,000 of the main Thames flow of 147 millions
gallons per day! The actual discharge in 1977 was only 16% of that permitted
for radium and other alpha and beta emitters. In addition there is a separate limit for the discharge of tritium, 41% of whose total was actually
discharged in 1977. Harwell has, from the beginning, easily met the severe
limits of the formula imposed on it by retreating high level effluents until
they are low enough to discharge. The remaining sludges, which amount to
some 70 cubic metres a year, are sent to a site at Drigg in Cumberland belong-
ing to British Nuclear Fuels, where the soil conditions are peculiarly
suited to avoiding any danger of the low activity leaching out; some sludges
are sealed in special containers and, in accordance with international agree-
ments, dropped beyond the N. Atlantic shelf from time to time.

The working limits for the airborne discharge of aplha and beta par-
ticulate activity and of iodine 131 from AERE are also low. The actual discharges have been 1% of alpha activity and 0.1% for beta activity, i.e. one-
hundredth and one-thousandth respectively of what would be acceptable under
the international code. Similar low limits have applied to the average

derived working limits for gaseous and tritium discharges. To back up these outlet measurements, milk and soil sampling is also undertaken. Milk samples are collected regularly from two farms within a 2.5 mile radius of the site and the activity regularly monitored. The strontium levels are well within the range expected from nuclear weapon test fall-out. Air sampling is carried out at three stations and soil core samples are taken for four points just outside the Harwell site. None of this has shown any significant activity escaping from the site. Such is the effort to protect the air and water of Oxfordshire that it may well be said that never in the history of science has so much effort been devoted to protecting so many from so little.

Impact on Oxford University

So far nothing has been said of the impact of Harwell on the University of Oxford. The University had been important to the choice of site; yet close relations did not develop easily. Of the first 130 contracts placed by Harwell with universities only sixteen were with Oxford compared with 26 with Cambridge and 32 with London. Indeed, in some years none went to Oxford at all. Some explanation of this distant relationship can be found in the attitude on either side. On that of Harwell, Cockcroft's determination that Harwell should have many of the features of a university tended in practice to pre-empt for Harwell work which others thought should have gone to a university. The wide scope for self-initiated research means that the first generation of Harwell scientists did many of the interesting things themselves rather than leave them to their academic colleagues. Sir James Chadwick, the discoverer of the neutron and our nuclear representative in the United States during the war, strongly criticised Cockcroft for placing so many important nuclear machines at Harwell rather than at the universities. However, there were genuine difficulties in that early time of specifying what part of the research should be delegated to universities, a difficulty to which the security problem added another dimension. On the side of Oxford University there was a distrust of big science and of big machines and an emphasis on small research teams which probably became more acute as Harwell grew bigger; also a leading theme at the Clarendon Laboratory was low temperature research.

An improvement came with the establishment of the Chair of Nuclear Physics at Oxford in the early 60's. In 1978 Harwell spent £178,000 on contracts with Oxford University out of a total of £434,000 on such contracts; and 60 students were attached from Oxford to Harwell out of a total of 270 attachments from all universities and polytechnics. Nevertheless, of the Oxford students, more than from other universities, most used Harwell facilities for training purposes rather than integrating themselves in joint programmes.

It was in the fusion and not in the fission field that the real collaboration with Oxford occurred. Here in the early years, the Clarendon Laboratory played a vital part in the development of the research. Thonemann and Von Engel carried out the first toroidal experiment in the Clarendon. After moving first to Harwell when it became necessary on security grounds, Thonemann subsequently became one of the first Division Heads at Culham and one can trace the genealogy of thought straight through to the present JET European experiment at Culham. The JET plan for centres of excellence in fusion design may well designate the University of Oxford as such a centre before long.

Conclusion

In conclusion I revert from the study of the impact of Harwell on its surroundings to history or rather to an historical "if". Suppose Halban and Kowarski had remained in Paris or broken down on their way to Bordeaux in

June 1940. The Nazis would have caught up with them; they would never have come to Cambridge and thence to Montreal and there would never have been an Anglo/French/Canadian project in Montreal. So there wouldn't have been a team to come home from Montreal to Harwell, and there wouldn't have been an obvious nucleus for an experimental establishment. Therefore the U.K. might not have set up an experimental establishment, then decided afterwards that it should produce some fissile material; then having produced some fissile material, decided to make a bomb with it. There might then have been an alternative, logical sequence of events. In that imaginary sequence Ministers might have decided to have a bomb or to have a nuclear power station (admittedly a little early for the latter decision). Then they would have decided to have a production establishment to make the material, and when they got the production establishment they would have seen that they needed an experimental establishment to produce the research data necessary to design the production lines. In that case, the experimental establishment would never have come to Harwell and would have been an adjunct of the northern factory sites. But after all, that would not have been the British way. So we turned the logic upside down and had the experimental establishment first, the production establishment second, the bomb next, and, a little later, nuclear power.

FOOTNOTE

1. In the event no production piles were built at Harwell, nor were Hanford type piles built in the U.K.

BIBLIOGRAPHY

1. Harlequin Vol. IV No. 1, July 1948, Chemistry 1953; Spring 1954, No. 22 1958 and No. 23 1958 and passim.

2. K.E.B. Jay, Atomic Energy Research at Harwell, Butterworth 1955.

3. Miss Heather Poulsford, Harlequin 1959.

4. Professor Gowing. Britain and Atomic Energy 1939-45. Macmillan 1964. Passim.

5. Professor Gowing. Independence and Deterence Vol. I and II, Macmillan Passim.

6. J.M. Turney, Thesis for the University of Hull, 1968.

7. Didcot, Abingdon, Wantage Transportation Study, Oxfordshire County Council. 1970.

8. Effluent and Water Treatment at AERE Harwell. Effluent and Water Treatment Journal, July, 1977.

9. Radioactive Wast Disposal by UKAEA Establishments during 1977 and Associated Monitoring Results. Flew, May 1978.

COLLEGE FINANCES AND PROPERTY IN THE TWENTIETH CENTURY

J.P.D. Dunbabin

The inhabitants of Oxford, or at least those of an older generation, generally use the term 'the colleges' when they mean Oxford university. Very naturally because the colleges both occupy and own a considerable area of the town. By any standard the colleges' impact on Oxford in the twentieth century has been significant. They are the principal tourist attraction. Their student body is a significant, and highly visible, element in the central city population. Their social self-sufficiency is sometimes perceived as exclusiveness and rather resented by local professional people (especially dentists). Directly and indirectly they offer a fair amount of employment. As landlords, the colleges have been involved in a number of celebrated planning controversies, from the development of the Cornmarket Woolworths to the Christ Church Meadow road. As Sir Norman Chester has reminded us, the university was until recently, by an arrangement only parallelled in Cambridge and Aldershot, represented on the City Council. And the view is widespread, though I think mistaken, that 'the colleges' can always get their way there. Lastly, though they are not outstandingly wealthy or munificent, the colleges represent a source of subventions that local cultural and artistic promoters are constantly seeking to tap.

Any proper assessment of the colleges' role in the Oxford region would concentrate on the above-mentioned topics. But I am afraid the perspective of this paper will be narrower, more an examination of their internal finances and development based largely on their accounts. In my experience, when one comes to accounts, one comes to disclaimers. I rather incautiously undertook the paper in the knowledge that Oxford had been the subject of at least three financial inquiries since 1918. And I imprudently assumed that all I had to do was to match these up. No so; for there had been an important change in their areas of interest. The 1922 [Asquith] Commission on Oxford and Cambridge Universities (1) was designed to provide reassurance that the colleges and their property were being efficiently managed, and that they could not indefinitely expand their support for the non-collegiate sector of the university. So it went into college finances in some detail. But by the 1960's this non-collegiate sector (which I shall in future term the University) had become overwhelmingly state-funded and considerably larger (in financial terms) than the colleges. And the immediate stimulus to the appointment of the 'Franks' Commission was criticism by the 'Robbins' Committee on Higher National Education of the slowness of the University's administrative proceedings, and by the University Grants Committee of the obscurity of its statistics. Franks was accordingly not primarily concerned with college finances, still less with college property. Times had changed, though people did not always realise it (2). So where the figures I wanted were not readily supplied by these various inquiries, I had to extract them myself from the accounts (3). But I am not an accountant. I was partially encouraged by observing the mistakes made by those who were, that is by Messrs. W.B. Peat and Co. who assisted the Asquith Commission. But this is cold comfort; and I would not claim any more for my own results than that they are of about the right order of magnitude.

One last preliminary point: in the course of the twentieth century the number of Oxford colleges has grown considerably, my own being among the new ones. This is an important development to which I shall return. But it presents the statistical problem of comparing like with like. So, for the greater part of my paper, I shall confine myself to the nineteen colleges of older foundation, which I shall term the 'historic colleges' [4]. To this day they constitute a majority, and in time past a great majority, of all colleges. I shall also concentrate mostly on the general picture rather than on the fortunes of individual colleges. Appendix I does, however, give some indication of how these fared over the half century after 1920: very broadly the range of collegiate wealth was compressed, and one or two rich new colleges were founded; but colleges did not rise or fall as much as might have been expected given their freedom to follow widely different financial policies.

So much by way of preamble. By 1914 the colleges were, of course, long-established. And the university regarded itself as a national (even an 'imperial') rather than a local institution, a point that distinguished it from most of the newer 'civic' universities and that was re-affirmed after the war by the Asquith Commission [5]. Nevertheless its finances rested firmly on real property: in 1913 at least two thirds of the historic colleges' gross income (on revenue account) came from land, house property or tithes. Such property was held in 47 counties in England and Wales. But (tithes apart) it was, as Table 1 shows, heavily concentrated in the Oxford region and around London.

TABLE 1

Agricultural acreage in 1918 - Total: 176,000 (192,000 on 1872)

Oxon	45,000	Northants, Kent,	between 5
Bucks	14,000	Wilts, Hants	and 10,000
Berks	13,000		
Glos	10,000	Total in the counties listed 112,000	

House Property

Oxon   2,405 dwelling houses, 357 working class houses, 69 tenements, 409 cottages, 56 inns, 110 shops, and 136 shops plus houses, 96 sundry

Middlesex   2,312 dwelling houses, 24 cottages, 2 inns, 96 shops and 362 shops plus houses, 21 sundry

London   591 dwelling houses, 7 blocks of flats, 2 inns, 14 shops, 33 sundry

Surrey   559 dwelling houses, 20 flats, 43 cottages, 3 inns, 16 sundry

Tithe - gross value £70,000 pa.

Essex	£11,000
Cheshire	7,000
Oxon } Yorks } each	6,000
Northumberland	5,000
	£36,000 (rounded)

These geographical details are derived from the Asquith Commission (6).
The pattern of land- (though not house) holding had probably changed little
since the 1870's. The point could in principle be tested, as the Cleveland
Commission on the Property and Income of the Universities of Oxford and
Cambridge also supplied a geographical breakdown of college possessions,
albeit in an impossibly dis-aggregated form (7). No post-1945 inquiry has
thought this necessary. And Oxford college land-holdings, though more
resilient than their Cambridge counter-parts, had sunk to about 119,000
acres in 1976 (8). So I fear that the remainder of my paper will be largely
the account of the colleges' progressive evolution away from both an Oxford
region and from a landed income base.

In some respects this was the state's doing, more especially in the
case of tithes, which constituted an appreciable part of Christ Church's
endowment and a minor one of that of most other colleges. By 1914 tithes
took the form of a rent-charge on land calculated with reference to wheat
prices over the previous seven years. Accordingly they responded automatically to the price rises of the 1914-18 war, in welcome contrast to most
other forms of income - Christ Church's increasing by £10,000 p.a. between
1914 and 1919. This, however, made them politically vulnerable, and during
and after the War the basis of calculation was adjusted more than once to the
tithe-owners' detriment. Matters came to a head with the depression of the
early 1930's, when tithe collection met with vocal and organised, if sporadic,
resistance. By now Oxford's exposure was rather lower, since a number of
colleges had prudently started to commute their tithes for cash. But collec-
tively the colleges took a firm line (as did the Bursar of King's, Cambridge,
J.M. Keynes): they would accommodate individuals in genuine financial difficulties, but not make across-the-board reductions. And they submitted evidence to the Royal Commission on Tithe Rent charge to show that in 1933 88%
of their tithes were paid in full, 5% witheld without good reason, and the
remainder adjusted to meet hard cases (9). By now, however, it was clear
that tithe would not last long; and in 1936 the Government commuted tithes
for gilt-edged stock, though it recouped itself by continuing to collect
tithe at a reduced rate for a further 60 years. After 1936, therefore, tithe
continued to feature in the college accounts, but only as an increasingly
minor financial transaction not as a link with land or agriculture.

Tithes, however, had never been as important as agricultural estates.
And among the concerns of the President of the Board of Education (a former
fellow of New College) in manoeuvring for the appointment of the Asquith
Commission, appears to have been the belief that these could be more profit-
ably managed (10). Certainly this was a topic that concerned the Commission,
and it produced a rather sketchy Appendix of 'Typical instances showing
increased interest secured [by seven colleges] by Sales of Real Estate [pro-
bably to the tune of some £400,000 in 1919-20].., and Reinvestment of Proceeds'. The Commission cautiously endorsed this policy, especially for the
smaller colleges (11). But, like much official advice, this came too late,
the best time for land sales having passed before the Commission reported in
1922.

One can go some way towards establishing how far the advice was taken
by looking at the colleges' Capital Accounts. This is a laborious process,
so I have confined myself to a selection of nine rich colleges. These account
for a high proportion of total land-holdings (and over 70% of all college
income from real property in 1964), but they are not a perfect sample.
Further one cannot always distinguish between transactions in urban and in
agricultural land, so I have had to lump both together as real property. I
have deliberately excluded tithe redemption, since in the event all tithe had

to be redeemed; I have unfortunately also had to omit capital expenditure on college estates, though in principle one can enhance one's landed income as readily by developing one's existing holdings as by buying new ones; and the table is subject to other (though I hope minor) caveats.

TABLE 2

Net sales and gross purchases of real estate by 9 colleges [12]

Sales		Purchases
£488,000	1920-24	£56,000
359,000	1925-29	343,000
839,000	1930-34	423,000
758,000	1935-39	669,000
316,000	1940-44	730,000
949,000	1945-49	1,642,000
1,382,000	1950-54	657,000
2,409,000 plus some £1,718,000 Town & Country Planning Act Compensation [13]	1955-59	495,000
4,702,000	1960-64	580,000
1,815,000 (£4,537,000 - 5-yearly rate)	1965-66	702,000 (£1,755,000 - 5-yearly rate)
9,570,000	1967/8-71/2	5,850,000
12,650,000	1972/3-76/7	6,840,000

The table largely speaks for itself. Land sales continued in the early 1920's, though not at the same rate as in 1919-20. Later in the decade falling land prices (presumably) brought about an equilibrium. There were again net sales in the early 1930's, followed by a swing back in the later 1930's and net purchases during and after the war. Since the early fifties the movement has always been away from real property, albeit at a distinctly slower rate in the early 1970's. One factor in this movement was the broadening of the permissible holdings of charities in 1954 to permit extensive investment in ordinary industrial shares at a time when equities' capital growth performance was at its most impressive. Another, though less important, factor was the good fortune of a few colleges in securing extensive compensation (under the Town and Country Planning Act, 1954) for not developing their green belt holdings: much of this money went into the stock market.

We shall note the effects of these changes on the sources of college incomes in a moment. But it must first be emphasised that not all these transactions reflected economic judgements. Some sales were forced by compulsory purchase or by an urgent need for the repair of college buildings. Many, particularly of land for development, were influenced by geographical accident. Also collegiate circumstances differed markedly, and so some colleges felt more need than others to diversify out of real property. Equally individual colleges have followed very different policies, some trading extensively and some very little. And their attitudes to land as an investment differ greatly: Balliol and Oriel have got rid of their agricultural land altogether; and another college, in response to a questionnaire, anticipated a steady reduction of its holdings whenever it secures vacant possession, partly as a reaction to recent legislation and partly because of land's low net yield. Several colleges, however, stressed land's potential for capital appreciation; a few regretted their sales of the 1950's; and one concluded, 'Agricultural land, in our opinion, should be held by investors wealthy enough to do so. "Perpetual" charities can benefit from long term situations regarding land.' (14)

Capital, however, does not come from investment alone. No account of college finances would be complete without some reference to benefactions. These are of all kinds - my own college was once offered $100, the interest on which was to be applied to the support of a Scottish student at an American university (15). Many gifts, though, are more substantial. Cecil Rhodes endowed first Oriel and then the University at the turn of the century. Lord Nuffield gave to Worcester, to the University's medical department, and then founded his own college, which by 1964 already had an endowment income second only to Christ Church. Monsieur Besse gave to a number of the poorer colleges, and founded St. Antony's. Sir Isaac Wolfson also contributed munificently to several colleges and founded his own. Green College is in the process of erection; and this very month (January 1979) Blackwell's have given £350,000 to promote a merger between St. Cross and Pusey House. I have not made any systematic survey of benefactions, indeed I doubt whether one could be made. But the profusion of post-World War II gifts both here and in Cambridge is striking (16).

Another phenomenon of the present era is the Appeal. Balliol had one before the 1914-18 War. But appeals then receded into the background - in 1938 the Treasurer of Christ Church could write 'that it has never been the custom, and I hope it never will be, for the Colleges [unlike the University] to appeal to their former members for financial assistance.' (17) In the last two decades most colleges must have done so, pressing into service any centenaries they could plausibly celebrate. (Perhaps the catalyst was the Oxford Historic Buildings Appeal of 1957, and Balliol's successful pursuit a little later of £1m.) The sums sought do, however, vary strikingly. New College is currently aiming for £2m., while a number of younger colleges have contented themselves with £0.5m.

Benefactions commonly, though of course not necessarily, involve buildings; and it is also the received wisdom that appeals are most successful when linked to some concrete object. So this is perhaps the point at which my talk can most conveniently overlap with Sir Norman Chester's. First a word of caution. Benefactions cannot be forecast. If anybody were to offer my college money to acquire, say, a hostel or hall of residence, we should take it and rearrange our thinking accordingly. And even without such upsets, forecasting is not easy. We have made two internal attempts at it in my college this decade, but to no purpose - but then the state did no better with its National Plan!

However I would not wish to suggest that colleges are individually unaware of some of the pressures on space that Sir Norman described. Their responses can perhaps be subdivided into the housing of their permanent employees and of their student members. When married fellows became common, many colleges acquired accommodation so that they might still live centrally. Such college houses survive, some of them very nice ones. But in today's conditions it is most improvident for those who can afford it not to buy a house of their own; and I should accordingly forecast that fellows will make diminishing use of college houses. Instead I should expect colleges to concentrate on assisting with loans those of their employees who wish to buy, while themselves acquiring houses for some of the others as a way of attracting and retaining labour. If so, they would simply be reacting to mitigate a situation that they cannot control.

College provision of student accommodation has a much longer history. There is now a league table kept of this, as well as of examination results, and the aim is to house a far higher ratio of junior members than is usual in most other universities. In 1923-4, 57% of all students were housed in college or college hostels, a total rising to 61% in 1938-9 entirely as a result of the increased provision of such accommodation for women (18). Increased numbers after the war sharply reduced the proportion (to 49% in 1948-9). Thereafter it remained stationary for a decade, began to climb in the early 1960's, and then rose steeply to 70% in 1976 (19). Clearly there has been a great deal of building of new (supplemented by a more limited purchase and conversion of old) property for students. But it is important not to exaggerate the university's power in such matters. Time was when undergraduate patterns of residence could be controlled. But it is no longer possible to stand in loco parentis, and a measure of laisser faire is the inevitable result. In particular the ban on undergraduates grouping together to live in flats had to be relaxed in the early 1970's, despite the knowledge that this would enable them to compete strongly on the limited local housing market instead of going to the old-fashioned land-ladies (of whom the supply is still said to exceed the demand). And should undergraduates ever decide against living in college - as for a brief time appeared likely in the later 1960's - the situation would be worse. On the other hand, the state might for economic reasons restructure student grants to compel students to attend their local university. Since Oxford's intake is not, in general, local, this might solve one problem, but create others.

We have thus far been chiefly concerned with the colleges' capital endowment (19a) and building stock. It is now time to turn to their Revenue Accounts and to changes in the shares of college income contributed by different kinds of property.

TABLE 3

Sources of 'historic college' income. (See also Appendix II)

	1913	1920	1938	1951	1963	1973-4	('Franks' form of accounts (20))
Land and tithes	41%	36%	21%	23%	17%	14%	Agricultural land and other
'Houses' - rent long lease	10 ⎱23 13 ⎰	9 ⎱19 10 ⎰	12 ⎱24 12 ⎰	17 ⎱24 7 ⎰	15 ⎱19 4 ⎰	17	Non-agricultural land
Dividends and interest	5	9	16	8	15	(35	- includes much of what previously features as 'trust and special')
Trust and special	7	7	9	9	8	(1	- Trusts of which the college is not the sole trustee)
Internal fees and charges	25	29	29	36	38	(32	internal fees only)
University contributions for services rendered					2	1	

208

The chief theme of this table is the gradual decline of the importance of
real estate. The relative significance of land and tithes increased
between 1938 and 1951 as a result of the purchases we have already noted.
Otherwise it fell, partly because of the forced conversion of tithes into
government stock in 1936, partly because of land sales, and partly because
land's chief attraction as an investment is in any case capital gain rather
than annual yield. (In real terms the produce of land and tithes was halved
between 1913 and 1920, since its money yield quite failed to keep pace with
inflation; in the same terms there was a recovery to 1938, followed by
another but less serious set back to 1951, and then a very slow increase).
'Houses' have been more constant, largely because the two different sectors
have tended to cancel each other out. The development of estates let on
long leases for houses had done much to ease the colleges through the agricultural depression of the later nineteenth century (21); but this form of
income proved almost totally inelastic during the 1914-20 inflation. There
was an improvement in money (and e fortiori in real) terms to 1938; but
thereafter inflation has become endemic, and income has again proved highly
inelastic. By contrast the produce of rented property (some of it, of
course, commercial) has invariably risen in money terms, and, except between
1913 and 1920, also in real ones. Taken together 'land and tithes' and
'housing' of all kinds accounted for 64% of gross income on revenue account
in 1913 and only 36% in 1963.

Other sources of income were 'trust and special' funds (of which there
is little to be said since they were fed both by landed and by investment
income), dividends and interest, and internal fees and charges. Dividends
and interest proved fairly buoyant between 1913 and 1920 even if they did not
quite keep pace with inflation. They then rose strongly to 1938, but were
run down absolutely (as well as relatively) to 1951. Thereafter they have
recovered strongly. But in gross terms they were still less than either
houses or land in 1963: in 1973-4 (by which time the yield of most trust
and special funds had been apportioned according to its source) they outweighed land and 'houses' combined. Moreover (unlike real property) they
will have occasioned comparatively little of the external expenditure which
varied from 42 to 25% of all external income (22).

My next category of income, internal fees and, so far as they were
brought into revenue account, charges, has been more stable. But these too
have tended to rise in percentage and (except between 1913 and 1920) also in
real terms - after all there are now more students to charge. Their salience
increases if we look beyond our sample of historic colleges to the colleges
in general. For the newer foundations have rarely owned much in the way of
real property: they accounted for only 1% of all college income from agricultural and 14% from non-agricultural land in 1973-4. So they depended
far more on other forms of investment, on internal fees and charges, and
(particularly in the case of the new graduate colleges Nuffield and St.
Antony's) research grants. As a result the two groups presented rather different financial profiles in 1973-4:

TABLE 4 [(23)]

	Net 'endowment' income	Fees	Sales Internal	Sales External	Other (mostly research grants)
'Historic' colleges	42%	32%	19%	5%	1%
Other colleges	23	42	22	6	7

TABLE 5

Approximate balances - historic colleges revenue accounts

	1913	1920	1938	1951	1963	1973-4
INCOME						
External, Trust and special	£426,000	£519,000	£670,000	£937,000	1,840,000	£5,262,000
Less external EXPENDITURE	179,000	193,000	204,000	382,000	565,000	1,296,000
	247,000	326,000	466,000	555,000	1,275,000	3,966,000
Internal Income (incl. tuition fees)	140,000	208,000	270,000	523,000	1,183,000	Fees ONLY 2,535,000 / Total 4,616,000 (also includes sales not recorded in earlier accounts)
	387,000	534,000	736,000	1,078,000	2,458,000	8,582,000
* *1963 pounds*	*1,843,000*	*1,027,000*	*2,230,000*	*1,609,000*	*2,458,000*	*(6,501,000)* *(3,253,000)*
INTERNAL EXPENDITURE (incl. college contributions and - fairly minor - loan repayments/ transfers to reserves)	382,000	521,000	752,000	1,173,000	2,537,000	8,601,000
Approximate number of (25) students in residence	2,500	3,700	3,750	4,950	5,573	6,386 (in 1972-3)

* *Until 1963 derived from the London and Cambridge Economic Service index of retail prices (all items), The British Economy. Key Statistics 1900-1970, (no date) p.8: for 1973-4 this has been supplemented by an internal adaptation of the Tress-Brown index of university costs.*

The function of college income is, of course, to support expenditure: table 5 attempts to cast an overall balance for the historic colleges since 1913. It will be seen that the colleges suffered in both world wars and their aftermaths, but more especially during World War I. These set-backs apart, real college incomes have risen steadily during the twentieth century. So however have their student numbers. 1913 was in fact an unusually prosperous time [24]. But the ratio of income per junior member (admittedly a very rough measure of well-being) would not seem quite to have recovered this peak either in 1938 (its second summit) or in the course of its long (but slower) post-World War II improvement.

Calculations of expenditure are more complicated owing to the number of special funds. Also there are, on any classification, significant residual items listed under such imprecise headings as 'maintenance of establishment'. So I have confined myself to comparing certain major items; and I should emphasise that Table 6 is concerned with their relationship to each other, not to overall expenditure.

TABLE 6

A comparison of certain major items of expenditure - historic colleges
(see also Appendix II)

a)

	1913	1920	1938
Heads of colleges	7%	6%	6%
Fellows, pensions, allowances (incl. high table), College Officers	22%	22%	20%
Tutors, lecturers, fees to Professors and laboratories (tutorial a/c)	16%	17%	15%
University purposes (incl. fellowships for professors etc.)	13%	13%	13%
Scholarships, exhibitions, studentships	16%	14%	16%
College servants (revenue a/c only)	8%	12%	12%
College buildings (current expenditure)	12%	12%	13%
Chapels	4%	3%	2%
Libraries	1%	1%	2%
	99% (rounding)	100%	99% (rounding)

TABLE 6 (cont.)

b)	1938	1951	1963	1973-4
Heads of colleges	5%	3%	2%	2%
Fellows, pensions, allowances (incl. high table), college officers	16%	13%	13%	27% (Fellows, tutors, lecturers)
Tutors, lecturers, fees tó Professors and laboratories (tutorial a/c)	12%	16%	16%	
University purposes (incl. fellowships for professors etc.)	10%	7%	4%	10% (College contributions scheme and residual University purposes)
Scholarships, exhibitions, studentships	13%	8%	6%	3%
College servants (revenue and catering a/c's)	15%	21%	23%	25% (Domestic, Office and Clerical Staff)
College buildings (current expenditure)	11%	11%	17%	15%
Chapels	2%	1%	1%	1%
Libraries	1%	1%	2%	2%
Supplies purchased for catering (catering a/c)	16%	19%	16%	14%
	101% (rounding)	100%	100%	99% (rounding)

The chief impression must be one of suprising stability. But payments to heads of colleges have generally tended to fall as a proportion of total expenditure. This is only to be expected, since college fellows, students and staff have increased in numbers and heads have not. Between 1913 and 1920 and again between 1938 and 1951 the pay of heads remained more or less constant in money terms, and so dipped sharply in real ones. Individual posts might keep the same nominal salary for decades - the stipend of the Dean of Christ Church was raised to £3,000 p.a. in 1899 and remained at that level until 1955 [26]. Between 1920 and 1938, and between 1963 and 1973-4 there was an appreciable general recovery in real terms. But college heads are not as well paid as in 1913; and the gap between them and college fellows must have narrowed in financial as well as in status terms.

Payments to fellows, tutors, lecturers and the like appear to have remained remarkably constant as a fraction of college expenditure. They fell sharply in real terms during the inflation of the 1914-20 period; this

inflation was the more damaging since the stipends of Fellows were generally
prescribed in fixed terms by college statutes, and it was only possible to
circumvent this to a limited extent by making extra payments out of the
Tutorial Funds. Again there was a recovery in the inter-war period, and a
recession (though a slightly smaller one) between 1938 and 1951. Thereafter
payments have risen steadily in real terms. But the significance of this is
clouded in two ways: on the one hand numbers of teaching staff have increased very considerably, but, on the other, a growing share of their remuneration is, as we shall see, borne by the University.

Scholarships and other awards remained fairly constant in proportional
terms until World War II, but declined thereafter with the advent of state
studentships. In the 1960's the Franks Commission (i pp. 90-1) urged a
drastic reduction in the number (and a limitation of the value) of undergraduate awards, with the aim of redeploying £100,000 p.a. towards the
appointment of more academic staff and the support of post-graduates. But
this recommendation encountered a good deal of opposition (in part as a
result of inter-collegiate competition). Some agreed moves have been made
in this direction, but they have been limited; and the redeployment that
has occurred probably owes as much to the progress of inflation as to
definite policy decisions.

Expenditure on college buildings increased sharply between 1951 and
1963. Rates and insurance apart, this presumably reflects some (though not
all) of the restoration set off by the Historic Buildings Appeal, which has
quite transformed the face of the university area. One has only to look at
old photographs to see how blackened and flaking everything used to be.
Since then building, restoration and internal conversion work has continued
at a high level, and the current emphasis on fire precautions guarantees
that it will remain so. The process has drawn into Oxford building firms
from a considerable distance, and constitutes an appreciable slice of the
indirect employment afforded by the colleges and the University.

Direct employment is of college servants, expenditure on whom has
risen steadily in money terms ever since 1871; in real terms there was a
very slight dip between 1913 and 1920, but not in any other of the infla-
tionary periods. Again interpretation is difficult, since we do not know
how much of the increased expenditure is accounted for by better wages, and
how much simply by more extensive employment.

Lastly chapels and libraries. Both, alas, will have benefited from
trust funds that I have not been able to bring into account. But it seems
that expenditure on college chapels increased only very slightly in money
terms from 1913 to 1951. From then until 1973-4 such expenditure broadly
kept pace with inflation - perhaps rather surprisingly since it must be in
this period that attendance at chapel services has fallen most sharply.
Library expenditure had just overtaken that on chapels by 1951. Therafter
it increased rapidly; and the Franks Commission (i p. 157) gave libraries
as the area where Oxford expenditure was most markedly higher than that of
other universities. Not all of this can be ascribed to the colleges - the
Bodleian is probably the largest university library in the country. But,
though it is possible to question the system of college libraries, it is
clear that they do make very extensive provision, at any rate for undergraduates.

The terminal date I have chosen, 1973-4, was just before inflation
really took off. Next year most of the colleges were in deficit, though the
subsequent slowing down of price rises has enabled them to recover. Inflation has two effects on college finances: it erodes the value of their
endowment - the real rate of return has generally been negative over the

last five years; - and it makes correspondingly more important internal fees and charges which can be adjusted annually. Such fees are not paid directly by central government, but either by the students themselves or by local government. And though central government interventions (from the raising of fees for overseas students in the 1960's onwards) have considerably altered the environment in which fees are determined, they were, until very recently, formally set by the individual colleges without any official public scrutiny. In practice the need for an accurate prediction of future costs, on the one hand, and of compliance with national exhortations for self-restraint in price increases, on the other, have led since 1971 to the emergence of inter-collegiate arrangements to recommend, standardise, and scrutinise - arrangements which clearly owe much to Whitehall interdepartmental committees and which tend to ape civil service language and acronyms. In the last couple of years things have moved further. For the Department of Education and Science, goaded by pressure from Public Accounts Committee, has determined that it is no longer tolerable that Oxbridge college fee increases should be unpredictable. Such uncertainty apparently makes the planning of public expenditure impossible! Accordingly, though the D.E.S. does not wish to be involved in the setting of individual college fees, it now negotiates with the representatives of the colleges an annual average increase. And it remains for the inter-collegiate arrangements to ensure either that all colleges keep to this figure, or that increases by some are balanced by decreases by others.

How this will work out in practice it is too soon to say. But either way it implies a major change in the status of the colleges. For should the system not deliver the goods, the D.E.S. will be compelled to intervene more directly - and it is interesting to observe the deep suspicion of Whitehall voiced by ex-mandarins now transmogrified into heads of colleges. But to make the system work, it will be necessary for the majority of colleges (or their representatives) to acquire powers, in the last resort, of coercion. At present all colleges are sovereign: and, though they agree rather more frequently than do members of the European Community to be bound by a majority vote, they do occasionally exercise this sovereignty - a carefully planned scheme for a transition to mixed under-graduate entry, phased to protect the existing women's colleges foundered on the intransigence of one (or at most three) colleges. Accordingly inter-collegiate arrangements, like the Estates and Domestic Bursars' Committees, have historically tended to be bodies for consultation, the exchange of information, and the occasional joint presentation of evidence to Royal Commissions [27]. Recommendations that would have involved a supra-collegiate authority, notably in the field of catering and purchases, have never made much progress [28]. Admittedly the volume of inter-collegiate consultation has increased sharply over the last decade and a half; but it looks as if we are, in the financial field, on the eve of a departure that would be different in kind.

For my final theme, relations between the colleges and the University, we must go back in time. It has been calculated that in 1870-1 the total income of the University was £48,600, that of the colleges £397,000. [29] By 1883 a system, the Common University Fund (C.U.F.), had been enacted to tax the colleges for the benefit of the University. And various reforms had been embarked on in the belief that college income from agricultural land would rise very considerably. Instead there was the so-called 'Great Depression'. How seriously this affected Oxford has proved controversial, my own, comparatively optimistic, view being that the reforms were carried out, in essence if not always in detail, but that 'they engendered a considerable sense of strain, and little margin was left for new developments. So the next wave of reformers came to look elsewhere for their money': a public appeal was launched in 1907 for £250,000, just under half of which had been subscribed by 1912 [30]. In addition, and rather to the Government's surprise, individual scientific departments started applying for the specific grants that it introduced at this time [31].

Nevertheless Oxford was not, in its own eyes, a grant-aided university. And in 1918 the Vice-Chancellor turned down an invitation to join a joint universities delegation to the President of the Board of Education (H.A.L. Fisher) to plead for more money. Eventually, however, through the deployment of his own Oxford connections, and aided by the impatience of a number of Oxford scientists for more support, Fisher manoeuvred the Vice-Chancellor into putting together a list of the university's needs. This he then treated as a formal application, observed that the Board of Education no longer gave specific grants, and insisted that both college and university finances must be examined by a Royal Commission before any block grant could be made [32]. The examination was in fact fairly friendly, and the C.U.F. college contributions scheme was accepted as evidence that the 'University has received from its constituent colleges the full contribution that they can properly be asked to make out of their resources.' State aid was therefore in order for the University (though not for the colleges); but by 1922 the state unfortunately no longer had any money, and the Commission could only recommend a continuing grant of £110,000 p.a. to 'meet the most urgent needs of the universities at the present time, leaving it to the future benefactors to provide for the less urgent needs and for future developments from time to time'.[33] And indeed the 1930's saw another University appeal. [34]

However even if state aid was less than some would have wished, it still amounted in the later 1930's to nearly a third of the University's ordinary income; and this afforded some margin for the redeployment of college contributions. One of the themes of the Asquith Commission, and indeed a continuing criticism of Oxford to this day, was that the load of undergraduate teaching was such as to drive college Fellows to neglect research. And accordingly in 1927 £10,000 p.a. was earmarked from the C.U.F. for the provision of 50 lectureships to rotate among the 200-plus college tutors so that each 'might hope to have one for a reasonable period in the course of his career and thus be relieved from financial pressure and be free to undertake research.' For technical reasons college contributions between the wars fluctuated greatly and amounted to a good deal less than had been intended; so this £10,000 p.a. became not only the first but also the principal charge on the fund, especially after its subvention of professorial salaries was reduced to £6000 p.a. in 1937.

After the war the University's finances were suddenly transformed by a massive increase in government grants from the University Grants Commission (U.G.C.): 1938-9 £108,000, 1945-6 £266,000, 1946-7 £330,000, rising over the next quinquennium to £1,215,000. At the same time the colleges were faced 'with a tremendous backlog of repairs which had to be carried out at inflated post-war prices, while the effect of inflation on every item in the college budgets had produced great financial stringency. There was consequently a general outcry against college contributions....' Fortunately the C.U.F. had accumulated a considerable surplus during the war, since its lecturers were away. And it was decided to devote the greater part of its current yield to the provision of C.U.F. lectureships for all college arts fellows. Then between 1949 and 1952 the U.G.C. agreed to assume the costs of this policy, less a standardised contribution from the C.U.F., with the effect that by 1962-3 the C.U.F. itself provided only £38,000 of the £313,000 involved overall [35].

We shall return to the major significance of this development in a moment, but we must first note that it progressively freed the C.U.F. to move

in other directions. Since World War II there has been considerable concern
about the financial position of the poorer colleges (broadly those of more
recent foundation, whose endowment did not begin to match those of most
historic colleges). Like the other Oxbridge colleges these were substantially (36) debarred from direct state aid - and in 1963-4 the Franks
Commission found that this debarment 'clawed back' the equivalent of half
Oxford's endowment income (37). But they had the same expenses as other
colleges, perhaps more since their building needs were greater. Thus the
1950's saw the establishment from the C.U.F. of a fund to provide cheap
building loans for colleges and the inauguration of a system (in fact soon
eroded by inflation) of University payments 'towards the cost of maintaining
college buildings from whose use the University derives advantage.' Then in
1962 the C.U.F. started to provide a £2000 p.a. grant to the five women's
colleges, which was soon increased and extended to the four poorest men's
colleges. The Franks Committee next recommended the discontinuance of C.U.F.
payments to the University (though this did not in fact occur until 1973),
and the concentration of the college contributions scheme on building up
the endowments of the poorer colleges. This process lasted until 1978-9, and
involved the distribution of some £5m. among ten colleges. The scheme will
now be continued at a lower level, with the immediate aim of assisting Linacre
to financial independence.

    All this generated a good deal of politics and has been of considerable
importance to the poorer colleges (among them my own). But it has had far
less influence on Oxford life than the provision of University-financed
C.U.F. lectureships for college arts fellows. This has meant a subsidy
of nearly one-third of their cost, ensuring both that college fellows are
better paid than they might otherwise have been, and that, over a significant area of undergraduate teaching, the primary initiative for appointment,
provision and development has been collegiate. This is in marked contrast
to Cambridge where Faculties are more important, no such automatic provision
of University posts for college fellows exists, and many fellowships are
therefore just temporary teaching posts for migrants. As the Franks Commission recognised, Oxford is (for better or worse) a collegiate university;
over the past half-century its collegiate and its University sector have
become increasingly integrated, and the C.U.F. lectureship system has been
one of the most important factors in bringing this about.

    Until recently, indeed, one would have regarded it as an arrangement
whereby the University, with its now superior financial resources, subsidised college autonomy. True there were pointers that things might work
out differently. In early 1955 there was a good deal of complaint when it
was realised that the University had without consulting the colleges,
negotiated with the U.G.C. on the general relationship between the pay of
college fellows and of academics in other universities (38). And in the
later 1960's University Faculties acquired the right of representation at,
and last resort veto over, the appointment of college C.U.F. fellows. But
probably neither of these developments will be as influential in the long
run as the University's financial embarrassments of the 1970's. For these
mean that the University can no longer automatically match college appointments with C.U.F.'s. In theory, no doubt, any college could now afford one
unsubsidised C.U.F. fellow (and, indeed, Mansfield hall has appointed a number): but in practice college appointments in new fields are coming to
depend on the ability to extract a matching post from the University.
Re-appointments are another matter, subject only to the rather general
establishment of a 'teaching need'. But if the present distribution of
University posts between colleges becomes frozen, its equity is bound to be
questioned by those colleges that have developed more recently and that
could not acquire posts while the going was good. In which case there may

have to be a system for determining whether College A should continue to be entitled to, say, two C.U.F.'s in a subject in which College B has none. And, as with college fees, this would imply some supra-collegiate authority, a distinctly new departure.

The other half of the integration of college and University posts is the question of college affiliations for the holders of University appointments - principally people in the scientific field or attached to specialised institutes. Here the story is, in proportionate terms, one of steady progress. In 1871 there were perhaps about 370 college fellows, but only fifteen of these also held University posts. Subsequently colleges became able to set off the cost of professorial fellowships against C.U.F. taxation; so their number increased. In 1922 the 66 Professors appear all to have had college attachments; but only just under half of the eleven readers and just over half the 64 University lecturers did so. The expansion of college (and undergraduate) interest in the natural sciences must have helped to close the gap, since most college science tutors must hold University appointments if they are to have access to laboratories (39). And in January 1965 two-thirds of readers and of University lecturers held college fellowships, though only one-third of demonstrators and senior research officers (40). University expansion, however, meant that in the early 1960's the absolute number of non-fellows (230-350, depending on one's definitions (41)) was perhaps greater than ever before. And college tradition and attractiveness, especially at lunch-time, was sufficiently strong for them to feel distinctly under-privileged. The outcome was mixed. Pressure was exerted, not unsuccessfully, on college to elect more as Fellows. Steps were taken to insure that, in future, posts were usually advertised with both University and college attachments. But the University would not accept that it should never create posts that colleges were not prepared to underwrite in this way. So in 1965 two last resort 'colleges of entitlement' were created by the University, with the aid of the richer colleges, for those who fell through the collegiate net. Gradually both have created a corporate identity for themselves as Wolfson and St. Cross.

This solution was expensive and not entirely satisfactory. But it does testify to the continuing importance attached here to colleges as a way of organising a university. This has been one of the most marked pecularities of Oxbridge. It influenced the first English universities to be deliberately founded - London and Durham - in the early nineteenth century. But it was then eclipsed by the much simpler model of the civic university, and only made a come-back in the 1960's when three of the new universities - Kent, Lancaster and York - adopted a collegiate structure. Their experience in this respect has not, I believe, been entirely successful, since nobody now starting de novo would wish to delegate to the colleges what appears to be the very high degree of autonomy necessary for their successful functioning.

I have suggested that two possible major challenges to Oxford college autonomy can now be dimly discerned. Certainly the collegiate system is still in full working order, and can be pointed to as a distinctive feature of the Oxford region. In other respects, however, the colleges would appear to have distanced themselves from that region. For they no longer derive their income mostly from real property (chiefly local), but from investments and charges. And they probably no longer feel quite the same local involvement. In 1921 the notion, pushed in connection with the Asquith Commission, that they should stop buying locally and pursue economies (42) by collective purchasing on the London market was given a very frosty reception, not only for its alleged impracticability but also because of its effect on the local economy:

'It is clear that the whole tendency of the recommendations...
must mean something like ruin to the Oxford retail market, and
is bound to cause an absolute breach of feeling between the men
who have served them so long'.

'if legitimate trade is taken out of the City, the power of the
tradesmen to pay rent, to the Colleges and others, and rates will
be diminished. Take away £5,000 legitimate profit, and up go our
rates.' (43)

The colleges of today would, I think, no longer rate their local
importance so highly. And, though inter-collegiate purchasing co-operation
has still proved elusive, no scruples operate to prevent the building of
individual cold stores and their stocking from wherever appears most
advantageous. And the current enthusiasm, as I am told, is for going in
with the London colleges to take advantage of the rather loose scheme of
rebates they have negotiated. So much from the collegiate angle. This
shift of perspectives has no doubt also been mirrored from the tradesman's
end. When I was young, my hairdresser, Victor Drewe, used to tell of the
number of Heads of House whose hair he cut. His successor does not. And
is there any modern counterpart to the celebrated sign in the Market,

'University, Family and Pork Butcher'?

APPENDIX I

To illustrate the comparative fortunes of individual colleges over the
half century after 1920, I have calculated for 1920 and 1973-4:

A. individual colleges' percentage shares of all college external incomes

B. individual colleges' percentage shares of all college internal expenditure

C. relative internal expenditure per junior member.

Two important qualifications need to be made. Firstly collegiate needs differ,
some colleges having to maintain a greater research establishment, or more
costly historic buildings, than others; and these differences of needs do not
show up in simple calculations of expenditure per junior member. Secondly
there is a greater chance that particular years will prove untypical for
individual colleges than for the average of all colleges (to which I have
restricted myself elsewhere in the paper); New College, for instance, had
an unusually bad year in 1973-4.

A. Percentage shares of all college external incomes

	1920	1973-4
18%	Magdalen	–
14%	Christ Church	–
10%	–	Christ Church
8%	All Souls	All Souls, Nuffield, St. John's
7%	New College, Queen's, St. John's	Merton
6%	Merton	Magdalen, Queen's
5%	Brasenose	Balliol
4%	Corpus Christi	Brasenose, Corpus Christi, Lincoln

A. Percentage shares of all college external incomes (Cont.)

1920	1973-4
3% Balliol, Jesus, Oriel University	(New College), St. Antony's, Wadham
2% Exeter, Lincoln, Pembroke, Worcester	Exeter, Keble, Oriel, Pembroke, University, Worcester
1% Hertford, Keble, Pembroke, Wadham	Hertford, Lady Margaret Hall, St. Anne's, St. Catherine's, St. Edmund Hall, St. Hilda's, St. Hugh's, St. Peter's, Somerville

Sources: 1920 (Gross income from estates less expenditure on estates) plus net income from trusts - as calculated in Appendix 16 of the Asquith Commission.

1973-4 'Net endowment income available for colleges' own purposes' plus college contribution payments. New College's share is untypically low.

B. Percentage shares of all college internal expenditure

1920	1973-4
13% Christ Church	
9% Magdalen	
7% Balliol, New College, Queen's	
5% Brasenose, Exeter, Merton, University	Christ Church, Magdalen, New College
4% Corpus Christi, Jesus, Oriel, St. John's, Trinity	Balliol, Nuffield, St. Catherine's, St. John's, University
3% Pembroke, Wadham, Worcester	all other colleges
2% Hertford	Hertford, St. Peter's

Sources: 1920 Repairs and improvements to college buildings, 'Establishment', Tuition, 'General' less payments to the University - as calculated in Appendix 16 of the Asquith Commission. Keble is excluded as its accounts (which include the cost of catering) were compiled on a different basis from those of other men's colleges.

1973-4 Statements 4 and 5 excluding the notional cost of fellows' room rents, plus (Statement 3 expenses of premises less contributions from Statements 4 and 5).

C. **Relative internal expenditure per junior member**
(undergraduate colleges only)

	1920		1973-4
180-140%	of average: Corpus Christi, Magdalen, Merton, Christ Ch. (in that order)	Over 140%	Merton
		139-130%	Corpus Christi, Christ Church, Magdalen, Queen's, St. John's
		119-110%	Balliol, New College, Oriel
109-90%	Balliol, Brasenose, New Coll., Oriel, Queen's, Trinity, Univ.,	109-90%	Brasenose, Jesus, Lincoln, St. Catherine's, Trinity, University
89-80%	Exeter, Jesus, Worcester	89-80%	Exeter, Keble, St. Edmund Hall, Worcester
79-70%	St. John's, Lincoln	79-69%	Hertford, Lady Margaret Hall*, Pembroke, St. Anne's*, St. Hilda's*, St. Hugh's*, St. Peter's, Somerville*, Wadham
69-60%	Hertford, Pembroke, Wadham		

1920:   expenditure per undergraduate

1973-4:   expenditure per junior member, a graduate being taken as equivalent
          to 0.45 undergraduates. The concentration of women's colleges
          (starred) at the bottom of the table will be noted; but they would
          presumably have occupied at least as low a position had it been
          possible to include them in 1920.

APPENDIX II

SOURCES OF INCOME AND PRINCIPAL ITEMS OF EXPENDITURE (HISTORIC COLLEGES)

a) Sources of Income

	1913	1920	1938	1951	1963	1973-4
Houses						
a) Rent	£ 56,000	62,000	114,000	241,000	450,000	£1,293,000 Non-agric. land
1963 pounds	*267,000*	*119,000*	*345,000*	*360,000*	*450,000*	*647,000*
b) Long Lease	73,000	75,000	114,000	107,000	135,000	
	348,000	*144,000*	*345,000*	*160,000*	*135,000*	
Lands, Tithes, etc.	230,000	265,000	202,000	342,000	537,000	1,094,000 Agric. land, etc.
	1,095,000	*510,000*	*612,000*	*510,000*	*537,000*	*556,000*
						17,000 'other'
Dividends and interest	30,000	66,000	154,000	121,000	460,000	2,744,000
	143,000	*127,000*	*467,000*	*181,000*	*460,000*	*1,373,000*
Trust and Special	37,000	51,000	86,000	126,000	258,000	mostly incorporated above. Also, from trusts of which the college is not the sole trustee, £112,000 - less £98,000 (1963 £33,000) for purposes external to the college
	176,000	*98,000*	*261,000*	*188,000*	*258,000*	
Tuition fees	56,000	89,000	105,000	222,000	411,000	2,535,000 (internal fees only)
	267,000	*171,000*	*318,000*	*331,000*	*411,000*	*1,269,000*
All other internal (mostly fees)	84,000	119,000	165,000	301,000	772,000	
	400,000	*229,000*	*500,000*	*449,000*	*772,000*	
Contributions from the University for services rendered					51,000	51,000
					51,000	*26,000*
Repayment from C.U.F.					12,000	
					12,000	
Sales - internal						1,515,000
						758,000
- external						430,000
						191,000
Other (mostly research grants)						136,000
						55,000

b) Expenditure – principal items only

	1913	1920	1938	1951	1963	1973-4	
Heads of colleges	26,000	27,000	37,000	39,000	57,000	£143,000	
1963 pounds:	*124,000*	*52,000*	*112,000*	*58,000*	*57,000*	*72,000*	
Fellows, pensions, allowances (incl. high table), College Officers	77,000	106,000	129,000	164,000	322,000	2,004,000	(Fellows, tutors, and lecturers)
	367,000	*204,000*	*391,000*	*245,000*	*322,000*	*1,003,000*	
Tutors, lecturers, fees to Professors and laboratories (tutorial account)	55,000	81,000	99,000	198,000	416,000	}	
	262,000	*156,000*	*300,000*	*296,000*	*416,000*		
University purposes i) Fellowships for Professors, readers etc.	31,000	37,000	47,000	45,000	38,000	38,000	(University objects)
	148,000	*71,000*	*142,000*	*67,000*	*38,000*	*19,000*	
ii) C.U.F. and other	14,000	28,000	35,000	42,000	71,000	681,000	(College contributions scheme)
	67,000	*54,000*	*106,000*	*63,000*	*71,000*	*341,000*	
Scholarships, Exhibitions, Studentships	57,000	70,000	103,000	98,000	152,000	230,000	
	271,000	*135,000*	*312,000*	*146,000*	*152,000*	*115,000*	
College Servants i) Revenue a/c only	28,000	59,000 }	119,000	268,000	594,000	1,874,000	(Domestic, Office Clerical Staff)
	133,000	*113,000*	*361,000*	*400,000*	*594,000*	*938,000*	
ii) Catering a/c only		1927: 35,000					
		100,000					
College buildings (current expenditure)	41,000	56,000	85,000	140,000	431,000	1,121,000	
	195,000	*108,000*	*258,000*	*209,000*	*431,000*	*561,000*	
Chapels	14,000	15,000	15,000	16,000	22,000	48,000	
	67,000	*29,000*	*45,000*	*24,000*	*22,000*	*24,000*	
Libraries	5,000	6,000	11,000	17,000	45,000	178,000	
	24,000	*12,000*	*33,000*	*25,000*	*45,000*	*89,000*	
Supplies purchased for catering (catering a/c)	125,000*		125,000	247,000	414,000	1,053,000	
	*240,000**		*379,000*	*369,000*	*414,000*	*527,000*	

*Asquith Commission estimate for the purchases of all (not merely of the historic) colleges

222

NOTES

1. Report, P(arliamentary) P(apers) 1922 x, and Appendices (separately published, 1922) - subsequently cited as Asquith and Asquith Appendix.

2. The Asquith Commission had already commented on this. Franks repeated the observation, and recommended the appointment of a University Information Officer (now at the University Offices, Wellington Square) to combat such 'erroneous ideas' - University of Oxford, Report of Commission of Inquiry, (Oxford, 1966) (subsequently cited as Franks), i pp.18-20.

3. University of Oxford: Accounts of the Colleges (Oxford, 1884 -); until the later 1960's they were usually bound up with Abstracts of the Accounts of the Curators of the University Chest.

4. University, Balliol, Merton, Exeter, Oriel, Queen's, New, Lincoln, All Souls, Magdalen, Brasenose, Corpus Christi, Christ Church, Trinity, St. John's, Jesus, Wadham, Pembroke and Worcester.

5. See eg. the section on the 'General position of the two Universities and their special value to the nation', Asquith pp.43-8; also the beginning of the Vice-Chancellor's letter of 19 Nov. 1918, Asquith Appendix p.217.

6. Appendix, pp.356-7. It should be noted, however, that the term 'sundry house property' can conceal some quite important holdings, like those of the Queen's College in Southampton.

7. P.P., 1873 xxvii Part 1 pp.197, 199, 203 (totals of Oxford and Cambridge holdings), Part 2 (details of Oxford) and Part 3 (of Cambridge holdings).

8. A. Harrison, R.B. Tranter and R.S. Gibbs, Landownership by public and semi-public institutions in the U.K., (University of Reading, Centre for Agricultural Strategy Paper no.3 - December 1977) p.44 - the figure is only approximate, having been ascertained by questionnaire, and (unlike the 1918 figure) related to college holdings only. On the same basis, Cambridge colleges and University held 127,000 acres in 1872 and 116,000 in 1918, and Cambridge colleges 57,000 in 1976.

9. Royal Commission on Tithe Rentcharge 1934-5, Statement of Evidence submitted by the Bursars of the Oxford Colleges, (1935) esp. pp.1, 12, Appendix 1.

10. Asquith Appendix, p.222.

11. Ibid., pp.358 (Oxford), 366 (Cambridge): the Cambridge sales were by 13 colleges and fetched about £550,000.

12. Merton, Queen's, New, All Souls, Magdalen, Brasenose, Corpus Christi, Christ Church and St. John's.

13. The accounting for receipts under this heading was extremely complex and the figure here given is correspondingly liable to error.

14. 'Perpetual' charities do, however, also enjoy considerable advantages when investing in stocks and shares. And one cloud on the colleges' financial horizons is the possibility of a legal redefinition of 'charitable status'.

15. Had we accepted this benefaction, the proceeds would have been constituted as a 'trust' fund. College accounts have been much complicated by the proliferation of such trust and special funds, whose origins are sometimes misunderstood. They result partly from the internal convenience of ear-marking certain sums (a process that external commissions pressed on the colleges in connection with 'tutorial' and 'catering' accounts), but chiefly from a wish to preserve the names and memories of benefactors, both in their own right and pour encourager les autres.

16. Of the gifts recorded on the Bodleian Library benefactors' board, 30 antedate 1914, 13 date from 1914-41, and 13 from 1946-78.

17. G.T. Hutchinson, 'Some aspects of college finances', Oxford Magazine v (1938) pp.81,75.

18. Perhaps by reason of the number of 'home students', rather fewer women than men were housed in college in 1923-4. But already by 1928-9 considerably more were. This contrast has continued, though over the last decade or so the ratio of men 'living in' has risen nearly to match that of the traditional women's colleges.

19. Franks, ii p.35, and an internal tabulation for Michaelmas 1976. The figures for all colleges, halls and university departments combined were: college 6828; college provided 1107; University provided 237; other (mostly privately rented) 3566.

19a. Figures for colleges' gross capital endowments are not available, and would in any case fluctuate considerably from year to year with changes in stock market values and accounting conventions. But we may note the following statement about one rich college: 'Magdalen's total endowment stands today at...14 million pounds and its annual income from interest, student fees and grants amounts to about...1.2 million pounds'; however building repairs 'scheduled to last through 1987' will come to at least £1½ m. and the total cost may be of the order of £2½ - 3 m. - N. Daniloff, 'Magdalen Great Tower Crumbles', The American Oxonian lxvi (1979) pp. 284-6.

20. The post-1967 'Franks' form of account incorporates far more catering and other internal charges than did its predecessors. But in this table I have omitted them to preserve rough comparability with the 1913-63 Revenue Accounts.

21. See my 'Oxford and Cambridge College Finances, 1871-1913', Economic History Review, 2nd series xxviii (1975), esp. pp.637-8, 633.

22. External expenditure as a % of historic colleges' external income: 1913 42%; 1920 37%; 1938 30%; 1951 41%; 1963 31%. On a slightly different basis external expenditure accounted for 25% of the historic colleges' 1973-4 external income.

23. 'Endowment' income here means Statement 3 'Balance available for college's own purposes' plus trust fund income available only for statements 4 and 5. All Souls, the 'historic' counterpart of Nuffield and St. Antony's, did not depend significantly on research grants.

24. See my article (cited above), esp. p.640.

25. Asquith, pp.26-7 gives 3,460 men and women students in residence in 1913. From this I have subtracted some 380 women (Asquith p.27) and a more arbitrary allowance for male students outwith the 'historic' colleges. In 1920 there were 4,651 students (or about 4,000 male students) in residence (ibid., and Asquith Appendix p.275), or 3344 undergraduates in the historic colleges (Asquith Appendix, p.325). Franks gives totals of 5,023 students or 4,147 male students in 1938-9 (ii p.12), and of 5,009 in the 'historic colleges' in 1948-9 (ii p.30), a year when total numbers were slightly higher than in 1951. The 1963 total comes from Franks (ii p.30) and the 1972-3 figure from the University Calendar.

26. Whitaker's Almanack. And for a further dozen years the college's supplement to the traditional sum received from the Chapter Fund remained comparatively minor.

27. The only exception is the Senior Tutors' Committee, established in 1946 to obtain uniformity between colleges on tuition fees and rates of payment for outside tuition - Franks Commission, Written Evidence Part 12, p.47. In its other activities, however, the Senior Tutors' Committee conforms to the general pattern.

28. For the Asquith Commission's recommendations, see its Report pp.146-55 and Appendices 9 and 10; the Franks Commission made comparable recommendations, but laid less stress on them (i p.169).

29. Franks, i p.282.

30. Dunbabin, article cited, esp. pp.643-4; see also A. Engel's 'Comment' on this article and my 'Reply' in Economic History Review, 2nd series xxxvi (1968) pp.437-49

31. Asquith Appendix p.221.

32. Ibid. pp.217-223.

33. Asquith, pp.203, 205, 215-16.

34. By 1935 this had already raised £526,000 (including Lord Nuffield's promise of £100,000 for the Physical Chemistry Laboratory) and a further £250,000 was being sought for general research and for improvements to laboratories and museums. The £220,000 for the New Bodleian was already secure - Oxford University, A Programme for Development (May 1938).

35. The two previous paragraphs are chiefly drawn from H.H. Keen's written evidence to the Franks Commission (Evidence, Part 2 pp.18-39).

36. Subject to very limited exceptions for the women's colleges.

37. Franks, i pp.157, 159.

38. Oxford Magazine, lxxiii (27 Jan. 1955) pp.162-4, 166.

39. A few colleges continued to maintain laboratories down to the Second World War; but University provision was already dominant by the beginning of the present century.

40. Franks, ii pp.36, 39, 253.

41. On 1 January 1965 there were 229 University academic staff without college posts, though many were fairly junior (Franks, ii p.253). There were also some 125 similar posts in University administration, in museums and libraries, and in the Press, though the Norrington Committee recommended fellowships only for the most senior (Further Report on the closer integration on university teaching and research with the college system, Supplement to the Gazette, January 1964, p.6). By February 1979 the number of actually or potentially 'entitled' persons without college fellowships was 33, and it will fall further with the advent of Green College.

42. Of some £11,000 on total purchases of £125,000 (Asquith p.149 and Asquith Appendix p.253).

43. Asquith Appendix pp.268-9.

ADULT AND FURTHER EDUCATION IN OXFORDSHIRE

F.V. Pickstock

The rate of technological and social change, and accompanying fears
of substantial long term unemployment is focussing attention on patterns of
living and especially on the shifting significance of work and leisure in
people's lives. Such changes do not, of course, occur suddenly and it
would be wise to reflect upon the ways in which people have
been responding to the substantial changes already experienced since 1945.
One of the responses to longer initial education, to less physically
exhausting work, increased leisure, occupational change and greater mobility
has undoubtedly been to seek opportunities to fulfil and to express educational, cultural and recreational needs and interests. Public provision
through organized adult education has rapidly expanded although it has for
a much longer time been a more generally accepted part of people's lives
than is apparently recognised. For instance, the Ashby Committee, appointed
by the government in 1953 to review The Organization and Finance of Adult
Education could report that since the 1919 Report of the Adult Education
Committee of the Ministry of Reconstruction it could not be said that adult
education as an organized activity had become either universal or lifelong.
It was true that because of its brief the Ashby Committee concentrated on
the work of the Responsible Bodies: University Extra Mural Departments and
the W.E.A. Surely it was myopic however not to draw attention to the much
larger volume of adult education under the local authorities, some 700,000
students as compared with the 100,000 or so in W.E.A. and University classes.

By 1974, the number of students in responsible body courses in England
and Wales had grown to 270,000, in Evening Institutes to nearly 1,600,000
(aged 18 and over), whilst the largely new Colleges of Further Education
enrolled over 470,000 in evening courses. (D.E.S. Annual Statistics. Vol.3).
The sheer volume of this adult education is the response of people to the
social changes mentioned. That this has not been registered in public con-
sciousness is partly due to the fact that it has not come about as a result
of deliberate public policy, and partly because of the variety of adult
education agencies at work, many of them masquerading under the official,
and to the ordinary public, technical, title of Further Education. Adult
education has not had the benefit of authoritative reports of the kind that
have influenced the rest of the educational system - Crowther, Newsom, Albe-
marle, Robbins, Plowden and James, nor has it had more than a marginal direct share of the great investment of resources ploughed into education in
consequence. Belatedly the Russell Committee was appointed in 1969, not to
examine the whole field but to examine "non-vocational" adult education
only. On its publication in 1973, it elicited no official response in the
form of a White Paper, and its influence on official policy and particularly
on the allocation of resources has been little more than cosmetic.

If there has been no generous public sponsorship to explain the great
growth of adult education, neither has there been any great movement, organizing and campaigning for adult education in the manner of the W.E.A. in the
earlier part of the century. The grandiose continental and American concepts
of education permanente and of lifelong education have had no resonance here
and certainly offer no explanation of the phenomenon of adult education growth.
The explanation is to be found in a long tradition of adult education, rooted
in a whole variety of institutions, which has expressed itself in the
opportunist adaptation of every institution at hand to meet the demands arising in consequence of social change. We may no longer pride ourselves on

our pragmatic genius as a nation, but adult education certainly is a shining example of that trait at its best.

ADULT EDUCATION

The history of English adult education, from the nineteenth century Mechanics Institutes and even earlier is a story of response to the particular needs and circumstances of a rapidly changing society and a tribute to the fertility of the soil it cultivated. A remarkable number of Britain's characteristic educational institutions and societies sprang from humble adult education beginnings. University Extension at the end of the nineteenth century was especially influential and amongst its other progeny it gave birth in the early 1900's to the influential W.E.A./University partnership which, with its prestigious University Tutorial Classes, and its network of voluntary branches, closely associated with the rising working class movement, was to exercise a profound influence, not only upon adult education but on society more generally. This was so dominant that the kind of adult education for which it stood, and still stands even to this day, is deemed to be the only one worthy of the title Adult Education. H.J. Edwards however has reminded us (The Evening Institute. N.I.A.E. 1961) that even in the heyday of the W.E.A. in the 1920's and 1930's for far more people – half a million or so – adult education meant the Evening Institute. It was symptomatic that local authorities, who were directly responsible for evening institutes, with few exceptions, paid much more attention to the adult education work of the universities and the W.E.A., to which many of them gave generous support. All the expansion and growth of adult education in the post 1945 period has come from the evolution of these institutions and structures established in the first half of the century. Even before the war, alongside the 'Evening Institute' and partly developing from it was the 'Technical College', which after the war was destined to become an important part of the adult education stream, although a large segment was to be hived off into 'Higher Education' to become de facto part of the university system.

The evolution of the technical colleges into Colleges of Further Education on the one hand, and into polytechnics and universities on the other needs special treatment and for the time being I will concentrate attention on the development of the W.E.A., university extra mural departments and the evolution of evening institutes into the adult education service of the local authorities.

In the post war world there was great qualitative change in the work of the W.E.A. and the university extra mural departments. Even in the immediate pre-war years there had been a broadening of its appeal and curriculum and this change grew rapidly in pace in the 1950's. There was a steep decline in the number of manual workers in classes and a corresponding growth in the number of women. The old staple subjects of university tutorial classes such as Economics, Economic and Industrial History and Politics declined almost to extinction and were replaced by English Literature, the Arts, Sociology, Archaeology and Local History, and to a lesser extent, scientific subjects. At the same time, the three-year University Tutorial Class lost its eminence and a great variety of types of course, including short residential ones provided a new flexibility to serve a new kind of clientele. Other changes affected this new flexibility. The decline of the ability of the W.E.A. to mobilize working class interest in adult education led to a severance of the formal partnerships between universities and W.E.A. districts which had been enshrined in Joint Tutorial Classes Committees. Extra mural departments came to be regarded simply as university departments responsible for the university's contribution to adult education.

This change coincided with a time of rapid university expansion and extra mural departments were able to call on a wider range of specialist resources to meet the more varied, and sometimes esoteric interests of the new clientele. We are not suggesting that the W.E.A. and extra mural departments went entirely different ways; in most areas they still co-operated closely and W.E.A. classes developed on much the same lines, and for the same reasons as extra mural ones.

Oxford was slower to adapt in any formal way than other universities, primarily because of its historic connection the the W.E.A. - which had started the whole working class adult education era in 1908 - and partly because its far-flung empire of Kent, East Sussex, Lincoln and North Staffordshire, as well as its home territory of Berkshire, Buckinghamshire and Oxfordshire, could not effectively be served by Oxford internal staff. It was not until 1962 that Oxford's Joint Tutorial Classes Committee with the W.E.A. was dissolved, and it was not until 1975 that the last of its distant territories, the county of Kent, was handed over to one of the new universities.

Neither the W.E.A. noruniversity extra mural departments acquiesced easily to the change of role which social change forced upon them. There was a feeling of guilt about devoting resources to more widely dispersed artistic, cultural, social and environmental interests, apparently lacking the more direct sense of social purpose which had hitherto informed their work. Their most striking response was co-operation in the development of educational work for trade unionists, in particular for shop stewards, and in this, as was appropriate, Oxford played a leading part. In the later 1960's, when the new T.U.C. educational scheme got into its stride, shop stewards' education and training became a substantial educational movement in its own right, though disappointingly lacking in the broader educational objectives at which the universities and the W.E.A. had aimed. The sense of guilt, as well as a recognition by extra mural departments of their new kind of responsibility to their university had one other beneficial effect: it led to critical examination of most aspects of the new work in which they were finding themselves engaged, and it would not be difficult to give examples of their contribution to the quality and range of teaching in a number of subjects, most notably in the fields of Literature, Archaeology, Local History and Environmental Studies, aspects of Sociology and of Industrial Relations. In a few cases, alas not in Oxford, research and studies in adult education have made a notable contribution to the development of adult education and the influence of this can increasingly be seen in the work of local authorities.

This widening of the range and variety of adult education, not only that provided by university extra mural departments, but also that provided by the W.E.A. and some L.E.A.'s, has been aided by two post-war innovations. The first of these was the establishment of short term residential colleges, largely from the inspiration of Sir Richard Livingstone, whose book The Future in Education, first published in 1941, went into a number of editions and was widely influential. Wedgwood Memorial College founded jointly by the three local authorities in North Staffordshire, the Oxford Extra Mural Delegacy and the W.E.A. early in 1945, was the harbinger of a network of similar colleges, which combined the preservation of historic houses with widening educational opportunity. Oxford combined with the Y.M.C.A., and the Kent County Council to provide a similar college in Kent and finally, in 1965, signalled its future concentration on its home territory by attractively converting Rewley House and its adjoining Victorian houses into a residential centre. The experience of the Oxford Extra Mural Department has been that these residential facilities have been indispensable to its capacity to innovate and to respond flexibly to the adult education interests and needs of present day society.

A second post-war innovation has been the creation of special purpose adult education centres, giving new opportunities and setting new standards for a form of education long accustomed to battling with the cold and discomfort of borrowed school rooms. Outside London the most ambitious development of such centres was in Kent, under the direction of Frank Jessup, then Assistant County Education Officer and a member of the Oxford Extra Mural Delegacy, later to become Head of the Delegacy in 1952. In the other Oxford areas outside Berkshire, Buckinghamshire and Oxfordshire, similar centres were established with local authority assistance in East Sussex, Lincoln and North Staffordshire. The only comparable centre in Oxford's home area is Rewley House itself, which before it was adapted for residential use had long become a fully-fledged University Adult Education Centre.

A different sort of contribution to adult education has been made by the expansion of the long established long-term adult residential colleges, Ruskin and Plater Colleges in Oxford, Coleg Harlech, Fircroft, Hillcroft, Newbattle Abbey, and quite recently the new College of the North in Yorkshire. The small stream of students from adult classes who attended these colleges before the war has broadened and deepened, providing not only intensive one or two year courses to equip adults for wider public service, but also an alternative high road for adults into the university and higher education system.

The local authority system of adult education, based for the most part on the ubiquitous 'Evening Institute', after the war began to benefit from the rapid expansion of secondary education with its expanded facilities of arts and craft rooms, laboratories, workshops and gymnasia, and later on, some enlightened authorities began to add special adult education wings. With some important exceptions however, local authorities in general acquiesced in the expansion of evening institutes as an adjunct to the school system, serviced them with miniscule professional staffs, and failed to develop adult education policies of their own. A number of local authorities, of which Oxford City was one example, paid little attention to guiding and developing evening institutes and made the Youth and Community Service, based on community centres the focus of interest. It was the unsatisfactory nature of this which led to pressure for a clearer definition of the City's role in adult education. With the growth of colleges of further education the overtly vocational aspects of the work of evening institutes more or less disappeared and so by the 1970's they were clearly engaged in adult eeucation, i.e., non-vocational education. With this change came the question as to whether they should continue to be regarded as an offshoot of the school system or follow the Kent pattern of an independent adult education service closely related to the work carried on by the W.E.A. and university extra mural departments. But, at the same time, colleges of further education, and this was particularly true of the Oxford F.E. College, alongside vocational courses, began to develop an attractive and extensive programme of non-vocational courses, in the daytime as well as in the evening. The City of Oxford was in the process of trying to sort out the problems arising from these changes before it was overtaken by local government reorganization. Berkshire did not have a similar problem since it had a policy of basing its adult education on its colleges of further education. Oxfordshire's adult education service had been influenced by the ideas of Henry Morris's Cambridgeshire Village College in which it was envisaged that all forms of education, primary, secondary, further and adult education, as well as social and recreational facilities, would be combined in one community centre serving a neighbourhood or a group of villages. The Oxfordshire version however, was much less ambitious and followed an opportunist policy of providing adult education rooms and other facilities in selected schools. These were under the control of lay management committees, normally with part time paid organizers, but operating independently with the assistance of some grant aid. In three cases, at Watlington, Sonning Common and Kidlington there were more ambitious schemes directed by a full-time professional adult education tutor. Besides this scheme for what were entitled Adult Education Centres, the technical colleges at Banbury and Witney each had adult education facilities and a professional adult tutor, with a rather undefined neighbourhood, as well as college, responsibilities. Oxfordshire thus attempted a co-ordinated adult education policy, but its limited resources and opportunistic character meant that it lacked consistency and comprehensiveness.

FURTHER EDUCATION

The 1944 Education Act (Section 41) used the term 'Further Education' as a generic one to include all post compulsory school leaving age education, including cultural and recreational activities. Without specifically saying so it thus included what had hitherto been known as adult education. Later the term, as used by the Ministry of Education and hence by local authorities came to be generally used, loosely and without precise definition, to describe lower level technical and vocational education, differentiating it on the one hand from universities, polytechnics and other colleges in what came to be called the 'Higher Education' system, and (implicitly) from 'Adult Education' on the other. (See 1966 White Paper, A Plan for Polytechnics and Other Colleges; Higher Education in the Further Educational System.) This confusion of language reflected a failure to face a problem which is more fundamental than the categorisation of institutions; it is a question of the role and character of adult education in a modern society. The issue had last been tackled by the 1919 Adult Education Committee of the Ministry of Reconstruction. The influential members of that Committee had been deeply involved both in the W.E.A. movement and in the development of the public education system following the 1889 Technical Instruction Act and the 1902 Education Act. They wished to see an adult education system in which technical and vocational education, the arts and crafts, and liberal adult education were integrally combined, but reluctantly came to the conclusion that it was "impossible to obliterate the artificial distinction between technical and non-technical subjects (without) a profound change in the motive and spirit of industry" (Section 294). Much present day adult and further (or technical) education is informed by this more universal conception of education which is so eloquently expressed in Sections 153 to 155 of the 1919 Report, but there are even more powerful forces at work bringing together adult and further education and obliterating distinctions imposed by old prejudices. As the 1919 Report said "Whether an education offers a liberal culture or not depends on the purpose to which it is directed, and the spirit in which it is carried on", and more and more, distinctions between vocational and liberal are becoming irrelevant to the impulses which lead people to pursue educational interests in their adult lives. There are also more specific factors. In a world of constant innovation, the value of technical knowledge and training in itself is short lived, and adaptability, not merely to technical, but also to social and organizational change is assuming a much greater importance. Traditional adult education on its part, from its long concern for social relevance, has also come to place more emphasis on motivations springing from people's lives as a whole, including their vocational and quasi vocational interests.

In the actual practice of educators, both in the adult education and in further education (narrowly defined) systems there has been a convergence towards a common conception of adult education. Adult education in consequence has benefitted from an unintended "spin off" of the concern of governments from the early 1950's onwards with the development of technical education, partly for reasons of "national efficiency", partly as a means of coping cheaply and rapidly with the rising demand for advanced education. After the 1956 White Paper on Technical Education and the designation of a number of Colleges of Advanced Technology, Circular 305 of the Ministry of Education made plans for three grades of colleges below the C.A.T.S. - regional, area and local. The adoption of the binary system in the later 1960's led to further changes with ten of C.A.T.S. becoming universities or university institutions, and twenty eight technical colleges being transferred into the higher education system as Polytechnics. Presumably, at least as regards formal designation, the hierarchy of area and local colleges has now been dropped and all of them whatever their actual titles are Colleges of Further Education.

The consequence of all this concern is that colleges of further education have received a lot of official attention from ministers and officers, from Regional Advisory Councils for Further Education and from local authorities. More important, substantial capital programmes have ensured the expansion and enrichment of their facilities whilst at the same time their revenue budgets and professional staffs have grown enormously. More recently, during a period when the rest of the educational system has been feeling the sharp edge of expenditure cuts, the maintenance and expansion of the programmes of colleges of further education have been sustained by contracts or earmarked training grants from the Manpower Services Commission.

The broadening and deepening of so-called vocational and technical education in response to social and technical change has implications for adult education, but apart from this, colleges of further education have enormously expanded their programmes of non-vocational or adult education to the extent that they account for approaching forty per cent of adult students in Oxfordshire. Unless adult education was to fall into complete chaos, with university extra mural departments, the W.E.A., the mainly school-based adult education work of local authorities, and colleges of further education, indiscriminately overlapping and competing in the same field, some review of the whole structure became imperative. This was attempted in the Russell Committee's Report - Adult Education; a Plan for Redevelopment, published in 1973. Locally, the new Oxfordshire County Council adopted in 1975 its own scheme based upon the Report of an Officers Working Party and it is to this I now turn.

A COMMUNITY EDUCATION SCHEME FOR OXFORDSHIRE

The new County of Oxfordshire, established in 1974 as part of comprehensive local government re-organization, inherited the northern half of the old County of Berkshire, the City of Oxford and the former Oxfordshire County. The part of Berkshire now included in Oxfordshire included the College of Further Education at Abingdon, which, in accordance with the old county's policy had a responsibility for providing adult education within the college itself as well as in satellite centres in the surrounding towns and villages. The Youth and Community Service of the county was mostly school-based and run separately. In Oxford City the Youth and Community Service was based mostly on purpose-built Community Centres though it also included under its wing school-based evening institutes. The Oxford College of Further Education, founded in 1960 to take over the less advanced work of the College of Technology, expanded prodigiously in the 1970's when it acquired a fine new site and building in the Oxpens. The accompanying extension of its adult education role caused Oxford City to review its whole adult education, community and youth service arrangements before (as previously noted) its plans were overtaken by local government reorganization.

The old Oxfordshire arrangements, with the small technical colleges at Banbury, Witney and Henley having firm but ill-defined adult education commitments, three ambitious, but experimental Adult Education Centres at Kidlington, Watlington and Sonning Common, and a number of school based adult education centres elsewhere, whilst having virtues of variety, experiment and scope for voluntary initiative, allowed little room for comprehensive educational leadership.

The University, now, with the loss of its far-flung territories, turned its attention to a more intensive cultivation of its "home" adult education area, and sought along with the W.E.A. to find a modus vivendi with the widening field of local authority adult education but found it difficult to make much headway despite much goodwill on each side. Nevertheless, in the late 1960's and early 1970's a group of individuals from the University Extra Mural Department, the W.E.A., the local authority adult education service and Colleges of Further Education were meeting fairly regularly to explore co-operation, particularly in the provision of training for full and part time adult educators. For this group, the reorganization of local government represented a heaven sent opportunity. They secured the benevolent patronage of the chief education officers of the three local authorities concerned in the establishment of the new Oxfordshire County Council and as a result they were commissioned as an official Working Group to prepare a report to provide the basis of a scheme of Adult and Community Education for the new County. Working against time they produced a thorough and practical report in time for it to be considered by the councillors elected in 1973 to establish the new County on April 1st 1974. Though the proposals of the Working Group were not accepted in their entirety, its main aim of establishing the principles of a comprehensive scheme of adult and community education, including colleges of further education, adult education centres of all kinds, university and extra mural work, and youth and community services, was adopted. The principle of delegating management to lay controlled community education management committees, co-ordinated by district committees, and by a County Advisory Committee reporting to the Further Education sub-Committee of the County's Education Committee was also accepted. The county jibbed at the Working Group's recommendation to integrate the colleges of further education completely into the scheme by giving them an educational leadership role in community education in each of the five County Districts into which the County's five Colleges of Further Education so conveniently fitted. They did so to allay two great anxieties which public consultations preparatory to the adoption of the scheme had revealed;

" i.   fear of loss of identity or disintegration of the
       present Youth Service as a result of being merged
       into a wider organization.

  ii. fear of decisions being taken by the new Oxfordshire L.E.A.
       which would give local Colleges of Further Education direct
       control of a developing area structure for the organization
       and channelling of public funds for adult and community edu-
       cation to voluntary bodies, local management committees and
       the like."

(Oxfordshire Education Committee. 9th January 1974.)

The Working Group had recognised the opposition its report was likely to encounter in giving the Colleges of Further Education such a central role, and it also recognised that the fears later expressed in the Education Committee's report were not entirely groundless, but they hoped that the prizes to be gained would be recognised. These were two; first, it would accelerate the broadening of the role of the Colleges which had already been so beneficial, and second, it would ground the new system firmly in substantial educational institutions, commanding adequate facilities and resources to enable them to provide the intellectual leadership and initiative required.

Despite its shortcomings, all too obvious to those who work in it, the Oxfordshire Community Education Scheme is a brave and bold venture. It could hardly have been born at a worse time; no additional money or resources were available and any changes or developments could only be secured through re-allocation of existing resources. Worse still county grants towards the cost of part time teachers and youth leaders have been sharply reduced and vacancies for full time staff in many cases have been frozen, at least for a period of time. Despite these handicaps the scheme is evolving hopefully, if slowly, buoyed up by a longer term sense of common purpose and assisted by a perceptible improvement of rationality in arrangements proceeding from the County's commitment to a comprehensive adult and community education policy. This commitment was confirmed by the establishment of a County Advisory Committee for Community Education, giving all the interests a forum where problems and difficulties can be aired and policies discussed with some hope that these may influence the County Council. In its first three years of existence, this Advisory Committee has already proved its usefulness and is gaining in cohesiveness and confidence all the time.

The University Extra Mural Department and the W.E.A., have played a critical part in the preparation of the initial report and in the establishment of Oxfordshire's Community Education scheme and have given substantial help in the training of adult and community education full time and part time staffs. They have not however, made much progress in integrating their activities with those of the other partners in the scheme. They are handicapped by their own traditions and the insistence of the Department of Education and Science that grants to responsible bodies are conditional on them being used to promote 'liberal education' as narrowly defined by the Department. It is to be hoped that time will bring about a change, for the University Extra Mural Department in particular can contribute significantly to the Oxfordshire scheme, not simply by bringing to bear the important educational resources at its command, but in certain critical areas, by exercising the leadership role for which its distinguished history fits it. Certainly, the long tradition of partnership with voluntary organizations which has marked the University's participation in adult education, ensures that its active engagement would engender confidence in the scheme, rather than suspicion.

From the universalistic view of adult education represented in this paper, there is no mistaking its size or importance of this scheme in Oxfordshire. In 1977 the five Oxfordshire Colleges of Further Education had a total professional teaching staff of 450, plus an equivalent of 100 teaching posts filled by part time staff. They had over 2,000 full time students, 7,000 part time day and over 8,000 evening students. Local Authority adult education centres account for another 17,000 students, mostly in evening classes. For this part of its service, which includes the youth service and much informal adult education, the County has a professional staff of 50. To complete the picture the University Extra Mural and W.E.A. programmes attract over 3,000 students, excluding the 2,000 who attend the Universities residential and short courses. The professional staffs of these two bodies are much smaller, totalling just over twenty, and with responsibility for

Berkshire and Buckinghamshire as well as for Oxfordshire.

These figures, it is suggested, reinforce the view that despite official neglect, adult education is an important part of our educational system , responding not to nurturing or encouragement from above, but to the insistent demand of people who attend voluntarily, gladly accept the onerous commitment of regular attendance and study and appear ready to pay the ever increasing fees which are demanded from them for the privilege. Though the public "invisibility" of adult education owes much to the indifference of governments, politicians and public officials, the conscience of some adult educators themselves must bear part of the blame. The large and growing volume of adult education provided in response to articulate demand is often regarded with something like shame, diverting resources and attention from the efforts which they feel ought to be made to reach out to those groups resistant to their blandishments, yet those lives could so obviously be enriched, as those of their grandfathers had been, for example, by participation in the work of the W.E.A. This passion of adult educators for improving mankind is not something to be discouraged, but it has to be tempered by a recognition of the limitations of adult education as a means of social, as well as of individual improvement. Adult education, to the great benefit of many people and to our society has been widely extended, a process which is likely to continue, but we have to recognise that it is unlikely ever to be universal in the sense of engaging all the adult population, all the time. The confident prediction that the process of expansion of adult education will continue, is based not just on the expected results of schemes like the Oxfordshire one, but because of the continuing process of social change, to which the extension of adult education is such an important response. Despite the evidence adduced in this paper, in these times of pessimism about the progress of humanity, those committed to adult education (as most of those engaged in it are) would be wise to be modest about its potentialities for human improvement, at the same time, pointing out relentlessly that it is one of the most productive areas of public investment, not just in cash terms, but in enabling our society to cope with the stressful changes of the modern world.

FINANCE AND STAFF

The seminal influence on modern adult education - University Extension - in the last decade of the nineteenth century acquired a reputation for dilettantism because it had to be self-financing and local centres had to attract large audiences in order to pay the fees charged by the universities. Oxford Extension unsuccessfully sought private or public endowment to enable it to appoint professional staff who could organize more consistent and purposive programmes on a local area basis. The founding of the W.E.A. in 1903 and the institution of government grants for tutorial classes solved the problem for them. The national network of branches which the W.E.A. created, each of them circled by affiliated societies and organizations, enabled the Association effectively to recruit amongst the emerging leaderships of local working class movements and to imbue them with the values of a liberal education of a high and serious standard. The astonishing success of this voluntary movement over a long period of time, supported by only a tiny corps of professionals, established a tradition which is still influential today. It is right that this should remain and flourish, but neither should it inhibit, nor disparage other arrangements as the basis for organizing the provision of adult education as times change. Many institutions and social movements today, as well as professional organizations, firms and public authorities, have become aware that adult education can contribute towards their specific purposes, and in consequence seek the co-operation and assistance of adult education institutions to provide programmes for

them. Such organizations, able and willing to pay for services of this kind
at a time when public grants have been severely curtailed, have assisted
materially in maintaining the impetus of adult education as well as giving it
new dimensions. Alas to many adult educators, steeped in the older tradition
of voluntarism, this extension has a taint of illegitimacy. Provided that the
educational institutions which engage in this new work retain their basis of
public finance and accountability, and thus are able to select their work on
sound educational and social criteria, this development of self-financing
adult education, arranged in co-operation with a variety of agencies, is as
beneficent an innovation as was the voluntary movement of the W.E.A. and
public grants for tutorial classes some seventy years ago.

To try to maintain their adult education service at a time of severe
public expenditure constraints, some local authorities, happily not including Oxfordshire, have sought to make it "self-financing" to the extent of
setting student fees at a level which will meet direct costs. This is
dubious economics since indirect or overhead costs, mainly maintenance of
buildings and of an organization and especially professional salaries, are
by far the largest items of expenditure. Fee levels which deter students
from enrolling merely increase average costs per student and result in sub-
optimisation of the value obtained by the community from the expenditure
actually incurred. Nevertheless, evidence of the past decade indicates that
it is possible to maintain fee levels at an appreciably higher level than
was previously thought desirable, without any noticeable effect on student
enrolments. For instance, in the 1930's, student fees for a university
extra mural tutorial class amounted to about 3% of the direct costs of the
class; in 1978 they amounted to nearly 50%. The readiness of students to
pay appreciable fees has therefore been one of the factors in maintaining
much of the growth noted.

Before concern about the growth of public expenditure reached its
peak in the 1970's some of the resources devoted by the government to university expansion, and some of great local authority outlays on school and
further education found their way into adult education in the form of firmly
establishing effective extra mural departments in the case of universities
and some form of adult education organization in most local authorities.
Each of these have been able to grow incrementally in response to internal
dynamism and the growing volume of work they have been called upon to per-
form. The establishment of a substantial corps of professional staffs in
this way has created a new and distinct, if still largely unrecognised,
profession of adult educators. Before 1939, apart from the hundred or so
W.E.A. and university extra mural tutors, administrative and organizing
staff, and a handful of local authority officers, adult education was largely
a part time occupation. Even then, there was a presumption that full time
work in adult education was an occupation for young men who were expected
to go on, as many of them did, to become university professors, dignitaries
of the church, senior local authority officers, civil servants, politicians
and the like. There are still vast numbers of part time tutors and lecturers, but there is now a sufficient number of career adult educators to mark
out a distinct profession. With the changes in society and in adult education, the role of these professionals too has changed. There are many
adult educators, particularly amongst W.E.A. and university extra mural
tutors who still work more or less as lone entrepreneurs and tutors with
voluntary groups and organizations, as their predecessors did in the early
days of the W.E.A. The typical adult educator of today however works more
as a member of an institution, planning programmes in co-operation with his
colleagues, consulting and advising client groups, devising courses with
specialist colleagues, commissioning and preparing special teaching materials
and other aids and co-ordinating teaching generally. To be successful he

has to deploy not merely versatile academic skills, but a whole range of pedagogic, social and entrepreneurial skills. The greater availability nowadays of premises with suitable equipment and facilities, the variety of course structures now open - day, evening, residential and so on gives adult educators great flexibility in arranging team teaching and in making use of specialists.

The tradition of adult education as a part time occupation, which still persists in some quarters, tended to obscure its special characteristics and subsumed it as a branch of school or university teaching, or of technical instruction, whereas, as I have tried to indicate, it calls for a demanding range of skills and expertise all of its own. Courses to develop this expertise and to extend training in the skills are growing in number, extent and sophistication but are still far from adequate in relation to the need. The approaches to training which have been sponsored by the Department of Education and Science have so far not been very appropriate and the greatest successes have followed initiatives by a few enterprising universities in co-operation with enlightened local authorities. Yet training is vital. The success of institutional changes, whether they be of the more general kind recommended by the Russell Committee, or of the kind adopted by individual local authorities such as Oxfordshire, will depend upon whether or not professional and part time staff understand and are committed to the aims and values which inform the schemes. In addition, they have to learn to deploy with confidence the range of skills, methods and resources which are indispensable to the modern adult educator.

Many institutions and firms, and particularly large-scale ones, have learned that one of the by-products of their adult education is often an improvement in communications between compartmentalised groups and different levels of their organization. This has been the case in Oxfordshire. Here, planning and taking part in training schemes has been the single most important factor in bringing together adult educators from all sections of a fragmented public service. It was in trying to understand each others' problems, aims and methods that they gradually became aware of the common characteristics, as well as of the particular features, of the activities in which they were engaged. Despite their achievement in establishing the basis of a comprehensive adult and community education service for Oxfordshire, and despite a number of valuable and successful training courses for both part and full time adult educators, the County still lacks the comprehensive training programme which is really needed. Above all, the missing feature is that of provision for systematic study and research into adult education and its relation to society. The long experience of the University of Oxford in this field, and its distinguished contribution to it surely marks it out as uniquely qualified to fill this gap. In so doing, it would render a great service to its local community as well as enriching educational studies within the University.

OXFORD ECONOMISTS AND THE YOUNG EXTENSION MOVEMENT

A. Kadish

The concern felt during the last third of the nineteenth century for the education of the nation's new rulers - the working classes, in the new age of democracy, resulted in various educational movements including University Extensions. These were aimed at bringing the National Universities - Cambridge and Oxford, to the people where the people were unable to come to the universities. This in turn, it was hoped, would bring two results. Firstly, the working classes would develop a sense of affinity towards the nation's traditional centres of scholarship thereby promoting the much sought after sense of national harmony and cohesion. Secondly, extending the benefits of higher education to the working classes would not only render them more competent to use the political power given to them, but would also point them in the way towards material and cultural progress so that they may, in that respect, catch up with the rest of the nation. Both results would mean a contribution to bridging the gap between classes, a cause for major concern during the late nineteenth century. The efforts to bridge this gap, caused by industrialization and its demeaning effect on the working classes, stimulated the growth of various movements, some religious, others secular. And although the University Extensions were secular in their work, the Oxford Extension preserved a religious, almost missionary zeal with which it tackled issues of higher education. Theirs was a national mission in which both ideology and means were an almost religious conviction, a characteristic noticed by Cambridge contemporaries whenever the two Extension Movements found themselves in disagreement.(1) The case of Oxford's young economists and the early years of the Extension Movement demonstrates the play between ideals and reality in the careers of four young men.

Although the basic ideology was shared by all Extension workers it may be said that Oxford's young economists attached to them further significance thereby intensifying their commitment to the Movement. The gap between the 'two nations' was not merely a figure of speech, a popular metaphor. It was the expression of a real difference in material, social and moral conditions. These conditions must be changed in order to preserve social cohesion and in order that proper means be employed for the necessary change they must be studied in detail and who was better qualified for both the analysis of material conditions and the suggestion of proper remedies than the professional student of political economy. Oxford young economists as a rule preferred the term Political Economy to the term Economics adopted by Marshall and his followers. By Political Economy they denoted a field of inquiry which included the social and moral aspects of material questions and applied itself not only to the analysis of what was but also to the question of what ought to be. More specifically they believed that both material improvement and the means of obtaining it should be instrumental in the moral elevation of the working classes and of society as a whole. Through material improvement obtained carefully with the aid of professional and social association (i.e. Trade Unions, Distributive and Productive Co-operatives etc.) England's working classes could be led to live a better, fuller life. At the same time the actual act of instruction, the willingness of university students to instruct working men in the path to material improvement, would serve to allay, at least to some extent, class antagonism and suspicion.

These beliefs,whether caused by a sense of duty, fear of social upheaval or feelings of guilt, found their strongest and therefore frequently quoted within the Movement, expression in the life and work of Arnold Toynbee (1852-1883). In addressing a radical and extremely vociferous crowd in London during January 1883 Toynbee, in highly emotional tones, pledged himself and fellow scholars to the service of England's working classes.

> 'We students, we would help you if we could. We are willing to give
> up something much dearer than fame and social position. We are
> willing to give up the life we care for, the life with books and with
> those we love. We will do this, and only ask you to remember this -
> that we work for you in the hope and trust that if you get material
> civilization, if you get a better life...you will really lead a
> better life.(2)

Following the lecture Arnold Toynbee collapsed and soon afterwards died thereby lending his message an added air of a sacred and almost religious mission. Toynbee's death was to be portrayed as a sacrifice and the lecturers of the Extension Movement as

> 'a large and enthusiastic band of University men, anxious to
> fulfil the pledges that Mr. Arnold Toynbee made to the toiling
> masses of England. (3)

Toynbee's own efforts in the dissemination of the benefits of higher education were mainly within the co-operative movement. Although there was in existence in Oxford since 15 June 1878 (4) a Standing Committee of the Delegates of Local Examination with the aim of organising extension work, probably on lines similar to the work done by Cambridge, it did little in initiating the creation of an organizational structure for such work. Instead the tendency was to rely on existing working men's organizations which had an interest in educational work, i.e. primarily the co-operatives. Arnold Toynbee and A.H.D. Acland, then Secretary to the Oxford Standing Committee of the Delegates of Local Examination, were instrumental in bringing the Co-operative's Union annual conference to Oxford in 1882 during which Toynbee presented his scheme for 'The Education of Co-operators.' (5).

Toynbee considered the co-operative movement to be the germ of a future industrial national society. The existing co-operatives, in his opinion, could and should present a model of a new type of social industrial organization by uniting in one corporate body education and industrial activity. Toynbee's concern was with promoting the education of the co-operator towards understanding and fulfilling 'his duties to his fellow-men and in what way union with them is possible'. This type of education, the education of the citizen as member of the highest existing form of human social organization, was considered by Toynbee to be significantly different from any other existing form of education including elementary, intermediate, higher, religious or technical education. In his address he outlined the contents of a citizens' education scheme as consisting of Political Education, Industrial Education and Sanitary Education, the last subject being a purely technical one concerned mainly with the working man's environment. For the study of Politics and Industry Toynbee suggested two complementary approaches - current analysis is existing systems and a historical analysis of the development of systems and their theories. In another address he stressed another aspect of such a scheme - its practical value:

> 'if I have shown working men that they should study economic science,
> if they would understand within what limits they can raise wages
> under present social conditions, and taking human beings as they are -
> if I have succeeded in doing this, then...I shall be content'. (6)

The combination of current and historical analysis and the emphasis on practical lessons became the dominant approach in all the courses in Political Economy given in the re-organized Extension regardless of whether the audience were co-operators or not. To this was added another component. In every case the practical aspects were considered with their moral implications. Practice was not confined to 'what can be done' but included 'what ought to be done' as well.

In discussing Toynbee's paper at the 1882 Co-operative Congress, A.H.D. Acland suggested, in the way of realizing Toynbee's scheme, that papers on relevant subjects be issued under the auspices of the Congress' Central Board and that Toynbee and like-minded friends form a committee to begin work on the papers under the direction and advice of the Central Board.[7]

Following Toynbee's death in March 1883 the committee's work was continued by Acland and Arthur Sidgwick (a former Master at Rugby and since 1879 a Fellow of Corpus Christi College, Oxford). Within a year they had drawn a systematic instruction scheme in the principals of co-operation and the duties of co-operators. The first class was inaugurated in London[8] and the southern Sectional Board adopted an Oxford plan for short three-lecture courses to be delivered by Oxford men at various co-operatives. In the 1883 Congress Acland was appointed chairman of the newly established Education Committee appointed by the United Board: 'to provide for the educational needs of the Movement, and to carry out the necessary work forthwith.'

The Education Committee, in turn, encouraged the establishment of local committees in each co-operative to which the Education Committee might recommend courses so that although courses and lecturers were made available through the Education Committee's recommendations the ordering of the courses was entirely up to the local co-operative societies. The Oxford active supporters of extension work sought to reach working men outside the co-operatives as well, and when Sadler set out to reorganize the Oxford Extension Movement during the mid 1880's he used the organizational system of the co-operatives as the model for a national organization. The hope was that eventually the movement as a whole would be endowed by the university or the state so that lecturing would not depend on local ability to raise funds and on the popularity of certain subjects. Early attempts at limited endowment may be found in the money left by T.H. Green in his will for the purpose of financing lecturers in industrial centres and in the Toynbee Trust set up after Toynbee's death by some of his friends. The purpose of the Trust was to combine endowed lectures in political economy with field research to be conducted by the lecturer who would reside in the area of lecturing for the during of the course. Here as elsewhere the lecturing depended on local organization and during the early 1880's the co-operatives were the only ones with such a network of local committees. Toynbee had realised that a perfect scheme should consist of 'an ideal which takes the imagination by storm and a definite intelligible plan for carrying out that ideal into practice' [9]. The ideal was present but it was up to his disciples to formulate the plan for its realization.

During the mid 1880's an Oxford graduate wishing to specialize in Political Economy was faced with dim prospects for a professional career. If he did not enjoy a private income he would have to combine lecturing, writing and coaching and at the same time enjoy a perfect health in order to survive. The pecuniary advantages offered by the profession were meagre and by no means certain (10). Most of the young graduates who wished to pursue an interest in economics identified with Toynbee's ideals and example but Extension work as a source of income was yet far from certain. This situation changed materially when M.E. Sadler was appointed on 20 May 1885 as Secretary of the Committee of the Delegates (11).

As a young undergraduate Sadler had been deeply impressed by Toynbee and a paper Toynbee had delivered at the radical liberal Palmerston Club proved to be a turning point in his views (12). He became involved in a small discussion group of undergraduates organised by A.H.D. Acland for studying social questions, known as "The Inner Ring" or "The Inner Circle" and to outsiders as the "Upper Suckles" (13). With Acland, Sadler became actively involved in the various memorial schemes which followed Toynbee's death. When, during a meeting at Balliol on April 15, 1883 a fund was set up which later became the Toynbee Trust, Sadler was appointed undergraduate member of the committee and assistant secretary (14). At roughly the same time Sadler became active in a counter-memorial scheme for the establishment of a university settlement in the East End. At first the settlement plan was suggested for the use of the money collected by the fund set up for a memorial, this was supported by the Rev. S.A. Barnett of Whitechapel, S. Ball of St. John's College and P.L. Gell, one of Toynbee's close friends(15). However, after it had been decided that the money would be used for the Lecture scheme, i.e. the Toynbee Trust, an independent effort was launched in favour of the settlement plan. During May 1883 a public meeting was convened under Sadler's presidency in which Barnett described the work which was to be done in the East End. Later that year a private meeting was convened in S. Ball's rooms at St. John's organized by S. Ball, A. Sidgwick and A.H.D. Acland with the members of the Inner Circle present. At the meeting Barnett drew a more detailed plan for an East End university settlement on which it was commented that it 'might serve as a home of the University Extension and Lecture Classes' (16). It was felt that such a scheme would require undergraduate participation not only in East End work but in running the movement as well. M.E. Sadler and G. Cosmo Lang who, with the other members of the Inner Circle, were present at the meeting, became leading figures in supporting the scheme within the Oxford undergraduate community and in a meeting held in Cosmo Lang's rooms at Balliol, he and Sadler were elected undergraduate university secretaries to the East End settlements' project (17).

Upon obtaining a degree Sadler began looking for a job which would enable him both to marry and to realize his social ideals. Having refused some job offers and upon failing to obtain a lectureship in Political Economy Sadler became active with A.H.D. Acland in co-operative lecturing. In 1885 Acland's decision to stand for parliament vacated the position of Secretary to the Committee of the Delegates to which Sadler, with the backing of Acland, was elected.

Sadler's election was a turning point in the history of the Oxford Extension Movement. The search for a national status for the movement and the eagerness to reach working men outside the co-operatives led to a new initiative in the re-organization of the movement. Efforts were made to encourage the establishment of local centres, courses were shortened and certificates were awarded for courses as short as six lectures thereby offering a cheap course with all the trimmings of the longer ones with the hope that short courses would create in the long run a demand for longer ones. The Oxford Extension Movement would send lecturers to practically anywhere to lecture on a wide variety of subjects while refusing to set any boundaries to its activities, thereby 'trespassing' on the 'territory' of the other Extension Movements. Most of Oxford's young economists were active in the East End settlements Association and the opportunity offered to them by the re-organized Extension Movement to carry on 'Toynbee Hall' type work on a national scale seemed at first ideal. A position within the Movement would allow them to teach Political Economy and Economic History to the working classes thereby contributing to the progress of society while at the same time forwarding their professional aspirations.

The Extension as a career option to young graduates was described by Sadler in the Secretary's report for 1886-87

'The greater part of the lecturing staff will always be composed of young graduates who are glad to have a University Extension engagement for a year or two after taking their degrees, partly because of the practical experience in teaching which they gain from it, and partly because it gives them in each year twenty eight weeks of unbroken vacation in which they can continue their studies more uninterrupted than would be possible in almost any other remunerated occupation.' (18)

Already, Sadler added 'University Extension lecturing has...provided for younger graduates an entirely new means of earning a livelihood during the first few years after taking their degrees'.

Beyond the usefulness of an Extension position in starting off a young graduate on a professional career as a teacher it was hoped that the University and the State would eventually recognize the national importance of the Movement's work and establish it as an endowed and academically recognized body of higher education with teaching activities in places too small for local colleges such as small towns and co-operative districts. It was anticipated that such recognition would give Extension lecturers formal academic status within the University of Oxford with teaching responsibilities outside it. Endowment would enable the Movement to reduce the cost of lectures and offer the lecturers a regular salary. Demand would still be regulated by local committees but it was hoped that these, in turn, would establish with the Movement's aid, local centres which would serve as permanent centres for local lecturing activity (19). Such a centre, it was envisaged, would include basic facilities for Extension lecturing such as a small library, a lecture hall and a classroom. Each centre would be able to accommodate a visiting lecturer who would remain in residence for the duration of his course, supervising local students who sought more advanced tutoring, promoting the ties between the local population and Oxford and at the same time using his stay to study local conditions. This was not intended as competition with the young local colleges but rather as a plan to fill a gap in national higher education by combining the Toynbee Hall principle of residency and Extension lecturing. At no time was it suggested that such centres would have a permanent academic staff or, for that matter, more than one or two visiting lecturers resident at a time.

The concept of a temporarily resident lecturer was realized by the endowed courses in Political Economy of the Toynbee Trust. The Extension under Sadler offered the Trust the local organization it otherwise lacked for the execution of the purposes for which the Trust had been set up. Towards the end of 1885 the Executive Committee of the Trust (20) approached the Extension Committee with the proposal of appointing L.L. Price as the first Toynbee Trust lecturer. Price was Sadler's contemporary at Trinity College and it is likely that the two were on close friendly terms since it was Sadler who proposed Price as member of Palmerston Club when both were still undergraduates (21). As an undergraduate Price attended Marshall's lectures during the four terms Marshall filled the position at Balliol vacated by Toynbee's death, and was considered by Marshall to be one of his most promising Oxford students, so that it is likely that Marshall's influence was instrumental in obtaining Price's appointment within the Toynbee Trust whereas Sadler almost certainly supported the Trust's proposal in the Extension Committee (21a). Price was to give two, twelve-lecture, courses at an industrial centre, the courses to be endowed mainly by the Trust with a small participation of the local committee (22). The lecturer would remain in residence for the duration of the courses, simultaneously conducting investigations into local economic and social conditions. It was agreed that the courses would be given at Newcastle-upon-Tyne where the local Extension committee was organized by one of the trustees - Robert Spence Watson - who had organized Toynbee's lectures at Newcastle in 1881 and 1882 (23). During his stay, Price collected material on migration of labour and on arbitration but eventually chose to concentrate on the latter (24), a subject on which Spence Watson was a local authority having served as an industrial arbitrator since 1864. On the basis of his investigations which included interviews with Trade Union officials and working men (25) Price compiled a report to the Trust published as a monograph titled Industrial Peace, Its Advantages, Methods and Difficulties (London 1887) with a preface by Marshall. A shorter version of the study was read, upon the recommendation of Foxwell (26), - another Toynbee Trustee, as a paper to the Royal Statistical Society.

Price's reports (27) to the Trust and to the Extension Executive Committee were enthusiastic and he did his best, through the use of his impressions, to promote the cause of Extension lecturing in Political Economy. In support of his impressions he included in his reports some of his students' comments on the courses. When, after the final lecture of one of the courses, a vote of thanks was moved, it was seconded by a student who declared that

> 'he had thought Political Economy was very dry and not used at all...but during the three months that the lectures had been going on there was not a day on which he had not read Political Economy.'

Another student wrote to Price confessing that -

> 'As a working man previously knowing nothing about Political Economics (rather with a prejudice against it) I think these lecturers have accomplished their end in my case and I do not stand alone.'

In his report to the Toynbee Trust (28) Price concluded by stating

> 'I need hardly say how interesting to myself and encouraging has been my first experience at teaching those who have been eager to learn and in removing so far as have been able, a prejudice felt (and perhaps not unnaturally felt in the light of the history of the past) against Political Economy.'

Such a change of attitude in a period in which Political Economy came under constant attack from various quarters (29) was considered a most promising sign. Price in his reports stated his satisfaction with the number of students who had submitted weekly essays and who had sat for the final examination. He found the general standard of their work high, their weekly essays 'clear and pointed' and their use of the travelling library, which accompanied the course, intelligent and assiduous.

The experience in resident lecturing was apparently considered encouraging. Even before the Price Newcastle course began, Sadler proposed that the principle of residential lecturiships should be raised with co-operative districts (30). Early in 1886 an Endowment Fund was established with the aim of developing a wider system of Extension teaching by establishing 'a system of higher education adapted to the needs of the working classes particularly in History, Natural Science and Political Economy.' (31) These hopes for early endowment resulted eventually in disappointment but at the time the positive experience of Price's Newcastle courses led to a similar arrangement during autumn 1886 - winter 1887 at Cornwall. As in Newcastle Price used his period of residence to investigate conditions of labour in the Cornish tin mines

reporting his findings to the Royal Statistical Society in a paper on the
system of work and wages in the mines (32).

The satisfaction with the experiment in resident lectureship was shared
by the Toynbee Trust which offered its second lectureship to H.Ll. Smith who
gave courses in Bradford and Halifax during autumn 1887. By 1880, Oxford's
young economists, most of whom were young graduates and a few of whom enjoyed
a college fellowship, formed the Oxford Economic Society with the purpose of
discussing economic and social problems presented as papers by its members.
Sadler, Price and Ll. Smith were all members of the Society as were a
number of other young Extension lecturers who chose to teach subjects other
than Political Economy. Thus the members of the Society were the natural
source for young lecturers in Political Economy. Before his Toynbee Lectureship appointment H.Ll. Smith had already given a trial course of six lectures
during spring of 1887, however it was the Toynbee Lectures which established
his position within the Extension circuit. Despite the various efforts at
attracting endowment, lecturers depended entirely on the demand of local
centres for their employment, a situation which made extension lecturing an
uncertain source of employment for young and unknown lecturers. The few
endowed lectureships in existence offered the young lecturer a chance to
make a name for himself while serving to stimulate interest in local
centres where demand for lectures may have been flagging.

As in the case of Price, Ll. Smith's reports (33) were enthusiastic
and optimistic. Average attendance at lectures given in Bradford reached
350-400 rising to 500 at the last lecture of the course. Because of the
size of the classes, usually held after the lectures for the purpose of
offering those interested a more detailed discussion of the lecture's subject,
another smaller discussion group was formed which stayed on for a further
session after the regular classes. Interest was such that Ll. Smith found
it necessary to add another twenty minute session before each lecture for
special instruction in essay writing. Some students found even this insufficient and combined to meet privately for weekly meetings during which they
went over the issues raised during the lectures with the aid of notes taken
by them during the lectures. Ll. Smith was told, and in turn informed the
Executive Committee, that some of the students were resolved to pursue a
more systematic study of Political Economy by forming "The Bradford Economic
and Statistical Society" in which papers were to be read and economic problems
discussed. 'I think', Ll. Smith concluded his report, 'that no more satisfactory outcome of such lectures is possible.' Like Price before him, he had
found much reassuring evidence of a change in the attitude of working men
towards the study of Political Economy. He quoted in his report some students
who had stated before the course that what was needed was a course on Party
Politics not on Political Economy but expressed after it the hope for more
courses in the future preferring educational to political ones. During his
term of residence Ll. Smith chose the subject of labour mobility for his
investigations (the same subject chosen initially by Price at Newcastle)
the results of which he published in a report to the Trust (34) whilst
continuing his investigation into the matter during his period of residence
at Toynbee Hall in the following year. However, despite Price's and Smith's
enthusiastic reports and Sadler's and the Executive Committee's efforts neither
the Oxford Colleges nor the State could be induced to endow the Extension's
lectures and resident lectureships were eventually discontinued with the
Toynbee Trust being absorbed by Toynbee Hall where projects of local investigations continued.

The appointment of young economists to Extension positions on the basis
of personal acquaintance and membership in the Oxford Economic Society continued
in the case of W.A.S. Hewins. Hewins, the youngest member of the Society had

won in 1887 a second class honours degree in Mathematics and planned to read for a second honours degree in History under the tuition of C.Firth. However within a few weeks Hewins, the son of an ironmonger, realized that lacking the security of a private income he could not afford to continue his studies. Like Sadler in 1885 he too wished, to marry and the usual Oxford solution for out of work graduates still in residence - coaching, proved a disappointment since by January 1888 all he had were two pupils (35). The Extension seemed the obvious solution, and so early in 1888, while continuing to read history and especially seventeenth century economic history, with Firth, Hewins offered himself to the Extension Executive Committee as a lecturer (36). A few days after the Committee had noted Hewins' application, Sadler approached him with an offer which would allow him a clear advantage in creating a demand for his courses among local centres. The wife of Hudson-Shaw, one of the Extension's most popular lecturers, had just died and replacements were required to complete the courses he had started. One of these courses - on Irish History at the Doncaster Co-operative Society, was an attempt at launching a new extension centre and the offer of the course to Hewins set him off on a promising start (37). But Sadler's help did not end here. While Hewins was giving his first lectures a committee was set up to organize Home Reading Circles. The new project was aimed at reaching those students who sought to further their interest in some subject but presumably suffered from the relative lack of demand for advanced courses. Such a student would be offered an introductory course after which he could continue his study through correspondence with an Extension teacher in charge of instructing students of a certain region in the appropriate subject. The student would conduct his study with the aid of a specially prepared syllabus and would occasionally meet the Extension teacher in regional classes. Hopes for this form of advanced studies ran high and some considered it as potentially requiring an organization independent of the common Extension lecturing (38). It was agreed that the scheme would be launched at a summer meeting of Extension students at Oxford, during which the introductory courses would be given and the students interested in more advanced studies would be given a chance to meet their teachers while strengthening their ties with the University as a whole. The Home Reading Circle Committee empowered Sadler to recommend 'a suitable organizing secretary' (39) to launch the summer meeting with the understanding that if the Committee should be satisfied with his work he would be asked to organize winter activities of the Home Reading Circles as well. Sadler offered the job to Hewins and Hewins accepted (40) thereby securing a job and a source of income for the summer - usually an inactive period for Extension teaching, with a chance of continuing to organize a new educational organization. Although the Home Circles amounted to less than it was originally hoped, the summer meeting proved a great success and Hewins was asked to continue organizing them for the next few years while lecturing during autumn and spring.

The young economists' Extension courses coincided on the whole with the guidelines laid down by Toynbee. Three types of subjects were given - introductory courses in current analysis of the structure of industrial economy, courses in economic history and courses in history of economic doctrines. All courses concentrated on "working class" issues and all contained a common theme - progress was historically a continuous process achieved only through gradual reform. All the young economists took definite positions on the concrete issues of the day, their courses were aimed not only at convincing their students of the usefulness and applicability of economic analysis but also at presenting them with the conclusions they themselves derived from the use of these methods. Hewins went as far as presenting a letter from a student professing conversion to Free Trade following a lecture on the subject by Hewins, as a statement in support of his candidacy to the Tooke

Professorship in 1891 (41). Similar use of Extension courses in support of the doctrine of Free Trade may be found in Ll. Smith's and Price's courses (42). Hewins was justly proud of the letter he presented to the Tooke Professorship electors since if offered proof of the attainment of the result towards which Extension lecturing in Political Economy by the young economists, strove. In it the student stated that Hewins' lectures –

> 'convinced me that Political Economy was not a sham but a very
> practical science, and that only on the lines indicated by you
> [Hewins] in your treatment of such questions as Co-operation,
> Trade Unionism etc. could we hope for real economic advance.'

The ideology the young economists tried to inculcate their students with, rejected revolutionary measures for the correction of present evils in the economic structure of society, while at the same time referring to themselves as Modern Socialists, distinct from the Continental Socialism of Marx and Lasalle. Their form of Socialism, wrote Price in one of his syllabuses suggested a process of gradual evolution and postponed the total change of society to a distant date (43). The definition of what they called Modern Socialism had been stated by Toynbee in his 1882 "Are Radicals Socialists?" lectures in industrial centres in Northern England (44), in which he argued

> 'We have not abandoned our old belief in liberty, justice, and
> self help but we say that under certain conditions the people
> cannot help themselves, and that then they should be helped by
> the State representing directly the whole people.'

The balance that must be maintained between self help through association and state through the use of political power, was dealt with extensively in the economists' courses. They all supported Trade Unionism, Distributive and Productive Co-operatives, Profit Sharing schemes, etc. but they were also careful to note that these measures were not absolute in their ability to transform present conditions. On the other hand they wished to make it clear that state interference should be limited in scope and applied only with extreme caution for fear that it may impede self help. The courses were meant to place in the hands of the working classes analytical tools, the practicality of which the lecturers emphasized, so that they may analyse for themselves the problems with which they were faced and inevitably reach the same conclusions as their teachers had as to the appropriate solutions. However material improvement was not a goal in itself but the means to a better moral and spiritual life of the working man. Therefore the means employed in the effort for material improvement had to be examined in the light of the final goal, i.e. their relation to the moral and spiritual betterment of the working classes. Accordingly the merits of Trade Unionism, Co-operatives etc. were not described as merely material and practical ones but spiritual and moral as well. All forms of labour association by fulfilling the principal of association 'which should be the basis of all social effort'(45) were simultaneously promoting both the material and moral improvement of the working man, teaching him to set the collective interest above his own narrow interests and providing him with a sense of pride in his trade and comradeship with his fellow workers.

Despite the great hopes all had for the young Extension Movement, immediate pressures forced all young economists lecturing in the Extension to seek additional sources of income which would not be dependent on the interest their courses aroused in the local centres. Upon entering Parliament in December 1885 A.H.D. Acland resigned from his Stewardship in Christ Church which, upon his resignation, he was able to secure for Sadler. The Stewardship offered to Sadler in March 1886 (46), secured his financial position. However the rules of the Stewardship forced him to give up his active work as an Extension lecturer thereby confining his lecturing to the summer Meetings. In 1887 Price was elected to a similar non-teaching position of Assistant Treasurer at Oriel which was followed a year later by his election to Junior Treasurer and Official Fellow of the college. H. Ll. Smith became a resident at Toynbee Hall in 1888 and during the same year was offered, through A.H.D. Acland, and accepted, the position of Secretary to the National Association for the Promotion of Technical Education. Similar attempts by Hewins to secure a steady source of income failed. By the end of 1888 he offered his candidacy to the position of Bursar at St. John's College, a position that had he been elected to would have allowed him to marry. During the following years, determined to make his way as an academic, he turned down offers by Rev. S.A. Barnett to become resident at Toynbee Hall and organize local classes in economics (as James Bonar had done in previous years). In 1891 he applied without success to the position of Secretary to the Publishing Department of the National Liberal Federation and later the same year to the Tooke Professorship at King's College, London which he lost to W. Cunningham (47). Only by 1892 with his popularity as an Extension Lecturer well established and with various contracts (48) for books signed did he feel secure enough financially to marry.

The fact that the Extension was unable to secure for its lecturers a steady source of income through lack of endowment was not considered by the lecturers to be a fault of the Movement and as long as that was the only problem with their Extension work they continued their lecturing while seeking elsewhere positions which would offer them financial security. The initial enthusiasm, which explains such dedication, was sustained during the first years of Sadler's secretaryship by the enthusiastic reports that as a rule followed courses given in Political Economy. The combination suggested by Toynbee of theoretical and historical analysis coupled with an emphasis on practical conclusions seemed to prove popular. During a conference of representatives of the local committees held during April 1887 one of the representatives, Mr. Greenwood of the Hebden Bridge Manufacturing Co-operative Society, stated that his reason for inviting a lecturer to give an Extension course in Industrial History was

'in order to guide working men into the way of acquiring knowledge conducive to their welfare. We thought it would bring us together and make us each think more particularly and directly of the causes which affect our position and the purpose which we are trying to carry out co-operatively.' (49)

As anticipated (50) the contact between the young economists and working class audiences proved to be beneficial to both sides in as much as it brought together the lecturer's theoretical and historical knowledge and the audience's practical experience. A fairly representative comment describing the knowledge gained by such an intercourse may be found in H.Ll. Smith's report following a course given at Ancoats, Manchester, late in 1888. Ll. Smith reported that the class, following the lecture, always took the form of a discussion

'from which I myself learnt much, as those who took part almost always brought knowledge of practical detail to bear on the points raised. I have never had an audience with whom it was such a pleasure to discuss Economic problems.' (51)

Following their first courses the lecturers were quick to detect a favourable change in the attitude of working men towards Political Economy and its uses, hence their optimism concerning the development of a demand for more advanced and systematic courses on the subject (52). It was hoped that promising students would continue their studies with the aid of the Home Reading Circles and would create a local demand which would manifest itself in orders from the local centres for longer and more advanced courses. In addition it was expected that endowment by the University would make it possible to use the certificates given at the end of courses as academic credits which would enable the ambitious student to eventually obtain a university degree. In the case of Political Economy these hopes proved to be groundless. Working men, it was true, were greatly interested in practical conclusions but on the other hand they had little patience for, or interest in, the theoretical arguments in support of these conclusions. They wanted clear statements on current issues rather than scientifically accurate ones. 'The English workman' Hewins observed early in 1890 (53) 'is a politician first and a working man afterwards.' Working men may not have seen the need to base support for Trade Unions, Co-operatives, sliding scales etc. on detailed theoretical and historical proof but for the lecturers to do otherwise would have undermined the scientific status of their subject and their own professional position (54). The issue was realized by H. Ll. Smith as early as 1888 when he pointed out that –

'Perhaps the greatest danger which a lecturer on Economics notices, lies in the tendancy of a popular audience to demand a degree of clearness and simplicity in Economic expositions which sometimes scientific accuracy does not admit of. They find a difficulty in looking at such questions from a historic point of view.' (55)

One result of this attitude was the inability of the Extension lecturers to stimulate a widespread interest in advanced courses in Political Economy or Economic History despite frequent recommendations in their reports to the local committees. This was, by no means, the case with other Extension course subjects and it must have been extremely frustrating to the Political Economy lecturers to observe cases such as Hudson Shaw's courses at the Oldham Co-operative which by 1891, for four consecutive years, drew crowds reaching five hundred men and classes of one to two hundred men (56). Courses in Political Economy were dropping both in relative and in absolute popularity. Whereas the Oxford Extension Movement enjoyed during the period 1885-1891 a steady high rate of growth in the number of courses delivered, attendance, and average length of courses, Political Economy courses never exceeded their number in 1886-1887 and there was no widespread demand for courses longer than six lectures. Contrary to early expectations the populatiry of the introductory courses did not lead to a demand for thorough and systematic courses in the large industrial centres and as Hewins observed in 1896 'no spontaneous demand for scientific training in economics can be said to exist.' (57)

Even the surge in popularity of other Extension courses was somewhat deceptive since a growing proportion of the crowds drawn by the courses were middle class, rather than working class, with a large proportion of women, a fact which became obvious during the summer meetings which were originally meant to strengthen the ties between working men and Oxford. This was a matter of great concern to the Movement as a whole and various explanations were attempted. Sadler and H.J. Mackinder in their book University Extension: Past, Present and Future (London 1891) (58) argued that the drop in working class attendance was due to the lack of continuily in subject matter from one course to the other. No attempt was made to utilize the interest aroused by one course by bringing another course on a related subject. Had such a sequence of courses been arranged, where interest had already been stimulated in a working class audience by one course, this interest could be maintained and stimulated. However such a scheme which aimed at the creation of a demand rather than responding to an existing one required subsidizing, i.e. endowment. To this they added another factor resulting from the lack of endowment – the continuous loss of the Extension's best lecturers in favour of a more secure income.

An article in the March 1893 issue of the <u>Extension Gazette</u> (59) gave three different reasons for the fall in working class attendance

1. The course fees were too high

2. Many of the lectures were given at too early an hour

3. The local committees were too often controlled by the middle class

which resulted in 'the very prevalent idea among working men that University Extension lectures are not intended for them at all, but for those who have had a higher education.' The first reason was considered as one other outcome of the lack of endowment while the second and third reasons required, if accepted, the reorganization of local committees so that at least half their members would be working men or their representatives, a task practically impossible in light of the decentralized system of the Extension since the Executive Committee had no authority over the local committees.

Although low attendance of working men was a cause for concern for the Movement as a whole, in the case of the young economists it rendered their Extension work pointless. It became apparent that not only did the Extension fail to live up to their early expectations in forwarding their professional careers, it was also the wrong system for educating the working classes in Political Economy. The fault was not entirely in the lack of endowment since the inclusion of Political Economy in the Technical Instruction Act by spring 1892, thereby allowing local councils to subsidize courses in the subject, did not result in a noticeable change in the demand for such courses.

By the end of 1890 the young economists were slowly drawing away from Extension work. Although H. Ll. Smith and L. L. Price were appointed during 1890 Extension Staff Lecturers, thereby entitled to higher fees for their courses, their careers led them elsewhere. After 1890 Price gave only two six-lecture courses up to his resignation from the Extension in 1900 and Ll. Smith's last Extension courses were given during the autumn of 1890. Hewins remained the only Oxford economist lecturing during the early 1890's who had started Extension work shortly after obtaining an Oxford degree. In 1891 he was joined by J.A. Hobson who had left Oxford upon graduation and thus had not been a member of the Oxford Economic Society, and whose early work was considered by Hewins to consist of fallacious arguments and untenable conclusions (60). The drift away from Extension work was not merely a technical change in employment. The direct relation between the young economists research, their extension work, and the contents of the courses was carried over to their new careers in which one may detect with the change in employment a change of direction in their work. In the cases of both Price and Ll. Smith it meant a move away from the Oxford school of thought. Price became one of the secretaries of the new British Economic Association as well as an ardent defender of the Marshall line in the debate concerning the nature of the study of economics which flared during the early 1890's. H. Ll. Smith whose residency at Toynbee Hall brought him into Charles Booth's Life and Labour project modified his views accordingly and adopted the position held by Booth and a significant contingent within the Statistical Society.

A perhaps more far reaching change, due to a large extent to the disappointment in the Extension and extension type projects, may be detected in the early days of the L.S.E., the first director of which was W.A.S. Hewins.

When Hewins left the Extension in 1895 in order to take part in the foundation of the London School of Economics and Political Science, the change was in position, not in direction. The L.S.E. was conceived at first as an extension type centre for advanced studies. It was not meant to fill the gap in the curriculum of Oxford and Cambridge by offering advanced courses in Economics and related subjects. Indeed at first not only were no degrees or certificates awarded, but in light of the original aims of the School no such degrees were planned. These original aims may be found in an entry in Mrs. Webb's diary of September 1894. The new institute was envisaged as a centre for educating the leaders of the working classes while at the same time a core of students working on special subjects would formulate schemes for reform (61). It was to serve as a think tank, the results of its work to be implemented through working class action. The working class was to be served with the fruits of the School's work through Extension type summer meetings. Both the idea and its purpose are explained by S. Webb in a letter of 9 September 1895 to Hewins in which he describes S.G. Hobson's (of the I.L.P.) idea

> 'that a "Summer Meeting" of a week, specially arranged, would probably draw some hundreds of Co-operatives, Trade Unionists and Socialists from the provinces.' (62)

The first Summer Meeting held in 1896 bears an understandable resemblance to the first Oxford Summer Meetings organized by Hewins. The lectures and conferences were held at Toynbee Hall and the programme consisted of specialized lectures in the mornings and general ones in the evening. The purpose described in Webb's letter was phrased in a more general manner as the offering 'to those who live at a distance from centres of systematic study, opportunities of obtaining guidance in their work.' (63)

However, by the end of 1895 the emphasis in the School's work had changed. Disappointment in the positions adopted by working men in general and socialists in particular caused Beatrice Webb to state that in face of the 'reaction' of the working classes, probably reflecting the differences in tactics and General Election policy between the London Fabians and the I.L.P., 'we have turned our hopes from propaganda to education, from the working class to the middle class.' (63)

What the change meant in actual terms may be gauged from a report drawn up by Hewins during 1896 in which he claimed that

> 'The lectures and classes have appealed especially to those who desire the guidance of experts on particular subjects. The students consist of graduates of British and foreign universities, women students of the universities, and are mainly engaged in the research department of the school, and of civil servants, local government officials, railway officials, young men and women engaged in business, bank managers and clerks, teachers and other persons engaged in public work.' (65)

No mention is made of the School's function as a centre for working class evening lecturers or as a training centre for the new class of public and business administrators with the purpose of

> 'promoting efficiency, diminishing social and economic friction and exerting the knowledge of public affairs.' (66)

To translate the change into the terms of Hewins' experience and ideology, the work of the economists in the Extension was over. Preaching Trade Unionism and Co-operation to the working classes had become pointless with the advent of the New Unionism and the I.L.P. As for further instruction the

Extension and early L.S.E. experience made it clear that the working classes did not choose to turn to the professional student but to the politician. And the realization that Trade Unionism, Co-operation etc. were limited solutions there was a danger that the working classes as a political movement would turn towards a policy of 'collective ownership and control of the means of production, distribution and exchange,' as adopted by the T.U.C. in 1893 (67). An alternative must be presented by way of an extensive programme of reform to be worked out through research by trained students and passed on to those whose job it was to serve society. From here politics was but a short step away.

The L.S.E. also created a much needed career alternative to the existing universities. During the early 1890's Oxford became for a while the centre of opposition to the main line in British Economics dominated by Marshall from Cambridge and represented in the Economic Journal, published by the newly created British Economic Association. One of the main bones of contention was the extent to which economists, using their professional status, should become involved in contemporaneous debates and use their position to pronounce on current issues. The dissent to Marshall's position was voiced by the Economic Review published by the Oxford Branch of the Christian Social Union and originally edited by three of the older members of the Oxford Economic Society - Campion, Carter, and Phelps. At Oxford the main advocates of the dissenting position included Edwin Cannan, whose private income allowed him to remain in residence without obtaining a job or fellowship. L.R. Phelps - fellow of Oriel, and Sidney Ball, fellow of St. John's and the founder of the Oxford Branch of the Fabian Society. Support from outside Oxford came from W.J. Ashley one of the founders of the Oxford Economic Society and its first secretary, who had left Oxford in 1888 for a Chair in Toronto, W. Cunningham the Economic Historian, and W. Smart of Glasgow. Despite the position of Oxford as centre of dissent, the University did not choose to reconsider the place of economic studies in its curriculum. Furthermore, the cause of dissent suffered a severe setback with the election of F.Y. Edgeworth, a strong supporter of Marshall and the editor of the Economic Journal to the Drummond Professorship in Political Economy in 1891. Edgeworth not only refrained from supporting the dissenters, he also avoided any confrontation on the question of the status of the study of Economics. As a result, with the subjective failure of the Extension no alternate career was available within Oxford or for that matter at most of the other English universities.

This changed with the L.S.E., as one jubilant friend wrote Hewins congratulating him on his appointment as Director of the new institute:-

'While the doors of universities are closed to dissenters in economics, they [the dissenters] will give fresh life to your young institutions.' (68)

Recruits to the L.S.E. included Cannan, Ll. Smith, Foxwell and others, and, in keeping with the Extension tradition, it sponsored the publication of its staff's work as textbooks or research monographs. Thus, within a relatively short period, the L.S.E. developed as an alternative academic centre to the study and investigation of current and historical economic problems (69).

On the whole the members of the Oxford Economic Society held in common a system of social and moral ideals. This ideology prompted those of its members who held college positions, such as W.J. Ashley (till 1888), L.R. Phelps, and S. Ball, to support the young Extension Movement from the sidelines with the occasional active aid in committee activity, lecturing and syllabus writing. The same ideology shaped the young Movement and thereby made it such an attractive career option to the Society's younger members, combining what they hoped would be the beginning of a professional career with a way of contributing to the progress of society. As young graduates they had little doubts as towards which direction progress was to be found and what were the means of achieving it. Their Extension experience did not shatter their basic convictions but it did shake their certainty about the means, and resulted in a change of emphasis from self-help to state aid. No more obvious career choice, similar to the Extension in the mid 1880's, was available, and as a result each turned to whatever opportunity offered. Yet it is possible to detect the survival of these ideals in the choices made. The Civil Service for H. Ll. Smith and Sadler, the L.S.E. and politics for Hewins and academia for L.L. Price.

The author would like to express his gratitude to Mrs. P.V.W. Gell, O.B.E., of Hopton Hall, Wicksworth, Derbyshire for permission to study and to quote from the Gell family papers, and to the staffs of Rewley House, Oxford, Oriel College Library, the Greater London Council Record Office, and Sheffield University Library for their invaluable help in conducting the res research on the paper's subject.

NOTES

1. For an expression of these ideals as well as one clash with Cambridge on the 'Missionary' issue see Report of a Conference of Representatives of the Local Committees, Oxford, April 20-21, 1887. (Oxford 1887).

2. Arnold Toynbee. 'Progress and Poverty, A criticism of Mr. Henry George. (London 1883) p.54.

3. Robert Halstead. 'Working Men and University Extension' in The Oxford University Extension Gazette, May 1893, p.108.

4. Minutes of Meetings of the Committee for University Extension in Rewley House, Wellington Square, Oxford. The Standing Committee included Prof. T.H. Green as Chairman and J.E. Thorold Rogers.

5. Arnold Toynbee 'Education of Co-operators' in Congress of Central Co-operative Board. (Manchester 1882), pp.17-21.

6. Arnold Toynbee 'Wages and Natural Law' given at the Mechanics' Institute, Bradford, Jan. 1880 and again in Firth College, Sheffield in Feb. 1882. Printed in Arnold Toynbee Lectures on The Industrial Revolution of the Eighteenth Century in England. (London 1884).

7. F. Hall and W.P. Watkins, Co-operation, (Manchester 1937), p.168.

8. Ibid. p.169.

9. A. Toynbee, 'The Education of Co-operators', op-cit.

10. See, in retrospect, W.A.S. Hewins 'The Teaching of Economics' in Journal of the Society of Arts, Vol.45, no.2298 Dec. 4, 1896.

11. The election took place on 30 April 1885. Michael Sadleir. Michael Ernest Sadler. (London 1949) p.69.

12. Ibid. p.30.

13. The first name appears in ibid. p.68 (photograph opposite p.80) and Sir Charles Mallet. Anthony Hope and His Books. (London 1935) p.47. The second name appears in J.G. Lockhart. Cosmo Gordon Lang (London 1949), p.39 (including the reference to the name 'Upper Suckles' and Wilson Harris, J.A. Spender (London 1946), p.9.

14. The Oxford Magazine, 9 May 1883.

15. Evidence for the controversy may be found in the Gell Family Papers, Hopton Hall, Derbyshire.

16. The Oxford Magazine, 21 Nov. 1883.

17. J.G. Lockhart, Cosmo Gordon Lang (London 1949), p.39.

18. Oxford University Extension Lectures. Annual Report for the year 1886-7 (Oxford 1887).

19. Minutes of Meetings of the Committee for University Extension, 12 Dec. 1885. In Rewley House, Wellington Square, Oxford.

20. Consisting of the Earl of Dalhousie, A.H.D. Acland, W. Markby, A. Milner, H. Sidgwick, H.S. Foxwell and R. Spence Watson. G.LC. Record Office A/Toy/1-2.

21. Price was elected in 9 Feb. 1883. List of members in the Bodleian Library, Oxford.

21a. The Trust's decision to employ Price was preceded by a number of futile attempts to arrange the Trust's first lectures through the Cambridge Extension Syndicate.

22. Minutes of Meetings of the Committee op.cit. 12 Dec. 1885.

23. Percy Corder, The Life of Robert Spence Watson (London 1914), p.165.

24. L.L. Price to A.H.D. Acland 22 May 1886 and 8 Oct. 1886 in the Gell Family Papers.

25. L.L. Price Miscellaneous Reminiscences, MSS. Oriel College, Oxford.

26. L.L. Price to A.H.D. Acland, 23 Oct. 1886 Gell Papers op.cit. A similar paper was also read at Oxford.

27. Oxford University Extension Lecturers and Examiners Reports 1886-7. Rewley House, Oxford. See also Committee for University Extension Minutes, op.cit. 11 March, 1880.

28. L.L. Price to A.H.D. Acland, 22 May 1886, op.cit.

29. E.g. in the Industrial Remuneration Conference (London 1885).

30. Committee for University Extension Minutes op.cit. 12 Dec. 1885.

31. Ibid. 24 June 1886.

32. L.L. Price 'West Barbary or Notes on the System of Work and Wages in the Cornish Mines', in Journal of the Royal Statistical Society, Sept. 1888.

33. Oxford University Extension Lecturers...Report 1887-8 op.cit.

34. H. Ll. Smith, Modern Changes in the Mobility of Labour (London 1891).

35. The Hewins Papers 41/156, 41/158, Sheffield University Library.

36. Committee...Minutes, op.cit. 23 Feb. 1888.

37. The Hewins Papers, op.cit. 41/100-101, 41/162-3.

38. Michael Sadleir, Michael Ernest Sadler, op.cit. pp.102-3.

39. Committee...Minutes, op.cit. 7 March 1888.

40. The Hewins Papers, op.cit. 41/168-9.

41. Ibid. 43/68-9.

42. See Syllabus to H. Ll. Smith course 'Wealth and Industry' in the collection of Extension Syllabuses in Rewley House, Oxford. Report on one of Price's Lectures in the Reading Mercury, 17 Dec. 1887.

43. Syllabus to 'Three Chapters of Economic History' in Extension Syllabuses, op.cit.

44. Printed in A. Tyonbee, Industrial Revolution, op.cit.

45. W.A.S. Hewins, Syllabus of 'The English Labourer Past and Present' in Extension Syllabuses, op.cit.

46. Michael Sadleir, Michael Ernest Sadler, op.cit. pp.87, 89.

47. The Hewins Papers op.cit. 42/15-17, 43/74, 43/45-49, 43/51.

48. With the Clarendon Press, 23 Oct. 1891 for the publication of the Whiteford Papers and with Methuen, 30 April 1892 for the publication of English Trade and Finance.

49. Oxford University Extension Lectures. Report of a Conference of Representatives of the Local Committees. Oxford, April 20-21, 1887. (Oxford 1887), p.72.

50. Ibid. p.96.

51. Oxford University Extension Lecturers Reports, op.cit. 1888-9.

52. E.g.Price's report on a course given at Godalming 23 Oct. 1888 - 22 March 1889 in Reports op.cit. 1888-9.

53. Reports op.cit. Vol. 5.

54. See Oxford Magazine 6 Nov. 1889.

55. Reports op.cit. 1888-1889.

56. 'An Ideal Working Mens' Centre' in Oxford University Extension Gazette 10 Aug. 1891.

57. W.A.S. Hewins 'The Teaching of Economics' in the Journal of the Society of Arts, vol. 45, Dec. 4, 1896.

58. See also Oxford University Extension Gazette, July 1892.

59. R.A. Gregory, 'University Extension Lectures and Working Men'.

60. W.A.S. Hewin's review of J.A. Hobson and A.F. Mumery 'The Physiology of Industry' (1890) in the Economic Review, 1891.

61. Beatrice Webb, Our Partnership, edited by B. Uralie and M.I. Cole. (London 1948), p.86.

62. S. Webb to W.A.S. Hewins, 9 Sept. 1895 in the Hewins Papers 44/91.

63. 'Summer Meeting Aug. 1896' in the Oxford Extension Papers, Rewley House.

64. B. Webb, Our Partnership op.cit. p.92.

65. Report quoted by Hewins in 'The Teachings of Economics' op.cit.

66. The Education Department. Special Reports on Educational Subjects, vol.2, H.M.S.O. 1898. p.80.

67. Henry Pelling. A History of British Trade Unionism (London 1970) p.107.

68. Hewins Papers 43/188.

69. W.A.S. Hewins. The Apoligia of an Imperialist (London 1929) vol.1, p.2.

EXTENSION COURSES GIVEN BY OXFORD ECONOMISTS AFTER 1890

		Spring 1891	Spring 1892	Autumn 1892	Spring 1893	Autumn 1893	Spring 1894	Autumn 1894
PRICE	Subject	Burke, Fox, Pitt		Making of Wealth	Social & Industrial Movements			Econ. aspects
	No. of lect.			6	6			
	Place			Prestwich	Keighley			
	Sponsor			Local Committee	Mechanics Institute			
	Attend.			65	59			
W.A.S. HEWINS	Subject	Eng. Labourer	3 centuries of work-ing class history	Econ. aspects of social questions		Econ. aspects of social questions	Econ. aspects of social questions	Econ. aspects
	No. of lect.	6	6	6		6	6	6
	Place	Rochdale	Bacup	Lincoln		Grimsby	Rochdale	Kidderminster (even)
	Sponsor	Local Committee	Mechanics Inst.	Local Committee		Local Committee	Local Committee	Local Committee
	Attend.	80	52	180		236	120	75
	Subject					Eng. Social Life	Econ. aspects	Econ. aspects
	No. of lect.					6	6	6
	Place					Llanelly	Kidderminster (aft)	Banbury
	Sponsor					Mechanical Institute	Local Committee	Local Committee
	Attend.					300	47	70
	Subject					Eng. Social Life		Econ. aspects
	No. of lect.					6		6(+2nd part given by J.A. Hobson)
	Place					Swansea		Grimsby
	Sponsor					Local Committee		Local Committee
	Attend.					300		235
	Subject							3 centuries of work-ing class history
	No. of lect.							12
	Place							West Brighton
	Sponsor							Local Committee
	Attend.							38
	Subject							3 centuries etc.
	No. of lect.							6
	Place							Puchlechurch
	Sponsor							Local Committee
	Attend.							47
	Subject							Eng. Social Life
	No. of lect.							6
	Place							Hyde
	Sponsor							Local Committee
	Attend.							285

Note: No. of lect. for the Spring 1891 "Eng. Labourer" course shows 100 (110) in the attendance region.

Name	Year of Birth	Matric.	College	Status	Mods.	Class	Final School	Class	Prize	BA	MA	First Fellowship
J.J. Bickerton	1840	23.5.1866	Charsley Hall				Law & Mod. Hist. 1870	3rd		1870	1876	
P.F. Willert	1844	20.10.1862 trans. 1864-7	Balliol ↓ C.C.C.	Taylorian Scholar. Scholar	Cl. Mods 1864	2nd	Lit. Hum. 1866	1st		1867	1869	Exeter 1867
W.A. Spooner	1844	18.10.1862	New. Coll.	Scholar	Cl. Mods. 1864	1st	Lit. Hum. 1866	1st		1867	1869	New. Coll. 1867
R. Ewing	1846	16.10.1866	Balliol	Exhib.	Cl. Mods. 1868 Math.Mods. 1868	2nd 1st	Lit. Hum. 1870	1st	Junior Greek Test. 1869	1870	1873	St. John's 1870
St. G.W.J. Stock	1850	26.10.1868	Pembroke	Scholar	Cl. Mods. 1870	1st	Class. 1872	2nd		1873	1875	
W.J.H. Campion	1851	10.6.1870	Univ.	Exhib.	Cl. Mods 1872 Math.Mods. 1872	2nd 1st	Lit. Hum. 1874	2nd		1875	1875	Keble 1882
A.W. Roberts	1851	25.10.1869	Lincoln		Cl. Mods. 1871	3rd	History 1873 Jur. 1873 B.C.L. 1875	1st 2nd 2nd		1873 B.C.L. 1875		
T.C. Snow	1852	19.10.1870	C.C.C.	Scholar	Cl. Mods. 1872	1st	Class. 1874	1st		1874	1877	St. John's 1875
L.R. Phelps	1853	22.10.1872	Oriel	1) Scholar 2) Exhib.	Cl. Mods 1874	2nd	Class. 1876	2nd		1877	1879	Oriel 1877
D.G. Ritchie	1854	26.5.1874	Balliol	Class. Exhib.	Cl. Mods 1875	1st	Lit. Hum 1878	1st		1878	1881	Jesus 1878
S. Ball	1857	19.10.1875	Oriel	1) Scholar 2) Ireland Exhib. 3) Robinson Exhib.	Cl. Mods 1877	1st	Class. 1879	2nd		1879	1883	St. John's 1882
O.M. Edwards	1858	15.10.1884	Balliol	Brackenbury Scholar			History 1877	1st	Stanhope 1886 Lothian 1887 (Arnold His. Essay 1888)	1888	1889	Lincoln 1889
W.J. Ashley	1860	19.10.1878	Balliol	Brackenbury Scholar			Mod. His. 1881	1st	Shakespeare 1880 Lothian 1882	1881	1885	Lincoln 1885
M.E. Sadler	1861	16.10.1880	Trinity	Scholar	Cl. Mods. 1882	1st	Class. 1884	1st		1884	1887	Ch. Ch. 1890
E. Cannan	1861	29.1.1881	Balliol		Cl. Mods. 1882	2nd	Pass 1884		Lothian 1885	1884	1887	
D.J. Medley	1861	19.10.1880	Keble				History 1883	1st		1883	1887	Keble 1884
A.J. Carlyle	1861	18.10.1883	Exeter	Exhib.			Mod. His. 1886 Theology 1887	1st 2nd		1886		Univ. 1893
J. Carter	1862	18.10.1882	Exeter	Exhib.	Cl. Mods. 1885	3rd	Class. 1887	2nd		1887		
L.L.F.R. Price	1862	15.10.1881	Trinity	Scholar	Cl. Mods. 1882	1st	Lit. Hum. 1885	1st		1885	1888	Oriel 1888
J. Tracey	1862	18.10.1881	Brasenose	Scholar	Cl. Mods. 1883	1st	Lit. Hum. 1885	1st		1885	1888	Keble 1887
F.S. Marvin	1863	14.10.1882	St. John's	1) Scholar 2) Senior Scholar 1887	Cl. Mods. 1884	1st	Class. 1886 History 1887	1st 2nd		1886	1889	
L.T. Hobhouse	1864	19.10.1883	C.C.C.	Class. Scholar	Cl. Mods 1884	1st	Class. 1887	1st		1887	1890	Merton 1887
H. Ll. Smith	1864	19.10.1883	C.C.C.	Scholar	Math. Mods. 1884	1st	Math. 1886	1st	Cobden 1886	1886	1889	
H.W. Blunt	1864	31.10.1882	Oriel	Scholar	Cl. Mods. 1883	2nd	Class. 1886	1st	Arnold 1887	1886	1889	Ch. Ch. 1889
W.G. Smith	1864	14.10.1882	St. John's	Scholar	Cl. Mods. 1884	1st	Class. 1886 History 1887	1st 1st		1886	1889	St. John's 1889
H.L. Withers	1865	10.10.1883	Balliol	Scholar	Cl. Mods. 1884	1st	Lit. Hum. 1887	1st		1887	1894	
W.A.S. Hewins	1865	27.10.1884	Pembroke	Scholar	Math. Mods. 1885	1st	Math. 1887	2nd		1887		

LIST OF ABBREVIATIONS

Matric.	– Matriculation	Jur.	– Jurisprudence
Mods.	– Moderations	Exhib.	– Exhibitioner
Cl. or Class	– Classics	C.C.C.	– Corpus Christi College
Math.	– Mathematics	New Coll.	– New College
Lit. Hum.	– Literae Humaniores	Ch. Ch.	– Christ Church
Mod. His.	– Modern History		

THE EXTENSION LECTURE'S SUMMER MEETING 1889

A section from a photograph taken in Balliol College gardens.
Oxford Summer meeting photograph album (Vol.1) Rewley House,
Wellington Square, Oxford.

1. J.A.R. Marriott
2. Jowett
3. M.E. Sadler
4. Sir W. Markby
5. W. Hudson Shaw
6. W.A.S. Hewins
7. H. Mackinder